MICROCOMPUTER TROUBLESHOOTING

MICROCOMPUTER TROUBLESHOOTING

James Perozzo

DELMAR PUBLISHERS INC. ®

Cover Photograph by: Joseph Schuyler Photography
Glasgal Communications Inc.

Delmar Staff
Administrative Editor: Mark W. Huth
Associate Editor: Jonathan Plant
Production Editor: Ruth East

For information, address
Delmar Publishers, Inc.
2 Computer Drive West, Box 15-015
Albany, New York 12212

Printed in the United States of America
Published simultaneously in Canada
by Nelson Canada
A Division of International Thomson Limited

10 9 8 7 6 5

Library of Congress Cataloging in Publication Data

Perozzo, James
Microcomputer–Maintenance and repair. I. Title.
TK7887.P47 1986 621.391′6 86-4447
ISBN 0-8273-2500-2 (soft)
ISBN 0-8273-2501-0 (instructor's guide)

Contents

NOTICE TO THE READER

Preface

Microcomputer Troubleshooting is a text for second-year electronics students and for those who, having the necessary prerequisites, wish to repair or maintain these amazing electronic machines. It is assumed that the reader is familiar with basic electronics and digital electronics and with computer numbering systems. My book *Practical Electronics Troubleshooting* is recommended for those interested in more details of troubleshooting to the component level.

There are four general classes of computers: the mainframe computer used by large corporations, usually located in a room by itself because of its large size. It is operated simultaneously by many terminals throughout the business. The minicomputer, about the size of a filing cabinet, is used by smaller businesses and serves fewer terminals. Because of its smaller size it can occupy a corner of an office space. The microcomputer, the subject of this book, is desk-top size, the associated monitor often sitting atop the system unit. The microcomputer is capable of most of the functions of a minicomputer. With the addition of a hard disk, the microcomputer is a serious contender in the minicomputer market. The last category of computer is the game computer often seen in homes. This small computer is lap-sized and, although it is capable of competent graphics and sound generation, it is not suitable for serious business applications due to the limitations on the maximum amount of memory it can use.

A computer technician competent in the repair of a microcomputer can easily learn the repair and troubleshooting techniques of any other class of computer. The use of ROM, RAM, data storage, monitors, and keyboards remains essentially the same for all computers.

Troubleshooting Microcomputers emphasizes the troubleshooting of computers mainly to the board level, since this is most often the level to which troubleshooting is done in the real world. Sufficient information is given here to enable a technician to troubleshoot effectively to the component level when necessary. Troubleshooting to the component level will make additional troubleshooting instruments necessary. These instruments and their use are also covered. A practical, real-world approach to troubleshooting is emphasized. Cautions are given when appropriate to help the technician avoid safety hazards and to prevent further damage to the computer being repaired. Recommendations of the tools and instruments to use are based upon the author's experience. Other tools and instruments may be used, of course, with differences in the specifications and use of those instruments.

The computer service technician will often need the information in Appendix A, the intercabling information. Cables must be made or purchased to operate printers and modems and to connect terminals to computers. This appendix gives the information necessary to help ensure that the right cable is used.

The block and schematic diagrams in this book are representative of microcomputers. With individual computers, these diagrams may not be accurate: the service and maintenance manuals for the computer under repair are the final authority.

Mastery of the material in this book will give the beginning computer-maintenance technician the confidence to begin troubleshooting on actual computers with a minimum chance of further damage to the equipment and a maximum chance of troubleshooting success.

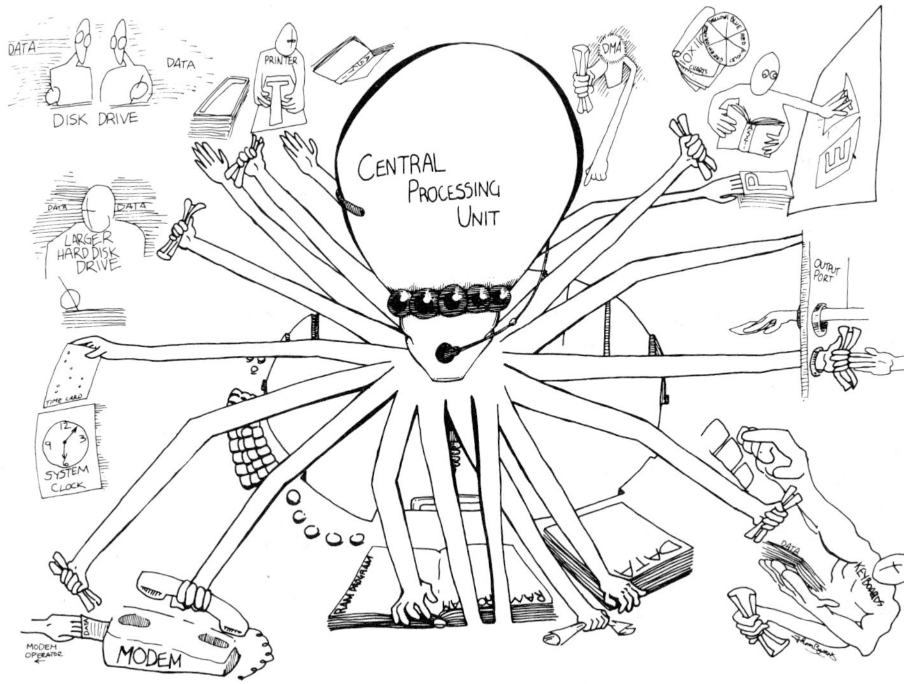

Courtesy Tom Burns

Acknowledgments

My special thanks go to those who have encouraged me, particularly my life's companion Vi Perozzo, my friends Robert Dudley, David Malland, and Bud Abbey, photographer for most of the photographs in this text.

Jim Walton, a fellow computer teacher at Renton Vocational Technical Institute, is a close friend and a major contributor to the material in this book. I owe much to his consistent interest and positive attitude.

Len Boscarine, Al Pierce, and Gary Davidson of Mannesmann Tally, printer manufacturers, gave me valuable information on state-of-the-art printers.

Bill Hunt of Huntron Instruments, Bill Long of Creative Microprocessor Systems, Ms. Elizabeth Dessuge and Rick Jorgenson of Dysan Corporation, and Ken King of Omnilogic each gave of their time and talent to ensure the accuracy of the information in this text.

The following reviewers provided valuable feedback during the development of this book: Don Forbes, National Education Center, Westwood Campus, CA; Willard Waters, RETS Electronic Institute, Birmingham, AL; George Sappington, formerly of Lyons Institute, NJ; John Amico, Renton Vocational-Technical Institute, WA; Daniel Moore, North Carolina State University; Reddy Talusani, Houston Community College, TX; Ralph Masciulli, Franklin Institute of Boston; James King, Joliet Junior College, IL; Glenn Buck, Pitt Community College, NC; Edward Hartwick, Johnson City Community College, KS.

About the Author

James Perozzo has over 25 years' experience repairing electronic equipment of many different types. After 20 years' service as a technician and officer in the Coast Guard, he broadened his experience by working in marine and aviation electronics, microwave voice carriers, and computer repair. A native of the Pacific Northwest, his qualifications include an FCC General Radiotelephone Certificate, Amateur Extra Class License, FAA Avionics Certification, and an Electronics Teaching Certificate. He currently teaches computer repair and robotics at Renton Vocational-Technical Institute in Renton, Washington. He has also written *Practical Electronics Troubleshooting*, (Delmar), 1985.

part one

An Overview of Computer Troubleshooting

chapter one

How Microcomputers Work

CHAPTER OVERVIEW

The new technician attempting a repair on a microcomputer can be nearly overwhelmed at all of the things that might be wrong with it. This chapter discusses in detail the way a microcomputer normally operates when nothing is wrong. Safeguards to prevent injury to the technician and to the microcomputer are included. Having absorbed the information in this chapter, the new technician will be able to better analyze computer problems and avoid causing additional damage.

WHAT IS A MICROCOMPUTER?

All computers operate in basically the same way, regardless of size, although the capability and speed of operation of the computer generally improve as the cost of the system increases (see Figure 1.1). Game computers costing less than a hundred dollars can process a limited amount of information and output it to a printer. A microcomputer, on the other hand, is a computer system designed to meet the needs of the professional who uses one at home or at the office, the small business operator, and the serious computer hobbyist. The microcomputer is often used to type reports and letters

Figure 1.1 Even a small computer is often capable of printing and other basic computer tasks. (Abbey Enterprises)

using word-processing software, to manipulate complex figures involving many variables using electronic spreadsheet software, and to keep track of multiple records using data-base management software. Although the microcomputer can certainly be used to play games, this is not its primary purpose.

The tremendous popularity of microcomputers has led to the standardization of several interface connections such as driving signals and plugs for disk drives and plug-in cards, and standardized keyboards and monitors that are interchangeable between computers of different manufacture. This is a big advantage to the servicing technician because a single item such as an option card or monitor can often be used as a spare for several different makes of computer. The usual configuration of a microcomputer system is shown in block diagram form in Figure 1.2 and in a photo in Figure 1.3.

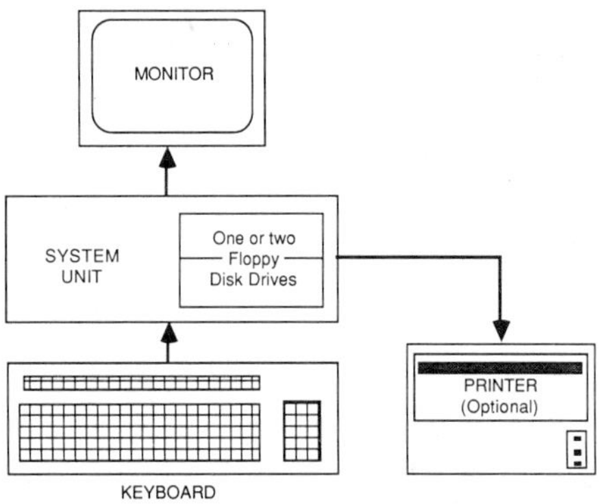

Figure 1.2 Block diagram of a typical microcomputer installation

Figure 1.3 A typical microcomputer setup, the computer system this text will cover (Courtesy of Corona Data Systems)

Figure 1.4 The mainframe computer processes information at a high rate of speed and can service the needs of many operators working at separate terminals. (Courtesy of IBM)

Microcomputers, the subject of this book, lie somewhere between the small computers shown in Figure 1.1 and the large mainframe computers used by large corporations (Figure 1.4). Mainframe computers have much more extensive data-storage capability than microcomputers do. They also usually have more RAM memory and are able to service inputs from many operators at essentially the same time.

Knowledge of the details of microcomputer operation will enable you to understand the operation of complex computers more easily. The troubleshooting techniques presented in this book, with appropriate modification, can be used to service any computer system. This book assumes the use of the very popular MS-DOS™ operating system for the operation of the microcomputer. With appropriate modifications of the commands, troubleshooting procedures can be translated into commands for other operating systems, such as CP/M™.

THE NORMAL OPERATION OF A MICROCOMPUTER

Most computer repair jobs require a certain minimum of knowledge to effectively localize the problem. The block diagram in Figure 1.5 presents graphically the internal workings of the computer.

When a computer is first turned on, it executes a program found in the computer's ROM chip, seen in Figure 1.6. This ROM program provides the following functions, shown in Figure 1.7:

1. Initializing the LSI chips used in the system (such as the 8255 PIO chip and the 8253 timer chip), which is necessary to set them up for later use. For example,

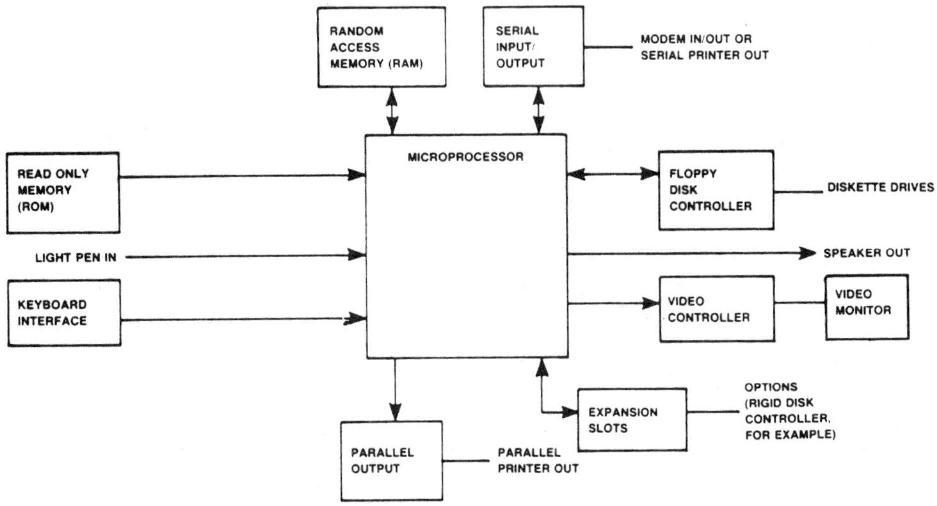

Figure 1.5 Basic block diagram of the internal circuitry of a microcomputer (Courtesy of Corona Data Systems)

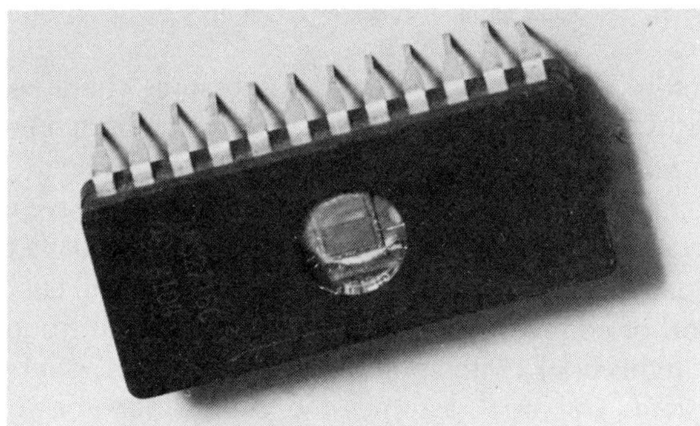

Figure 1.6 The ROM chip that gets the computer going (Abbey Enterprises)

the 8255 input/output chip is initialized for appropriate directions of data flow—in on some pins, out on others.

2. Reading of the system peripheral switches and setting of the system parameters accordingly. This step lets the computer know what resources are available, such as what kind of monitor (color or monochrome) is connected and how many disk drives are installed.
3. The power-on diagnostics then tests up to 14 items, among them checks of the CPU, ROM, RAM, video display card, keyboard, and floppy disk drive system. Normal execution of this part of the ROM program results in the no-error signal of a single beep from the computer and accessing of the floppy disk drive A where a loading program (called a *bootstrap loader*) loads the operating system.

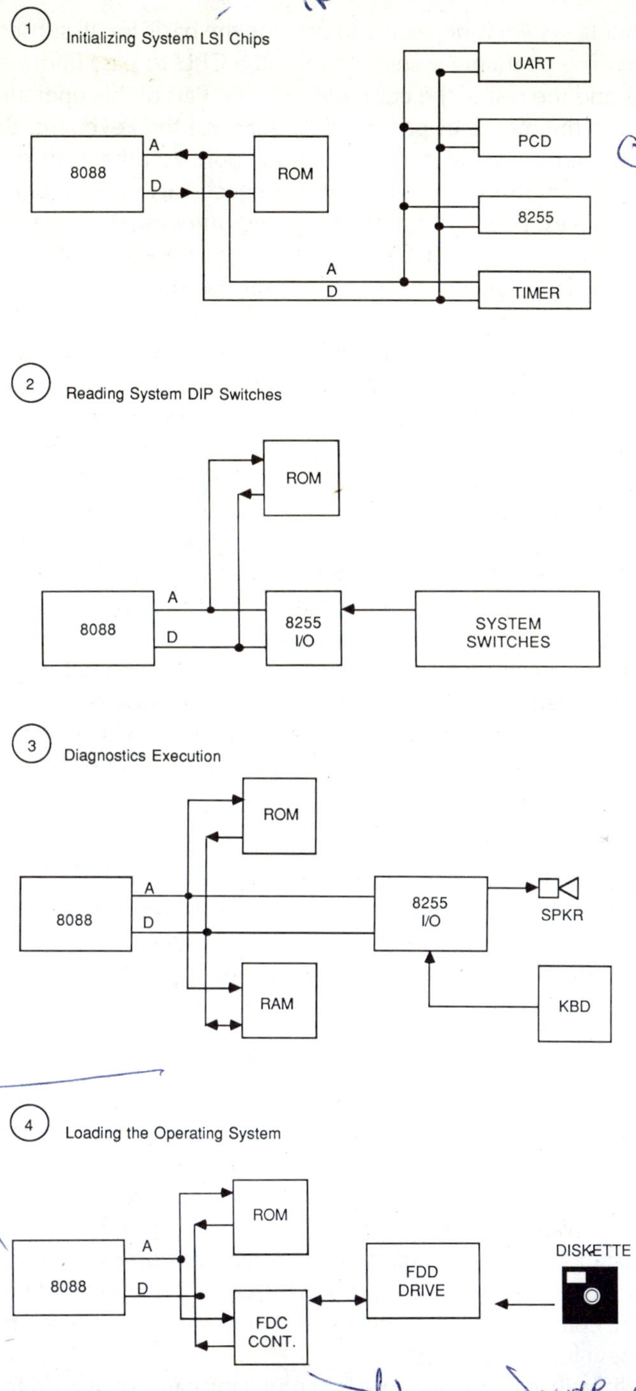

Figure 1.7 Steps in powering up microcomputer (Stephanie Enterprises)

An operating system is necessary to provide the basis for all subsequent applications programs. The operating system enables the CPU to pass information between the disk drives and the rest of the computer system. Part of this operating system, the BIOS, establishes the means of passing data between the keyboard, the printer, the monitor screen, and the serial communications port. Another part of the operating system, the DOS portion, provides the software necessary to read and write information to the disk drives. Different operating systems are available for microcomputers, notably Microsoft MS-DOS and CP/M from Digital Research. The details of ROM programming may be available in assembly language format in the computer instruction book.

After the operating system has been loaded into RAM the CPU begins execution of that program directly from RAM. When the computer is then ready for keyboard input it exhibits on the monitor the DOS prompt, the letter A followed by a "greater than" math symbol, the ">". This prompt shows which disk drive is the default drive and also signifies that the computer is operating at the DOS level. (Programs other than DOS use different prompts such as a dash [-] or an asterisk [*]).

At this point the computer may be used for such housekeeping tasks as looking at the directory of a diskette, changing the name of a file on a diskette, copying or erasing files, and the like. This is also the point at which more advanced programs such as word-processing or data-management programs may be loaded into the computer.

Any problems occurring *prior to* reaching the DOS prompt will mean that the technician will initially be relying on the numerical error codes and audio cues provided by the ROM diagnostics to localize a problem in the computer. If, however, a problem appears only *after* the computer reaches the DOS prompt, the diagnostics diskette becomes the primary troubleshooting tool.

An Overview of Computer Repair. There is a marked difference between troubleshooting electronic equipment such as stereo or radio equipment and treating computer problems. Almost anyone can operate stereos and radios, and only a little audio equipment has the modularized construction (plug-in circuitry) most microcomputers do.

Most computer problems are the result of operator error or software problems, with only a very small percentage involving electronic failures. Computer hardware repairs, perhaps all but 10%, are accomplished simply and rapidly. Repairs of computer hardware problems involve isolating the problem to a certain circuit or possibly a disk drive and then replacing that card or disk drive (see Figure 1.8). Chapter 2 will help you decide whether there is a problem within the computer or whether it lies elsewhere.

A defective card should be sent back to the factory for replacement or repair if the card is still under warranty. If the warranty period has expired, the cost of technician time versus that of getting a new card from the manufacturer will affect the decision. On those few occasions when a replacement card is not available and continued operation of the computer is extremely important, it may be necessary to troubleshoot to the component level (Figure 1.9).

It is not difficult to learn the process of replacing cards or disk drives to alleviate a computer problem. Much more detailed knowledge of digital circuitry is necessary if

Figure 1.8 Most internal computer repairs are accomplished by the simple replacement of a defective card or disk drive. (Abbey Enterprises)

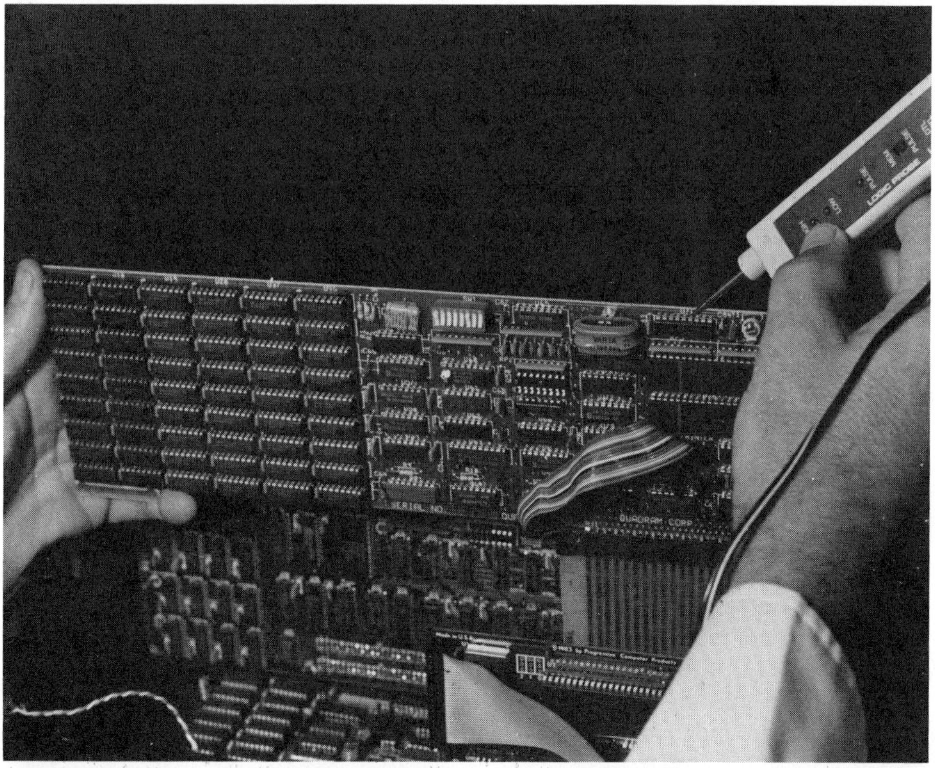

Figure 1.9 Troubleshooting to the component level requires additional electronic knowledge. (Abbey Enterprises)

the technician is expected to troubleshoot to the component level. In the usual case, where sufficient replacement circuits and disk drives are available, the technician will seldom need this level of troubleshooting expertise. When component-level troubleshooting is necessary, it is sometimes possible to use a replacement circuit to enable the computer to return to service while the technician takes the defective circuit back to the shop, where it can be worked upon at more leisure. Once back at the shop the technician can install the defective circuit in an otherwise working system and commence troubleshooting procedures there. Troubleshooting to the component level requires a thorough knowledge of digital circuitry and the use of digital test instruments.

SAFETY AND CAUTIONS TO BE OBSERVED DURING COMPUTER REPAIR

When a computer is received for repair the technician must make sure that no further problems are introduced into the equipment through carelessness. To this end, observe the following cautions at all times when working:

- Never close the door of a double-sided disk drive without either a diskette or a dummy cardboard shipping diskette installed in the drive like the one seen in Figure 1.10. To close the door with nothing in the drive invites chipping of either or both of the glasslike read/write heads. A chipped drive head can ruin any other diskettes inserted and rotated in that drive.
- Always take special care of floppy drive diskettes, keeping them in a protective jacket when not installed in a diskette drive. Don't leave unprotected diskettes lying about the work area (Figure 1.11). They are sure to be contaminated with dust, dirt, or physically damaged by tools or other objects. Use only felt-tipped pens to write on diskette jackets: ball-point pens can easily put a dimple in a diskette, ruining it.
- Never remove or attach connectors, or remove or insert any option card or IC into the computer, while power is on (Figure 1.12).
- Likewise, never touch any internal portion of a computer's power supply while it is attached to the power source (Figure 1.13). If voltage measurements are necessary, exercise extreme care to prevent shock hazards and/or damage to the power supply. Certain circuits within monitors also contain dangerous voltages, a subject discussed further in Chapter 12.
- Always observe the static-electricity safety measures for integrated circuits. Keep the new components in their static-free packaging until ready for installation (Figure 1.14). Ground your body to the equipment under test before installing a new chip into the board. If possible, work at a static-free work station that includes grounded metal surfaces and an antistatic floormat.

These rules should be followed at all times, until they become second nature.

Figure 1.10 Be sure to install the shipping cardboards when transporting diskette drives. (Abbey Enterprises)

Figure 1.11 Don't leave unprotected diskettes lying about when working. (Abbey Enterprises)

Figure 1.12 Always turn the power off when working inside the computer, for your safety and to prevent damage to the computer. (Abbey Enterprises)

Figure 1.13 Keep your fingers and tools out of the power supply when the power is connected, whether or not the power switch is on. (Abbey Enterprises)

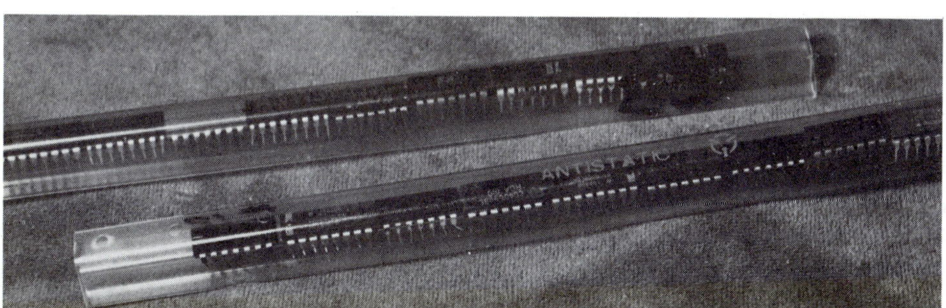

Figure 1.14 Leave good ICs in their original packaging until actually needed. (Abbey Enterprises)

CHAPTER SUMMARY

This chapter has focused on the microcomputer. The servicing technician must understand how the microcomputer operates normally to be able to analyze abnormal operation. Basic rules to prevent a technician from causing additional damage during an attempted repair were also given.

REVIEW QUESTIONS

1. What is the advantage of standardizing interface connections for units of a microcomputer?
2. Name the basic units of a typical microcomputer system.
3. Where are the initial instructions found in a computer after it is first turned on?
4. What is the basic difference in the operation of BIOS and DOS portions of an operating system?
5. What must the technician rely upon for troubleshooting information if a problem occurs before the system prompt appears?
6. A technician is troubleshooting a computer that is able to boot up as far as the appearance of the system prompt. At this point, what is the best troubleshooting tool to localize a problem to a specific hardware unit of the computer?
7. What is usually done with a computer card that is determined to be defective?
8. What is the principal difference in the treatment of a single-sided and a double-sided diskette drive during transportation?
9. What special quality should the floormat of a computer maintenance shop possess?

chapter two

A Computer Problem or Not?

CHAPTER OVERVIEW

Some very important questions must be answered to begin correcting a suspected microcomputer problem. Seldom is the electronic portion of a computer the real problem. More often, the power line supplying the computer, the diskettes and software on them, and the computer operator are the real problems. This chapter gives the new technician guidelines for a logical approach to field repair problems.

EXTERNAL POWER PROBLEMS

Computer malfunctions may be the result of power problems. Power is usually supplied to microcomputers by 120VAC power mains—the wall outlet—by no means a 100% reliable source. Computers require constant power to avoid the malfunction called a computer crash. Some computers are more tolerant than others with regard to short periods of power interruption because they have large capacitors in the power supply. Large filter capacitors can store enough energy to ride through the missing cycles of input AC power (see Figure 2.1).

Such power interruptions, if long enough, are detectable by the computer operator, who may report "The lights blink and then the computer keyboard locks." Longer periods of power interruption are obvious, since the lights in the working area usually go out for some time. There can also be a power interruption in the computer supply line and not in the power lines supplying lighting. In this case the computer screen may go dark for a moment, or it may blink off and then bloom momentarily when the power comes back on again. At the other extreme, a power interruption may be so short that the operator is not aware of the outage and knows only that the computer has ceased to function properly. At any rate, the interruption of input power is a major concern for computer operators.

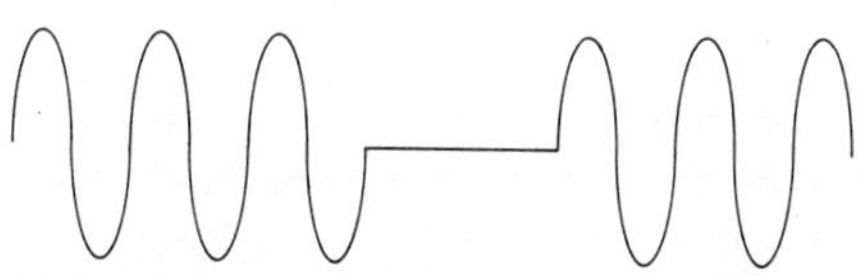

Figure 2.1 Short-term power shortages of a few cycles may or may not affect the computer, depending on the capacity of the power-supply filters.

The ultimate cure for power problems is to provide a backup source. The computer operates on a battery supply during periods of low or no alternating current from the power lines. In normal operation the battery is charged continuously from the power line (Figure 2-2). An alternate way of accomplishing the same result is to trickle-charge the battery at a low rate sufficient to maintain a full charge without any load on the batteries. An alternate path for power to operate the computer is provided through the contacts of a fast-acting switching arrangement such as a special relay. When the power-line input drops to an unacceptable level, the power source for the computer immediately switches to the battery circuit for continued operation. The switching time should be less than the period of a 60 Hz cycle, or 16.6 milliseconds. Typical switching times are from 6 to 12 milliseconds. Figure 2.3 is a block diagram of this type of backup power supply.

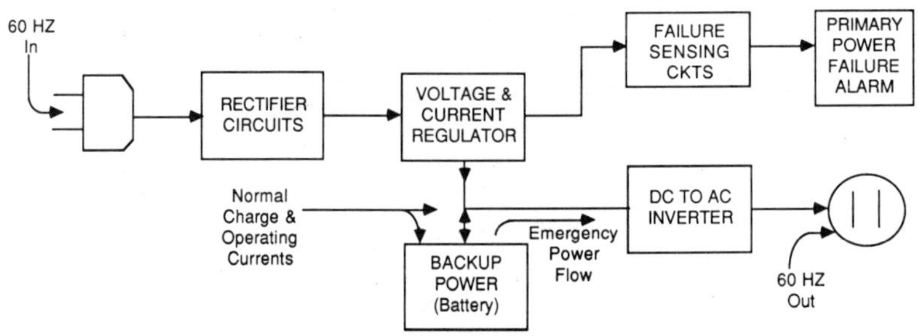

Figure 2.2 This type battery backup system provides a no-break system capability.

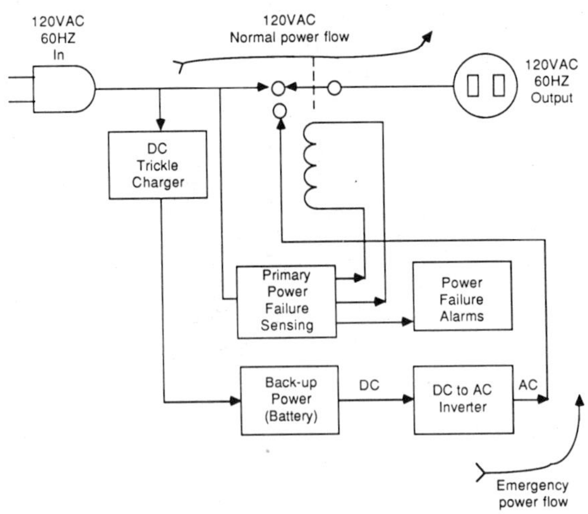

Figure 2.3 This type of power supply trickle-charges the battery and switches rapidly to use the battery power if the 120VAC lines fail. The transition time from 120VAC to the battery power must be very short to avoid disturbing the computer.

If for any reason the AC lines should fail to provide acceptable power, an alarm will sound to alert the operator, whose proper response will be to immediately put whatever data is in the computer's RAM onto storage media such as diskettes. As much as 15 minutes or more of operation may be available to accomplish this, depending on the power requirements of the computer and the amount of energy stored in the batteries (Figure 2.4).

Another common power-line problem is a temporary increase of line voltage, called *voltage transients*. These are caused by such other loads on the line as heavy loads being connected, electric motors starting up, or lightning striking power lines in the vicinity (see Figure 2.5). These transients (also called *spikes*) can be especially damaging to electronic equipment. Where a momentary loss of power may only cause a computer to crash, an overvoltage situation can cause overstressing of the power-supply components, stressing of the chips within the computer, and in severe cases damage that must be corrected by a technician.

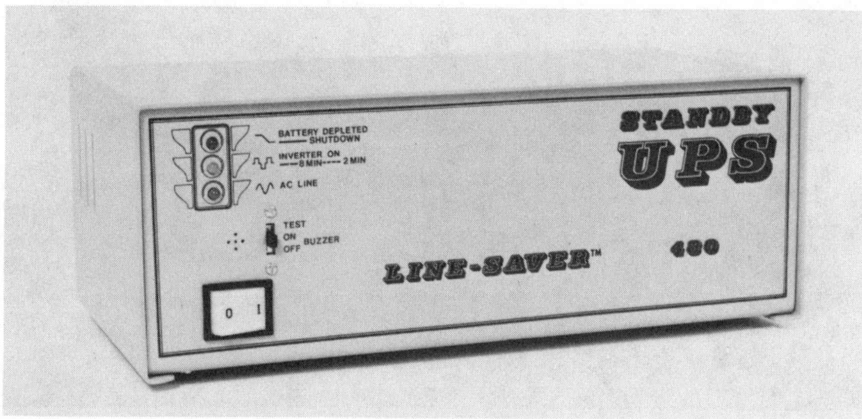

Figure 2.4 A commercial battery-backup power supply (Courtesy of Kalglo Electronics Company)

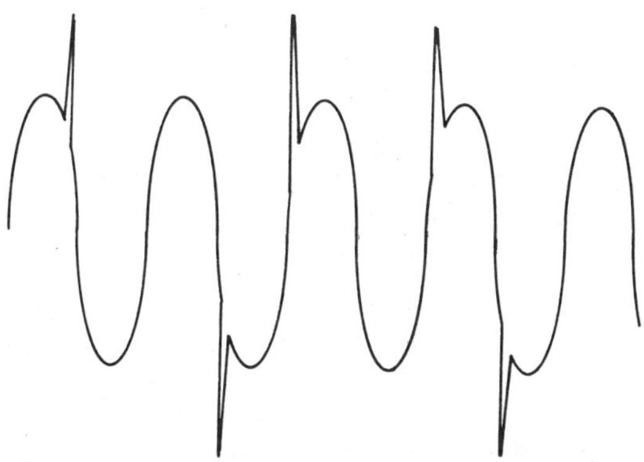

Figure 2.5 Voltage transients can be very damaging to computers.

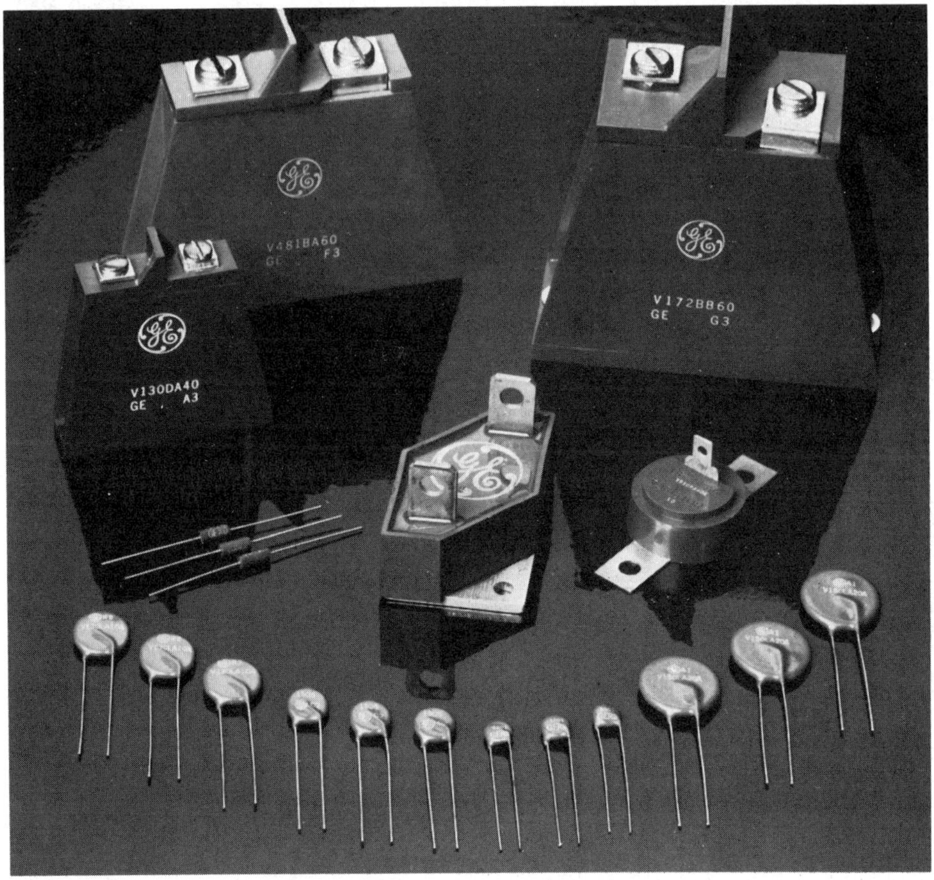

Figure 2.6 Commercial line-voltage spike suppressors often use Metal Oxide Varistors (MOVs) to clip voltage transients to safe levels. (Photo reprinted with permission of GE Semiconductor, General Electric Co.)

An economical method of providing transient overvoltage protection is to use a special outlet attachment that has internal components designed to absorb supply-line overvoltages. The component that does the actual work is a metal oxide varistor, or MOV (see Figure 2.6). The MOV is connected directly across the AC supply line. With normal voltages the MOV is effectively an open circuit. If the supply voltage exceeds normal levels, the varistor will immediately conduct heavily, loading the power line severely, thus protecting the computer from the surge (Figure 2.7). Varistors have power limitations, however, and a sustained overvoltage condition can cause them to fail by opening, thus no longer providing protection.

The battery backup power supply of Figure 2.2 can also provide a computer a great deal of protection from overvoltage. In the event of a severe enough surge, the

Figure 2.7 Commercial line-voltage transient suppressors (Courtesy of Kalglo Electronics Company)

backup supply might be damaged but the computer itself will probably not be harmed, since the computer is effectively isolated from the surge by the very low impedance of the battery. The backup supply of Figure 2.3 does not provide this isolation from surges.

DISKETTE PROBLEMS

Another source of possible problems that may not be a fault within the computer itself is the floppy diskette, the most common medium for storing data on microcomputers. Since information is stored on diskettes by tiny magnetic fields, any disruption of these fields can hopelessly scramble the recorded information (Figure 2.8).

There are two different types of diskette information: the program you are running and the data required by that program. These diskettes are usually placed in the A and B drives, respectively. An example would be a word-processing program that would be inserted in the A drive. All of your typed correspondence, on the other hand, might be accessed in the B drive. If a program from a diskette used in the A drive

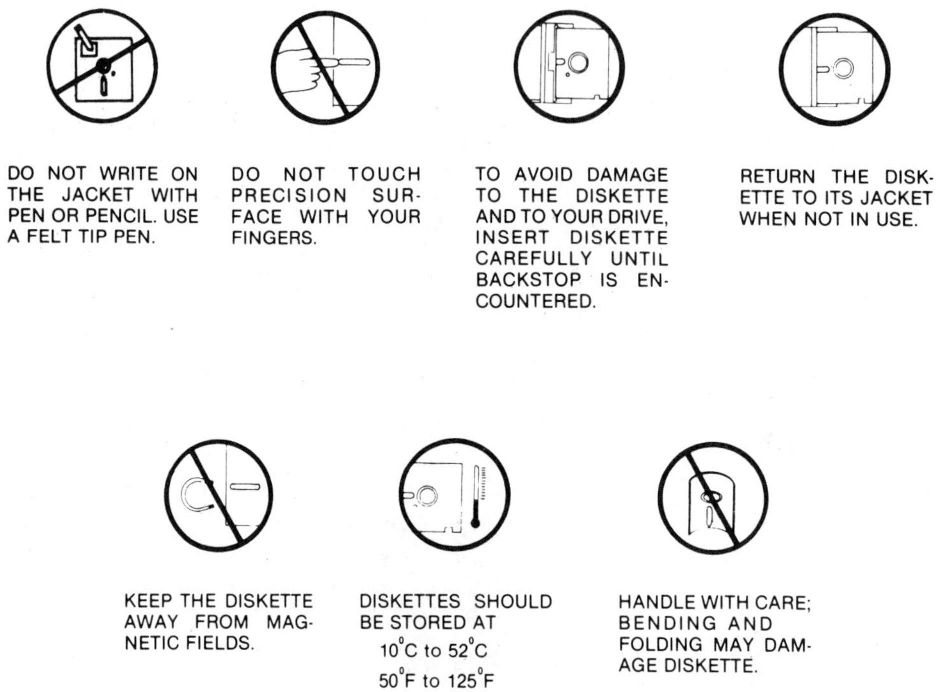

Figure 2.8 Mishandling of the diskette can cause apparent computer problems. (Tandon Corporation)

becomes damaged, the computer will cease to operate or will behave very strangely; often the computer will not respond to keystrokes at the keyboard. Bad data (usually from the diskette in the B drive), in contrast, is usually indicated by a failure of the drive to access data from the diskette or perhaps the appearance on the screen of inappropriate characters. If a diskette is the likely cause of a problem and if a backup diskette had been made of the now-suspect diskette, recopy the backup onto the suspected diskette. (Backup copies should be made on a routine basis for all important data and for all purchased applications software such as word processing and database programs.) In the event that the diskette data must be recovered from a damaged diskette at any cost, the DOS utility program CHKDSK with a /F option or RECOVER should be investigated.

Diskettes may have been damaged by being placed or held close to magnetic sources. A diskette dropped onto a pair of scissors, for instance, can be damaged by the magnetic field often present in such an instrument, and even paper clips can damage diskettes. Keep steel objects away from diskettes. Another cause of diskette problems is the contamination of the diskette surface through carelessness (see Figure 2.9).

Floppy diskettes should never be bent. It is easy to bend a diskette by forcibly inserting it into the computer disk drive. Handle diskettes carefully—and take your time inserting them. Store diskettes at normal office temperatures. Keep them out of

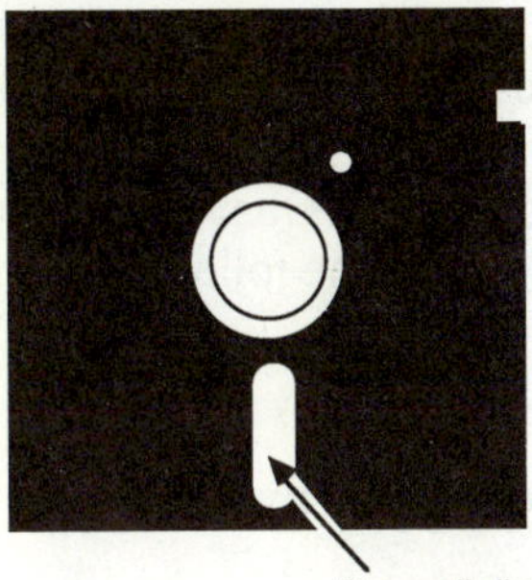

Figure 2.9 Keep fingers and any other contamination away from exposed portions of the diskette.

direct sunlight, where they might overheat and warp. Remember that the interior of a closed car on a hot day may become hot enough to warp diskettes. (Chapter 15 discusses software problems in more detail.)

IS IT A HARDWARE OR A SOFTWARE PROBLEM?

When a malfunction of the computer occurs it is necessary first to determine whether the problem is one within the computer (a *hardware* problem) or a matter of providing a correct program and data (a *software* problem) to the computer. Put a known good diskette with the operating system on it into the A drive and turn on the computer. Note whether the problem occurs before or after the A> prompt appears.

Hardware Problems

Problems occurring *before* the DOS prompt A> are usually hardware problems. Many microcomputers have an internal self-test, executed each time the computer is turned on, called the power-up diagnostic, power-on self-test, or ROM diagnostic. Execution of these routines is normally evident from a pause after turning on the computer's power followed by a short beep at the successful conclusion of the tests. Indications other than the short beep mean a problem has been detected and must be corrected before using the computer. The ROM diagnostic program may take from a few seconds up to a minute, depending upon the amount of installed RAM memory.

For the IBM PC only: If there is no DOS diskette the IBM will load BASIC from special ROM chips and display the following:

```
The IBM Personal Computer BASIC
Version XXXX Copyright IBM Corp 198X
XXXX Bytes free
Ok
```

Note: A failure of the A diskette drive to load DOS will result in the above display and is a very good indication of an A disk-drive malfunction. See Chapter 11 for disk-drive repair.

Problems detected by the ROM diagnostics may, depending upon the computer manufacturer, produce error codes similar to the following, which are those used by IBM.

REPRESENTATIVE ROM DIAGNOSTIC ERROR CODES

Normal Indication

Cursor appears somewhere on the monitor

One beep

Drive A is accessed as shown by the activity light on the drive illuminating

DOS prompt A> is displayed

Note: If the DOS diskette in A has a file on it called AUTOEXEC.BAT, the computer will load and execute the programs listed within that file automatically. Testing a computer for proper operation is best done with as simple a program as possible, preferably the operating system alone.

Abnormal Indications

Audio Error Codes

No beep, no display. Probable power-supply problem. Check the plug and the wall outlet for power availability. See Chapter 5.

Continuous or repeating short beeps. See Chapter 5, since a power-supply problem is likely.

One long, one short beep indicates a problem with the system board. See Chapter 8.

One long, two short beeps indicate a problem with the monitor circuits. See Chapter 12.

Normal beep with no display. Probable monitor problem. See Chapter 12.

Two short beeps indicate a possible problem reading the keyboard. See Chapter 9.

Numerical Codes

101 or 131 indicates a problem on the system board. See Chapter 8.

XXXX 201 indicates a memory problem. The XXXX portion is a numerical code assisting the technician in localizing the defective chip. For details see Chapter 8.

PARITY CHECK ONE

There is a RAM memory failure detected on the system board.

PARITY CHECK TWO

There is a RAM memory failure detected on one of the memory expansion boards. Either of the above error messages may be preceded *momentarily* by a numerical code that indicates the bank in which the error occurred. Watch carefully for this code and write it down when it occurs. The code may appear for only a second and then be replaced by one of the above messages. See Chapter 8 for details of troubleshooting memory problems on the system board and Chapter 7 for similar problems on the option boards.

301 indicates a problem with the keyboard. See Chapter 9.

601 indicates a problem with one of the disk drives. See Chapter 11.

1701 indicates trouble in the fixed (hard disk) drive.

1801 indicates a problem in an external expansion unit, a separate chassis into which additional option cards may be plugged when all of the internal expansion sockets are filled.

If the normal indications occur, you may assume several things. If the beep sounds, the RAM has passed a test that should show any permanent gross defects in the RAM chips. Operation to this point also confirms that the power supply is producing the necessary voltages, mainly +5 volts, to operate the computer. Depending upon the kind of RAM chips used, other voltages required by those chips are also present. If the A> prompt shows, the computer has been able to find and load the necessary software, usually from the A diskette. (Some systems have other sources for loading system software, such as hard disks.) The presence of the prompt also indicates that the source for the data, usually the A disk drive, is working properly.

A computer working to the DOS prompt has largely eliminated the majority of common problems, those of the bad power supply, bad RAM memory chips, and the bad or out-of-alignment diskette drive (only the drive used to boot up the computer). It also clears the possibility of a bad copy of the operating system in the A drive.

Software Problems

Computer problems occurring *after* the DOS prompt A> are largely disk-drive, peripheral, or software problems. An error code on the CRT screen such as READ

ERROR, BAD COMMAND OR FILE NAME, or CANNOT OPEN FILE means that the information expected to be on a diskette is not available for one reason or another. In addition to mistype of a command, these errors may be shown if the requested file is simply not present on the diskette specified: you cannot expect a computer to find something that is not there. There are two hardware causes for this kind of failure: (1) The diskette drive is defective and unable to retrieve data properly recorded on the diskette or (2) the diskette has been damaged or improperly recorded upon by a misaligned drive. The problem must be examined further to determine which possibility is the actual problem.

To determine whether a problem is in the hardware or the software, substitute another diskette as the next logical, easiest step in troubleshooting. Assume that data on a diskette cannot be read, but putting a different diskette in the same drive produces normal indications. (For instance, the word-processing files on one diskette cannot be read but a second diskette works normally, with all files apparently accessible after you have performed several random reads from the "new" diskette.) It is reasonable to assume that the first diskette has been damaged somehow and that the diskette drive is all right.

A caution is in order in making such an assumption, however. In time, a diskette drive may slowly drift out of mechanical alignment. If an out-of-alignment drive is used to format and record information, the diskette used will be readable with the out-of-alignment drive. As the alignment gets worse, if the drive is still used to record and read, the information on the diskette can still be readable *with that drive*. Repeated problems reading with a particular drive strongly indicate an alignment problem with that drive. The possibility of a misaligned drive can be checked by using a diskette in known good condition, such as a diskette that has been recently purchased with a program or data already recorded on it by a drive assumed to be in good condition. Such a diskette can be used as a standard for this test. Insert it into the suspect drive and attempt to read the files. If there is still a problem in reading the diskette, the drive must be suspected as too far out of alignment to read properly recorded information in spite of the fact that it may still read information recorded by that drive. The correction of drive misalignment is covered in Chapter 11.

If you suspect a hardware problem, see Part 2. Software problems are covered in Part 4.

CHAPTER SUMMARY

This chapter has traced the normal operation of the ROM diagnostics and provided direction to appropriate chapters in the event of a detected problem. Since many computer problems are detectable by the ROM diagnostics, you should become familiar with the concept of error codes and what they might indicate.

REVIEW QUESTIONS

1. Name two possible symptoms of a computer crash due to a momentary interruption of power.
2. What should the computer operator do if the alarm on the computer battery-backup unit sounds?
3. What is the component used to limit voltage spikes on AC lines called?
4. Name the two types of information contained on a storage medium such as a floppy disk and the usual drives into which they are inserted.
5. If a computer problem occurs *before* the system prompt appears, what type of problem is it most likely to be?
6. What are the likely causes of problems occurring *after* the system prompt appears?
7. Servicing an IBM microcomputer, you find that BASIC loads rather than the operating system on the diskette in the A drive. What does this indicate?
8. What are the two types of error indications that might be given during a ROM power-up diagnostic routine?
9. Suppose that a computer won't load a program from a specific diskette. What is the next troubleshooting check to make?
10. What is indicated if two computers use their own diskettes without problems but the diskettes will not interchange between computers? (Assume, of course, that the computers are of the same kind.)

part two

Troubleshooting Computer Hardware Problems

chapter three

Common Computer Problems

CHAPTER OVERVIEW

Computer problems tend to fall into specific categories. This chapter will help you recognize common problems and put them into rather neat categories that have definite cures or ways of being dealt with. The troubleshooting approach to an intermittent problem, for instance, may be random—or it may progress very logically if you recognize it for what it is.

COMPLETE FAILURES

The complete failure is the easiest microcomputer problem to identify. Everything is inoperative: the monitor screen is blank and the computer cooling fan is silent. Almost anyone could begin to troubleshoot this problem. Be sure the plug is in the wall, the fuses are good, and the circuit breakers are closed! Checking the availability of proper voltage is important. Substitute a lamp or other electrical load to see if the outlet is supplying power.

Then check the power cord, substituting another cord if one is available. Check the fuse, sometimes accessible on the rear panel of the computer. The next check would be to remove the cover of the computer and check the power supply within the computer. (Chapter 5 deals with troubleshooting the power supply circuits.)

TAMPERED EQUIPMENT

Some people are naturally curious and like to look inside their computers. There is no problem with that. The trouble starts when people begin to tinker inside with a screwdriver, particularly with the disk drives. The chances are very good that such efforts will be rewarded with opposite the desired effect, and by the time a technician gets the equipment it may be inoperative. The servicing technician should watch for such telltale signs of tampering as screwheads torn up by a poor-fitting screwdriver or missing screws, nuts, or other parts.

INTERMITTENTS

The key to repairing any kind of intermittent problem is to make the equipment stay inoperative long enough to pinpoint the cause. Nothing is to be gained by working on an intermittent problem when the failed symptoms will not appear.

The Mechanical Intermittent

A mechanical intermittent responds to a mechanical thump or pressure applied to a circuit board or connector. By very carefully noting the area of the equipment or the printed circuit board that is most sensitive to mechanical stress, it is possible in many cases, to narrow down the problem to the defective component. Take special note of the direction of flexing and the amount of force required to make the computer fail when tracing a mechanical intermittent. As you get nearer the source of the problem, the amount of force necessary to cause the symptoms will decrease.

The Thermal Intermittent

The typical symptom of a thermal intermittent problem is occurence of the problem after the equipment is operated for some time. If the computer is turned off for a time, the problem is often gone when the power is applied again. This thermal cycling can be simulated by the application of heat and/or cold in an effort to duplicate the problem. By selectively directing the heat or cold to smaller and smaller areas of the equipment, it should eventually be possible to isolate the defective component. Wide-area cooling and heating is best done with a commercial freon-based aerosol product specifically manufactured for this purpose and the use of a heat gun or possibly a hair dryer.

The Erratic Intermittent

The erratic intermittent is perhaps the most difficult problem to repair: the symptoms seem to magically disappear when the technician appears. The erratic intermittent is also the source of many customer disputes. The customer may assume the technician can't find the problem through incompetence, and the technician wonders if there really *is* a problem because no unusual symptoms appear when the computer is in the repair shop. Even if the technician believes the diagnosis of the customer, all he or she can do with this kind of intermittent is make an educated guess, replace a suspect card within the equipment, or replace a likely cause of the problem as the operator describes it. The erratic equipment will not respond to changes in heat or cold or to thumping. The problem is just there at some times and not at others.

One of the first things to question is the quality of power available to the computer on site. Low line voltage or such other disturbances as nearby heavy electrical load changes will cause computer failures that will not occur while the technician is working on the computer in the shop. Field service technicians should be especially alert for erratic problems from these causes.

Suggestions for curing the erratic intermittent include operating the equipment for long periods while running a looped diagnostics program. Diagnostics programs will probably have an audio indication of a failure, a beep or series of beeps to alert the technician—who can then be working on other equipment without having to continually watch the suspected computer.

The erratic intermittent may respond to twisting of circuit boards, pulling and pushing of wiring as it enters plugs and jacks, or the cleaning of plug contacts. Some plugs are prone to breaking contact between mating connectors. These contacts can sometimes be resprung so that their mating surfaces again fit tightly together. Methods of bending to restore normal tension in the contacts will be left to your ingenuity since there are many different types of connectors. Once a means is found to make the equipment inoperative, normal troubleshooting can commence.

Hint: The common pencil eraser makes a very good abrasive to clean contacts, especially the edge connectors of printed circuit boards. Printed circuit boards are subject to mechanical stresses where long connector posts go through the board. Pushing and pulling on the wires that connect to these posts can easily cause a hairline break in the circuit underneath where it *should* attach to the post. Inspect such post and wire arrangements very carefully, using a magnifying glass if available. An example of this sort of problem is often found where the keyboard connector is soldered to the system board of the computer. These connectors are often not mounted in any other way, depending upon the bond between the circuit wiring and the board to absorb all of the stress of plugging and unplugging the keyboard cable to the connector. Stressing the connector back and forth *gently* can sometimes reveal a break like this.

Field effect transistor (FET) gates and digital complementary metal oxide semiconductor (CMOS) integrated circuits will behave very erratically if an input is disconnected for any reason. Be aware of this unique possibility when dealing with erratic intermittents in circuits with FETs and CMOS ICs. In digital circuits, a voltage level between the acceptable high and low logic levels can cause erratic intermittent symptoms. Such levels can be detected with an oscilloscope or a logic probe. If any intermittent is general (that is, everything seems to be affected), the power supply is a likely suspect (see Chapter 5).

APPLICATION OF VOLTAGE IN THE WRONG PLACE

A technician using a probe or any metal tool within equipment while it is in operation runs a very definite risk of shorting a pair of IC pins or printed circuit traces together. Often this does no damage, but once in a while the wrong combination comes up and in a few milliseconds a great deal of damage is done. As a simple precautionary measure do not use anything to probe into live circuitry other than a test probe designed for the job. A good probe like the one in Figure 3.1 will be needle-sharp at the tip and very small in diameter. Ideally, it should be small enough not to short IC pins together if placed between them.

If the computer suddenly emits a beep or strange noise, or smokes or otherwise ceases operation when the technician "slips," there is a very good chance that a big job

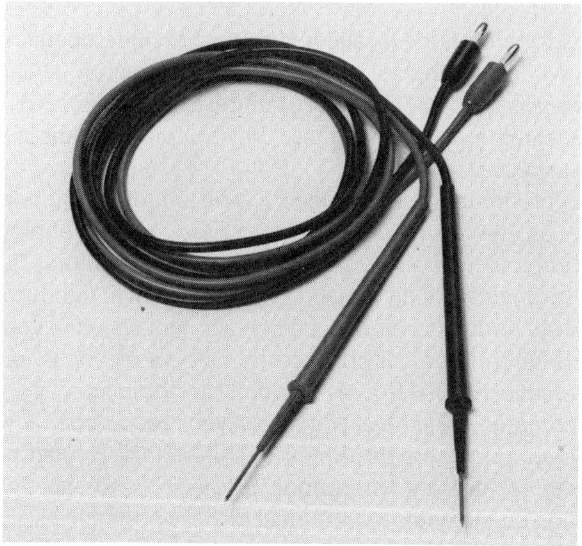

Figure 3.1 Only very sharp, small-diameter probes should be used to test computer circuits. (Courtesy of Huntron Instruments, Inc.)

lies ahead just to get back to the original problem. A slip of a tool like this can cause a string of many circuits to die an instant death. TTL ICs, for instance, will not tolerate 12VDC applied to them without permanent damage; a slip from input to output pins of a regulator could accomplish this in the twinkling of an eye. Be careful! Investigation into the problems caused by such an accident should begin by noting exactly where the improper voltage was applied. Carefully note what those points are on the schematic diagram and what components would most likely be damaged. These components will include ICs, regulators, transistors, and electrolytic capacitors. Other components are more tolerant of such accidents. Troubleshooting should then proceed to replace or verify as good those components that were possibly damaged by the accident. This may require stage-by-stage signal tracing.

TRANSIENTS

Transients are voltage spikes or momentary surges of the primary power source. These surges can cause the instantaneous voltage applied to the computer's power supply to increase enough to trigger failures of almost any of the ICs in computers, the filter capacitors in the power supply, and other semiconductors in the computer.

Typical equipment failures that may point to possible transient damage include shorted rectifier diodes and bridges. Most well-designed equipment operated from 120VAC or 240VAC lines will include some form of transient suppression. These suppression components should be tested for proper operation if other semiconductors may have been damaged by transients, as the suppressors may be open or otherwise not performing their intended function. See Figure 3.2. Most of these failures

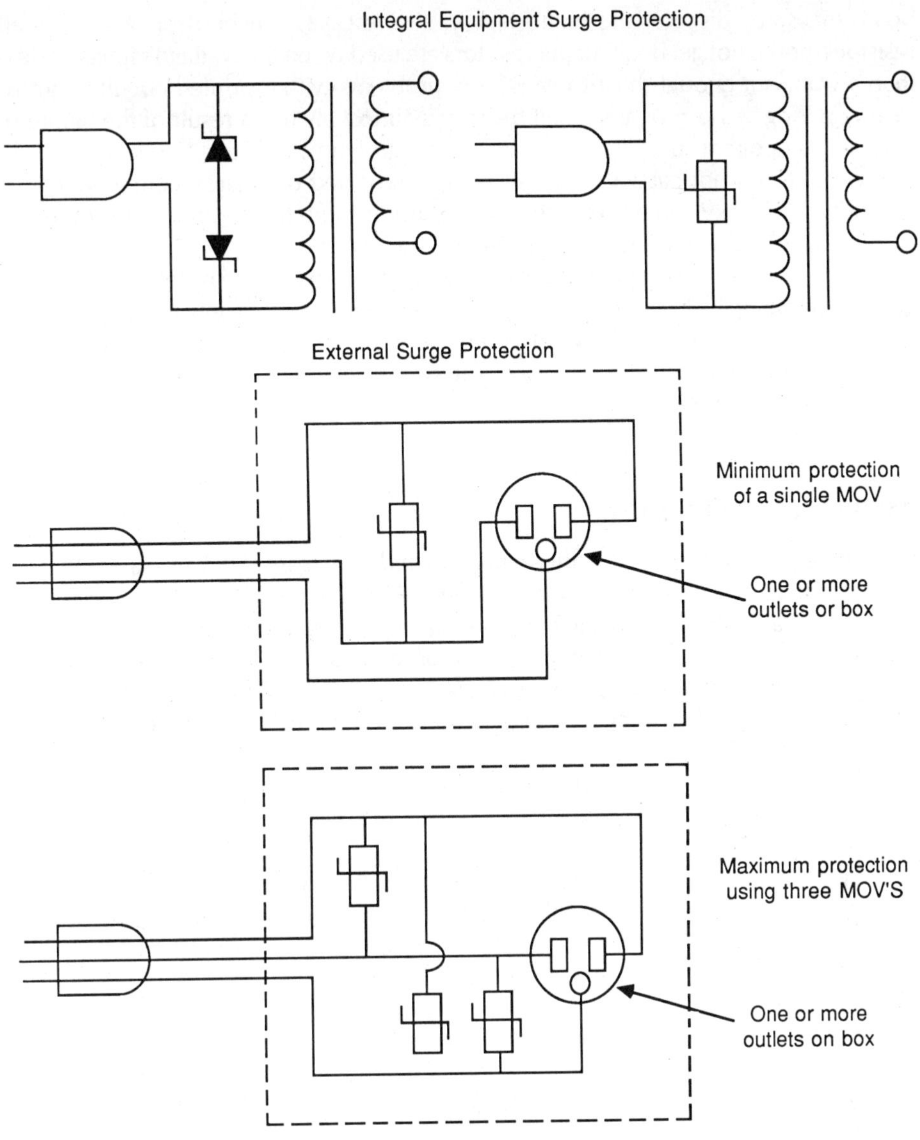

Figure 3.2 Circuits having transient voltage-suppression protection

may be found by following the techniques discussed in Chapter 5. (Figure 2.6 shows some of the more common transient suppressor components.)

OVERHEATED PARTS FAILURES

Resistors are made to throw off heat. The bigger they are the more heat they can safely get rid of without burning up. If hot resistors are mounted directly on a circuit board they may discolor the board and in severe cases can burn or char it. Small resistors should not get hot. Smaller resistors are used when the wattage ratings are less than a watt, not enough heat to cause any problems with a printed circuit board or nearby wiring. A burn of any small resistor is almost always a result of the failure of another component, usually a transistor or electrolytic capacitor. Capacitors should not feel hot. If a hot capacitor is not being overheated by nearby components it is probably very leaky. When replacing a capacitor be sure that no associated failure is causing too much voltage to be applied to the capacitor.

If you suspect a component is overheating you can obviously get a good idea of gross overheating by holding your finger on the component for a few moments. If your finger is not sensitive enough to feel a merely overwarm component, immediately put that finger to your upper lip, just below your nose. The upper lip is extremely sensitive to minute temperature changes.

MULTIPLE PROBLEMS

Once a problem is identified and repaired it is reasonable to expect that the equipment will work properly when assembled into its cabinet. This is, sadly, not always the case. Once in a while the technician may introduce further problems in the course of finding and curing another. The most common second problem is probably the broken wire. When equipment is opened and circuit boards dismantled from the chassis the wiring takes some punishment. Watch for this to happen when dismantling and reassembling computers. It is a sure indication of a technician-induced problem when the equipment was working fine after the repair but ceased operation when inserted into the cabinet. Watch also for pinched wiring, which could cause a short to ground.

Multiple problems may be indicated if a definitely defective component is discovered and replaced and yet the equipment does not work properly. Perhaps the technician has replaced a failed component that was a secondary failure and neglected to find the principal cause of the problem. Troubleshooting must continue to find the second problem. If the second problem found bears no relationship to the first failure and there is little if any chance the technician somehow caused the second failure during the troubleshooting procedure, the technician should suspect a possible voltage transient as the source of this problem and perhaps additional failures, too.

THE TOUGH PROBLEMS

Every technician occasionally encounters a problem that defies all identification efforts. Nothing seems to go right, and all the usual procedures don't help at all. What to do then? Consult this checklist carefully, and you may find the problem:

1. Be sure there is not an operator problem or software problem that could make the hardware seem defective when it really isn't. Suspect people and software

before you suspect the computer. Over half of the reported computer problems are nonhardware-related; power-line transients, operator error, and software are much more likely to be the problem.

2. Check the test equipment test leads for intermittents or opens that may have occurred since starting the troubleshooting procedure.
3. Did you change ranges on the test equipment and forget to change it back?
4. Try substituting known good test equipment for the test equipment in use, which might have failed. Try the same with the board or computer under test. Remove the suspected unit and substitute a known good piece of equipment to verify the symptoms you are getting.
5. If you have access to a good computer of the same type as the defective one, try comparing readings from good to bad unit to help in isolating the problem in the bad. This procedure involves applying power to both units and taking voltage reading back and forth between them. If you are making dead-circuit checks, you would of course not apply power to either unit.
6. Get away from the problem for a while. It is possible to get too involved and begin making dumb mistakes.
7. When you go back to the job make notes on paper as you go to keep the facts straight. This is of particular help when you are taking many readings.
8. Get the help of another technician. No one, no matter how experienced, has all the answers all the time. You could be overlooking something very simple that another technician might be able to point out.
9. Start your troubleshooting all over again and take all your readings again. Something may have changed as you were working that could scramble any logical approach you are trying to maintain.
10. Are you sure there was a problem to start with? Some microcomputer boards are turned in for repair when there is nothing at all wrong with them.
11. Consider that the documentation you are using might be in error. Be sure you are working on *exactly* the same model as your documentation, particularly when it comes to schematics. Production changes are very often made to hardware without updating the documentation.
12. Consider the possibility that the instruction manual might be wrong. Inaccurate documentation can indicate symptoms that are extremely confusing.
13. It is not unusual to have more than one problem in a piece of equipment. Remember that the symptoms of two different failures may together cause symptoms that cannot be explained by a single failure.

CHAPTER SUMMARY

This chapter has covered some of the types of circuit problems the computer technician might see in the course of a day's work. Familiarity with these problems and an ability to identify them instinctively will increase any technician's working speed.

REVIEW QUESTIONS

1. What simple method could be used to verify the presence of electrical power at an outlet?
2. What is the key to troubleshooting any kind of an intermittent problem?
3. Name two desirable features of a test-probe tip for troubleshooting in dense circuitry?
4. Where could you find a handy checklist to help you when a particular problem is frustrating you?

chapter four

Troubleshooting to the Unit & Board Level

CHAPTER OVERVIEW

The typical hardware repair of a computer consists of replacing a printed circuit card or a diskette drive or other peripheral. This chapter will enable a technician to attempt a typical computer repair with confidence by discussing such a repair and suggesting ways to isolate the cause of a problem. Simple repairs are given for common situations: lack of good primary power to the computer, cabling problems; and failure of a diskette drive, monitor, or printer.

CHECK THE SIMPLE THINGS FIRST

Before assuming that the computer is at fault, check out the simple possibilities first (Figure 4.1):

1. Be sure the power plug is inserted into an energized outlet. Remember that some outlets can be switched off at a wall switch. If possible, change the power cord to the computer to be sure that the cord isn't open.
2. A proper operating system program must be inserted into the booting up diskette drive. Without the proper programs on the diskette (covered in detail in Chapter 15) the computer cannot be put into full operation. Try other diskettes with the operating system installed. If that is not practical, use a fresh copy of the backup diskettes to see if that cures the problem.
3. Be sure that operator error is not the cause of the problem. Operate the computer yourself, using software with which you are familiar, to eliminate this possibility.
4. If the computer has recently been opened and changes made within it, there is an excellent chance that these changes are the cause of the problem. For instance, if an option card has just been installed and the computer then refuses to work properly, it is a good bet that something involving what has just been done is now causing the problem. Think over what has been done and retrace the steps to the point where the computer was working properly before the changes were made. For instance, an option card often requires that the system

Figure 4.1 The servicing technician must be able to perform fundamental operations with the computer in order to troubleshoot the computer system effectively. (Abbey Enterprises)

board option switches be changed. If they are changed to a wrong combination, the computer may not work at all. For this reason, it is always a good idea to write down switch settings *before* any changes are made so that this step can be retraced with minimum effort.

TROUBLESHOOTING TO THE UNIT LEVEL

Once the simple items above are eliminated the next step is to see which of the computer units are causing the problem:

Printer and monitor cables

Printers

Disk Drives

Monitors

Keyboards

The system unit (the computer itself)

These items have been listed in the approximate order of their likelihood of causing a problem. Since the printer is a mechanical device and goes through a great many motions in doing its job, it is probably the most troublesome component of a computer system. At the other extreme, the computer circuits themselves are very seldom the cause of a problem. Not mentioned in this list are the two major causes of computer problems: the operator error and the software problem. Eliminate these two common

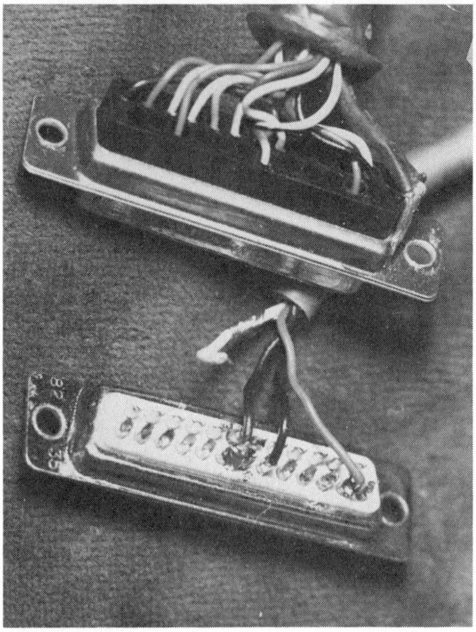

Figure 4.2 Nonrepairable and repairable connectors (Abbey Enterprises)

causes of problems, using Chapter 2 as a guide. Specific problems with software are covered in Chapter 15.

Printer and Monitor Cable Problems

The cables between a computer and such peripherals such as monitors, printers, and modems are subject to a considerable amount of mechanical damage. They can be caught between desks and the wall or other furniture, burned by cigarettes, or crushed by the weight of heavy computers and printers. Perhaps the greatest stress is placed on a cable by pulling on the cable harness instead of directly on the connectors at either end. Some connectors are securely fastened to the computer or the peripheral equipment by a couple of small bolts. Since the plug cannot come loose, the cable takes any pulling stress directly on the wires at the point they enter the connector. This is the most frequent cause of cable failure. Some plugs can be repaired, while others are meant for a one-time permanent attachment to the cable. A defective cable of the latter type must be replaced as a unit. See Figure 4.2.

Printer Problems

Printer problems can be localized to the printer itself by invoking the self-test found in many printers. The method of starting the self-test routine varies in detail, but often consists of turning on the 120V power while at the same time holding down a specified key. The self-test consists of having the printer print each of the characters that it is capable of printing, over and over (Figure 4.3). Often, only turning off the printer will stop the routine. The self-test should be run *without* the cable connected to the

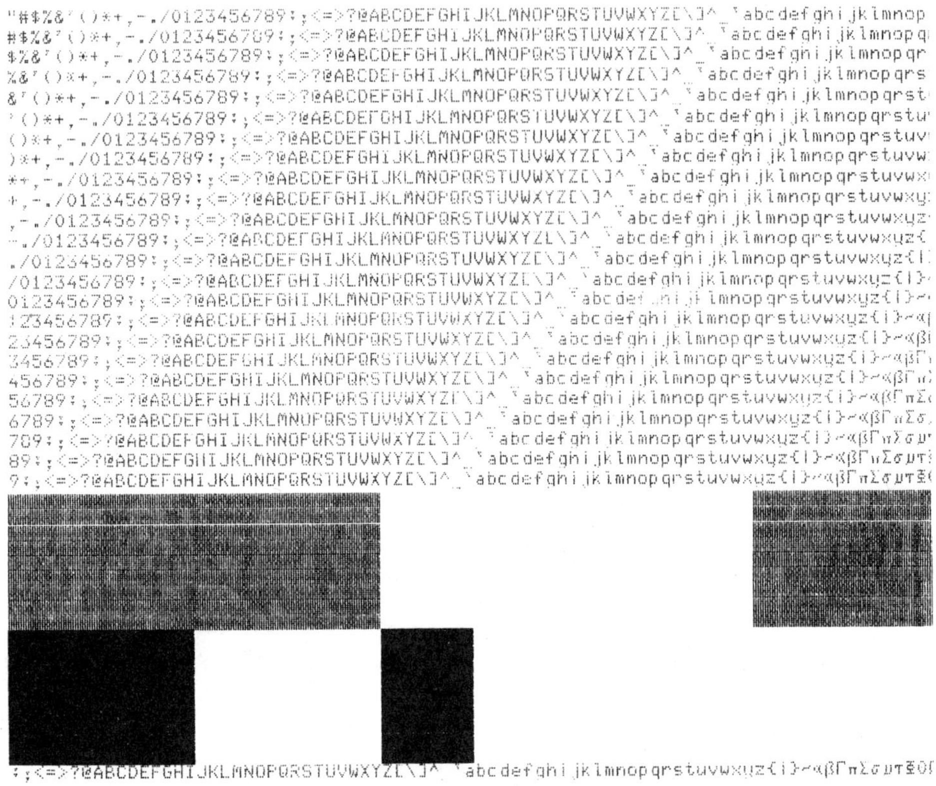

Figure 4.3 Typical result of a printer's built-in self-test (Mannesmann Tally)

computer, and it is preferable to disconnect the cable at the printer so problems in the cable cannot affect the printer.

A second test is to substitute another printer for the suspected one. If the second printer runs without error, the first printer obviously was defective. Be sure to check the cable to the printer for problems such as broken or stressed connections where the wiring goes into the connectors at both ends.

If two printers of identical manufacture are compared and only one works, be sure to check any internal setup switches which may be inside the printer to be sure the settings are the same.

For further printer troubleshooting refer to Chapter 13.

Localizing a Problem to a Disk Drive

The following items indicate a probable diskette drive problem:

1. Frequent error messages on a specific drive, such as CANNOT OPEN FILE
2. Diskettes written by one drive cannot be read by another drive.

3. The operating system will not consistently load, if at all, from a particular drive. (Be sure you have a good system diskette for this test.)
4. Lack of an LED activity indication and inability to access files on a drive.
5. IBM PC computers only: If an IBM PC's A diskette drive is the drive used to load the operating system, a bad drive there will cause the computer to miss loading the system, of course, but the computer will then default to loading BASIC from the ROM chips within the IBM. Only the IBM PC has these ROM chips.

The appearance of:

```
The IBM Personal Computer BASIC
Version XXXX Copyright IBM Corp 198X
XXXX Bytes free
Ok
```

is a sure indication of an A drive problem or a floppy diskette problem in that drive.

Either mechanical or electronic problems will cause malfunctions. To verify whether a drive is defective, be sure that the drive motor is operating when the drive is accessed for data and the diskette is revolving within its envelope. See that the activity LED is lighting at the same time. There are two common ways of confirming the condition of a suspected drive. The first method is to substitute a known good drive (if one is available) for the suspected drive; the other is to switch between drives A and B to see if the problem also switches location.

Opening a Computer to Switch the Diskette Drives or Change One. Always unplug a computer before removing the cabinet. It is very easy to cause an accidental short with the cover of some computers, which could severely damage them.

Take the case off a computer slowly while watching for anything that might get caught on the cover and be damaged (including the edges of the option cards). Some computers are provided with connectors on items such as speakers, which must be disconnected to remove the cabinet.

Be particularly careful not to scratch the equipment. Do not stack equipment without intervening protective material such as cardboard or rugs to prevent damage. Take removed cabinets or covers and place them where they will not be knocked over.

Keep in mind when disconnecting wiring that if the parts needed for repair are not available, it may be some time before the equipment is reassembled. If there is any chance at all that wiring might not be placed on the same terminals from which they came, write down the layout of the wiring and where it connects. Keep these notes with the equipment.

When removing screws from equipment, be careful to note the length of each as it is removed. Some screws need to be shorter than others to prevent them from going too far into the equipment and causing damage.The best way to save the bolts and to be sure they are returned to the proper holes is to take off the covers and immediately put the screws back into the holes from which they came. This is an especially good idea if the equipment may not be reassembled for some time. A second-best alternative is to put the bolts into a small container that can be put with the equipment. The worst thing that can be done with loose screws is to lay them somewhere on the workbench. At least one will find its way onto the floor and will be lost.

Once the cover is off it may be possible to find the problem quickly by a close visual inspection. Look for burned or broken components or anything else out of the ordinary, such as loose or broken wiring and poor soldering joints. Look closely at the center of each IC for raised dimples indicating overheated and probably shorted circuits. The smell of burned components may also lead to the problems. Resistors and transformers have their own characteristic smell when burned and the technician will come to recognize them.

Switching Diskette Drives to Verify a Suspected Bad Drive. The technician may decide that it would be a good idea to substitute the normal B drive of the computer for the normal A drive. If the software is then readable in the new A drive it can be assumed that the original drive A was indeed defective.

To change the B drive temporarily to act as the A drive you must turn off the computer and remove its cover. When the cover is off, the signal plugs to the A and B drives are removed (see Figure 4.4).

The cable that originally went to the A drive is then placed on the PC connector of the B drive.

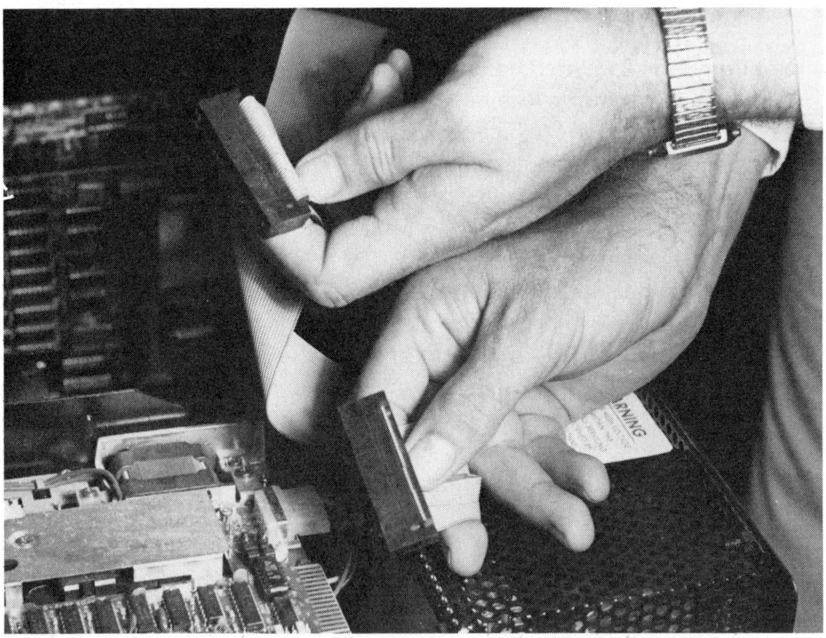

Figure 4.4 Exchanging the A and B drives is a fast method of determining where a floppy diskette drive problem lies. (Abbey Enterprises)

The two drives may have a set of jumpers which must be examined before the drive can operate properly (Figure 4.5). These jumpers may be exactly the same on the two drives, the original A and B drives. If so, they may be ignored. If they are different, write down exactly how they are before you make any changes. Then change the original B drive jumpers to match those of the A drive. The jumpers of a Tandon™ drive are explained in Figure 4.6.

The final item item to check in swapping the drives is the terminating resistor, which is installed only on the last drive on a control cable string. In most cases the cabling comes from the floppy disk controller card to the B drive first, then the A drive. Thus, the A drive will have a terminating resistor installed. This resistor often resembles an ordinary IC (see Figure 4.7).

Although resistors may be installed into a circuit either way, the terminating resistor array in the IC case is not necessarily reversible. Note any markings indicating pin #1 of the IC and place it into the socket correctly. Now that the original B drive has the terminating resistor and its jumpers are the same as the original A drive, it should perform as the booting drive. Place an appropriate bootable diskette in the drive, apply power, and see if the computer now loads the program properly. If it does, the original A drive is probably out of alignment or otherwise defective and should be further repaired. See Chapter 11 for details of alignment and testing of disk drives.

Figure 4.5 Make note of the jumper positions before changing them. (Abbey Enterprises)

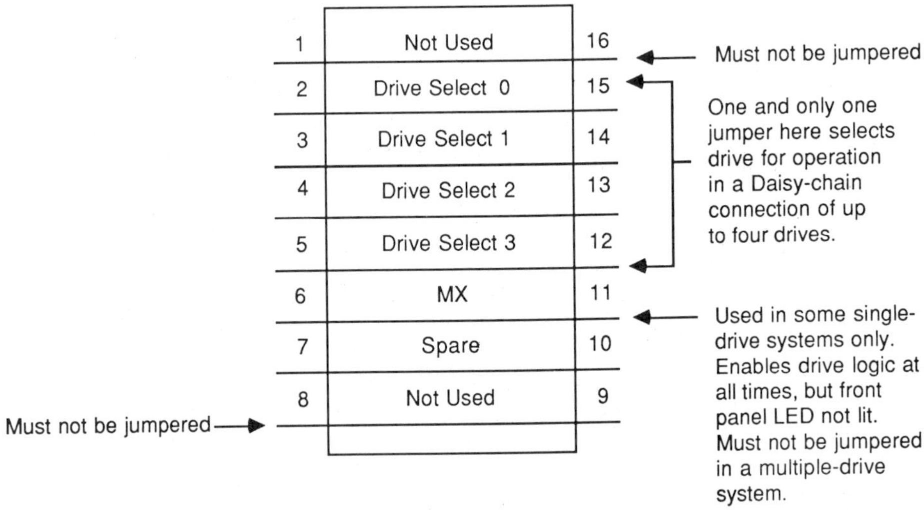

Figure 4.6 Jumpers on the diskette drive enable the drive to be customized to a specific installation.

Figure 4.7 The terminating resistor should be installed on the last drive of the connecting cable. (Abbey Enterprises)

If the computer still does not load a program properly, the problem may be with the disk controller card. Substitution of the controller card is the best way to eliminate or confirm the controller card as the cause.

Monitor and Cable Problems

The accidental moving of the brightness or contrast controls of a monitor may make it seem dead when there is no problem other than operator error (Figure 4.8). Be sure to check the settings of these controls *first* when a monitor problem occurs.

Monitor problems can best be localized to the monitor unit itself by substituting another monitor known to be in proper working order. A similar monitor *must* be used, monochrome for monochrome and color for color. If possible, the good monitor should get its signals from the same connector on the computer that the original used. It is possible that the good monitor may still malfunction, indicating a problem most likely in the monitor adapter within the computer. This will necessitate the removal of the computer case to get inside the computer. The monitor adapter should be changed with a known good monitor card to localize the problem to the old card. Few computers use a TV screen for a monitor, but those installations that do will have an extra RF modulator unit which may also be causing video problems.

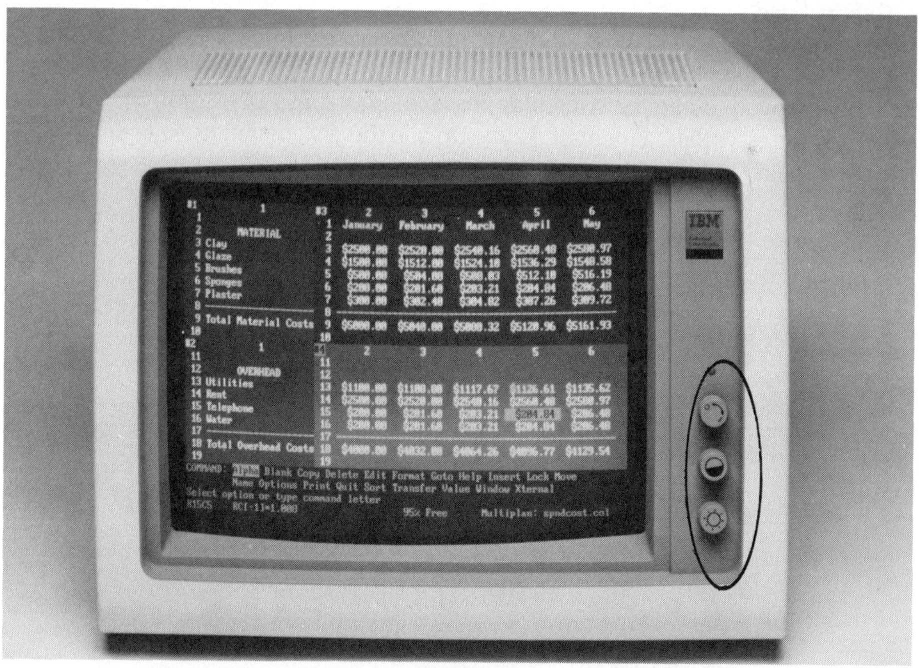

Figure 4.8 Be sure that the operator hasn't accidentally turned down the brightness or contrast controls of the monitor and then reported that the monitor has failed. (Courtesy of IBM)

If the monitor has a removable cable, the cable can be changed to eliminate it as a possible problem. Often, however, the monitor has a permanently connected cable, which requires that the cable be considered part of the monitor. Chapter 12 gives more details on monitor troubleshooting.

Keyboard Problems

Keyboard problems can be most easily verified by connecting another keyboard to the computer. Problems in the keyboard are most often one of two types: the cord is apparently intermittent, or one or more keys are stuck or don't seem to make contact reliably. Further keyboard troubleshooting is covered in Chapter 9.

Localizing Problems Within the System Unit

Manipulating Hardware to Localize the Problem. Once such external units as printers, monitors, and keyboards are eliminated as causing the problem it becomes necessary to localize problems inside the computer.

The best way to localize problems within the computer is to remove nonessential cards from the computer and attempt to run the computer without them. Whenever cards are to be removed from or installed in a computer, make certain that the power is *off* before handling them! This is absolutely necessary to prevent damage to the boards from minute electrical charges. If the computer has option cards such as additional RAM, clock-setting hardware, hard disk controllers, and game interface cards, these may be removed to eliminate them as possible problem sources. Strip the computer system to the essentials: a monitor, keyboard and the system unit itself (Figure 4.9).

Figure 4.9 It may be necessary to strip the system to the minimum possible configuration. (Abbey Enterprises)

Figure 4.10 The system board switch settings must be checked and reset when option cards are removed. (Abbey Enterprises)

Once the nonessential cards are removed from the computer, *write down* the settings of the system board selector switches before changing them. These switches are "read" by the computer during power-up to tell it whether or not certain options are present, such as the number of disk drives installed, kind of video monitor installed, and the amount of RAM memory provided. Changing the installed options requires careful checking and probable resetting of the system board switches (see Figure 4.10).

Understand the switch settings thoroughly before changing them. Documentation on the specific computer should give all the information required to set the switches to new values as the option cards are removed. Here is an example of setting the system switches to a minimum configuration. Before any cards were removed from our sample computer, it had the switch settings for S1 and S2 as shown in Figure 4.11. After removing all cards except the video card and the floppy disk drive controller card, the switch settings would need to be changed to those of Figure 4.12.

After all the nonessential option cards are removed, attempt to operate the computer. If the computer operates properly, the original problem was likely to have been caused by one of the cards removed. Continue to run the computer for some time to be certain that the problem is now gone. After convincing yourself that the computer is still operating normally, turn it off and reinstall *one* of the cards you have removed. Be sure to reset the appropriate system board switches so the computer will know of the presence of the new option board. Again run the computer. If it now fails, the card you just installed is causing the problem. If it does not fail, run the computer for a while

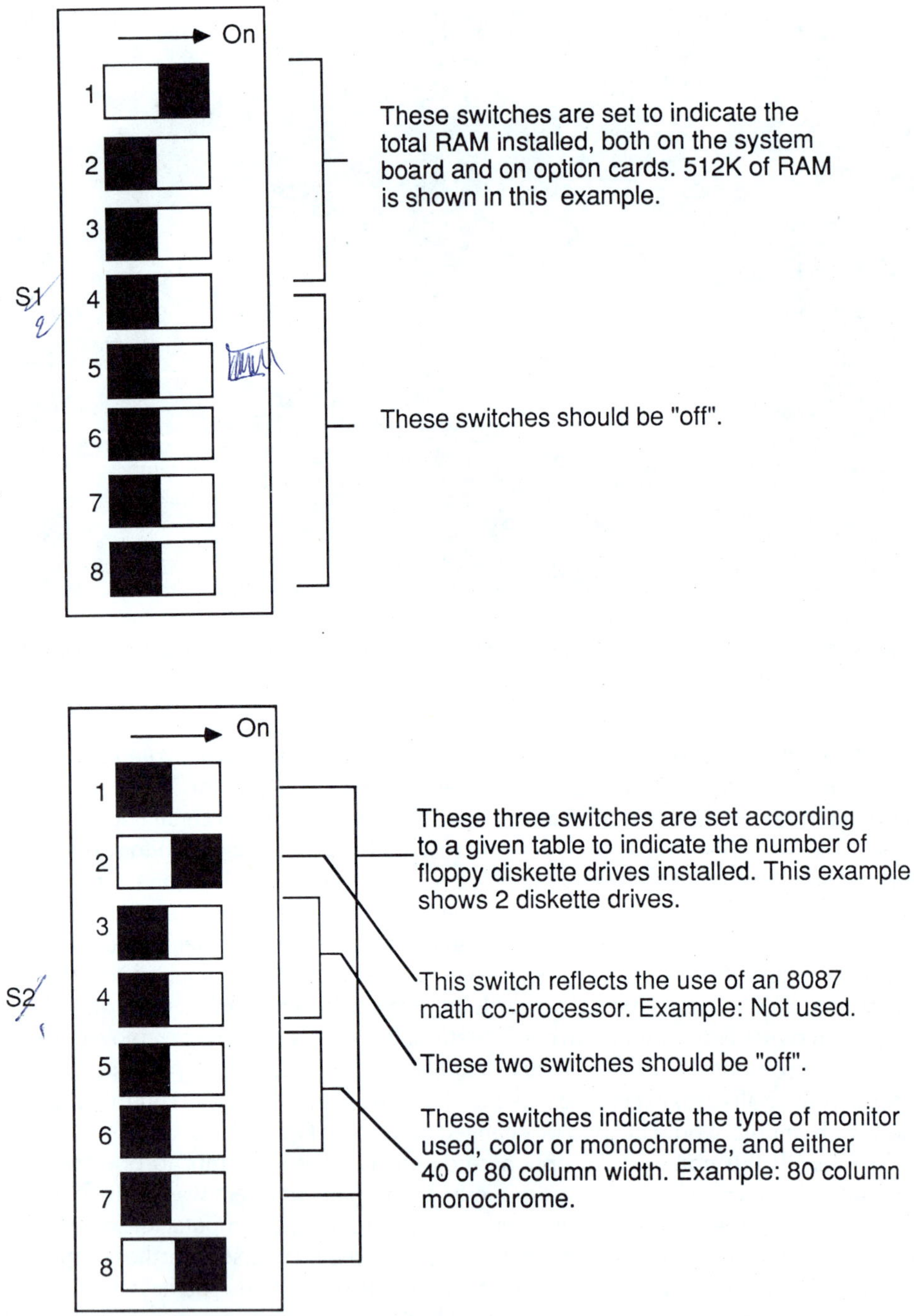

Figure 4.11 Representative example of system switch settings before changing them to the simplest configuration possible (Stephanie Enterprises)

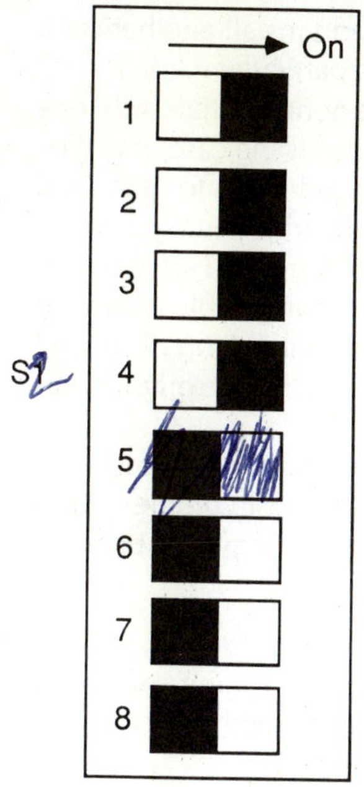

System switches after changing them to show a minimal system. Example: 64K of RAM memory now shown.

These switches still "off".

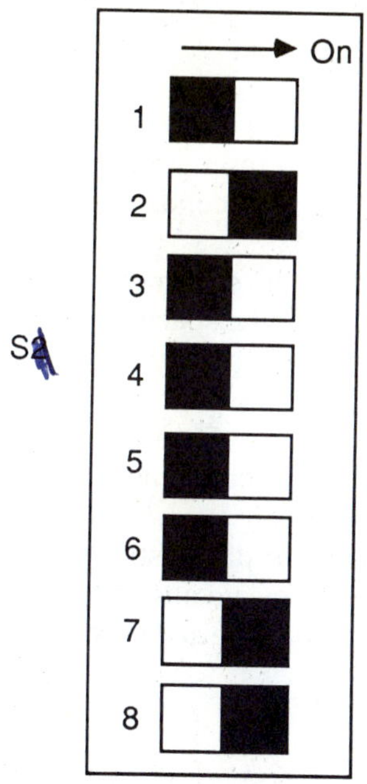

Still no co-processor:
These switches still "off".

Changing one of these three switches reduces the diskette count to only one.

Note: The use of "negative logic" in these representative system board switch settings. When a switch is in the "on" position, that function is "off". This is common practice in system switching.

Figure 4.12 New switch settings show only 64K of memory, one diskette drive, and a monochrome monitor (Stephanie Enterprises) to be certain that there is still no problem, then shut it down and install another card. Repeat this process until the problem appears after installing a particular card.

If the computer refuses to operate after the removal of the nonessential cards, one of the necessary option cards may be causing the problem. If this is the case, it will be necessary to borrow or otherwise obtain substitute, known-good cards to insert and test. When installing a new board, be sure that it is compatible with your system (an identical replacement if at all possible) and that the switches on the board are properly set as was the original board. Installation of a board that is not compatible with your computer can easily cause extensive and expensive damage. Installation of a good board and the resulting proper operation of the computer confirms that the original was indeed defective.

If the computer will not operate properly after substituting the essential cards it is likely that the problem is within the system board. This is the most complex, most difficult board of all to repair. Chapter 8 covers troubleshooting of the system board to the component level.

Memory Problems. Programs are retrieved from storage on diskettes, tapes, or hard disks and copied into RAM, where they are then executed. If there is a failure of any bit within the RAM (and there could be millions of bits in a computer with a lot of RAM memory installed) the missing bit could easily cause a computer crash.

The ROM diagnostics program may tell which specific chip is defective out of all of the installed chips. It might do this by flashing a numerical code on the screen for a *brief moment*, then showing:

PARITY ERROR

It is necessary to note the brief numerical code to help identify the bad chip. If you miss getting it, the computer must be turned off and restarted again to reset the system. When performing this check, leave the computer off for about 10 seconds to help reduce electrical stresses of rapid off-on switching of the power.

If the ROM diagnostics give a coded location for the bad IC, the documentation for the specific computer will further assist in decoding to identify the specific chip. Once the defective chip has been identified, it should be removed and a good chip installed with care. If you are fortunate, the IC will be installed in a socket. If not, it will be soldered into the board and must be unsoldered to remove it. (See Chapter 10 for soldering details and tips for removing ICs without damage.) Be sure that the new chip is properly oriented before inserting it into the board or the socket.

Memory problems that are not evident during the power-up diagnostics may present a particularly difficult problem to troubleshoot because they are intermittent. These problems may be evident to the computer operator by an unexpected message during normal operation such as:

PARITY CHECK ONE

or

PARITY CHECK TWO

or a complete computer crash. Parity check one means that there was an error in recalling information stored in the system board RAM. Parity check two points to a similar memory error in the RAM installed on an option board.

The most efficient way to troubleshoot intermittent memory problems is to run a diskette diagnostic memory test program for however long it may take to identify the bad memory chip. There are many different ways to test memory chips. One method is to put alternating 1 and 0 patterns into the RAM chips then go back to verify that all of the bits read back as they should. Then, alternate the pattern with a 0 and 1 pattern and again recheck it. Other patterns can also be used, such as all 1s and all 0s, rechecking results as above. Each pattern is written to memory in one-byte units (8 bits). Most microcomputers use nine bits for each byte, the ninth bit being used to keep track of the even or odd status of the other 8 bits written into memory (Figure 4.13). The ninth bit is set or cleared to make the sum of the bits come out to always be the same, always even or always odd, depending upon how the parity was set up originally. If the read value including the ninth bit is not consistently even or odd as determined by the software, there must have been an error between what was written and what was later read from a specified location.

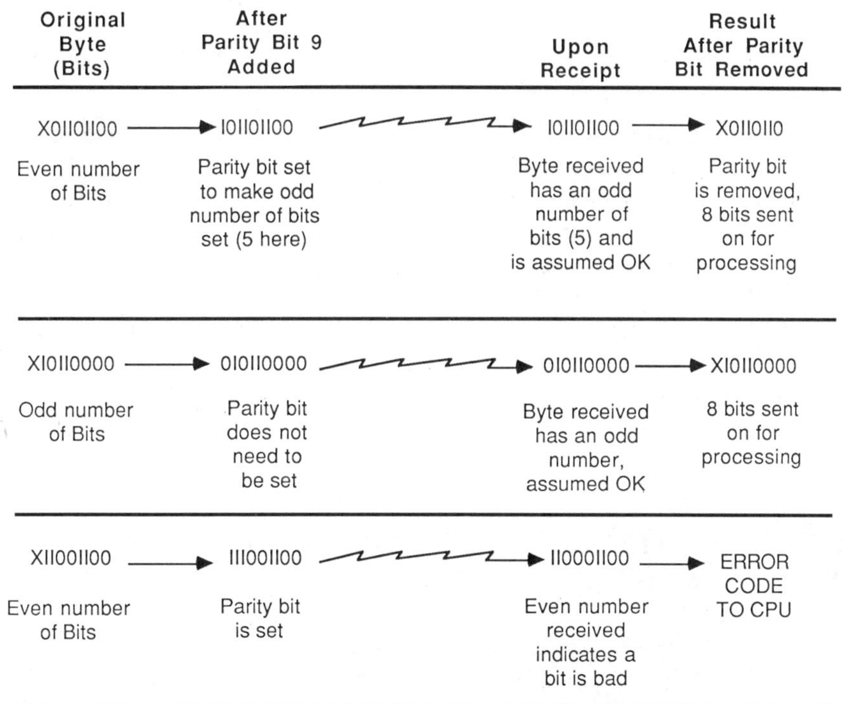

How a parity bit is used to detect a bad byte of data. This system was initiated for 8 data bits and odd parity checking.

Figure 4.13 The use of a ninth bit with each 8-bit byte is an effective means of detecting single-bit errors between write and read operations.

System board RAM has a single line which, if pulled up, causes an interrupt routine to place the PARITY CHECK ONE message on the screen and halt the processor. Any data that was held in RAM will be lost, since the computer must be restarted from a cold reboot, which does not leave any option of continuing where the program left off when the error occurred. This kind of failure is very frustrating to a computer operator. RAM expansion cards have a similar separate line which causes a PARITY CHECK TWO message to appear before halting the processor. There is no practical way to identify a specific defective chip during program execution. Only an indication that there is a problem is possible; this is where the diagnostic program proves invaluable. The diagnostic program can be left running for days, if necessary, to identify a defective chip. There are many RAM diagnostic programs available such as the programs offered by Quadram™ to check the RAM chips on their own memory expansion option boards. The details of the installation and running of the programs and their error codes must be obtained from the software instruction manuals.

TO REPAIR OR NOT TO REPAIR?

It is often cost-effective to troubleshoot computer problems only to the board level or to find that replacing a cable cures the problem. Once a card is determined to be causing a problem, several choices are available:

1. A defective board may still be under the manufacturer's warranty and should be sent to the factory for repair.
2. Return the card to the factory to have it repaired. This is often a wise move, and the factory can often repair a card at less expense than a technician's time would involve. Or, if the card is not too expensive, it may be cost-effective simply to replace it and discard the old card.
3. Referring to Chapter 6 or 7, it might be worth while to attempt shop repair of the circuit down to the component level. If the bad card is not absolutely necessary for a specific computer application, perhaps it could be eliminated from the system without severely limiting the use of the computer until the card can either be repaired or replaced.

USING THE DISKETTE DIAGNOSTICS PROGRAMS TO LOCALIZE PROBLEMS

The diskette diagnostics program is used to locate a problem in a computer (Figure 4.14). This program is more detailed than the ROM diagnostic program and allows the servicing technician many different options as to what to check and how to check it. In essence, the computer is used to troubleshoot itself at high speed rather than requiring a technician to attach oscilloscopes or other test instruments and then to interpret the instrumentation results.

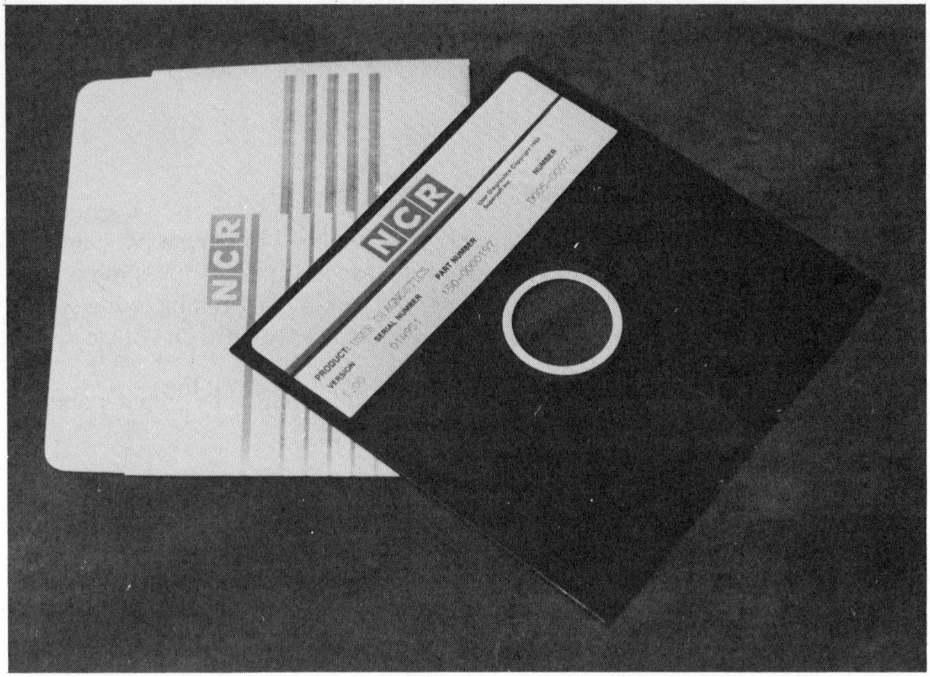

Figure 4.14 A diagnostic diskette is a valuable troubleshooting tool. (Abbey Enterprises)

If the computer is operational enough to load the diagnostic program from a floppy disk drive, the following items can be analyzed with the program to find specific problems in these areas:

The system (mother) board

System memory

The floppy drives

Monitor problems

Parallel or serial ports

The game port

Note that the diagnostic program does not test devices such as printers or modems. In fact, it may be more effective without such peripherals being connected to the computer. Before running the diagnostic program be certain the monitor and the system unit are plugged into a power outlet and that the necessary cables to the computer are secure at both ends. A technician who assumes that the monitor isn't getting a signal, accounting for the dark screen, would be embarassed to find out later that it hadn't been plugged into an outlet. If there is a possibility that the outlet is not energized for any reason, plug in a lamp or other device to assure that power is available.

Learning and Loading the Diagnostic Program

When first learning to use a diagnostic program, learn to run the program on a computer in good operating condition and how to respond to the various prompts and the options available along the way. Load the program by first getting to the system prompt, A>. Then type the name of the diagnostic program (such as DIAGS) to invoke it, then hit the RETURN key.

The diagnostic program may list the items installed with the computer and ask whether the list is correct:

```
THE INSTALLED DEVICES ARE:
   1 SYSTEM BOARD
   2 xxxKB MEMORY
   3 KEYBOARD
   4 MONOCHROME & PRINTER ADAPTER
   5 COLOR/GRAPHICS ADAPTER
   6 x DISKETTE DRIVE(S) AND ADAPTER
   9 PARALLEL PRINTER ADAPTER
  11 ASYNC COMMUNICATIONS ADAPTER
  12 ALT ASYNC COMMUNICATIONS ADAPTER
IS THE LIST CORRECT?
```

This listing allows the technician to see what the computer is reading from the system setup switches and will indicate what should be installed inside an unfamiliar computer without removing the cover, assuming that the switches are set correctly. If there is an obvious error in the installed devices, correct the switch settings and cold reboot the system. This usually means turning off the computer power for about ten seconds and then turning it back on. This causes the computer to reread the switch settings during the ROM initializing routines. Some computers may have a system reset button that accomplishes the same result without the necessity to remove power from the computer. Note that this rebooting does not refer to a warm reboot which is done by striking three keys at once—typically the Ctrl/Alt/Del keys.

One popular advanced diagnostics program then offers several options:

```
0 - RUN DIAGNOSTIC ROUTINES
1 - FORMAT DISKETTE
2 - COPY DISKETTE
3 - PREPARE SYSTEM FOR RELOCATION
9 - EXIT TO SYSTEM DISKETTE
```

The technician will usually select the 0 option. Options 1 and 2 are similar to the DOS programs for formatting a diskette and copying one. Option 3 is of negligible value at this point. Option 9 is a way out of the program back to the operating system.

Once option 0 has been selected, the following options may be made available:

0 - RUN TESTS ONE TIME
1 - RUN TESTS MULTIPLE TIMES
2 - LOG UTILITIES
9 - EXIT DIAGNOSTIC ROUTINES

Option 0 is the one the servicing technician usually uses. During the following checks, this option requires input from the technician, such as pressing the keys of the keyboard to test individual keys. More detailed troubleshooting can be done using this mode than using option 1. The technician must be present to catch and interpret some problems, such as incorrect characters appearing on the screen. Option 1 is better used in a case such as repeated automatic checks of memory to find an intermittent problem. This option relies on the computer to catch all errors that might occur. Option 2 allows the setup of a printer to keep track of intermittent problems in a completely unattended mode. Option 2 is used to log errors detected by the diagnostics program. Option 9, of course, exits the diagnostic routines and returns the technician to the operating system.

By this time the technician should have an idea where the problem lies within the whole computer installation. More detailed troubleshooting is covered in chapters devoted to specific hardware areas:

Chapter 5 Power supplies

Chapter 7 Option cards

Chapter 8 System (mother) boards

Chapter 9 Keyboards

Chapter 11 Floppy disk drives

Chapter 12 Monitors

Chapter 13 Printers

CHAPTER SUMMARY

This chapter has presented the practical approach to troubleshooting computer problems to the unit or board level. Use of these procedures will enable the technician to rapidly pinpoint the problem to a specific defective unit or board. Once the problem is localized, what must then be considered is whether or not to go further into the problem to the component level or to leave the actual repair to the manufacturer of the unit or card at fault.

REVIEW QUESTIONS

1. Name the four steps to accomplish before assuming that a computer's hardware is at fault.
2. Name a common troubleshooting step to eliminate a printer as a problem cause.
3. Name two ways to eliminate a suspected diskette drive as being a problem.
4. The terminating resistor pack of a diskette drive should be installed only on the ________drive of a series of drive.
5. What is the best way to determine if the floppy diskette drive controller is causing a problem?
6. What is the quickest way to determine if a keyboard problem is in the keyboard unit?
7. What precaution *must* be observed to prevent further damage to the computer when circuits are plugged in and unplugged from it?
8. You are contemplating changing the system board switches after removing several of the computer's option cards as a troubleshooting step. What should you do before changing the switch settings?
9. What is the significance of a number flashed briefly on the computer screen during a ROM diagnostic memory check which then results in a PARITY ERROR showing on the screen?
10. What is the difference between PARITY CHECK ONE and a PARITY CHECK TWO indication?
11. Why are nine memory chips used in each bank of memory rather than the eight required for a byte of memory?
12. What two common peripherals are commonly not checked by a diagnostics diskette?
13. What is the principal troubleshooting tool in determining which unit or board of a computer is at fault?
14. What is recommended as a means of familiarizing a technician with the *normal* indications while running diagnostics routines?

chapter five

Troubleshooting the Computer Power Supply & Cooling Fan

CHAPTER OVERVIEW

Only rarely does a computer power supply cause a problem, but this chapter discusses them in some detail. This gives the new technician a feeling for the danger of working in these innocent- appearing circuits that may produce voltages over 300VDC during normal operation. It also explains the practical side of using a DC voltmeter during any kind of troubleshooting so that the readings obtained will really mean something instead of creating confusion and doubt. This chapter also introduces the concept of using a soft fuse to prevent further damage to an overloaded power supply. Confusing symptoms sometimes present when a power supply is overloaded are explained, avoiding wasted time looking for a problem where there is none.

This chapter also covers troubleshooting techniques used when working with the high voltage circuits of the power supply. The two kinds of power supply, standard transformer/rectifier and the switching power supply, are covered. Dangers of working on these circuits are also emphasized. Only experienced technicians should attempt the repair of these dangerous circuits. As always, the expense of working on a computer power supply must be weighed against simple replacement of the supply as a cure.

DANGER: HIGH VOLTAGE!

Cautions to observe when troubleshooting inside the power supply:

1. Always troubleshoot high voltage circuits with one hand behind your back or in a back pocket. This simple action will prevent an accidental shock from passing a current through the chest, where it can cause heart failure.
2. Always have another technician or at least a person knowledgeable in first aid in the vicinity in case of an accident. In other words, never service dangerous circuits while alone.

3. Use test leads that are insulated to the tips to help prevent accidental shorting of circuitry.
4. Be sure your test meter is on the voltage scales when testing live circuitry to avoid damage to your meter.
5. After you take voltage readings and before touching any components, turn off the equipment and discharge any large electrolytic capacitors in the power supply by shorting their terminals together. This must also be done before using an ohmmeter.

The first step in troubleshooting a power supply is to look for an improper voltage. There may be no voltage where there should be, voltage where it doesn't belong, or the voltage measured is not as much as it should be. Voltage troubleshooting procedures assume that the computer is plugged in and turned on.

GENERAL DC TROUBLESHOOTING

Voltmeter Test Probes

The probes used with a voltmeter should be sharp and either be of very small diameter or have a long, narrow taper with insulation down to the very tip (Figure 5.1). The sharp tip will pierce any contaminants or coating on a microcomputer board, including residue of soldering flux. The sharp tip is also very good to prevent the probe from slipping from one trace to another—or, worse, shorting two traces together. Standard test probes can be fitted with insulation such as heat-shrinking plastic.

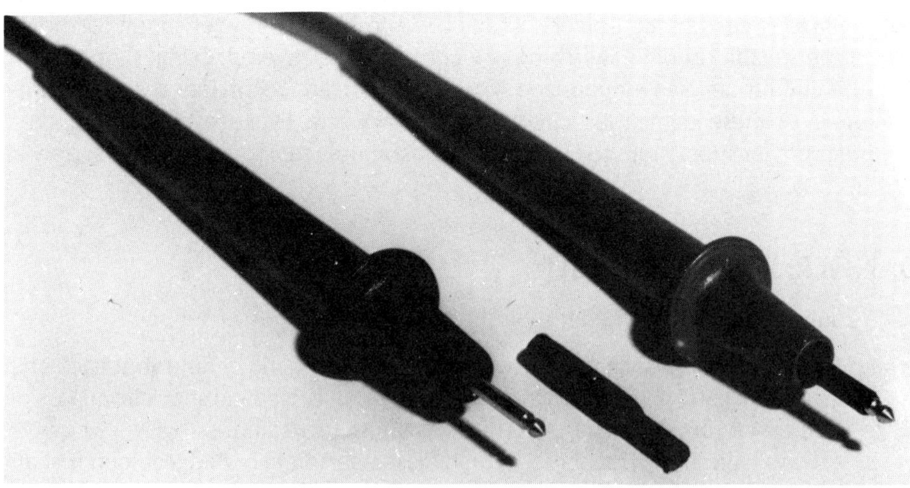

Figure 5.1 Insulating test probes to the tip helps prevent circuit damage due to accidental shorting.

Test leads should be checked occasionally for continuity, using the lowest ohms scales. Short the leads together and gently pull on the wires, especially where they enter the terminations on each end. A reading of more than 1 ohm indicates bad leads.

You may wish to install a small alligator clip on the black (negative) lead of a voltmeter. It is often convenient to attach this lead to the circuit common. This leaves one hand free to leaf through schematics and the like, while the other hand is occupied in taking voltage readings with the red (positive) lead.

Using a VOM for Voltage Readings

The volt-ohm-milliammeter in Figure 5.2 (hereafter called a VOM) is an instrument in common use. The VOM is more than adequate for tracing problems in power supplies. A digital multimeter would be preferred for critical voltages, however, due to its greater accuracy.

Using a Digital Multimeter for Voltage Readings

Today the digital multimeter (DMM) is probably the best all-around meter to use. On the voltages ranges, it has very little loading effect, typically 10 million ohms. See Figure 5.3. A good-quality 20,000-ohm/volt VOM, by comparison, has an input resistance of only 60,000 ohms on its 3-volt range.

A meter such as the one in Figure 5.3 is also recommended because it is auto-

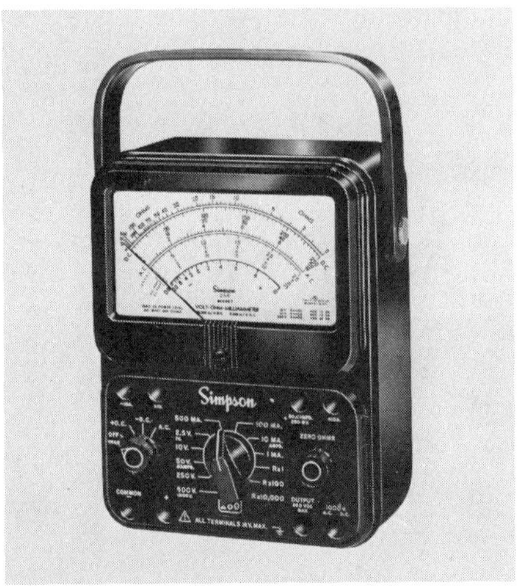

Figure 5.2 A high-quality VOM such as this will be very useful when troubleshooting a power supply. (Courtesy of Simpson Electric Co.)

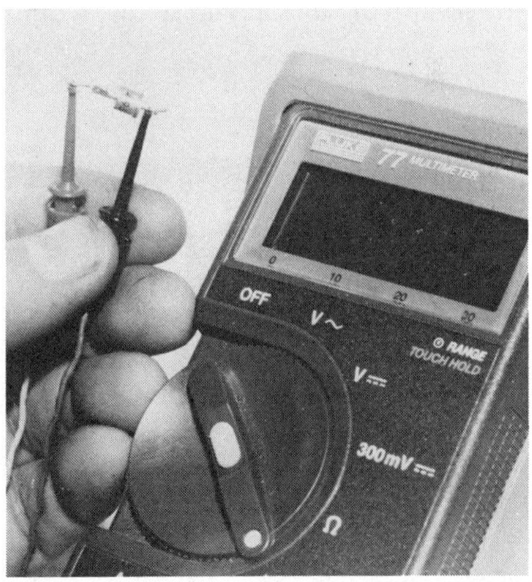

Figure 5.3 A digital multimeter is a primary tool for the troubleshooter. (Courtesy of John Fluke Manufacturing Co.)

ranging. The technician does not have to switch voltage ranges and can better concentrate on the work as a result. This particular meter will also hold a reading for later observation so that the technician can devote entire attention to the circuitry and avoid an accidental short.

Using an Oscilloscope to Measure DC Voltages

The DC coupled oscilloscope in Figure 5.4 provides voltage readings with moderate accuracy. It should not be used to take voltage readings directly on the power lines because one side of the probe circuit is grounded. This could cause a short if the ground is applied to the wrong point in a nonisolated power supply.

The vertical positioning control should normally be adjusted so that the center of the screen represents ground. If the circuit under test has no negative voltages to measure, it will give pictures twice the size to set the ground level at the bottom of the graticule (gridwork) of the screen rather than at the middle.

A test is necessary to be sure the trace position is stable when changing vertical sensitivity ranges without having to reset the vertical positioning each time it is changed. Set the input switch to GND; this prevents outside signals from affecting the amplifiers of the scope. Put the trace in the center of the screen with the vertical positioning control. Change the range switch through all its settings. The center position should not change appreciably. If it does (and sometimes the trace can even leave the screen because of gross misadjustment), find the adjustment called DC BAL—usually a screwdriver adjustment. Proper adjustment of this control will minimize the shifting of the trace as the range switch is changed.

The oscilloscope should be used with an appropriate probe for measuring DC voltages. With a good probe, the full gain of the vertical channel can be used without the pickup of hum and noise that would occur if the oscilloscope were used with two

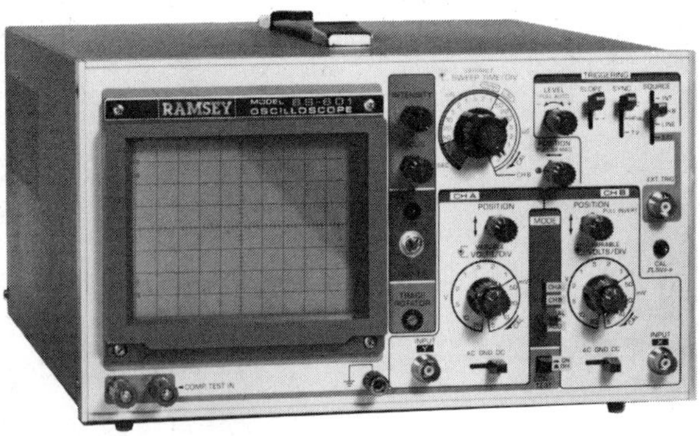

Figure 5.4 The DC coupled oscilloscope can be used for most DC voltage measurements. (Ramsey Electronics Inc.)

wires for the input and ground connections. If a probe is not available, two wires can be used, but noise and hum pickup may be excessive at high-gain settings.

The oscilloscope has one big advantage over a DC voltmeter for measuring voltages during troubleshooting: it will show AC signals riding on DC levels. In some cases the unexpected AC signal on a DC level as shown on an oscilloscope can lead the technician directly to the cause of a problem, which might otherwise escape notice for some time if only a voltmeter is being used.

Using the VOM/DMM for Current Measurements

Current measurements are very seldom used in computer troubleshooting. A possible exception is the use of the current tracer instrument, covered later. *Caution:* Do not apply voltage to an ammeter. The internal resistance of an ammeter is near zero. Besides shorting the voltage source, the full current capability of the source is forced through the instrument.

Using the VOM/DMM for Resistance Measurements

Using the VOM or DMM resistance functions on active circuits is a common way to damage the test instrument or the circuit under test or perhaps both. Never apply voltage from any outside source to the probes of a resistance meter. Testing circuits with the ohmmeter is restricted to dead circuits only.

TIMELY SHORTCUTS

If the computer seems to be without any power at all, be sure to check the outlet in use. Use a lamp or other 120VAC item to test for the presence of power. A check with an AC voltmeter is a good idea, too. The input to a typical microcomputer, for instance, must be within the limits of 104 to 127VAC.

The internal power supply of a microcomputer usually provides four outputs. For a typical microcomputer, Table 5.1 lists what these voltages might be:

Table 5.1 Typical system board voltages for a microcomputer

+5VDC at 2.3 TO 7 Amperes, for all TTL ICs within the computer
+12VDC at 0 to 2 Amperes, for diskette drives & RS-232C circuits.
−5VDC at 0 to 300 milliamperes
−12VDC at 0 to 250 milliamperes for RS-232C circuits

Failure of just the +5VDC output will disable the computer entirely, since it feeds the majority of the circuitry. Failure of the +12 VDC output will disable the disk drives, where the voltage is used to operate the drive spindle motors. These two voltages are easily checked at the connector to the diskette drives (Figure 5.5).

The +5VDC is also available at the expansion sockets on pins B3 and B29. The +12VDC supply can also be checked there at pin B9. The other two power supply

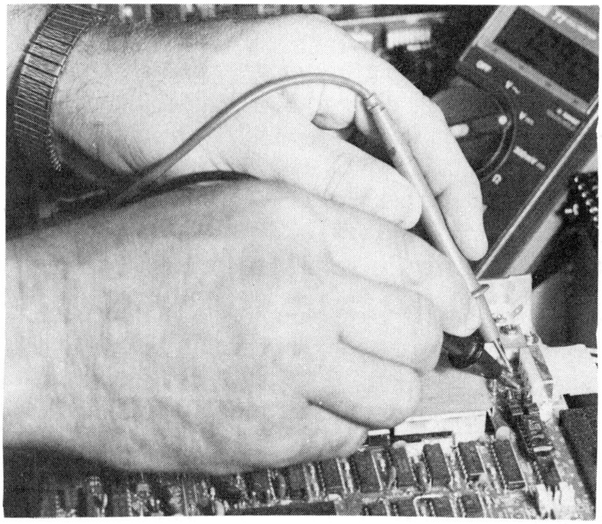

Figure 5.5 The diskette drive powe. ..ur provides a convenient place to check the +5VDC and +12VDC power supply output voltages. (Abbey Enterprises)

outputs, −5VDC and −12VDC are accessible at pins B5 and B7, respectively, of the expansion slot connectors.

The system board power connector has all these voltages present. This connector may also include a TTL Power OK signal to the system board from the power supply. Table 5.2 lists what these connections are in the IBM-PC:

Table 5.2 Voltages at the system board power connector of an IBM-PC computer

Common Pin	Active Pin	Reading
5,6,7,8	1	TTL High, 2.4 to 5.25 VDC (power good)
5,6,7,8	10,11,12	+4.75 to +5.25 VDC (+5VDC circuit)
5,6,7,8	4	−10.8 to −12.9 VDC (−12 VDC circuit)
5,6,7,8	7	+11.5 to +12.6 VDC (+12VDC circuit)
5,6,7,8	9	−4.5 to −5.4 VDC (−5VDC circuit)

The right rear corner of the system board, looking at the front of the computer, is pin 1 of the power connector. The power supplies used in some computers have an automatic resetting circuit breaker, requiring only the removal of power for about five seconds for them to reset themselves.

Some oscillating power supplies will shut down in the event of an overload and immediately recover when the short is removed. This is a particularly attractive feature of an oscillating power-supply since the slip of a test probe can easily short a power-supply output voltage. Shorting the power-supply output *may* do no harm, resulting in

Figure 5.6 Removing the drive connectors will eliminate them as a possible overload on the computer's power supply. (Abbey Enterprises)

only a restart of the computer from a cold start. This feature can also make a power supply seem defective when it is not, since a short anywhere in the circuitry of the computer would simply shut down the power supply.

The computer's ROM diagnostics may indicate a power-supply problem if there is a series of short beeps, a continuous beep, or an error code of 02X, where the X indicates any number.

The keyboard and all of the option cards can be removed to eliminate them as the possible cause of an overload. If this does not result in removal of a suspected overload, the diskette drive power connectors can also be removed to see if they are causing the problem. Under these conditions you could not expect the computer to operate, but the power-supply output voltage should again read normal if you remove an overload on the power supply outputs. (See Figure 5.6.)

ANALYZING FUSE FAILURES

A few computer power supplies may still rely on fuses to protect the circuitry. Fuses can open in normal operation and current surges can progressively weaken them, particularly when turning on equipment. The inrush of current may weaken a fuse to the point that it eventually fails, usually when the equipment is turned on that last time. This kind of failure is more or less normal and is corrected by putting in another fuse of the *same* rating. Look at the fuse that is removed. If it has a clear glass center, you can get a clue as to why it failed by visual examination. If the fuse element (the tiny wire inside) is simply broken or has been melted into tiny globules, the chances are good that the fuse simply weakened as explained above. If, on the other hand, the fuse has vaporized and coated the inside of the glass with a silvery mirrorlike deposit, there has been a gross overload on the fuse, and replacing it without finding the cause is wasteful. A new fuse will blow very quickly.

If the fuse has blown violently there is a good chance that the problem can be found with the use of an ohmmeter. Using an ohmmeter or solid-state tester if you have access to one, check the power-supply filter capacitors for short circuits. Test also for shorts across the voltage output terminals and test each of the rectifiers for shorts.

Don't install a fuse of higher rating than that installed by the manufacturer! Use a fuse of the same type, slow- or fast-blowing, too. General rule: replace with the *identical* type and current rating recommended by the equipment manufacturer. Keep in mind that the fuse removed may not be the proper size when installed by the manufacturer. The fuse may have been changed to one of an incorrect rating by some technoid in the past.

A open (blown) fuse may or may not look bad. If there are no indicators such as a glass center, an open fuse may be detected quite readily by using a voltmeter (not an ohmmeter) across the fuses while power is applied. The meter must be set to the proper scale for the voltages involved with the fuses. The load normally fed by the fuse *must* be connected and turned on. (See Figure 5.7.) If power cannot be applied for one reason or another the open fuse may be located by using an ohmmeter or a solid-state tester. However, *be sure* the power is completely off before using either of these instruments! Use the lowest scales, RX1 or LOW, of these instruments.

A series 120VAC lamp (on 120VAC input lines) can be used as a "soft fuse." If there is a short in the power supply the input current simply lights the lamp rather than damage the computer under test. The lamp should have a rating of approximately the power input of the equipment. Thus, if you are troubleshooting a computer with a power supply capable of 65 watts, use a 60-watt lamp in series. (This is not a hard-and-fast rule, as there is considerable leeway.) Using a lamp of twice this rating will allow more current to the equipment under test if you so desire, and a smaller lamp will reduce the maximum possible current flow to less than that of the larger lamp.

While the power supply has a short the soft-fuse lamp will light with near normal brilliance. When the short is removed the lamp will dim or go out, depending on the load on the output of the power supply.

Using DC Voltage Measurements to Find the Problem

If a voltage is measured and found to be too low, there are just five possible reasons shown in Figure 5.8 why this might be so:

1. The source itself is low in voltage
2. The resistance across (in parallel with) the voltmeter probes is too low or zero (a short)

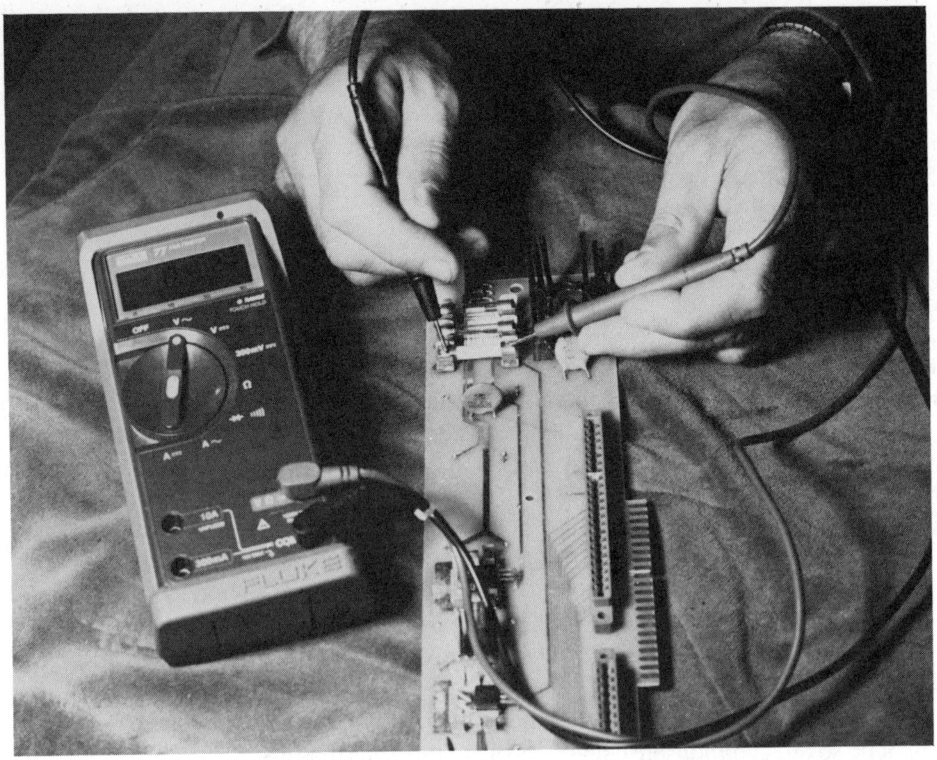

Figure 5.7 An open fuse can be verified with a voltmeter if the appropriate switches are turned on and power is applied. (Abbey Enterprises)

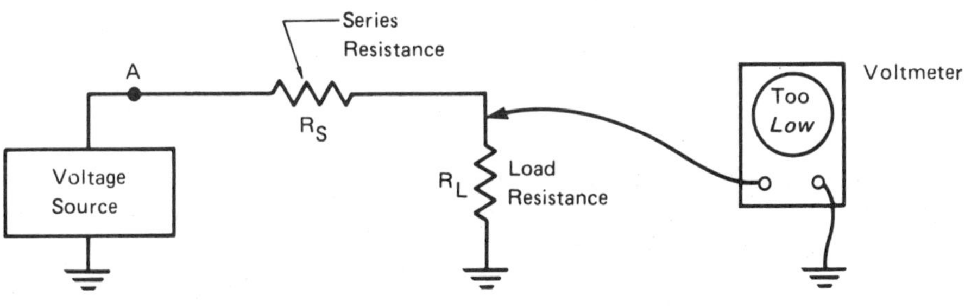

Figure 5.8 Voltage troubleshooting can always be visualized as variations on this basic circuit.

3. The resistance back toward the source is too high or open
4. The voltmeter is loading the circuit down
5. The voltmeter is defective

Possibilities 1, 2, and 3 warrant particularly careful attention, since they are by far the most common causes of low voltage readings in electronic circuits.

Possibility 1 is that the source itself is too low in voltage. Check the source at point A for abnormally low voltage. This may be low line voltage or weak batteries. The internal resistance of the source itself may have increased and be causing the problem. (This is what happens with worn-out batteries.) A good voltage reading at the source also eliminates possibility 5.

Possibility 2 occurs when the circuit resistance in *parallel* with the meter, RL (across the meter probes), has *decreased*. This is the case where a circuit has an overload on its output or, in the extreme case, a dead short across it.

Possibility 3 is that a resistance in *series* with the meter (looking back toward the voltage source) has *increased* in resistance or has opened. Rs of this circuit represent any resistance in series external to the source and includes poor ground returns.

Possibility 4 should be considered when using a VOM with its inherent low resistance across high-impedance weak circuits, especially on the lower voltage ranges. Some circuits such as FET and CMOS circuits are very high-impedance and susceptible to this type of error. (High impedance is defined in Chapter 1.)

Possibility 5 is that the meter has been overloaded (had its needle slammed into either end-stop), dropped, or is otherwise giving readings that are too low because of problems within itself. Or the meter needle may be dragging on the meter glass. The best check of this possibility is to substitute a known good meter for comparison of readings.

If a voltage is measured and found to be too high, the five possible reasons this might be so are commonsense reversals of the previous reasons:

1. The source itself is too high in voltage
2. The resistance across (in parallel with) the voltmeter probes is too high or open
3. The resistance back toward the source is too low or shorted
4. The voltmeter is not loading the circuit down enough
5. The voltmeter is defective

Possibilities 1, 2, and 3 again warrant careful attention for the reasons as previously mentioned. Possibility 1 is that the source is too high in voltage. Check the source itself for abnormally high voltage. A good voltage reading at the source also eliminates possibility 5.

Possibility 2 would be the case where the circuit resistance in *parallel* with the meter, Rl (across the meter probes), has *increased* or opened. This is typically the case where a circuit has an open or reduced load on the voltage source.

Possibility 3 is that a resistance in *series* with the meter (looking back toward the voltage source) has *decreased* in resistance or has shorted. Rs of the circuit represent any resistance in series external to the source. Practically speaking, this is often a voltage source filtering resistor or a voltage regulator's pass transistor shorting collector to emitter.

Possibility 4 should be considered when using a digital voltmeter or FET amplifying meter with its inherent high impedance across high-impedance circuits. There are still a few schematics around that specify the use of a lower impedance meter for taking voltage readings in fairly high-impedance circuits. In this case, the readings given depend upon a certain amount of loading by the meter. Use of a better meter will read a truer voltage, although higher than specified on the schematic.

Possibility 5 is again that the meter is giving readings that are too high because of problems within itself. The best check of this possibility is again to substitute a known good meter for comparison of readings.

POWER SUPPLY CIRCUITS

Transformer Type Power Supply

Transformer type power supplies shown in Figure 5.9 are reasonably standardized. Some computer AC power-supply input circuits consist basically of a transformer, rectifiers, filters, and regulators (see Figure 5.10). Other computers may use the switching power supply, covered later in this chapter.

Power-Supply Transformers. The computer power transformer performs two functions: it provides the required decrease in voltage from 120VAC and it provides voltage isolation between the 120VAC and the secondaries.

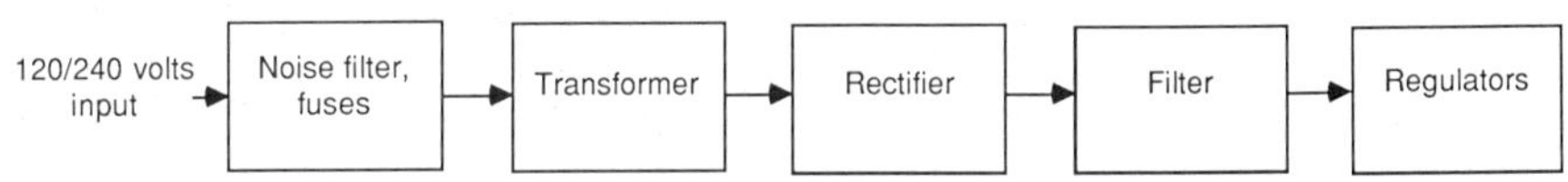

Figure 5.9 Block diagram of a transformer power supply.

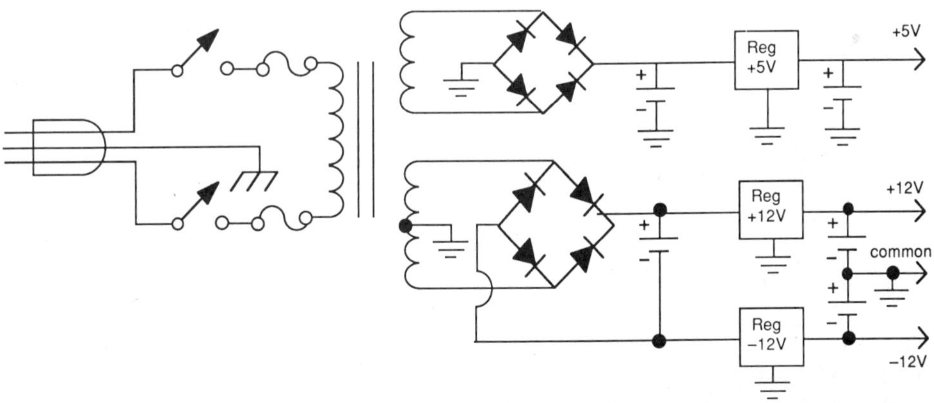

Figure 5.10 A "standard" transformer power supply with IC regulators.

During any dead-circuit troubleshooting remember that the windings of power transformers have a very low resistance and will appear to be shorted on the ohmmeter. This is a good reason to use live-circuit output voltage testing of power transformers. Transformers rarely fail by themselves. They more often fail because of some other circuit failure that overloads them, such as a shorted rectifier, power transistor (inverter type), or power-supply filter capacitor.

Rectifiers. Power-supply rectifiers conduct at the proper times to convert the pulsations of current from the transformer into one-direction output current. In voltage-multiplier rectifier circuits the diodes conduct at such times as to add the voltage across multiple capacitors that are connected in series. The shorted rectifier diode will place a short across the transformer secondary at least half the time, depending upon the circuit used. This will usually cause the power transformer to overheat and may cause the transformer's eventual failure if a fuse does not open to protect it from damage.

A voltage-doubler power supply contains several diodes. Troubleshooting is probably best done by turning off all power, *thoroughly* discharging the capacitors in the power circuits, and then using an ohmmeter.

Power-Supply Filter Capacitors. These capacitors are easily identified. They are the largest capacitors in the computer power supply. An electrolytic capacitor should show no signs of overheating. If it does, you may suspect a short circuit within it. Electrolytics most often fail by shorting. Occasionally electrolytics can fail by drying out and becoming an open circuit. In this case there will be a large AC ripple voltage across the capacitor. Electrolytic capacitors can blow up quite violently if they are internally shorted and if power is relentlessly applied to them. Protect your eyes from possibly shorted capacitors.

Switching Power Supplies

These power supplies operate on high voltage DC derived from the AC input. Using a jumper arrangement, the computer can be operated from either 120VAC lines or from 240VAC lines. Figure 5.11 shows a block diagram of this type of power supply.

The high voltage input DC is then applied to a pair of transistors, where it is chopped into a square wave that is then applied to a heavy winding on the power transformer. These two transistors are a free-running push-pull oscillator. Another winding provides the positive feedback necessary for oscillation.

Troubleshooting the switching power supply begins with checking for proper DC input voltage to the transistors. If one is available, a variable AC voltage input could be used to "ease up" to the proper input voltage. If the input DC voltage to the transistors is correct, the next step is to eliminate the transistor side of the circuit as a problem. Remember that if the switching power supply is overloaded there may not be sufficient feedback for the transistors to oscillate. This gives this supply a very desirable current-limiting feature. Overloading of the power supply may be eliminated as a possibility by disconnecting the load on the transformer output and substituting a resistive load to absorb the output of the transformer for a few moments, long enough to verify whether or not the transistors and associated circuitry are oscillating properly.

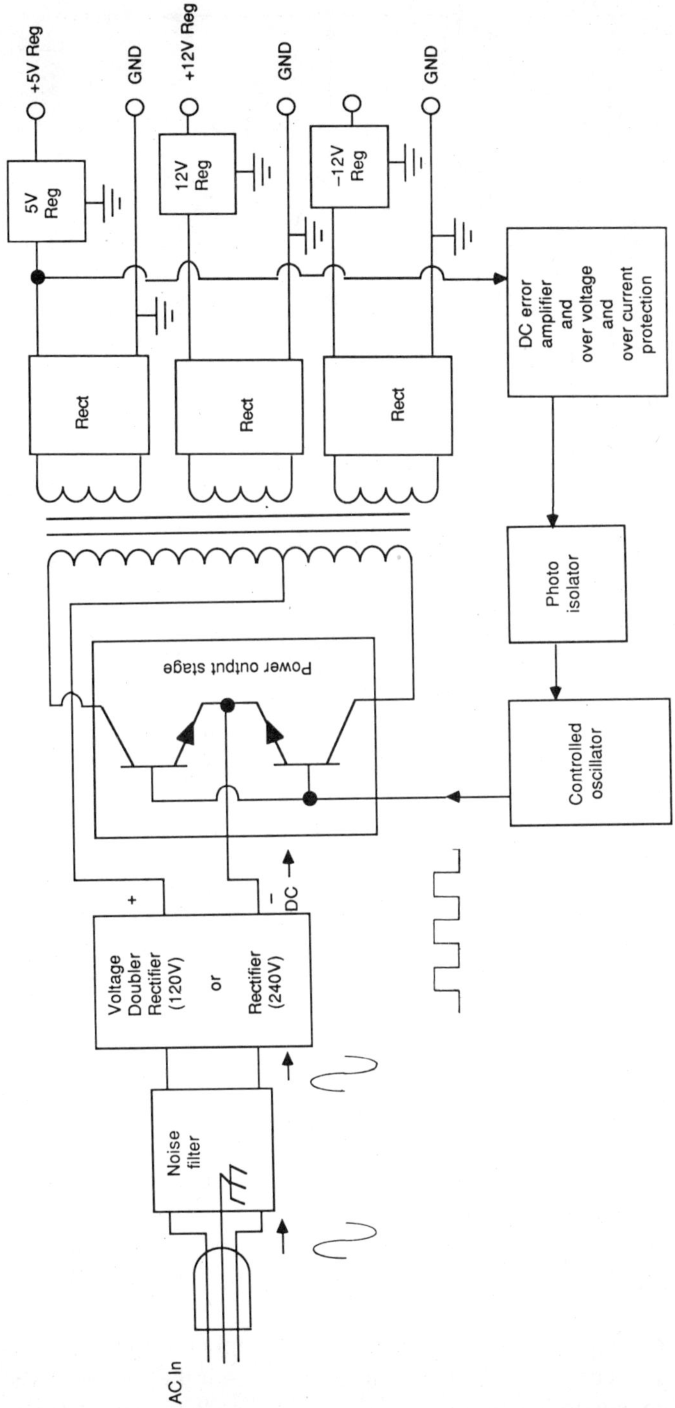

Figure 5.11 Many computers use the inverter power supply.

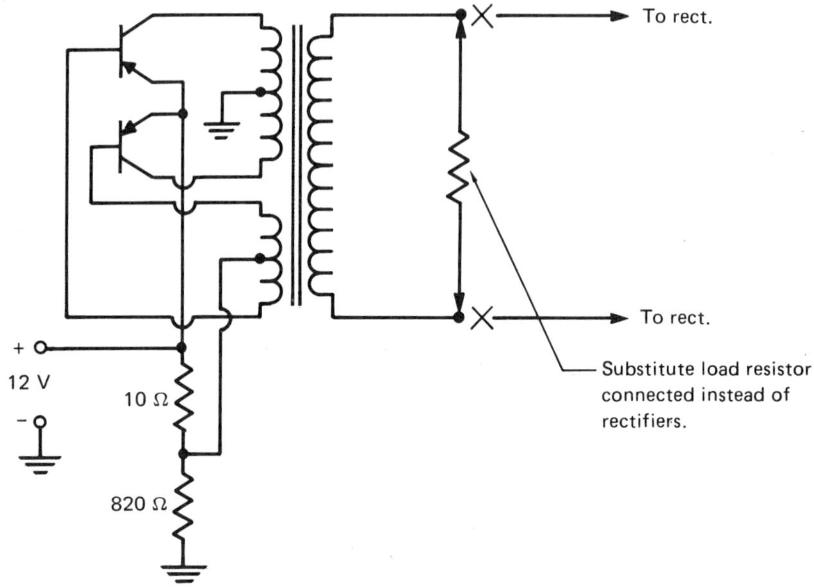

Figure 5.12 Substituting a resistive load on the power supply will provide a definite indication of where the problem lies.

For instance, if the supply is rated at an output of 5VDC at 10 amperes, a suitable load would be a resistor of 0.5 ohm capable of 50 watts dissipation. Such a load would not have to operate the inverter at 100 percent load, but should load to at least 50 percent of full load to ensure that the inverter is capable of reasonable output power. Figure 5.12 shows this principle schematically.

If the transistor side is defective, the transistors should be checked first as the most likely cause of the problem. If the transistors drive the resistive load on the transformer normally, troubleshoot the power-supply output circuits as explained in the following discussion of troubleshooting an overloaded (shorted) power supply.

THE OVERLOADED POWER SUPPLY (SHORTED)

A shorted or overloaded power supply may be evident from one or more of these identifying clues: blowing fuses, a louder than normal hum coming from the power-supply, overheating of any of the power supply components, smoking from anything in the equipment, and (sometimes) small crackling or frying sounds. An overloaded oscillating power supply may appear to be open due to its lack of oscillations and no output voltages. If the technician is using a soft fuse, bright lighting of the lamp indicates a shorted power supply.

The following procedure to trace a short in a power supply is basic to the art of troubleshooting. Disconnect the circuit in the middle and see if the problem is still there. Depending on the outcome of this test, the decision is made as to which way to

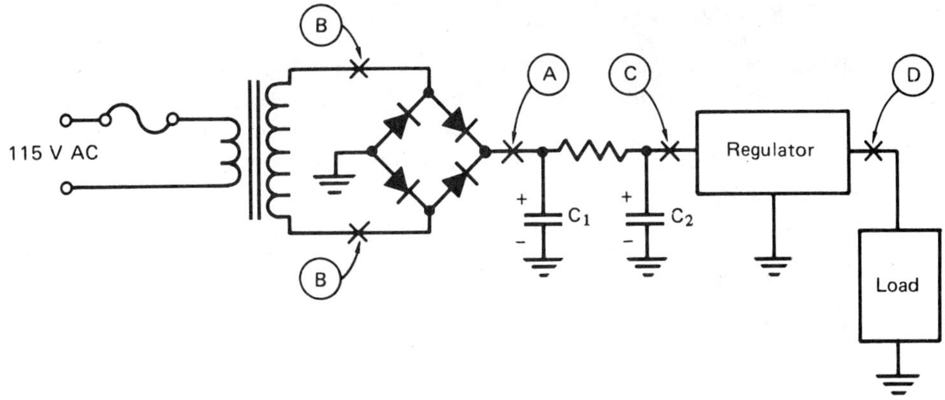

Figure 5.13 Dividing a defective power supply into sections allows logical troubleshooting.

go with another half-split, narrowing the problem down to a fourth of the equipment, and then again to an eighth, and so on, until the defective component is found. The first step in localizing a power-supply problem is to remove the load on the power supply. This is conveniently done in some computers by pulling out all of the printed-circuit boards or by pulling plugs from the power supply to the circuit boards. If the overload is still present, the problem is in the power supply. If the load is gone, the problem is somewhere within the load—the circuitry of the computer. For the following discussion, see the schematic diagram of a typical power supply in Figure 5.13.

Apply power through a soft fuse to the power supply so that the overload is shown as a bright lighting of the lamp. Turn off the power supply. Break the circuit between the rectifier and the filter, at point A. This step breaks the circuit into two parts, the left and the right, and makes a break in about the center of the circuitry. Apply power again and see if the overload is still present. If it is still overloaded, either the rectifier or the transformer is causing the problem. The short cannot be in any of the components to the right of the point A, because they have been eliminated by breaking the circuit. If the overload is still there, turn off the power. Reconnect point A and break the circuit between the rectifier and the transformer at point B. Again reapply power and see if the overload is still there. If it is, the transformer is shorted; if not, the rectifier is shorted.

If the overload was gone when point A was first broken, the overload had to be caused by something that was disconnected, a component to the right of point A. This might be the filter, the regulator, or the load itself. Reconnect point A and break the circuit at point C. Reapply power and see if the circuit is overloaded. If it is, the filter capacitor C1 or C2 is shorted; if not, either the regulator or the load is shorted. If you have determined that the overload is in the regulator or the load, turn off the power and reconnect point C. Break the circuit at point D and make the overload test again. If the overload is gone, the circuits beyond the power supply are overloading it, but if the overload is still there the regulator is causing the problem.

THE INOPERATIVE POWER SUPPLY (NO OUTPUT VOLTAGES)

Some failures are evident from the fact that the power supply has little or no voltage output. Be aware of the current-limiting circuitry (covered later in this chapter), because the output of a current-limiting power supply will seem to indicate that the power supply is defective when it is really just idling along, preventing any damage by reducing its voltage output to a safe level.

If the power supply has no voltage output at all, check the fuse carefully. Next see if the power transformer has any AC output voltage from the secondary winding. If it does, check the rectifiers for a proper DC output; if it does not, the transformer may be open. This can be checked by verifying that 120VAC is present at the input of the transformer, measured as physically close to the transformer primary winding as possible. Input voltage and no output is conclusive proof that either the primary or the secondary winding is open. Do not discount the possibility that the transformer was burned opened because of an overload. Before replacing a power transformer *be sure* to test the rectifiers and filters for shorts. If the rectifiers of a power supply have an AC input voltage but no output DC, two or more of them are probably open. Give thought as to why they might have failed. They may have opened due to a short circuit farther down the circuit. This possibility can be checked with an ohmmeter.

TROUBLESHOOTING THE DC VOLTAGE REGULATOR

Regulators come in two general types, series and shunt (see Figure 5.14). The shunt regulator is used in many noncritical applications by itself or as a voltage reference for a series-type regulator. The series voltage regulator will be stressed here since it is the type most used in computers.

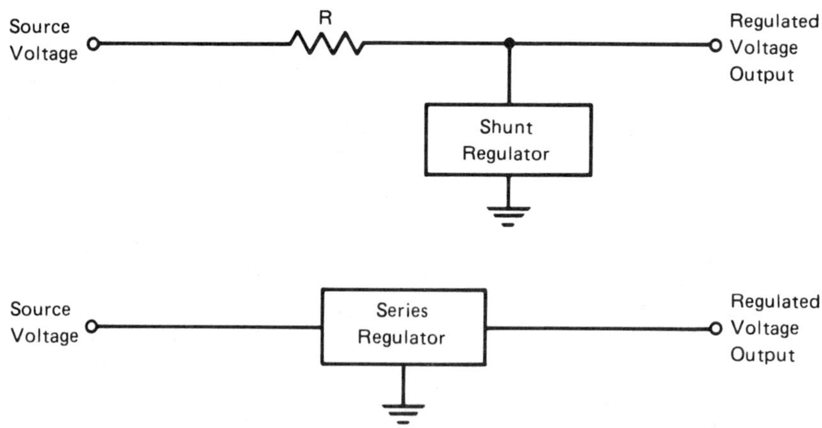

Figure 5.14 The two basic voltage regulator circuits are the series and shunt.

Details of the Series Regulator

The series regulator is, for all its apparent complexity, a variable series resistor between the power supply output and the load. This series resistor is a power transistor (in this case called a pass transistor). It may also be a power transistor contained within a regulator IC. By sampling the output voltage and comparing it against a fixed reference, the resistance of the series element is varied to maintain a constant output voltage. Amplification makes the output stable at a specified voltage at all normal load currents. See Figure 5.15.

The first step in analyzing failures of series regulators is to measure the input and output voltages. If the output voltage is too high, the regulator is defective. If the input voltage is correct but the output voltage is too low, the regulator may or may not be doing its job. Before assuming that the regulator is defective, the possibility of current limiting must be considered. Some regulators sample the output current and reduce the regulator output voltage if the current drawn is excessive. See Figure 5.16.

The current foldback circuit is self-resetting. This circuit will reduce both the regulator voltage and the output current to very low values if the regulator has seen an overload. This essentially turns off the power supply so that no further damage will occur, yet leaves enough current flowing to sample the overload. If the overload is removed from a foldback power supply the output voltage recovers. These circuits may make it necessary to break the circuit between the regulator and the load to ascertain which is causing the problem. Open the circuit, apply power, and measure the output voltage of the regulator. (It may be necessary to connect a reasonable load to prevent oscillations in the regulator). Be sure that any load attached does not also overload the regulator or these limiting circuits will keep the output voltage low.

Series regulators most often fail by opening or shorting the series power-handling element. This IC or discrete pass transistor is often required to throw off a substantial

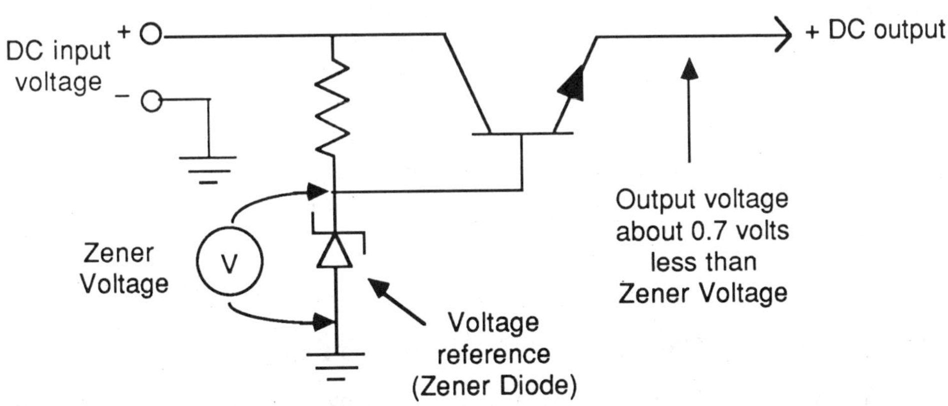

Figure 5.15 The series regulator maintains a constant output voltage with varying current demands.

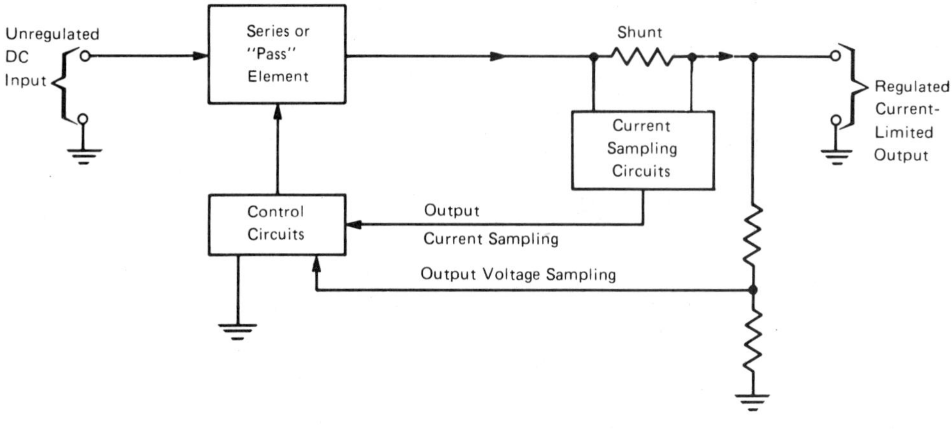

Figure 5.16 The current-limited power supply is protected against damage if the load becomes excessive.

amount of heat, which contributes to the high probability of failure. A check of defective series-regulator circuitry should include checking the reference voltage and checking for the proper bias on each of the discrete components. A rare possibility that may cause power-supply problems is an oscillation either in the regulator or in other outside circuitry that is influencing the output of the power supply. An oscilloscope connected to the power supply will detect this rare defect. It is most often caused by the lack of sufficient output filter capacity and should indicate that the output filter capacitors connected to the regulator are probably open.

The Switching Regulator

Rather than varying the resistance of a series transistor to regulate the output of a power supply, this transistor can be turned full-on and full-off at a very rapid rate, then filtered to accomplish the same thing: control of the output voltage. An inductor and a relatively large capacitor across the output of the regulator smooths out the pulsations to a DC level. This method has an advantage over the variable-resistance method in that the series transistor runs much cooler, since it is either on or off. The regulator is therefore more efficient, wasting very little power as compared to the variable-resistance method. The switching regulator must turn the series transistor on and off at a rate high enough to allow easy filtering. An oscilloscope will show the switching waveforms. See Figure 5.17.

TROUBLESHOOTING FAN AND COOLING PROBLEMS

The fan included in the power supply of many computers is not generally intended for internal repair. The bearings are sealed and in some cases the motors cannot be taken apart without damaging them. The whole fan and motor assembly is to be replaced if it develops noise due to bad bearings or if it no longer attains proper

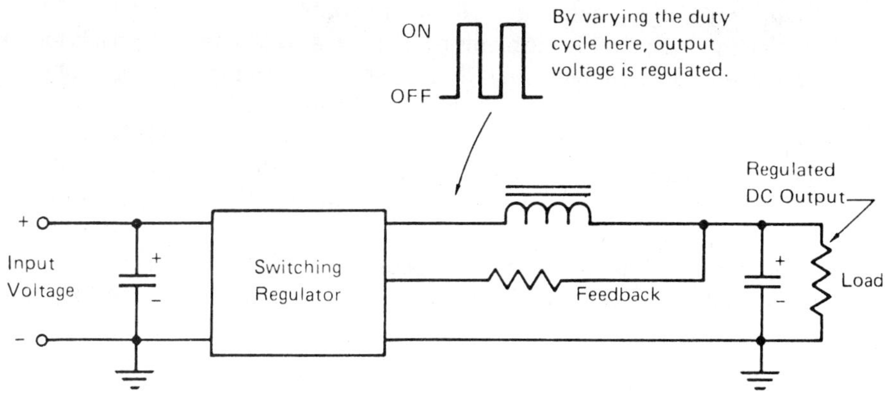

Figure 5.17 The switching regulator is more efficient than the regulator using a series pass transistor.

speed. One of the benefits of having a fan in a power supply is that it indicates whether there is 120VAC available at the wall outlet. If the fan works, power is available. If it does not, the fan may no longer be turning because it is defective. In such a case, the technician should measure the voltage available right at the wires of the fan before replacing the fan.

CHAPTER SUMMARY

This chapter has dealt with troubleshooting problems in computer power supplies. The principles of troubleshooting by the divide-and-conquer or half-splitting method were presented. Also included was the valuable concept and use of a soft fuse. Discussions of power supply and regulator failures and their sometimes misleading symptoms will help the new technician avoid wasting time troubleshooting in the wrong area for a problem. A thorough knowledge of the principles of this chapter will enable you to troubleshoot power supply problems with confidence.

REVIEW QUESTIONS

1. What is the danger of using an oscilloscope for viewing AC power lines and voltages not isolated from these lines?
2. What adjustment on an oscilloscope will nullify changes in vertical positioning when the vertical sensitivity is changed?
3. How many DC output voltages does a microcomputer usually have? What are they?
4. What is the usual symptom if the output of an oscillating power supply is shorted?

5. What is a soft fuse, and when is it used to troubleshoot a problem?
6. Name the five possible problems resulting in a voltage reading that is too low.
7. What resistance reading should you expect across the secondary of a transformer that normally delivers 4 amperes of current at 5 volts?
8. You are working on an oscillating power supply and suspect that it may be defective. However, you realize that a short in its load can make it seem defective when it is not. How can you verify whether the problem is in the power supply or not?
9. Name the two types of voltage regulator.
10. What is the most common failure of a series regulator using a pass transistor?

chapter six

Digital Troubleshooting Instruments and Techniques

CHAPTER OVERVIEW

A great many test instruments can be used to troubleshoot the circuitry and mechanisms used in microcomputers. The more common instruments are discussed in this chapter to help the new technician decide which instrument is needed and understand what it does, how it works during a troubleshooting session, and what the indicated readings might *really* mean about the circuit under test. Since this chapter is intended to help you troubleshoot to the component level, the tools and references necessary for the job are also discussed. This chapter further helps guide the troubleshooting job by suggesting initial checks to make on the computer and recommending the instruments to use.

PREPARATION

To be effective in component-level troubleshooting, you must have a good working knowledge of many subjects, including but not necessarily limited to:

Computer numbering systems

Computer schematic symbology

Detailed knowledge of digital IC operation

Use of digital test equipment

It will be necessary to have reference manuals available to identify the purposes of each of the pins of the ICs under investigation. Information on small-scale ICs can be located in manufacturers' data books such as the MOTOROLA SCHOTTKY TTL DATA manual #DL121R1 and MOTOROLA CMOS DATA manual #DL105, both available from Motorola. For a very practical and easy-to- understand approach to ICs Figure 6.1 shows two available books, the TTL COOKBOOK and the CMOS COOKBOOK, by TAB Books.

References must also be available for LSIs (large-scale integrated circuits) such as the floppy disk controller, direct memory access controller, the CRT controller, and the

Figure 6.1 Reference data books for the ICs used within a computer (Abbey Enterprises)

input/output port chips. These data books are used not only to identify the pins of the IC but also to explain in detail how the chip operates.

Troubleshooting begins with a review of the block diagram for the circuit in question. Such block diagrams may be very difficult to obtain from the manufacturers, who generally prefer to have boards returned to them for repair rather than repaired in the field. Careful study of the block diagram and consideration of the symptoms shown by the computer problem should indicate the area of the computer at fault. As an example, if the serial port coming from the system board is not working it would be reasonable to suspect a problem in the UART chip or its supporting circuitry.

THE DIGITAL SCHEMATIC DIAGRAM

Once the block diagram has served its purpose, it is time to progress to the schematic diagram where details of the circuit can be obtained. The schematic is necessary to identify which ICs are used in the circuit and what their pin connections are. It is useless to try to troubleshoot a computer without a complete schematic.

The digital schematic diagram is really a combination of standard gate symbols and an interconnection diagram. Some of the blocks may not be labeled in a way that you can tell what the functions of these blocks might be. See Figure 6.2 for an example of a mixture such as this. When using a schematic such as this, pencil in important information. The use of the IC, such as a "divide by 10" should be right on the schematic, where the information can be used. Usually all that has been provided is something like a circuit symbol U3, which doesn't tell what the chip is doing in the circuit.

The functions of U_3, U_4, and U_5 are easy to understand and troubleshoot because of their shape, which defines their use.

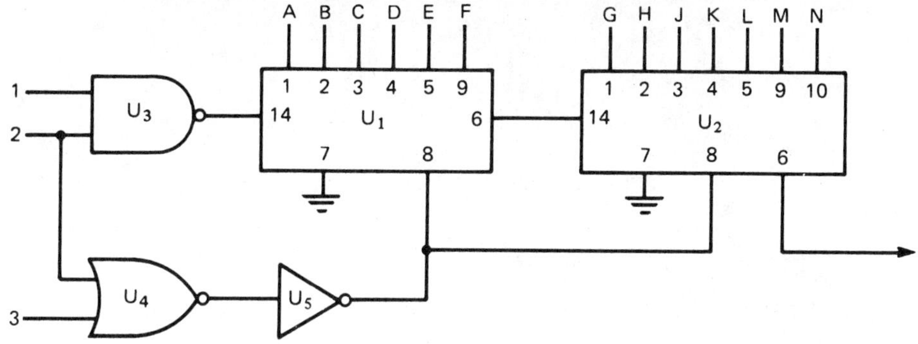

This circuit could not be intelligently signal traced until U_1 and U_2 were identified as to their use, their inputs, and their outputs.

The lines A through N could be either inputs or outputs. Only proper identification would determine their use.

Missing PIN numbers on a schematic may be unused or they may be very important. Look up *all* PIN numbers for troublesome circuits.

Figure 6.2 Many IC schematic symbols give no indication as to what they do in the circuit.

Another aid in troubleshooting is to color-code the various signal flows through the ICs. Change color when the signal takes on new significance. Colors can be alternated and repeated further down the line.

It is not unusual for the manufacturer of the equipment to connect unused input pins of the IC to either Vcc (the positive supply) or to ground them without making any notation to that effect on the drawing. Often the pins supplying power to the IC and providing a ground are not shown on the schematic at all.

FIRST CHECKS

The diagnostic tests that should have been among the first checks made on the computer will help narrow a problem to several of the computer's ICs.

Once the cover is removed from the computer, determine the use of each of the option boards installed. Consultation with the owner of the computer may produce the instruction manuals for the option cards. These instruction manuals will be of value, particularly if one of the cards is defective.

After you open the equipment and get the card in question in hand, give the board a thorough visual inspection. The ICs should be carefully inspected for any signs of overheating, such as discoloration or a raised dimple in the center of the IC.

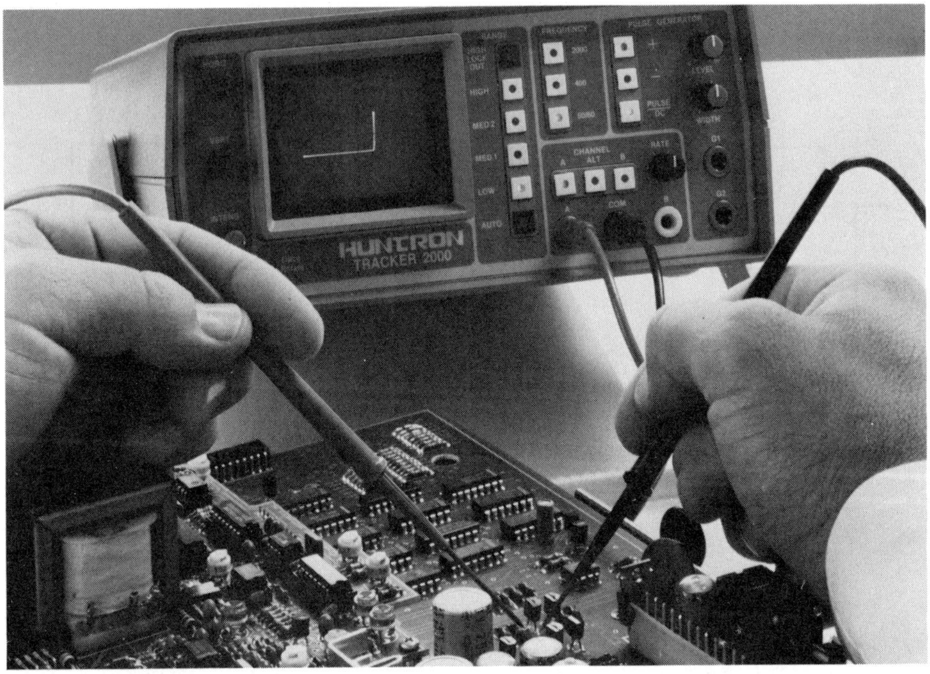

Figure 6.3 The solid state tester will test circuitry by exercising its components and showing a graph of the resulting E/I curve. (Courtesy of Huntron Instruments Inc.)

The solid state tester can be of great value at this point. This instrument is used to test circuitry without applying power. In this way it is similar to an ohmmeter. The solid state tester, however, tests components by applying AC rather than DC. This AC exercises the circuit under low voltage and shows a picture of the resulting E/I curve on a cathode ray tube screen. See Figure 6.3.

Semiconductors can be tested for proper front-to-back resistance readings using the solid state tester. ICs can be tested for internal opens, shorts, and crystal structure fractures. The instrument comes with an excellent reference book that explains the meanings of the scope presentations. If a solid state tester is not used, the next step would be to apply power to the board and check the voltage of all the DC voltage sources to the board. A digital multimeter is desirable for this check. The 5-Volt supply used by transistor-transistor logic (TTL) circuits is particularly critical and must be within the range of 4.75V to 5.25V. It should be adjusted for 5.00VDC if an adjustment is provided. CMOS circuits will operate on supply voltages from 3V to 18V and therefore are not as critical of supply voltages as TTL circuits. The output of all regulators should be checked to ensure that the proper voltages are present. While the circuit is in operation, check the ICs to see if any are overheating. While some ICs may run at a moderately warm temperature, none should operate so hot you cannot comfortably hold a finger on them.

INTRODUCTION TO DIGITAL TROUBLESHOOTING INSTRUMENTS

Oscilloscope

An oscilloscope is often used to trace signals through simple logic circuits such as logic gates and counters. This has been the traditional approach because the oscilloscope will show the logic voltages plotted over time. Using a scope to measure voltage is adding a dimension to troubleshooting over using a voltmeter, the dimension of time. The major limitations to an oscilloscope in digital troubleshooting is the fact that it is useful to view only one or two input signals and that it triggers on a single-triggering event (voltage level).

The Oscilloscope Probe Loads the Circuit. The perfect, nonloading attenuator probe does not exist. The common 10X probe has a circuit-loading capacity of about 1 pfd. This capacity will be placed in parallel with the logic circuit. In so doing, the rise time of the voltage observed will be longer than it is when the probe is not attached. There will be more effect in high-impedance circuits. Although this loading effect may lengthen the rise time of a logic signal, it should not present any particular problem from a troubleshooting standpoint. If, however, a circuit behaves differently when the probe is applied, this effect should be kept in mind before immediately assuming that there is a circuit malfunction. Remember also that defective open inputs may be affected by the probe or any other changes in circuit loading. This is particularly true of CMOS ICs.

Quick Signal Tracing Scope Settings. Use of the oscilloscope on digital circuits requires more skill in the use of the instrument than that needed for routine low frequency or RF troubleshooting. The technician must be very familiar with the triggering controls, particularly the level and mode controls. Improper triggering of the oscilloscope can make pulses appear when they should not and disappear from the screen when they should be there. Although automatic triggering mode may be used for simple troubleshooting where either the presence or absence of a signal is being observed, sophisticated use of the oscilloscope requires skilled use of the triggering controls.

Oscilloscope Timing Analysis. When analyzing digital signals, use the oscilloscope's *triggered* function in preference to the *automatic* triggering mode. This will help ensure that the pulses displayed will have the proper timing relationships and will not drift across the screen in a random manner if their repetition rate is very low.

To test whether the triggering circuits are properly set for digital troubleshooting, temporarily remove the source for the trigger. In the absence of a triggering signal there should be no trace. If there is a trace, the triggering adjustments are still not correct. To set the triggering circuit properly, proceed as follows:

1. Set the triggering source switch to the appropriate setting. If a separate signal will be used to trigger the oscilloscope, use the *external* position of the trigger source switch. Provide the trigger via a proper oscilloscope probe to the

external trigger connector. If the signal will be provided by one of the signals to be observed on the screen, set the trigger source appropriately to select *internal* triggering source and set appropriate switches to select the proper oscilloscope input channel for the trigger.

2. AC triggering can usually be used.
3. Attach the triggering source probe, either the external probe or the vertical channel probe for internal triggering, to a point in the circuit where the trigger will be sampled.
4. Next set the *trigger polarity*. For most troubleshooting work this will be the (+) or *positive* position. If desired, this control can be changed to (−) or negative later on to take advantage of the scope's ability to trigger on negative-going waveforms.
5. The last adjustment is to set the *triggering level*. This control is turned from the left or CCW end to the right until the scope produces a trace. Note the point at which the control is set when the sweep begins to trigger reliably. Then continue turning to the right until the sweep again disappears. Note the position of the control again and reset the control to a point midway between the two. This level should trigger the oscilloscope sweep when the triggering source is approximately halfway between its low and high logic levels. As the triggering source probe is then moved throughout the circuitry the scope should produce a sweep whenever there is a good logic signal at the triggering probe and no sweep when the probe is disconnected or grounded.

The triggering signal chosen from within the circuit is of considerable importance. The trigger must occur at the same time or slightly before the event to be observed. The triggering source and sweep speed are adjusted until the desired presentation appears on the screen. A thorough familiarity with the oscilloscope controls is required to set them up quickly for the best picture.

If you have some difficulty in obtaining a stable presentation on complex waveforms, the use of the holdoff control may stabilize the sweep. Using the vertical channel switching options of alternate or chopped sweeps (Figure 6.4), on a dual-trace oscilloscope requires a bit of understanding when using the instrument for timing checks on digital signals. Although on analog circuits it doesn't make much difference which mode of vertical switching is used because the signals are always there on both channels, on digital circuits the signals are often *not* there at the same instant of time on each trace. The use of the alternate trace option makes the oscilloscope beam sweep across the full width of the screen while displaying the signal of one channel. When that sweep is concluded the sweep begins again, displaying the signal of the second channel. This can result in missing some of the events occurring on one channel while the other channel is being observed.

A better choice of sweep mode for digital troubleshooting would be channel 1 or channel 2 input only, when using a single probe for digital signal tracing, or the chopped sweep function when using two vertical channel inputs at the same time. The use of the chopped vertical channel display provides essentially simultaneous sampling of both the input channels. The rate of sampling between the two channels is fast

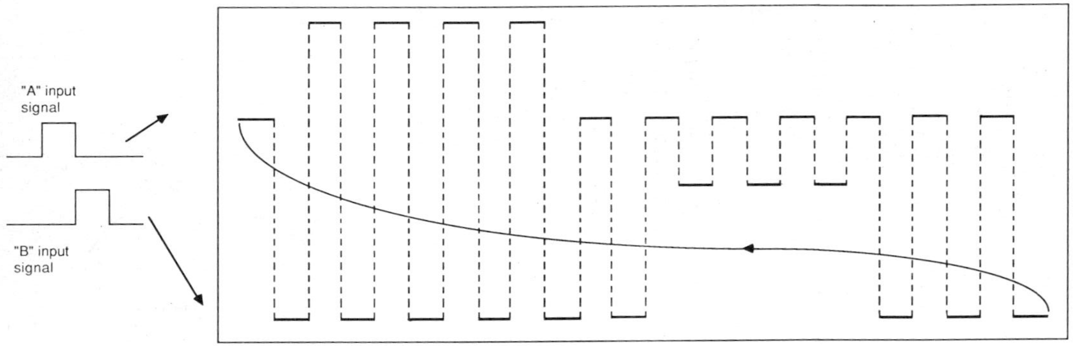

The chopped mode is actually a single sweep which samples each input signal for a very short time, then switches to the other input extremely rapidly and samples it for an equal amount of time. Since it is actually one sweep, only a single trigger shows the timing relations of both signals.

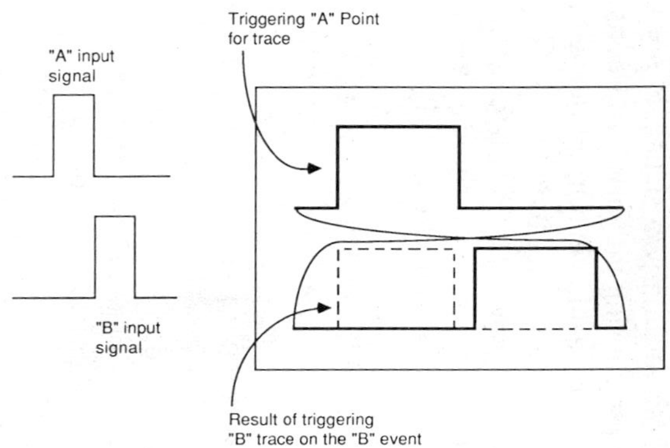

The alternate mode completes one trace before switching to the other channel. As long as both traces are triggered by a common trigger event the timing shown between the two traces will be accurate. Use of separate trigger sources on "alternate" will cancel any true timing indications between the two traces as represented by the shifting of the trace of "B".

Figure 6.4 Using the alternate and chopped sweeps properly.

enough for the two signals to appear on the screen apparently simultaneously. The sampling rate between the two signals is not synchronized with either signal and therefore will drift, causing the missed portions of a waveform due to the switching during one sweep to be filled in during succeeding sweeps.

Oscilloscopes with more than two vertical channels may be available for troubleshooting, but they may not be worth the effort in setting them up because of single-point triggering limitations. The technician will often end up using them as a single or dual trace instrument for routine digital signal tracing.

Oscilloscope Bandwidth Versus Risetime. To determine if a specific oscilloscope is suitable for use with a waveform of a given risetime, it will be necessary to calculate the approximate risetime of the oscilloscope in question and compare the oscilloscope's risetime with that of the signal under test. This is done by dividing the bandwidth of the oscilloscope's vertical amplifier (given in megahertz) into a constant of 350. This will give the approximate oscilloscope rise time in *nanoseconds*.

As a rule of thumb, the risetime of the oscilloscope should be less than one-fifth the risetime of the signal to be observed. This will result in no more than a 2 percent error in the observed signal over its actual waveshape.

An example: An oscilloscope with a vertical amplifier rated at 20Mhz would have a risetime of about 17.5 nanoseconds (350/20). This scope would be good for viewing any waveform with a risetime of 90 nanoseconds or more (17.5 × 5).

A Third Input for a Dual-Trace Oscilloscope. The external triggering input may be used as an extra input to the oscilloscope. With a dual-trace scope this would give three inputs, enough to test many of the commonly used gates. See Figure 6.5 for an example of how to use the scope to test the two inputs and the output of a NAND gate.

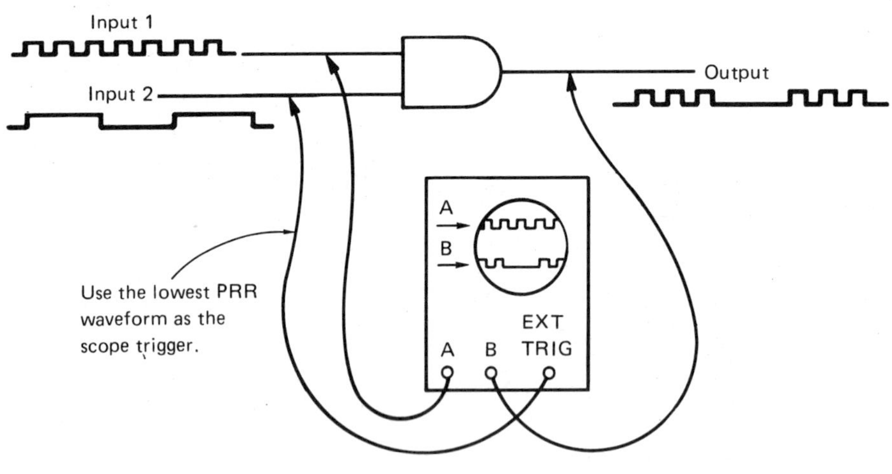

Figure 6.5 The trigger input can be used as a third signal input.

To obtain timing relationships between two or more signals, at least two inputs to the oscilloscope are required. If a signal is observed without an external triggering source it is shown at the left of the screen, since it is its own triggering signal. If the probe is then shifted to another signal, that new signal will also be shown at the left of the screen. This can lead the technician to assume erroneously that the two signals occur at the same time.

To observe time differences a minimum of two probes is necessary. One of the probes will be connected to each of the signals in question, and the oscilloscope must be set to trigger on one of those signals.

There are other instruments available to trace most signals through digital circuits with more speed and efficiency than the oscilloscope.

Setting Up a Scope for Signal Tracing. The vertical channel of an oscilloscope should be set up for DC input signals and the zero-reference line should usually be at the center of the scope. Set the sensitivity of the oscilloscope so that the maximum voltage (Vcc) is at the top line of the scope. (ECL circuits would set − 5.2VDC at the bottom).

A mark on the oscilloscope face to remind you to look for unacceptable levels is a big help. For TTL circuits this requires a mark on the scope face at 2.4V and one at 0.8 volts. Any voltage falling *between* these lines (if you are using ICs that are not three-state) is a bad level and should be regarded as a definite indication that the cause of the problem is close by. CMOS circuits should be set up at the 30 percent and 70 percent values of the Vcc supply. Three-state ICs may have apparently "bad" levels, however, if their outputs are floating and not used during the "bad" time interval. (Three-state ICs are treated separately later in this chapter.)

The marking on the CRT can be a small piece of very narrow black tape such as is used to lay out printed circuit traces. An alternative is the use of any one of the special pens for marking on glass and plastic. If the oscilloscope face is plastic, this marking must be done with care to prevent scratches.

When looking for simple missing signals, the internal triggering circuits and auto triggering may be used.

Static Stimulus Tester

While some of the digital circuits of a computer can be tested using traditional means, the problem of dealing with high-speed, three-state operation can greatly complicate troubleshooting of the address and data bases of a computer. This can be the most difficult of computer problems to troubleshoot.

An innovative solution to this problem is offered by Creative Microprocessor Systems for 8-bit computers. The concept is very simple: Remove the microprocessor and plug into its place a system of switches. With these switches any desired address may be set up and data either passed to or obtained from that address.

This company offers a small static stimulus tester (Figure 6.6) which replaces any of four microprocessors, the Z-80, 8080, 8085, or 6800. Using this tester, problems in computer address decoders, control bus lines, and data lines can be isolated with relative ease. The voltage levels on the microprocessor lines are held steady for as long

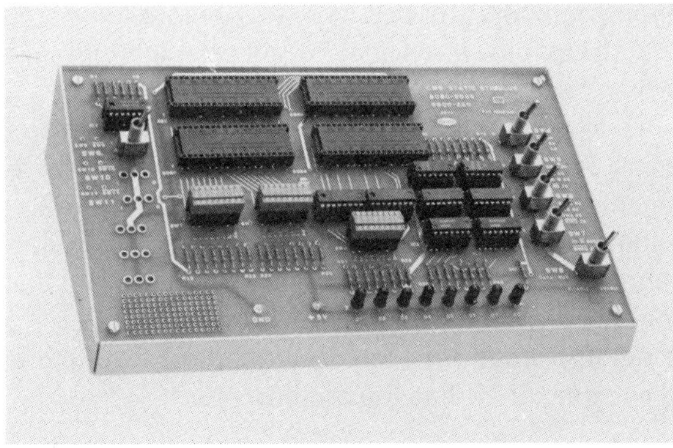

Figure 6.6 This instrument replaces the CPU for static troubleshooting of all address and data lines. (Courtesy of Creative Microprocessor Systems)

as the technician desires, making them suitable for signal tracing with conventional digital means, even a simple voltmeter.

The use of the static stimulus tester is well documented in the instruction manual that comes with the unit. Step-by-step instructions are provided for performing four basic tests:

1. Reading a data byte from a memory location
2. Writing a byte to a memory location
3. Reading data from an input port
4. Writing data to an output port

Every bit of each of these bytes can be individually traced from origin to destination. Each of the above tests involves the computer's address decoding, I/O port decoding, and support chips involved in these functions. Thus most of the chips on the mother board of an 8-bit computer become accessible to DC voltmeter troubleshooting.

Because of the DC approach to troubleshooting the SST provides, it is an excellent tool to use on computers that cannot run diagnostics because of a drastic problem. The SST fills a special troubleshooting gap in lieu of sophisticated, expensive equipment such as signature analyzers and logic analyzers. The static stimulus tester is also an excellent tool for learning the details of microprocessor operation.

Logic Probe

The logic probe (Figure 6.7) is so handy for single-point logic-level testing that it has been called the digital screwdriver. It is a small probe used to make go-nogo decisions throughout the circuitry. It will detect a digital logic level and can stretch very short pulses out so that the technician is aware they have occurred. It will also show bad levels (between high and low), or three-state buses. Every digital technician should have one of these instruments available. The current price of about $30.00 is well worth the investment.

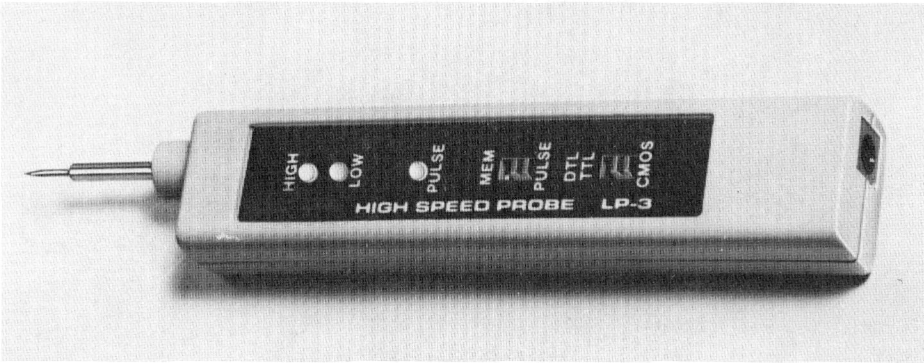

Figure 6.7 The logic probe is a very handy single-point digital signal tracer. (Courtesy of Global Specialties)

The logic probe has a selector switch to choose between the TTL and CMOS families. This switch defines the acceptable high and low levels of the two logic families. Remember that TTL circuits use 0.8V and below to define a low, 2.4V and above a high, where CMOS uses a Vcc percentage of less than 30 percent as a low level and more than 70 percent as a high. The logic probe's only other control is a switch to set a memory that can be used to detect the arrival of a single pulse. When the MEM/PULSE switch is pushed to the MEM position, the pulse LED goes out and remains out until the receipt of at least a single pulse, whereupon the pulse LED lights and remains lit. Ordinarily, this switch is left in the PULSE position, where the pulse LED flashes at a slow rate to indicate that there is signal activity at the probe tip.

The normal operation of the logic probe is as an indicator of signal activity. Two LEDs are used to indicate the level of the voltage at the tip, one for high levels, the other for low levels. If the probe is connected to a static voltage, one of the LEDs lights accordingly. If that level changes at a low rate, the other LED lights to indicate the change. At faster rates, the two LEDs alternate in step with the applied signal. At high rates of change, both LEDs appear lit, but at reduced intensity, roughly in proportion to the duty cycle of the applied waveform. At very high rates (more than about 100 kHz) the two high and low LEDs dim out and signal activity is shown only by the pulse LED's slow blinking. Any change of input level will cause the pulse LED to light, up to a frequency of about 10 mHz.

Power for the logic probe may be obtained from the equipment under test using any positive DC voltage from 5V up to 30V.

The logic probe can be used with existing circuit signals or with the logic pulser as a source of digital pulses.

Logic Monitor

This small instrument, pictured in Figure 6.8, is attached by straddling the IC in question. It then shows the high or low status of all 14 or 16 of the pins simultaneously. It

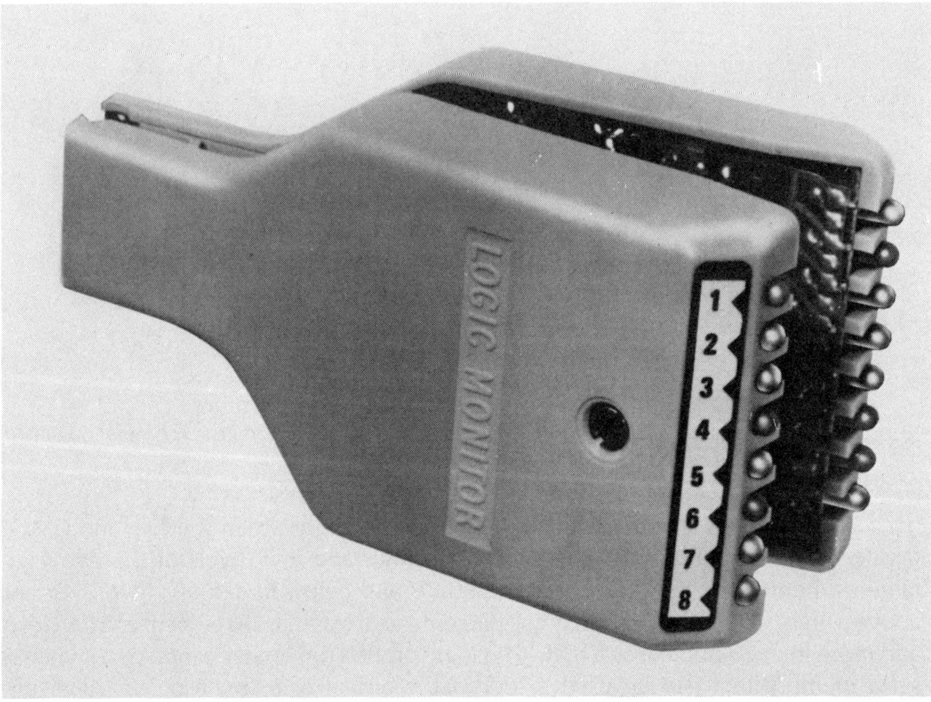

Figure 6.8 This logic monitor is particularly useful in tracing signals through counters if they can be single-spaced (Global Specialties)

may be attached to either TTL or CMOS chips. It finds the supply and ground leads to power itself without any effort on the part of the operator—all is automatic within the monitor. The status of all 14 or 16 of the remaining pins are shown on the LEDs on the top. A corresponding pin that is high will have the LED on, and vice versa. A partially lit LED in a circuit operating at full speed indicates that the IC pin associated with that LED has an active digital signal on it. The amount of the LED brilliance compared to the LED on the supply pin of the IC will give a rough indication of the duty cycle of the signal. A short duty cycle signal may not be visible because the logic monitor has no pulse stretcher to make the signal detectable.

This logic monitor can be used with TTL and CMOS up to 15VDC. No switching is necessary when changing digital families. The logic monitor may be used to check truth tables if the incoming pulses can be halted and the IC held in a static condition. The state of each of the pertinent pins is noted and the IC allowed to advance a single count. This is best done using a digital pulser, to be discussed next. The new state of the pins can then be observed for proper indications.

The logic monitor will exhibit a lighted LED on any pin that has more than 2.0 VDC on it, regardless of the IC family involved.

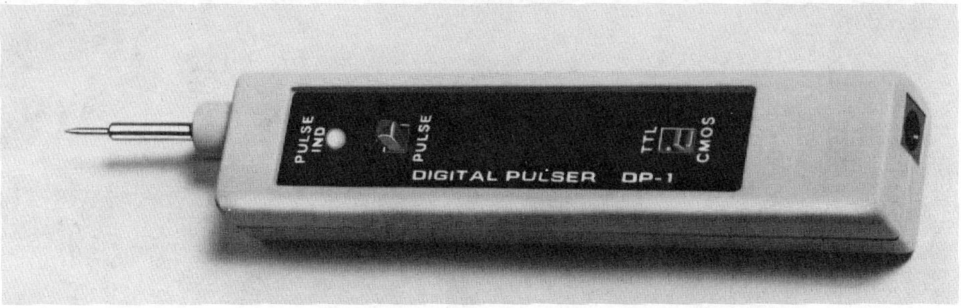

Figure 6.9 The logic pulser is sometimes used with the logic monitor to single-step a digital circuit. (Global Specialties)

Digital Pulser

The digital pulser is a digital instrument used to inject signals into digital circuits for troubleshooting purposes (see Figure 6.9). It is designed to pulse signals into circuit traces without disconnecting any of the ICs. Due to the very short duration of the pulse the output stages of the ICs are not harmed by the pulses.

This instrument can be used on TTL or CMOS circuitry. It is connected to the circuit's supply bus for power and will operate on any positive voltage up to 25VDC. As a result of the ingenious circuitry within it will pulse a high circuit low or vice versa without the attention of the operator. It will also provide the proper pulse width for the circuit under test, giving a shorter pulse for TTL than for CMOS. This shorter TTL pulse is required to overcome a saturated transistor yet not provide enough energy to damage the transistor.

The digital pulser is most often used as a quick signal source for digital circuits and is very useful when used with a current tracer to track down short circuits on boards or to clock ICs. The operation of the pulser is simplicity itself. Push the button and you get a single pulse. Hold it down longer and the pulser emits a string of pulses at about 100 Hz.

Current Tracer

The current tracer (Figure 6.10) is usually the final instrument to be used during troubleshooting. This instrument will trace the flow of pulsed current along a circuit trace. It is a valuable tool in finding shorted traces due to solder bridges or other board faults or shorted ICs. The reason the current tracer is so valuable is that conventional voltage-measuring instruments cannot effectively find the exact location of a short when there are many possible paths. The voltage instruments are useful for finding which trace is stuck, then the current tracer must be used to find the specific component responsible for the short.

Normal digital circuit currents are usually quite low. If a short occurs, the driving stage will try to drive considerably more current than normal into the short. The current

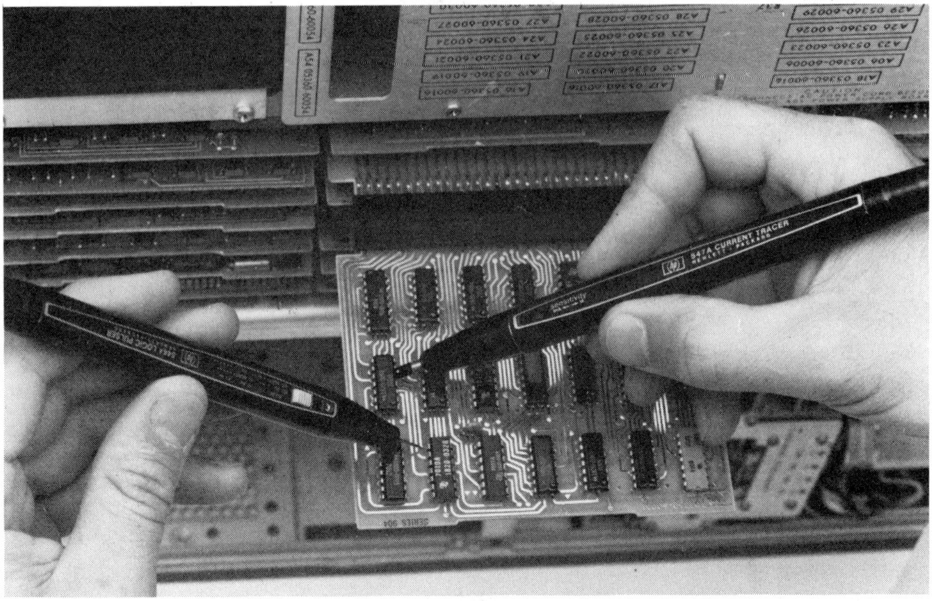

Figure 6.10 The current tracer can be used alone to find circuit shorts using normal signals or in conjunction with a digital pulser, as here. (Courtesy of Hewlett-Packard Co.)

tracer can detect these increased currents in operating circuitry using the circuit's existing signals.

Another way to use the current tracer is to use the digital pulser as a pulsed current source and follow the relatively heavy current path with the tracer to find the short.

The current tracer also has a pulse stretcher so the operator can see the relatively short pulses that the tracer is following.

Logic Comparator

This instrument (Figure 6.11) allows a technician to verify whether an operating circuit is occasionally missing pulses or is erratic in such a way that other instruments miss the cause of the problem. Its principle of operation is quite simple. A duplicate IC of the type under test is inserted into the comparator and, by means of a multipin clip, is compared in parallel with the one in question. The IC used as a good comparison is driven by the same input signals as the IC under test. If the IC under test varies at all in output from the good one, the comparator latches an LED on to indicate a discrepancy.

The Logic comparator is particularly good for finding missing pulses, glitches, and other intermittent problems caused by defective ICs. A good stock of known-good duplicate ICs is needed to use as standards.

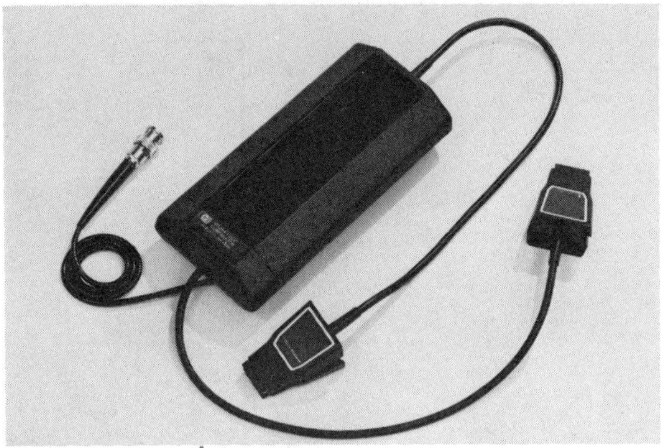

Figure 6.11 The logic comparator will show timing errors and many other subtle discrepancies at full system-operating speeds. (Courtesy of Hewlett-Packard Co.)

Figure 6.12 Signature analysis equipment can troubleshoot entire computer systems at full speed using special software. (Courtesy of Hewlett-Packard Co.)

Signature Analysis

The signature analysis method of troubleshooting microprocessor circuits is an innovation of the Hewlett-Packard company (see Figure 6.12). The principle of operation is similar to that in an analog system, where a library of normal oscilloscope waveforms is obtained within specific equipment under test while operating with a standard input signal. Signature analysis uses a standard digital input to a microprocessor system and gives an alphanumerical display is be compared with normal values recorded in separate documentation.

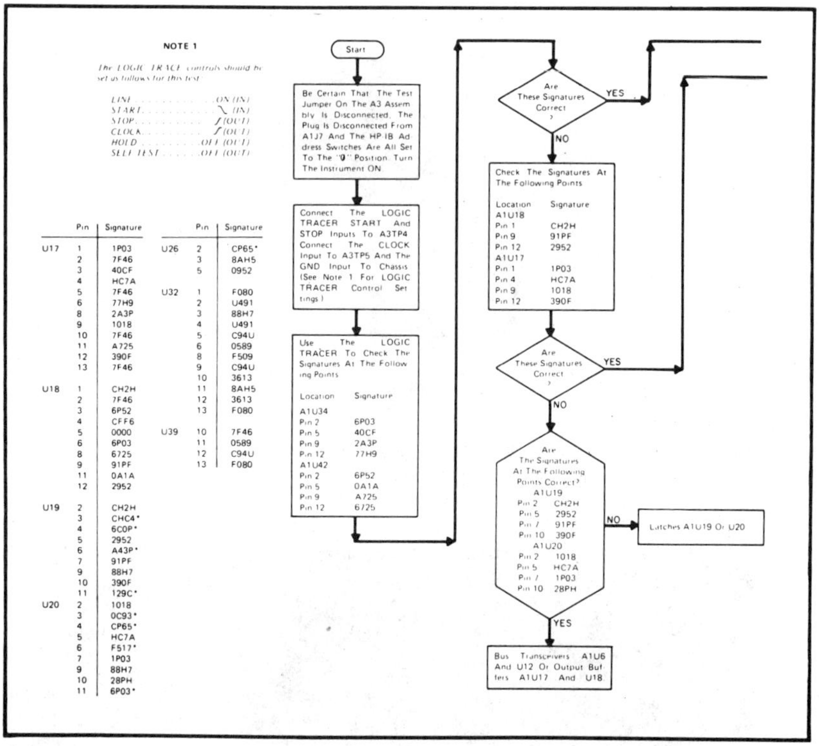

Figure 6.13 The signature analysis troubleshooting tree can lead directly to the cause of a computer system failure. (Courtesy of Hewlett-Packard Co.)

An advantage of signature analysis is that the troubleshooter, with proper software and documentation, can quickly tell which circuit is malfunctioning. The biggest disadvantages are that the equipment under test must have documentation with which to compare readings and must be operated using specific software for the run. Those few technicians fortunate enough to have this test equipment available for use will, however, find it a very fast and efficient way to troubleshoot documented microprocessor equipment.

Troubleshooting using signature analysis test equipment consists of following a printed troubleshooting "tree" to find the defective part while running special test signals designed to exercise the circuits. Figure 6.13 is an example of such a tree.

Logic Analyzer

Although the oscilloscope and the other instruments discussed so far in this chapter may be a good choice to troubleshoot simple gates and counter circuits, the detailed analysis of a complex computer-driven circuit requires not only the recording of voltage levels over a period of time, but perhaps 8, 16, 32, or more different voltages must also be monitored simultaneously to pinpoint a problem. This adds an entirely new dimension to troubleshooting over that of even the oscilloscope. Although multipoint troubleshooting might not require the extreme voltage resolution of an oscilloscope, needing only a simple determination of high or low logic levels, and the actual frequency of operation might be only a few megahertz, the sheer number of inputs required becomes a burden. For proper analysis of the information, the digital levels must also be stored for a terribly slow (relatively speaking) human to make the required observations.

How the Logic Analyzer Works. Reduced to understandable terms, the logic analyzer works like this: the logic levels of the circuit under test are interpreted as highs or lows and continuously placed into a high-speed RAM memory. Since the analyzer would soon run out of memory at the computer speeds used and the recording of extraneous information is useless, the special high-speed memory used in the logic analyzer is operated in a continuous circle. Data is written into the memory to the end and then begins writing over old data at the beginning. Once the digital information from the circuit under test is in RAM, it may be used in several different ways. It can be displayed as pictorial logic levels rather like timing diagrams, shown as binary 0s and 1s or shown in hexadecimal, recorded on a diskette for future reference, or even analyzed for statistical information.

The gathering of this data is under the manual control of the operator. Once a signal is given the analyzer gathers data and continues to do so from then on. This method of gathering data gives no indication of when it is gathered. A triggering point is needed from which data can be compared. This triggering point for a logic analyzer is an extension of the type of triggering of the oscilloscope. Where the scope triggers on a single event, the logic analyzer can be programmed to watch for a specific logic condition of a group of input logic levels. In other words, the logic analyzer watches for a specific binary *trigger word* in the string of data being sampled. This trigger word is entirely at the discretion of the technician, who may select the word bit by bit by requiring high, low, or "don't care" levels for as many as 16 or 32 bits.

As the logic analyzer is writing data into its circular memory it is also looking for the occurrence of the trigger word among the sampled levels. Upon recognition of the trigger word the analyzer begins counting a specified number of samples after the trigger and then stops sampling. This action gives a "window" of data that often contains the trigger word in the middle. A typical example of the data collected with the instrument shown in Figure 6.14 consists of 500 bytes of data collection on either side of the trigger word. Therefore, the data both before and after the trigger is now a matter of record in RAM.

Using the Logic Analyzer. The logic analyzer is the only sensible instrument to use when troubleshooting computer equipment. It is the only instrument that will gather the quantity of data necessary to determine exactly what is happening in multipoint circuits. Once the pertinent digital levels are obtained by the analyzer they can be displayed on a CRT screen or even printed out for leisurely troubleshooting. Only a few minutes' use will convince any technician that here indeed is a useful instrument for computer troubleshooting to any required level.

Figure 6.14 The logic analyzer records a great many simultaneous digital signals and later displays them for detailed analysis and troubleshooting. (Courtesy of Omni Logic)

DIGITAL TROUBLESHOOTING PRINCIPLES

It is interesting to see a graph of the means by which ICs fail (see Figure 6.15). Digital circuits must be turned on or off. Any voltage level between full on and full off is a bad level and points to a problem. These partial voltages and voltages that should be changing but aren't are what the technician looks for in troubleshooting. Voltages that won't change are shorted to either ground or the supply bus and are commonly called *stuck busses.*

Two special digital circuits are an exception to the rule that digital circuits require either high or low signals: The Schmitt Trigger and the delay multivibrator. A digital circuit called a Schmitt Trigger will accept any voltage input between 0 and the maximum voltage (Vcc) for the family and will give an output much like the mechanical action of a snap-action switch. Once the voltage reaches a critical level the circuit snaps on very rapidly. The output will remain in this state until the input voltage falls to a lower level than that at which it turned on. At this lower level the circuit snaps off and remains there even if the input voltage fluctuates slightly positive again. The input must reach the higher critical on voltage before the circuit will snap on again. This chip is particularly useful for "cleaning up" analog inputs so that they are suitable for the pure on/off conditions required by digital logic. Figure 6.16 illustrates this snap action.

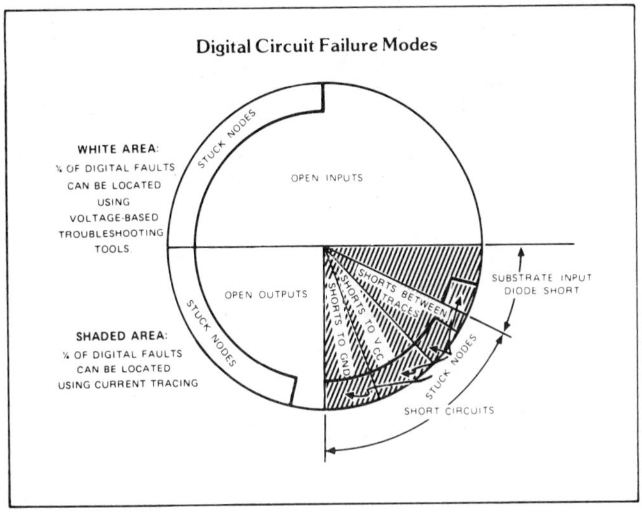

Figure 6.15 There are many means by which an IC might fail. (Courtesy of Hewlett-Packard Co.)

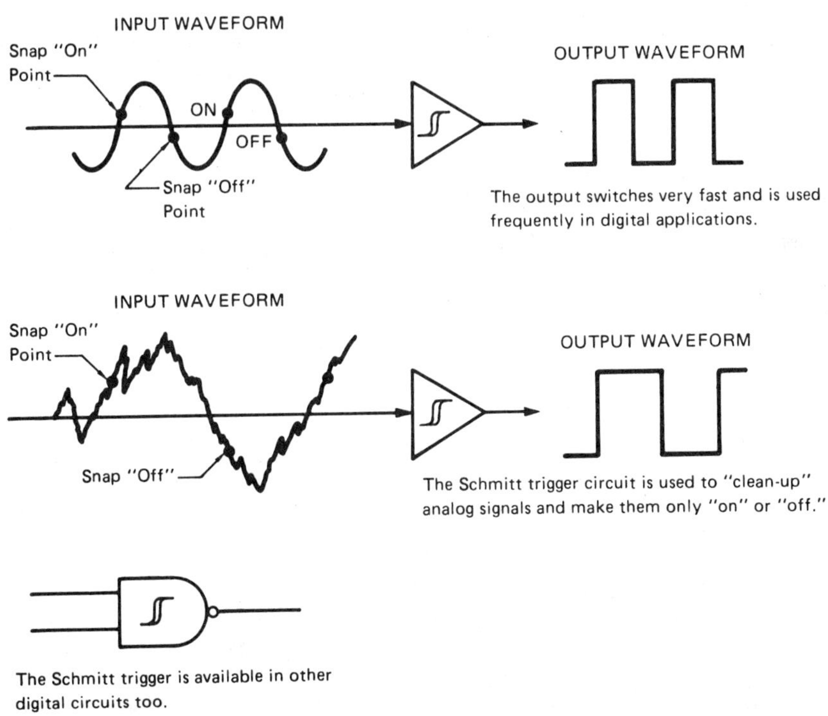

Figure 6.16 The output of the Schmitt Trigger is always high or low due to the snap action of the circuit.

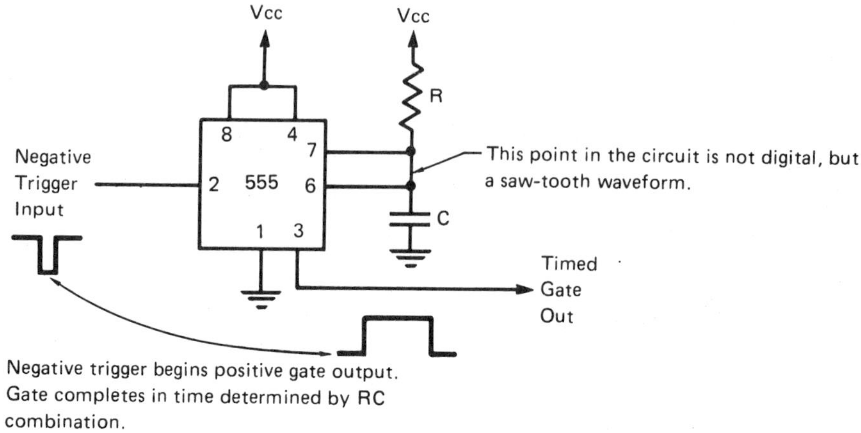

Figure 6.17 The delay multivibrator will have a sawtooth waveform at the timing pin.

The second exception, the delay multivibrator, has a special pin that has a capacitor and a resistor connected to it. This pin is used to sense the voltage across a capacitor as it charges and produce a fixed delay based upon that time. This pin is also used to discharge the capacitor to repeat the timing cycle (see Figure 6.17).

Of all the digital families available, two should be familiar to the microcomputer servicing technician, the transistor-transistor logic (TTL), and the complimentary metal oxide semiconductor (CMOS).

TTL Family Characteristics

TTL family characteristics dictate that the supply voltage (Vcc) for the entire family be very close to 5.0VDC, between the limits of 4.75VDC and 5.25VDC. Voltages over 7VDC may damage the ICs. A logic low signal for TTL is 0.8 volt or less. A logic high is 2.4 volts or more. Note that the logic levels are *not* as might be expected, 0 volts and 5.0 volts (see Figure 6.18).

TTL ICs are not as susceptible to static discharge as CMOS, being by nature low-impedance devices. TTL requires a small amount of power to operate: a typical TTL chip may dissipate about 60 milliwatts. Several families within TTL have characteristics tailored to such special uses as lower power requirement, higher current output, faster response, and so on. Table 6.1 explains the characteristics:

Table 6.1 Table of comparison between members of the TTL family

Family	Speed	Power/gate	Max Freq
Regular TTL	10 ns	10 mw	35 Mhz
High-Power TTL	6 ns	22 mw	50 Mhz
Low-Power TTL	33 ns	1 mw	3 Mhz
Schottky TTL	3 ns	19 mw	125 Mhz
Low-Power Schottky TTL	10 ns	2 mw	45 Mhz

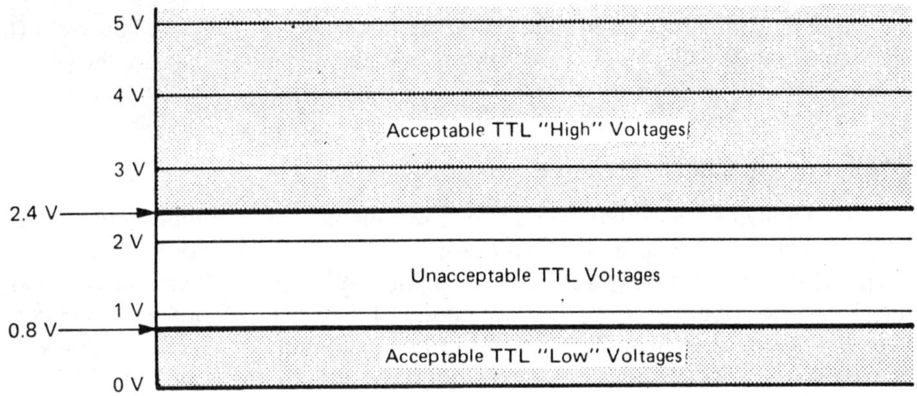

Figure 6.18 Good and bad TTL voltages are easily defined.

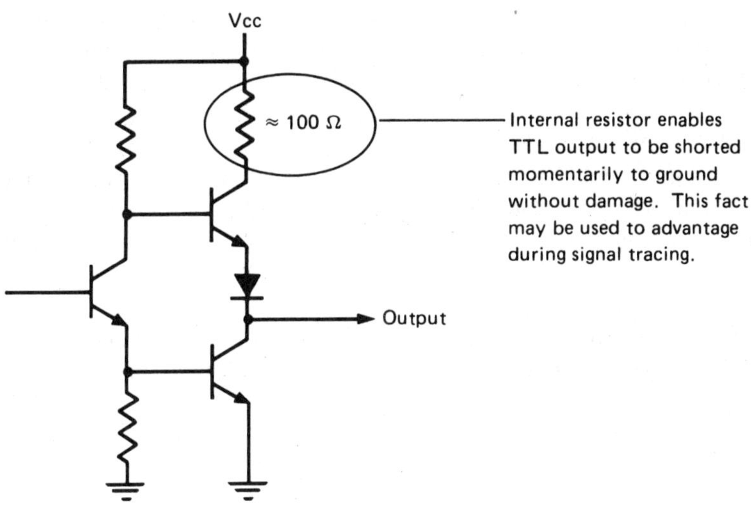

Figure 6.19 The internal resistor of a TTL IC will allow the technician to safely ground the output of an operating chip for troubleshooting purposes.

The TTL family can be identified by a numbering system that begins with either 74XXX or 54XXX. Details of the TTL numbering system and what they signify are well covered in the TTL COOKBOOK, Sams Publishing Co. #21035 and TTL data books from various manufacturers. The cookbook is an excellent reference manual for technicians who work with TTL circuits. The more common ICs are explained in detail, along with typical applications. It is an interesting note that due to an internal resistor in TTL ICs the output can be shorted to ground without disconnecting the IC from the circuit for testing purposes. This fact can be used to advantage to kill a digital signal, forcing a logic 0 at the output of the IC. See Figure 6.19.

Another particularly interesting characteristic of a TTL IC is that a "floating" TTL input pin will usually float high, producing an internal high input signal for the IC.

CMOS Family Characteristics

This family of ICs is identified by the 4XXX identification-number series. Most CMOS ICs will operate with a supply voltage of from 3 volts up to 18 volts. This family is not critical as to power supply requirements. Some CMOS chips, when idling, draw as little as .5 nanoampere—0.0000000005 ampere! This is because of the open-circuit internal structure of the ICs. During full-speed operation additional power is drawn, comparable to the power dissipation of a TTL IC, from 2 to 35MA per IC. The logic input levels to CMOS chips are defined as a percentage of the supply voltage. See Figure 6.20.

A disconnected CMOS input will be erratic and will produce unpredictable outputs from the chip. All unused inputs should be tied either to supply or to ground.

For all of the power advantage of the CMOS line of ICs, they do have one major disadvantage. CMOS is very susceptible to damage by static-electric discharges. A good CMOS reference book will go into considerable detail about a static-free place to work with these ICs. Whether or not the technician abides by these rules is analogous to the regular use of an automobile seat belt. To be safe, follow the rules. It is possible to get away with not taking the proper precautions sometimes, but is not recommended. Do the job right and avoid static damage by following the rules.

Briefly, CMOS should be handled only in their original packaging, which is designed to protect the IC from static discharges. Use a grounded workbench and touch the bench before picking up a CMOS device. Don't use static-generating materials such as nylon or styrofoam around CMOS. Connect only properly grounded test instruments to CMOS circuits. Insert or remove CMOS chips only when the power to the board is *off*.

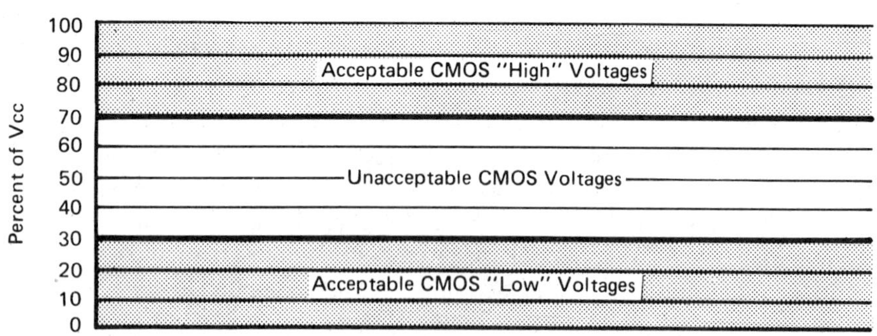

Figure 6.20 The acceptable logic levels of CMOS lie above 70 percent of Vcc and below 30 percent Vcc.

Figure 6.21 The extender chip is necessary for working on high-density IC boards. (Abbey Enterprises)

Several special tools will be needed frequently during troubleshooting digital ICs, and the job will be easier if they are at hand:

1. Good test probes (see Figure 5.1)
2. The extender clip (see Figure 6.21)
3. An IC puller

Look for Missing Signal Activity First

Existing circuits have already been designed to take into account the delay of signals as they progress through the ICs of a digital circuit. The rise- and fall time of circuits has also been considered. A service technician is not ordinarily expected to troubleshoot such problems. If the troubleshooting work is in research and development of circuits, however, this may not be the case. The engineering assistant technician may have to find these kinds of problems in the normal course of work. A solid foundation in normal troubleshooting, the topic of this book, will be absolutely necessary.

The pins of ICs are the best test points. They are accessible from both sides of the board, a handy feature in itself. It takes a bit of practice to remember to count *clockwise* on the bottom of the board and *counter-clockwise* on the TOP. Chips are usually laid out on the board so that all of the 1 pins of the chips are toward the same edge of the board—but check the ICs to be sure!

All signal readings should be taken at the IC pin on the top of the board, when practical. The reason is that, whether or not there is a socket, one leg of an IC can be bent under, not making contact with the board. (This is a common problem with automated component insertion machines at the factory.) Sockets can also develop bad connections to produce the same symptoms. Reading on the top of the IC pins will make detection of these problems easier to trace.

One way to begin troubleshooting a large digital board is to divide the schematic into two sections and then verify the presence of all signals crossing the line. With the schematic at hand, draw a light line down the approximate center of the schematic, between any ICs. This will be the beginning of the half-splitting method of signal tracing. Identify each of the ICs on either side of this line as to their use and location on the board. With the aid of any references available, identify all of the output pins of the ICs producing signals crossing this line, along with the termination pin numbers of the load ICs. See Figure 6.22.

With the schematic as a guide, first determine if signals are present where they cross the vertical line you drew. Depending upon whether or not the signals are all present where they should be, it may be necessary to half-split again in one direction or the other.

Full-Speed Testing of Digital Circuits (Not Three-state)

Full-speed testing is simply using the existing signals of the circuit, running at their normal speeds, to look for missing signals. Using either an oscilloscope or a digital logic probe, look at each of the lines that cross the center line of the schematic. Look for normal signal activity at each of these lines.

If You Find a Missing Signal

When you find a pin which apparently has a signal missing, consult the circuit diagram to verify that the signal should indeed be there. In microprocessor applications it is possible that that particular chip is not being called upon by the microprocessor chip, and certain signals shouldn't be there.

Be sure to check the special pins on the chip that originates a signal. Be sure that it is not being disabled by another input to the chip such as Set, Reset, Enable/Disable, Chip Select, or, in the case of the microprocessor itself, an Interrupt line. All of these inputs must be correct for the chips to work.

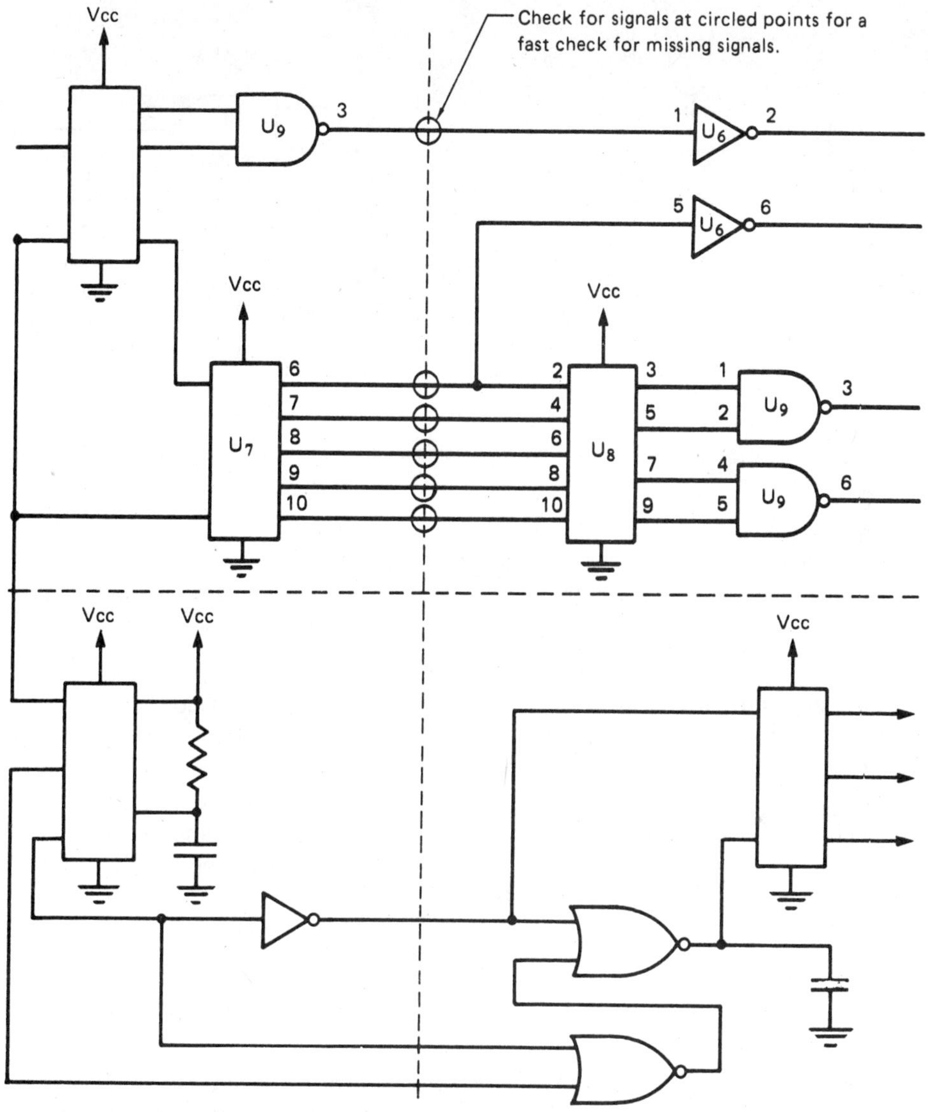

Figure 6.22 Layout of the schematic in sections can sometimes help in localizing a problem.

If a Pin is Stuck High or Low

The next things to check are the circuit inputs. If the input signals are not OK, you will obviously have to continue tracing backward through the circuit to find out why.

If the inputs are good and the output of the chip is bad, several possibilities exist:

1. There may be an internal short in an input to an IC connected to the bad pin.
2. There may be an internal open inside the source IC.

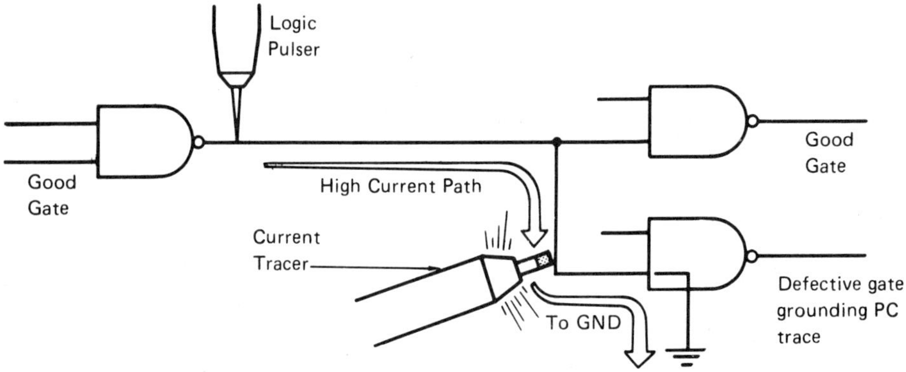

Figure 6.23 The digital pulser and current tracer combination finds circuit-board shorts on dead circuits easily and quickly.

3. There may be a short on the PC board, external to any IC.
4. The proper input conditions of a gate may not be present to produce any output. This should be verified using an oscilloscope, logic analyzer, or logic comparator.

The next step is to turn off the power and measure the pin that has no signal with an ohmmeter. Measure from the pin to the supply voltage bus and then to ground. If the lowest resistance is less than 1 ohm, look carefully for a short on the supply voltage bus and then to ground. If the lowest resistance is less than 1 ohm, look carefully for a short on the circuit-board trace. If the lowest resistance is a few ohms, either the source or one of the load ICs is shorted. Either of these shorts may be traced efficiently with the pulser/tracer combination of instruments. See Figure 6.23.

If there is no short circuit according to the ohmmeter, the source IC is most likely open internally.

If a Pin is Stuck at About 1.5V (TTL Only). This can occur when a TTL output open-circuits. The following input circuits will pull themselves to this approximate level, which is easily detectable with the oscilloscope, logic probe (neither the high nor the low LEDs light up), or even a voltmeter. It should fall right in the middle of the no-man's land, between the acceptable logic limits.

Watch for a CMOS Open Circuit

An open-circuited CMOS input will be extremely sensitive. The circuit output may or may not change state with the slightest input circuit disturbance such as a finger touching the board or the application of a probe. The chip may also vary its output at a 60-Hz rate due to hum pickup.

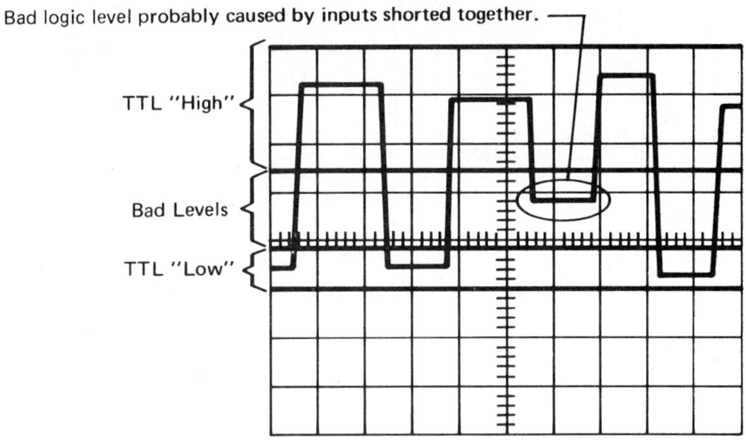

Figure 6.24 Intermittent bad logic levels are difficult to identify, but the oscilloscope can detect them.

If the Signal Level is Bad Only Part of the Time. A short between inputs within an IC can tie two other circuit outputs together. When two outputs are accidently tied together, they sometimes "fight" each other when they disagree. If they do agree, the output level will of course be acceptable. (See Figure 6.24.) Look for the chip or circuit-board short that is tying two inputs together. You should be able to identify another output signal that has a similar problem and then identify the chip that has an input from each of these two signals.

If all the signals appear normal down the center of the schematic, move to the right and draw another line similar to the one you drew down the middle. If you find many signals missing, trace them back to their source. Continue this half-splitting as necessary to find the single common problem causing the whole mess.

Special Considerations of Troubleshooting Three-State ICs

Bus-oriented circuits such as are commonly used in computers often connect two or more IC output circuits directly together. The circuits depend on logic levels applied to the chip select or chip enable of each to prevent more than one of them being selected at the same instant. This connection of chips may make the associated bus voltages look a bit strange when viewed with an oscilloscope (see Figure 6.25).

Since the bus is connected to several output lines, the tops of waveforms in particular may be stepped rather than flat. This is acceptable in view of the actual voltage levels involved. Remember that *any* level above 2.4V is acceptable as a high for TTL circuits, and more than 70 percent of Vcc for CMOS circuits. A bit of roughness on the tops or bottoms of the three-state digital waveform is normal. A three-state similar situation applies for logical lows—or less than 0.8V for TTL and less than 30 percent of Vcc for CMOS levels. The ramped portion of the waveform marked with the

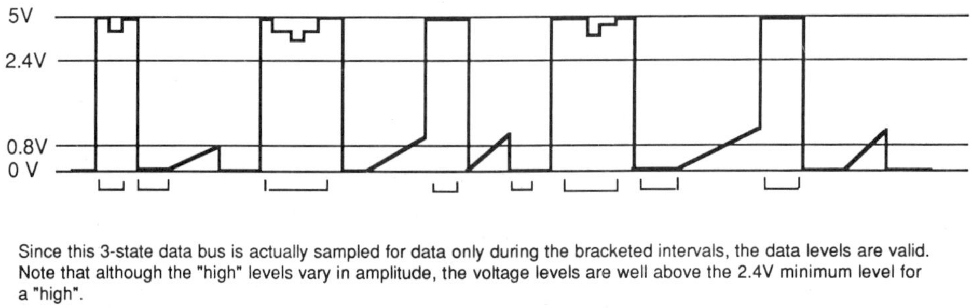

Figure 6.25 Logic levels on a three-state bus may not look acceptable yet may be quite workable.

X in Figure 6.24 is probably acceptable, too. This is typical of a bus voltage waveform when no chip is selected. Duyring this time the bus is "floating" and simply not in use and the voltage on it is of no concern.

If You Don't Find a Missing Signal on the Board

If all the signals on the board appear normal from one end of the circuit to the other, here is a clue as to what may be causing these symptoms: an AND, NAND, XOR, or XNOR gate with an internal open input can mask a problem. The output will be ignoring one of the inputs. The reason this can happen is that, with some internal failures, one of the inputs will pull high *inside* the chip. There will be no response to the outside signal which is normally being applied. The chip will assume that that input is always high. Thus the OR and NOR gates cannot cause this problem—they will "lock up" and won't pass signals if one of the inputs goes high.

Other, more complicated chips can cause similar masked problems. A counter, for instance, could have shorted or open circuitry and still be producing an output, although the output would not be correct. This possibility could be checked by testing each of the chips except those mentioned above for proper truth-table output. Although this wouldn't be too difficult to do with the simple AND, NAND, XOR, and XNOR gates, it could become a bit tedious with the counters and other chips when operating at full speed. Using a comparator at this point would be a very good idea: all the outputs and inputs of a good and a suspected IC are compared during full-speed operation. Remember the possibility of two inputs of a single chip shorting together, causing a poor level part of the time when the two inputs conflict. An oscilloscope can help verify this as a possible problem.

Single-Stepping Logic Circuits

In order to detect counting problems at a rate that will allow analysis of actual counts you may have to stop the normal counting of a circuit. Then the circuit can be single-stepped to check it for proper counting sequence. This can be done easily, without breaking the microcomputer trace or removing a clock circuit component, if

Figure 6.26 The digital pulser and logic monitor make an effective combination to troubleshoot defective counter and decoder circuits. (Courtesy of Hewlett-Packard Co.)

you use a circuit card extender. Some extenders have switches installed to break selected traces for troubleshooting purposes. If the extender board in use does not have such a feature, a bit of transparent tape on the appropriate pin of the board may accomplish the same purpose. (Don't forget to remove the tape at the end of the job!) Remember that a TTL output can be safely grounded to stop the normal counting signal.

The digital pulser can then be used to single-step circuits for counting. This is also a good time to use the multipin monitoring capability of the logic monitor (see Figure 6.26). The logic probe can also be used to monitor counter pins on a one-at-a-time basis.

A Digital Test Instrument Summary

A summary of the uses of the various instruments covered in this chapter according to the kind of trouble being experienced might look like this:

Completely inoperative circuit (power supply problems)

Digital multimeter, DC-coupled oscilloscope

Signal tracing through simple digital circuits

Digital pulser (source instrument)

Logic probe, oscilloscope

Bad counts from simple digital circuits

Digital pulser and logic monitor combination

Digital pulser and logic probe combination

Logic analyzer

Erratic operation

Logic comparator, logic analyzer

Timing errors

Logic analyzer, logic comparator

Wrong signals

Logic analyzer

Decoding I/O or addresses

Logic analyzer

Static stimulus tester (8-bit microprocessor circuits only)

CHAPTER SUMMARY

This chapter has covered the general procedures to follow in troubleshooting digital circuit boards. The technician should be able to repair 95 percent of the digital cards with these procedures if the proper schematics, test instruments, and tools are available. The remaining 5 percent or so of digital problems involve obscure problems such as timing errors and circuit glitches that may be very difficult to find. Such circuits are probably best returned to the manufacturer for repair.

REVIEW QUESTIONS

1. What is the most common method of making a computer repair?
2. What kinds of reference are necessary to identify the use and pinout of the ICs used in a computer?
3. To localize a problem within a computer, the ________ diagram is of great help.
4. Name an instrument that will give an E/I curve of a component under a small operating voltage while the rest of the circuit is dead.
5. What is the next step in troubleshooting once power is applied to a suspect circuit card
6. What is a typical capacitive loading effect of a 10X oscilloscope probe?
7. What is the danger of using the alternate oscilloscope sweep mode when checking circuit timing between two channels?

8. What is the risetime of the vertical channel of an oscilloscope with a maximum frequency specification of 20 MHz?
9. You have a dual-channel oscilloscope but need an additional input to test a logic gate. What could you use for the third input?
10. Above what voltage is considered a good TTL high?
11. Below what voltage is considered a good TTL low?
12. On what kind of computer might a static stimulus tester be put to good use in troubleshooting, for instance, a decoding problem?
13. What four functions can be performed using the static stimulus tester?
14. What does the TTL-CMOS switch of a logic probe do?
15. Assuming that the logic probe has two LEDs as indicators, what is the indication of a bad logic level?
16. What does the logic probe show to indicate logic-level activity in an operating circuit?
17. The logic monitor (or logic clip) is especially useful on logic circuits that can be ________.
18. What is the digital pulser used for?
19. What does the current tracer do?
20. What is the operating principle of the logic comparator?
21. How is the alphanumeric output of a signature analyzer utilized?
22. The logic analyzer, as compared to an oscilloscope, triggers on a trigger ________ rather than a trigger event.
23. Name two digital circuits that may not have true on/off signals present at the pins of the IC.
24. Which member of the TTL family has the fastest speed of operation?
25. A disconnected TTL input will be interpreted as a ________ so far as the output of that chip is concerned.
26. A disconnected CMOS input will be ________ in a similar situation.
27. CMOS ICs are very sensitive to ________ damage.
28. Name three pins of an IC that must have proper signals for the chip to work at all.
29. If the logic level of a standard TTL output is sometimes bad during normal operation, what should the technician look for?
30. What instrument can be used to single-step a logic circuit through its paces?

chapter seven

Installing & Troubleshooting Option Card Problems

CHAPTER OVERVIEW

This chapter provides guidance for a technician who is expected to either install or troubleshoot the plug-in printed circuit boards of a microcomputer, cards sometimes referred to as option cards. The installation of option cards is a major service of the computer technician. Some of the pitfalls that may occur are given and steps suggested for correcting them. Seldom can the installation of an option board be accomplished by simply plugging in the board and walking away. Software may be necessary to utilize the new card, or problems may be introduced by causing a port collision. The new technician will find the information given here very helpful in troubleshooting problems that may arise.

WHY USE OPTION CARDS?

Option cards are necessary to add operational capability to the basic microcomputer system. The microcomputer is often sold "bare bones," with only the system board and power supply mounted within the computer enclosure plus a keyboard. See Figure 7.1.

Figure 7.1 Some computers are sold "bare bones," without many necessary circuits such as a video adapter card. (Courtesy of IBM)

The block diagram in Figure 7.2 will help visualize the extras that may be necessary to make a usable microcomputer system.

INSTALLING OPTION CARDS

Some CommonSense Cautions

Whenever its cover is removed there is potential for damage to computer through carelessness. Static discharge into the sensitive circuits of the computer is the prime danger. The technician should be sure that any static buildup is discharged to the outer case or chassis of the computer before reaching into the enclosure for any reason. Simply touching the frame of the computer, particularly if the case is grounded to a wall outlet, is sufficient.

Always turn off the power before removing or installing any connections, including the option cards, inside the computer. This principle applies also to the connections of cabling to the computer's external input/output ports.

When installing option boards be sure that the components beneath the lower edge of the option card are not being forced down onto the system board when the option card is pressed downward. More pressure is required on the end of the option card with the connector than at the other end. Some components may be in the way of the card, such as small filter capacitors, which should be pressed aside gently to clear the card.

The documentation provided with an option board is the best source of information for the installation and the operation of any option card. The servicing technician *must* be very familiar with the documentation for any options cards that are to be installed. Failure to read and heed the instructions, or failure to understand the sometimes complex instructions provided, can lead to apparent problems with the new option card. The technician must remember that if the computer was working fine before adding the new card and the computer does not work properly after the card is installed, it is very likely that the instructions have not been followed. Blame the human element before blaming the new hardware.

Option boards often have several circuits built upon a single board. The more complex boards, those having more than a few functions (for example clock, RAM expansion, a serial port, a parallel port, and a game port on a single card), are becoming very popular. These cards provide some valuable extra functions at the expense of using only a single expansion slot in the computer. The following discussions consider each of these functions independently, however, for the sake of clarity.

Installing Additional I/O Ports

Depending on the specific microcomputer, it may or may not be supplied with parallel or serial input/output ports coming directly from the system board. These ports may be necessary to connect external equipment (peripherals) to the computer, such as a printer. The addition of more ports (Figure 7.3) using the expansion slots of the system board can be deliberate to get ports that are needed, or they may be available merely

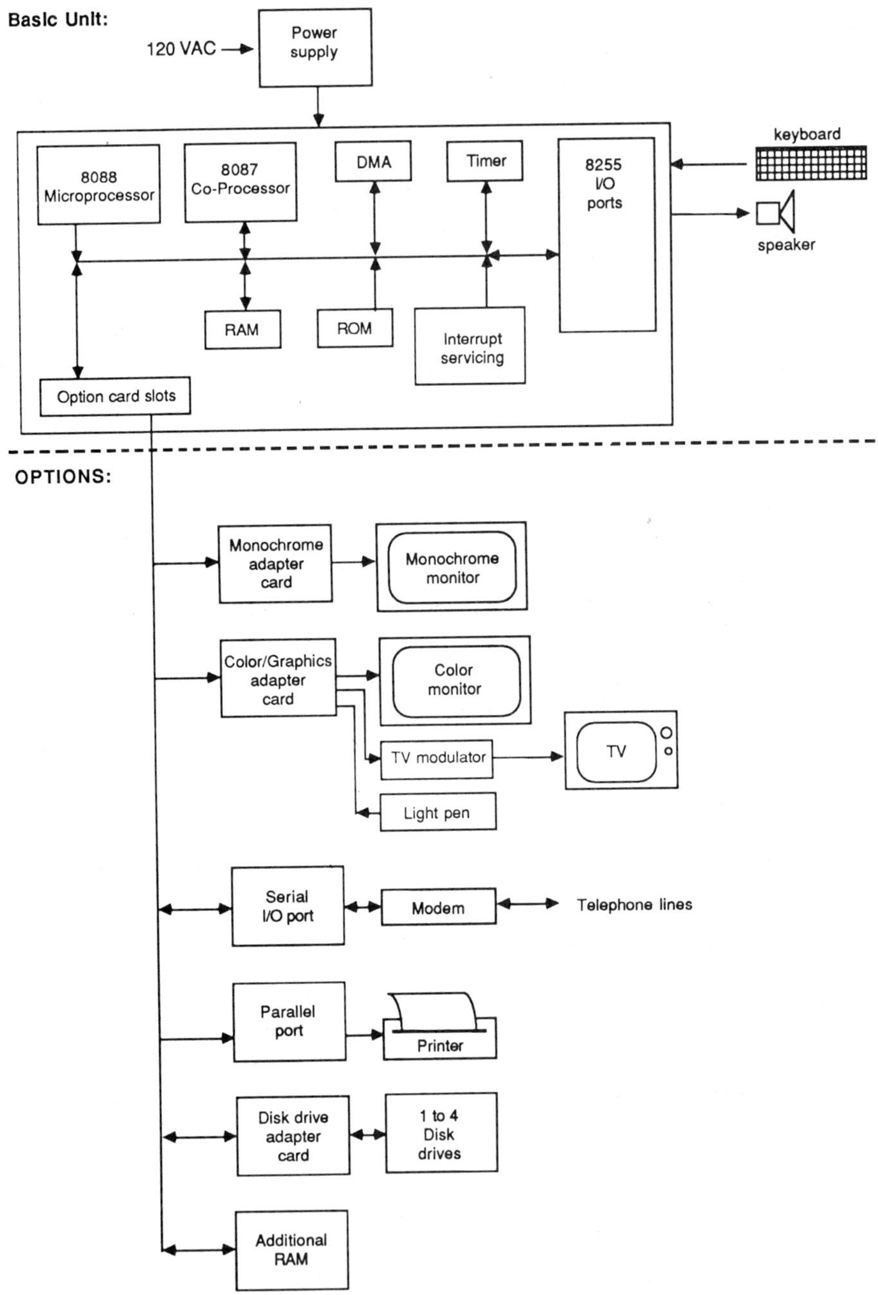

Figure 7.2 The microcomputer is purchased as a separate unit that often does not contain the necessary options to perform as a usable tool. Additional option cards may be required.

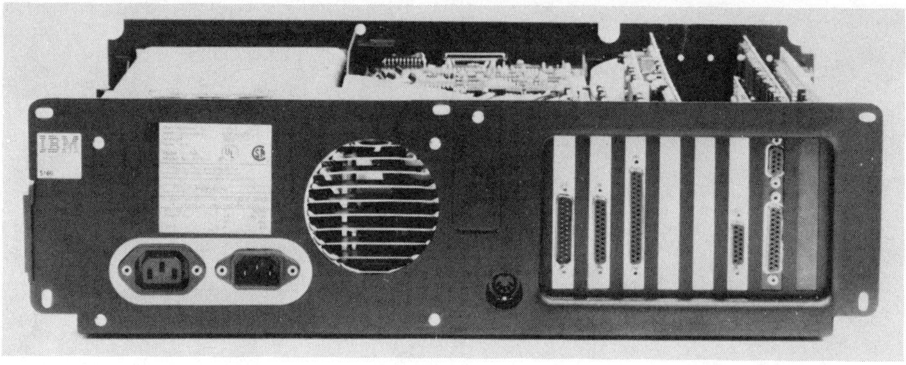

Figure 7.3 A microcomputer may have several parallel and serial port outputs. (Courtesy of IBM)

because they were extras on a board that was installed for another reason, such as for additional memory.

In any case, the addition of an expansion card port has the potential of disabling an existing system board port if the new port has the same address. This case is called a "port collision." For this reason, option ports are usually provided with strapping or a jumper to change the address of the new port or to disable it entirely. See Figure 7.4.

MS-DOS has provision for five outputs, three parallel ports and two serial ports. To differentiate between them in the various items of documentation, they have designations as follows:

Parallel Ports:

LPT1 = Line Printer 1

LPT2 = Line Printer 2

LPT3 = Line Printer 3

Serial Ports:

COM1 = Serial Port 1

COM2 = Serial Port 2

Each of the designations above refers to a specific address in the software used with the computer. As most software is supplied, LPT1 is the default printer output port used for printer operations. Additional ports become LPT2 and LPT3, respectively. Once an additional port is installed, operation of the original and the additional ports should be verified to be sure that there is no port collision. A port collision usually results in no operation at all of a printer connected to one of the ports involved.

On the other hand, if more than one port is used, signals can be rerouted from a parallel port to a serial port using the MODE command of MS-DOS. For instance, if a

Figure 7.4 Additional ports may require proper setting of an address jumper to prevent a port collision. (Abbey Enterprises)

dot-matrix printer is connected to LPT1 port and a serial letter-quality printer is connected to COM1, the normal software output to the printer (LPT1) will drive the dot-matrix printer. The printer information could be rerouted to the serial printer by two commands:

```
MODE COM2:12,,7,1,N
MODE LPT1:=COM2
```

The first MODE command sets the proper serial transmission parameters. The second command is the one of interest at this point. This command will take all the parallel printer data and redirect it to the address of the serial port, COM1. The parallel data is converted from a parallel format to a serial format as required.

There are two principal uses for the parallel port, that of running a write-only peripheral like a printer and that of using the parallel port to send and to receive data. These are covered using the Centronics and IEEE-488 communications standards, respectively.

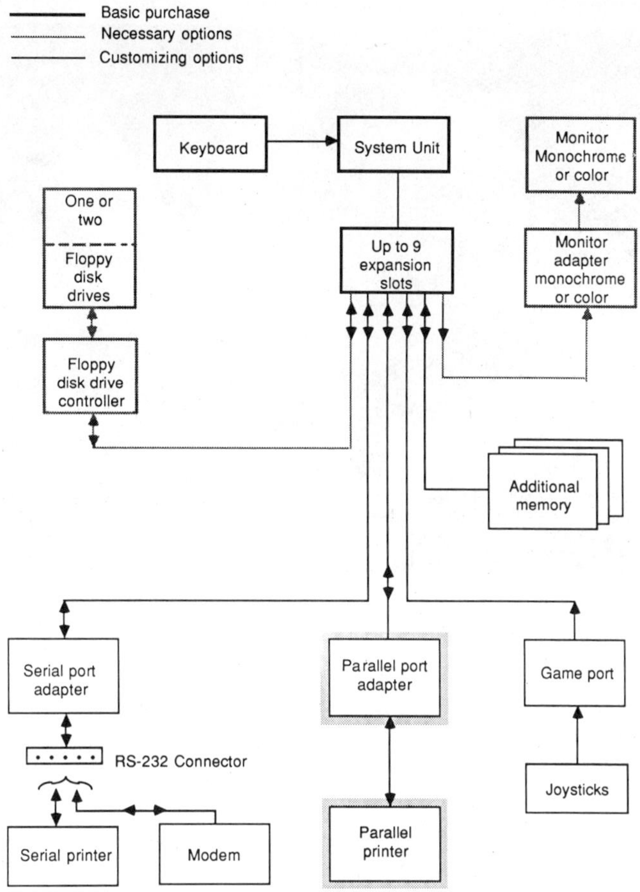

Figure 7.5 The parallel port is usually used for connecting a printer.

The Parallel Output Port. The parallel port fits into the whole computer system as shown in Figure 7.5. The Parallel port is sometimes easily identifiable by its standard connector usually located on the rear of the computer (see Figure 7.6). The electronic circuitry of a parallel port must be capable of both sending data and receiving handshaking signals from that port (see Figure 7.7). Operation of the parallel port consists of decoding the appropriate address for the printer port and then providing for either a write (send) or a read (receive).

The Centronics printer standard is used most often for the connection of a printer to the computer. This port allows the transfer of eight bits of data at a time, one each of eight separate lines. These bits share a common ground connection interspersed between the data lines in a ribbon cable. Besides these output data lines there are at least two other lines that receive handshake information back from the printer. See Appendix A for a breakdown of the Centronics port standard connections.

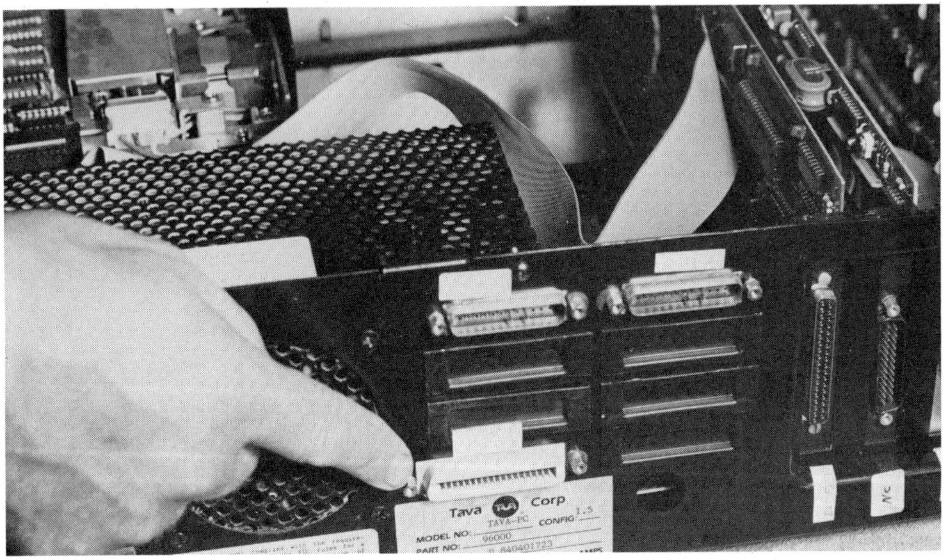

Figure 7.6 The Centronics or parallel port is easily identified. (Abbey Enterprises)

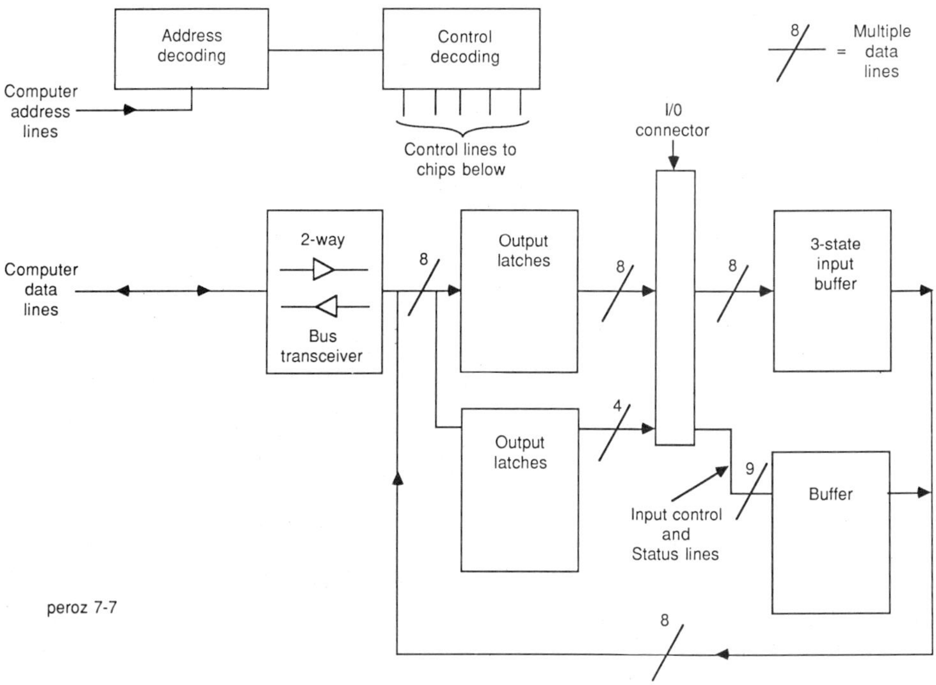

Figure 7.7 Block diagram of the parallel (Centronics) printer port.

Figure 7.8 The Amphenol Centronics and DB-25p connectors are the most widely used connectors for connecting microcomputer parallel printers. (Abbey Enterprises)

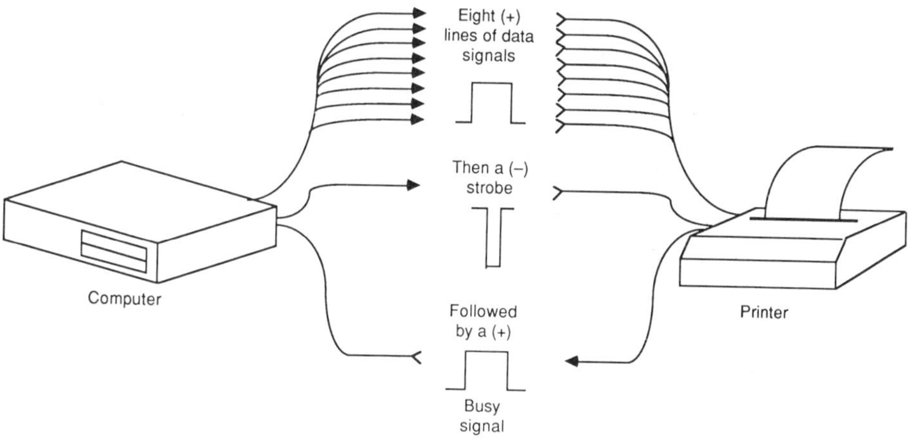

Figure 7.9 The connection of a parallel printer to a microcomputer usually uses the Centronics interconnection standard.

Many printers used with microcomputers are the parallel type and most of these use the Centronics wiring standard. They also usually use one of two types of connector, the traditional Centronics plug (a 36-pin Amphenol # 57-40360 plug fits it) or a 25-pin Amphenol D connector, DB-25P. See Figure 7.8.

The Centronics signals are covered in Appendix A. A typical connection between the computer and a printer is shown in Figure 7.9.

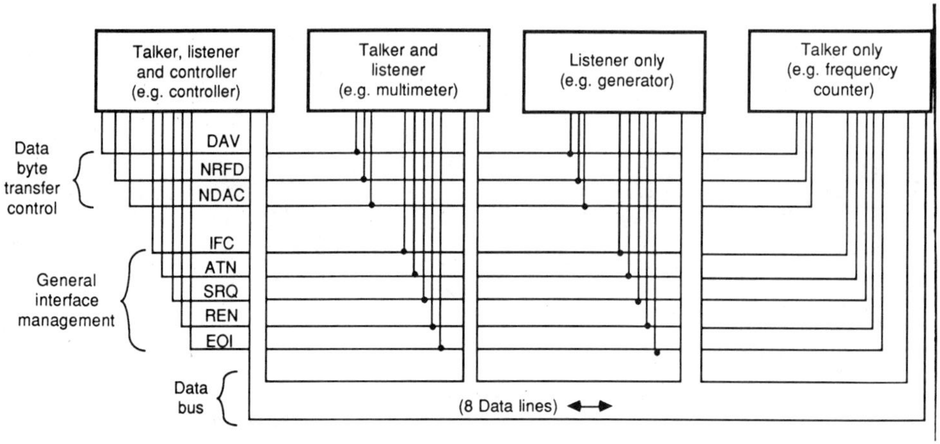

Figure 7.10 Concept of the IEEE-488 or GPIB interface bus for the transmission or reception of data in a parallel format.

The IEEE 488 Input/Output Port. The IEEE-488 port is also a parallel port but is used for both output and input purposes. The IEEE-488 standard was originally intended for use by a computer that needed to be connected to peripherals which themselves could either only accept data, originate only it, or both accept and originate data. Figure 7.10 shows the basic setup of this bus standard.

A good example of a use for the IEEE-488 interfacing standard is in a computer connected to electronic testing equipment. A signal generator could be "told" by the computer (here called the controller) to generate a particular frequency and amplitude. A voltmeter, on the other hand, might take a voltage reading and send this information back through the port to the computer. These two instruments illustrate a listener and a talker function in the IEEE-488 interface standard. The IEEE-488 input/output standard is also called the General Purpose Interface Bus, or GPIB. It can be used for other purposes besides electronics instruments, of course. The software used with the computer determines the details of how it operates. Appendix A gives the details of the individual pins of the IEEE-488 standard. All data passed back and forth on the data bus is under the control and/or supervision of the system controller, often a computer. Many sophisticated modern electronic instruments are compatible with computer control and are designed in accordance with the IEEE-488 standard.

Serial Input/Output Ports. The serial port is most often used for one of three purposes:

1. As a computer-to-computer port over telephone lines (using a modem)
2. As a printer port
3. As a computer to computer port, wired directly

In contrast with the parallel port, the serial port sends information a single bit at a time. This allows the computer to use only a few wires, usually three, to communicate to other computers over short distances (such as in the same building). This is the method used to communicate from smaller computers or "dumb terminals" to mainframe

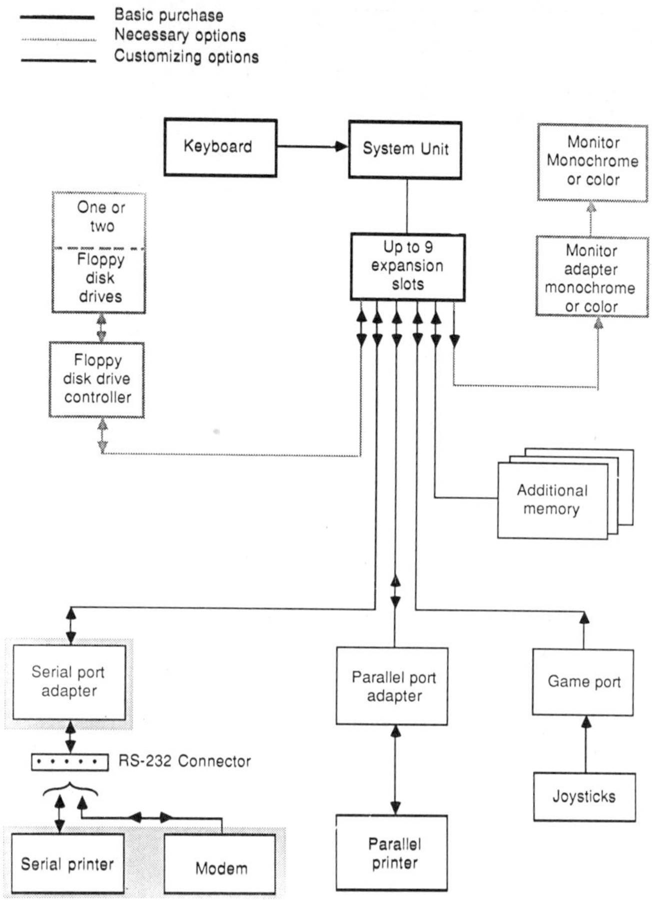

Figure 7.11 The serial port is usually used for connecting a printer, another computer, or a modem.

computers. With the addition of more hardware to convert the digital information to compatible signals, computers can also communicate to one another using a telephone line. This allows computers to communicate with each other over very long distances. The serial port fits into the computer system as shown in Figure 7.11.

Software determines the number of serial bits that define a byte of information, the speed of transmission and reception, and when that byte is completed and the next one begins (see Figure 7.12).

The principal IC used in the transmission of serial data is the UART, or universal asynchronous receiver-transmitter. This chip converts parallel bytes of data from the system data bus into a string of bits, one at a time, in a FIFO format. A similar IC on the receiving computer converts the data back into parallel bytes for the receiving computer to process further (see Figure 7.13). Detailed troubleshooting of the serial port may require the technician to review the operation of this sophisticated chip.

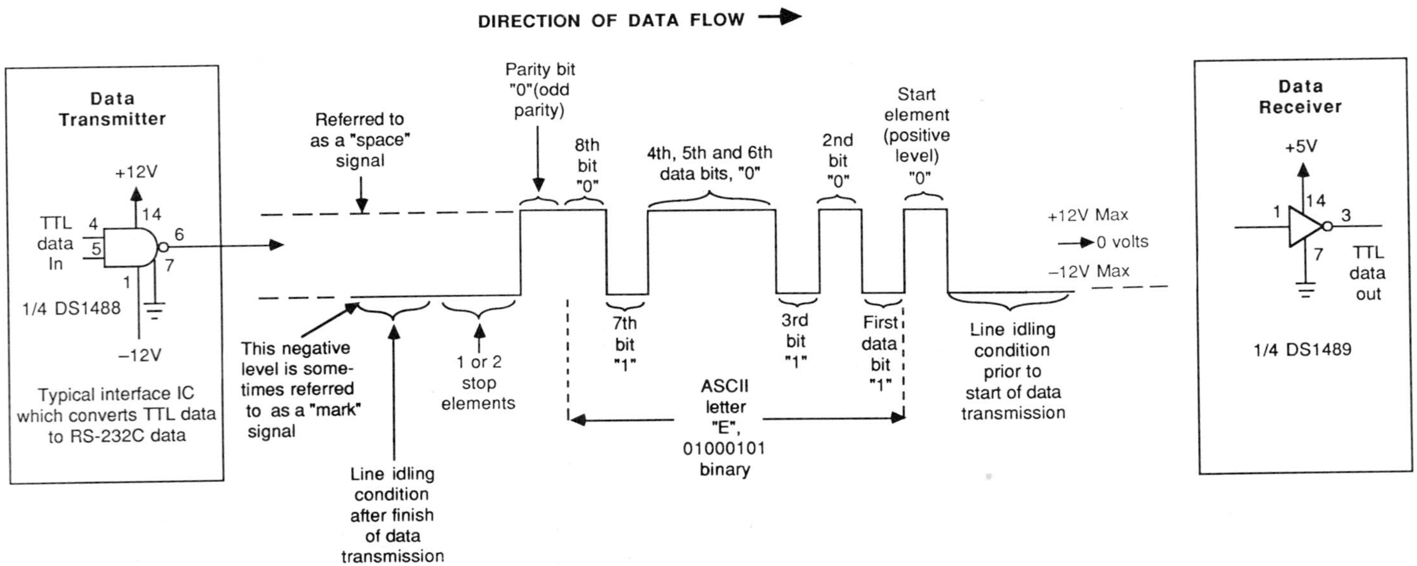

RS232C serial data transmission standards. Note the major points:
Data is inverted to a negative-true convention;
The least significant bit is sent first, most significant bit last;
Voltage levels are either positive or negative, not zero;
Line level idles at a negative voltage.
Control signals, not shown, are positive-true convention and use the same voltage levels as above.

Figure 7.12 Serial data transmission parameters are determined by the software used.

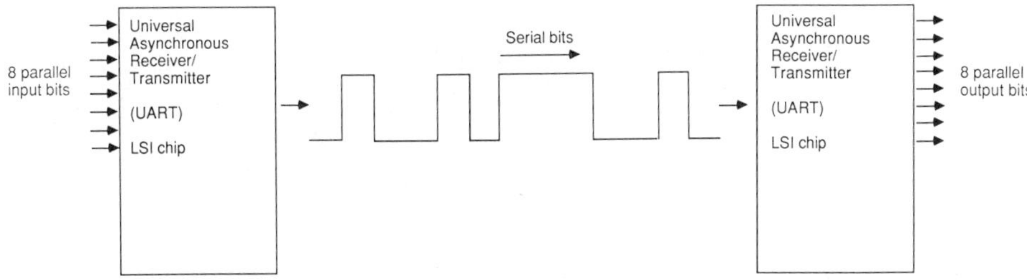

Figure 7.13 The UART chip is the heart of serial data transmission.

The serial transmission of data began in the days of the teletypewriter. These machines were set up in a loop, a common current being passed around among all the machines for communications. Data was encoded by making and breaking this current with relays. A vestige of this method of transmission, called the 20-milliampere current loop data transmission system remains today.

Telephone lines can be used to pass computer data if the data is encoded properly. The use of telephone lines requires the use of a modem to do this encoding. The original use for modems was to encode the data to and from a data terminal consisting of a CRT, keyboard, a minimal amount of memory, and a mainframe computer. (See Figure 7.14.) A microcomputer can be connected to the telephone line with a modem and can be used to communicate with other computers. A common use is to check into bulletin boards and to subscribe to electronic data services such as a physicians' medical data bank. Appropriate software must be used to transfer this data from one computer to another. The transmitting computer must be able to put appropriate information either directly from the keyboard or possibly from a disk file out to a specified serial port, and the receiving computer must be ready to receive it and place it into an appropriate place, either the screen in front of a live operator or onto a disk file for later access. Software such as PC-TALK (available from FREEWARE, P.O. Box 862, Tiburon, CA 94920) is such a program.

The RS-232C serial data transmission standard came into use to connect the data terminal equipment (DTE) with the modem, which the standard calls data communications equipment (DCE). Although many lines are designated in this standard, only eight are commonly used (Figure 7.15).

Note in Appendix A that the pins have unique names for the signals, regardless of whether the connection is being made to data terminal (DTE or terminal) equipment or data communications (DCE or modem) equipment. For instance, the transmitted data line, 2, of a DTE is connected to the *input* of a DCE. This is a bit confusing since now we have an *input* line called "transmit." Therefore, in order to make some sense of this connection it is necessary to know if the equipment in question is set up to act as DTE or DCE. It may be some help to know that the standard way of wiring a DTE is with a male connector and a DCE with a female connector. Thus, if the equipment is set up according to the standard, a male connector would have data coming *out* of pin 2. A female connector should indicate a DCE equipment with data coming out of pin 3. (See Figure 7.16.)

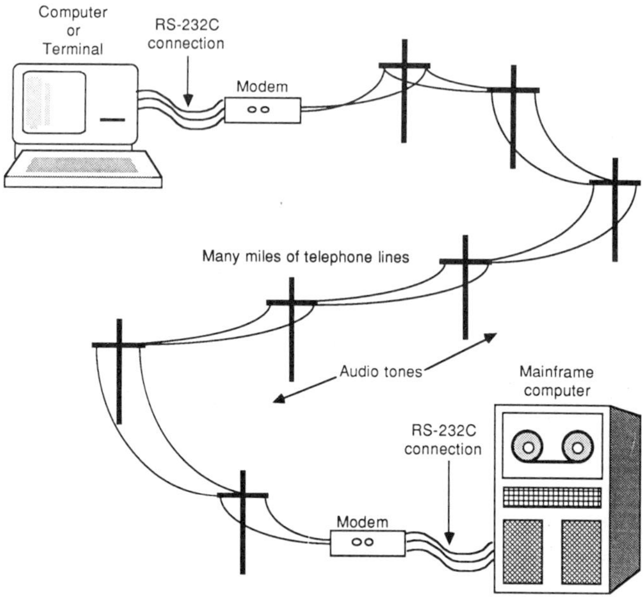

Figure 7.14 Serial data transmission is used in passing information over telephone lines between data terminals and mainframe computers.

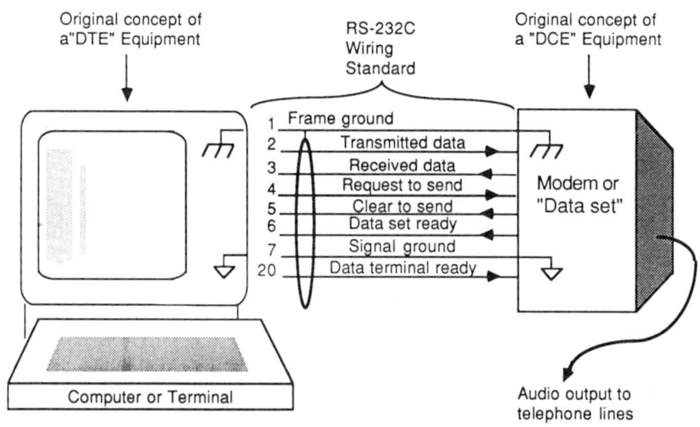

Figure 7.15 The most commonly used pins of an RS-232C connector.

For a clearer idea of how the signals of an RS-232C port compare with normal TTL levels, see Figure 7.17. One of the advantages of using the RS-232C standard is that no matter what might happen accidentally, no damage to either equipment can result if the intervening wires should be shorted or opened. The RS-232C circuits have been deliberately engineered to be "goofproof."

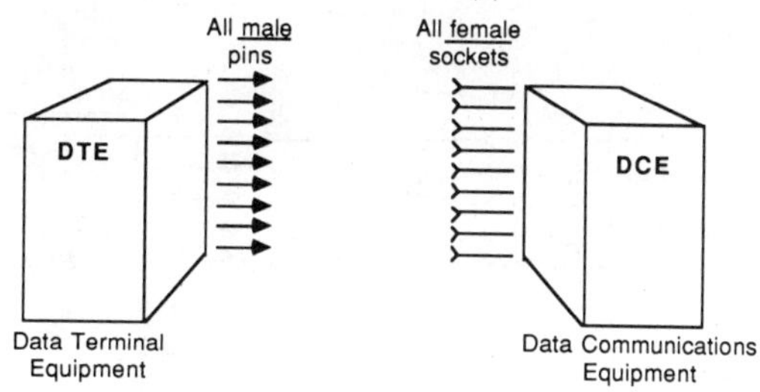

Figure 7.16 The presence of a male or female connector should indicate whether the equipment is configured as DTE or DCE equipment for the purposes of the RS-232C standard.

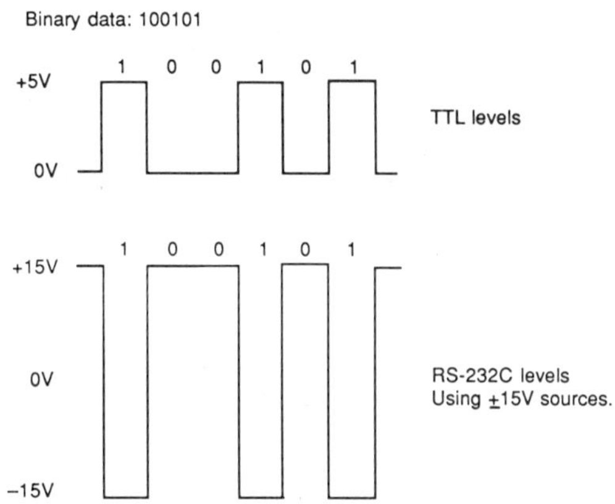

Figure 7.17 How RS-232C signals differ from normal TTL voltages.

Using this serial method of data transmission, two computers may be able to send data back and forth with only a few wires between them. Such an arrangement is shown in Figure 7.18. Note that each of the computers is configured as a DTE, where information comes out of pin 2. Since they are configured the same, a crossover cable with female connectors on each end must be used. This kind of cable is sometimes called a null modem cable because no modem is used in communicating between computers. (On the other hand, two computers configured as DCE could also be connected together with a similar connection using male connectors on the ends of the cable.)

Serial Printer Connections

Some printers use an abbreviated version of an RS-232C connection in passing data from a computer to the printer since data flows only in one direction. Only a few wires are required, generally three: a ground, a data line to the printer, and a handshake line (Figure 7.19).

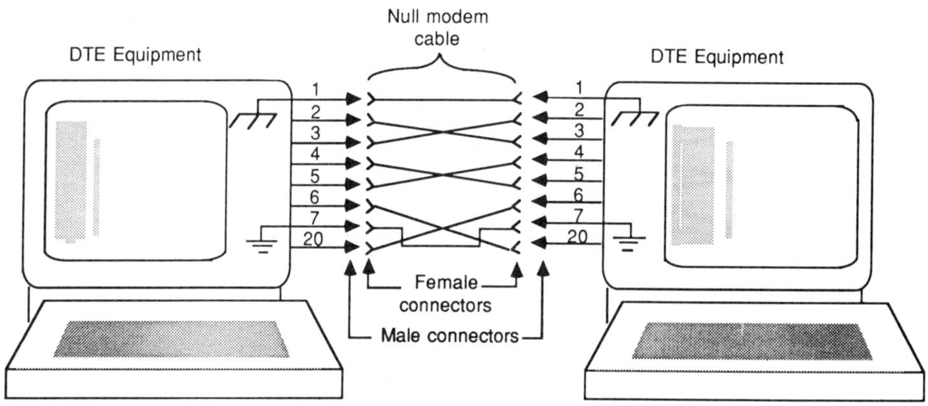

Figure 7.18 Two DTEs such as these computers can be cross-connected with a null modem cable with female connectors on each end.

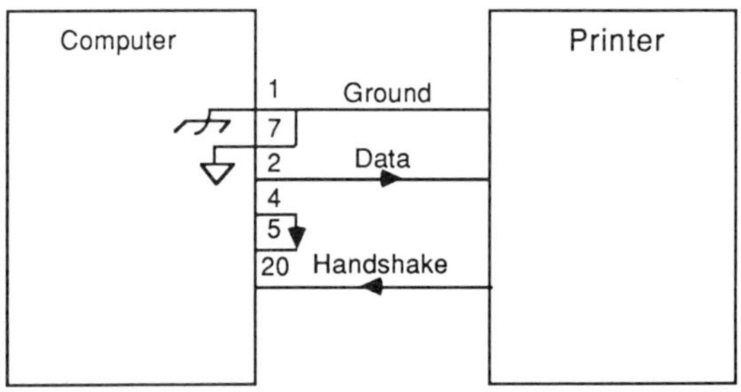

Figure 7.19 Using a serial printer allows the connection of only a few lines between the computer and the printer.

Installing Monochrome (B/W) Video Boards

Installing a monochrome video adapter board is about the simplest of all option-board installation jobs. Install the card edge guide as shown in Figure 7.20 and insert the new card. Connect the monochrome monitor to the jack provided on the adapter card, often a D connector having nine pins as in Figure 7.21 or a single RCA jack for a composite video output. The computer and monitor can then be turned on for a test to see if the screen is correct. The MODE utility command is available to shift the screen presentation a little each way horizontally.

Installing Color Video Adapter Boards

The job of installing a color video adapter card is as easy as installing a monochrome adapter. The nine-pin connector taking signals to the monitor is shown in Figure 7.22.

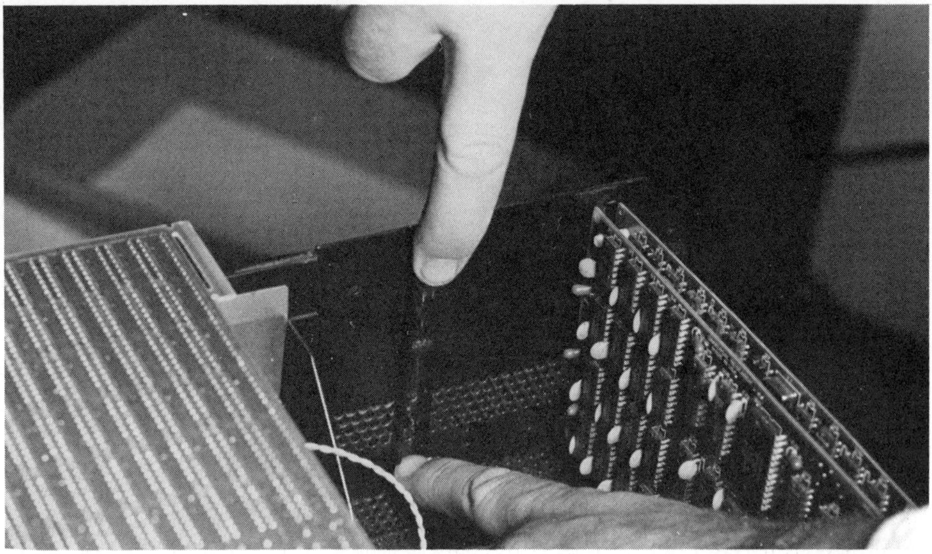

Figure 7.20 Install the card edge guide before installation of the card itself. (Abbey Enterprises)

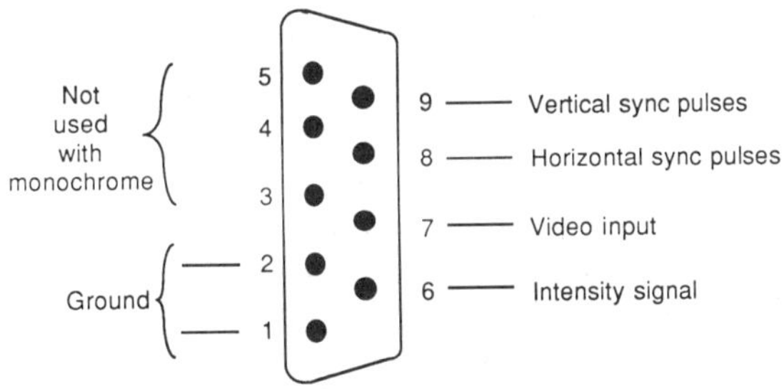

Figure 7.21 Monochrome pinouts for a 9-pin monochrome monitor.

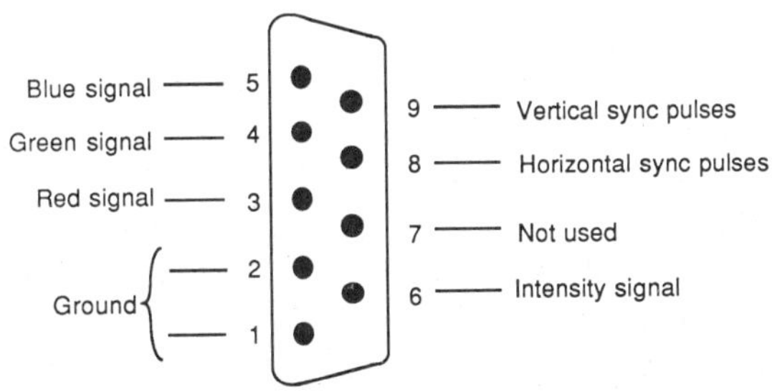

Figure 7.22 RGB color pinouts for a 9-pin RGB monitor.

Figure 7.23 A typical game controller for use with a microcomputer. (Abbey Enterprises)

Installing Combination Color/Monochrome Cards

The installation of a combination color and monochrome card may involve the setting of a switch or jumper to determine whether the computer will boot up in the color or in the monochrome mode. The instruction manual for the option card will explain the setting of this switch. After the computer is in operation the selection of either color or monochrome can be under software control. On occasions where the operator may wish to change from one monitor to the other, the MODE program can be used to switch.

Installing Game Options

The installation of a game option consists of plugging in an interface card that provides switched and analog resistance inputs to the computer. A typical game controller is shown in Figure 7.23. The game port can be an additional feature on a card that has other hardware. In case the game port is not to be used, it should be disabled with the jumpers provided for that purpose on the interface board.

Installing Modems

A modem is connected to a computer to use the telephone lines as a link to other computers. The installation of the modem requires the use of a multiwire cable between the modem and the computer. The telephone line connects to the modem by a separate connector, usually a modular telephone connector. See Figure 7.24.

The RS-232C cable to be used between the computer and the modem may be provided with the modem. If it is not, the technician can make up a cable by referring to the information above, or a cable can be ordered from manufacturers who specialize in computer interface cabling.

Software is necessary to operate a modem. A program such as PC-TALK, mentioned earlier, is used for this purpose. Such software may have such capabilities as storing frequently called telephone numbers or dialing them automatically, storing incoming data files on a diskette, or provision for two-way keyboard communications between the operators of the two computers.

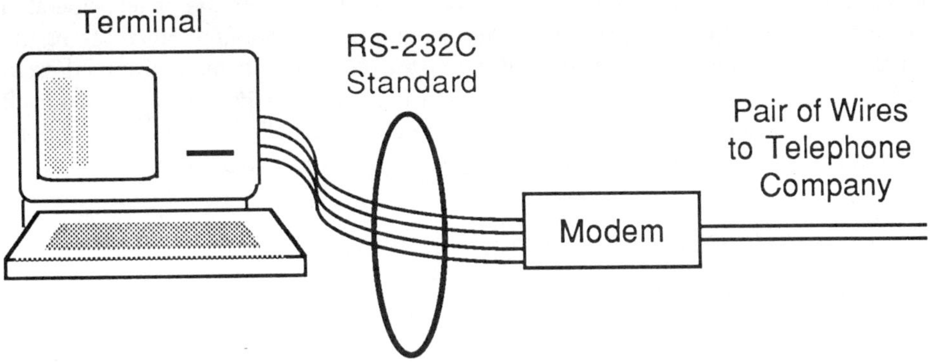

Figure 7.24 The modem is installed between the computer and the telephone line.

Figure 7.25 The rechargeable battery identifies the time-of-day clock circuitry.

Installing Clock Options

Once set to the correct time by the operator, the system-board clock offered with many of the microcomputers depends upon the uninterrupted flow of power from the power receptacle to keep accurate time. When such computers are first turned on, there is no way of knowing the correct time and date. The computer starts from 00:00 for the time and begins with a date of January 1, 1980. The operator may set this date and time from the keyboard each time the computer is booted up or an option can be installed to do the job automatically each time the computer is used. This clock option card keeps time once it is set, whether power is available or not, because it has a crystal-controlled clock that runs on a small rechargeable battery. The time-of-day clock option is easily recognized on an option card by the presence of the battery that maintains time when external power is turned off (Figure 7.25).

Software is necessary to get the correct time and date from the battery-operated clock and load it into the computer system when power is applied. Since setting the clock this way involves as much work as setting the date and time manually, it is best to operate this software from an AUTOEXEC.BAT file and have the computer load itself automatically upon power-up. If there are two clocks installed because the options cards are installed for other purposes, one of the clocks must be disabled.

TROUBLESHOOTING OPTION CARD PROBLEMS

Troubleshooting Notes

Detailed Documentation will be Required. It will be necessary to have at least two items of documentation available to troubleshoot to the component level on option boards: the schematic of the circuit, and a parts layout diagram. In addition, the theory of operation and a block diagram are very helpful. See Figures 7.26, 7-27 and 7.28.

Many of the option card circuits can be exercised by using the diskette diagnostics program.

Using a Board Extender. Test instruments will be necessary to troubleshoot option cards to the component level with the exception of RAM problems, which the computer can usually troubleshoot itself. Attaching test probes to appropriate circuitry is often impossible without getting the option card up in the clear, away from the other boards and the sides of the computer. See Figure 7.29.

These board extenders sometimes allow a circuit card to be reinserted into the circuitry backward, so they must be used with care. It is a big help to mark on the extender board the identification of all of the traces. These make ideal places to check for signals and voltages. Be sure to use the same lettering and numbering scheme as on the circuit card or socket connector.

Problems with Option Board RAM

Problems Detected by ROM Diagnostics Before the System Prompt. The RAM used by the computer is contained at least partly on the system board. Additional RAM may be installed by plugging in option cards having sockets for additional banks of memory chips. See Figure 7.30.

All of the systems memory is tested during the ROM memory checks each time the computer is turned on. A memory error will usually be detected during this check, and the location of the problem may be indicated by a message: PARITY CHECK ONE indicates a problem with the system-board RAM, while a PARITY CHECK TWO message indicates a problem in option-card RAM. Troubleshooting of system-board RAM is covered in Chapter 8.

When a RAM problem appears on an option board the fact may be confirmed by removing the suspected card and resetting the system board DIP switches to reflect the reduction in memory quantity. An appropriate diagnostics program should then be run to test the remaining memory. If there are two or more option boards with additional

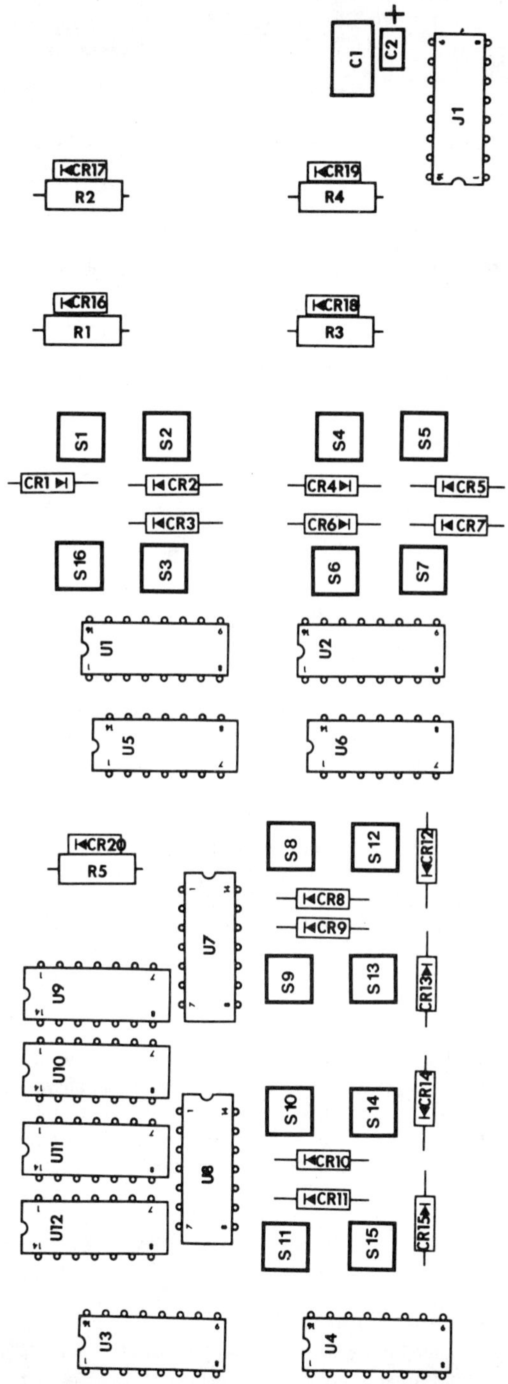

Figure 7.26 The parts layout is needed when repairing to the component level. (Courtesy of Datasouth Computer Corp.)

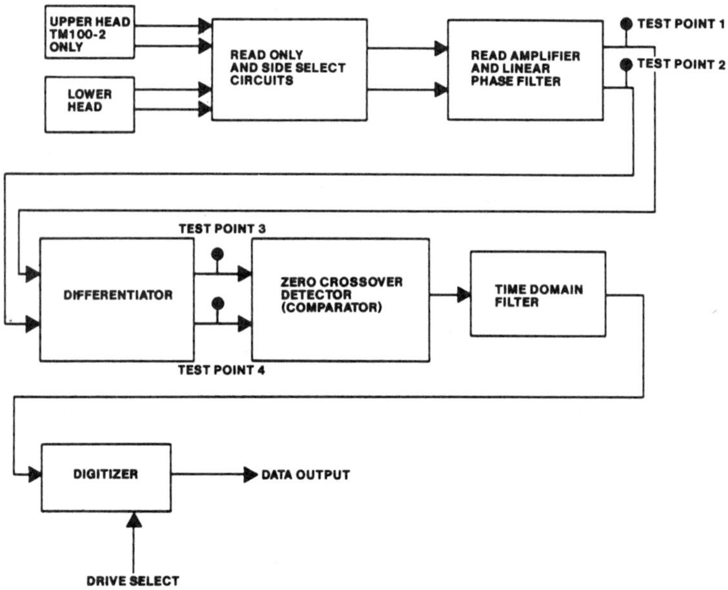

Figure 7.27 Troubleshooting is easier if the block diagram is also available. (Courtesy of Tandon Corp.)

Crystal controlled oscillator X1 operates at 15.9744 MHz. The oscillator output is buffered by UB13. The oscillator circuit output at a normal 16 MHz is used as 62 NSEC timing signal and is also used to clock 4-bit synchronous counter UB11 (on the positive edge of the clock) to develop additional timing signals of 8, 4, 2, and 1 MHz.

The 8 MHz is inverted by UA11 and becomes the dot clock (DOT CLK). One of the destinations of DOT CLK is Shift Register UA14 (Sheet 4 of the Schematic); UA14 is positive edge sensitive which is the reason for inverting DOT CLK. The active edge of DOT CLK is also the active edge of signals that follow at lower frequencies or lower rates. UA14 will load synchronously with the rising edge of DOT CLK when a load pulse (H COUNT*) Active low is indicated by (*). is applied. H COUNT* is generated by decoder UB1 (Schematic, Sheet 2). UB1 Pin 9 will be active during the counts E to F of counter UB11 which generates H COUNT*.

The Memory Counter is UD3. During the time H COUNT* is active synchronous with the rising of the 8 MHz clock, Shift Register UA14 will load new data from the video circuitry. The character on the screen is bracketed by the H COUNT* pulse which sets an inflexible limit in timing. A horizontal display line consists of 64 pulses including video retrace blanking which leaves 52 characters visible. Each character time is very nearly 1 microsecond, so that the vertical frame rate is in full synchronization with the AC line (60 cycles).

At the decoder UB1 (Schematic, Sheet 2), there is an active low CHAR CLK* at Pin 15. CHAR CLK is inverted by UE12 (Schematic, sheet 8). The other two . . .

Figure 7.28 The theory of operation explains in detail the use of each of the digital circuits and is also extremely valuable as a troubleshooting aid. (Courtesy of the Osborne Computer Corp.)

Figure 7.29 The extender board is used to bring the card up to a working position where test leads may be attached. (Courtesy of the Vector Electronic Co.)

Figure 7.30 Computer RAM memory chips are often contained partly on the system board with additional RAM available on option boards. (Courtesy of the Emulex Corp.)

memory installed, removal of a memory card must not result in a "hole" in the continuous addressing of RAM. In other words, removal of a memory expansion card in the middle address of RAM will mean resetting the addressing of the higher memory cards to lower addresses. Memory must be continuous from the lowest RAM address to the highest address used.

Once the offending memory expansion card is identified, it is necessary to identify the bank of memory chips responsible for the problem. At least one manufacturer has provided his card with a row of LEDs that latch on, indicating the row that triggers the memory defect. As many as six banks might be installed on an option card, each bank typically providing 64K of memory. The most efficient way to find the offending bank is to set the system-board switches to include only a single bank of the option card memory. There may also be DIP switches on the option card to switch in or out the number of banks in use, beginning from one end of the banks of memory and progressing to the opposite end. See Figure 7.31.

For instance, if an option card is producing a memory problem resulting in a PARITY CHECK TWO error during power-up ROM diagnostics, it is easy to set the system-board memory switches to show the maximum system board memory of (for example) 128K and run the ROM diagnostics again. Turn off the computer, wait for about ten seconds, and turn it on again. (A cold reboot switch accomplishes the same result as turning off the computer and is a bit easier on the equipment.) If the RAM problem is indeed on the option card, the computer should now detect no memory error and should load the operating system from a diskette.

The next step will be to set the system board switches to correspond to an additional 64K of memory (assuming 64K memory chips are used). This done, the switches on the option board must also be set to allow only one bank of memory to be used. Again, the computer is turned off or cold rebooted to run the ROM diagnostics. If the PARITY CHECK TWO error appears, the problem is contained within the eight or nine chips of the first bank cut into the system. If the PARITY CHECK TWO error does not appear, turn off the computer and again set the system switches to show another 64K to be cut into the memory, and set the switches of the option card to allow the second bank to be used. With this procedure the computer should eventually identify the bank of offending chips. The individual chip that is causing the problem can then be located by replacing the entire bank with known good memory chips, verifying them as operating satisfactorily by running the ROM diagnostics again, then replacing the known good chips, one at a time, with one of the chips from the bad bank. Each time a known good chip is removed, replace it with one of the suspected chips and run the ROM diagnostics program again. Eventually the bad chip will show up. When the chip is identified (the last one installed before the error message appeared again), bend the leads of the chip under to identify it *before you put it down*. (This is important to identify the chip if it gets mixed with the good chips.) It should then be safe, assuming only one chip was bad, to replace all of the known good chips with the originals with the exception of that one bad chip. Be sure to run the ROM diagnostics a few more times to be sure that all of the bad chips have been identified and replaced.

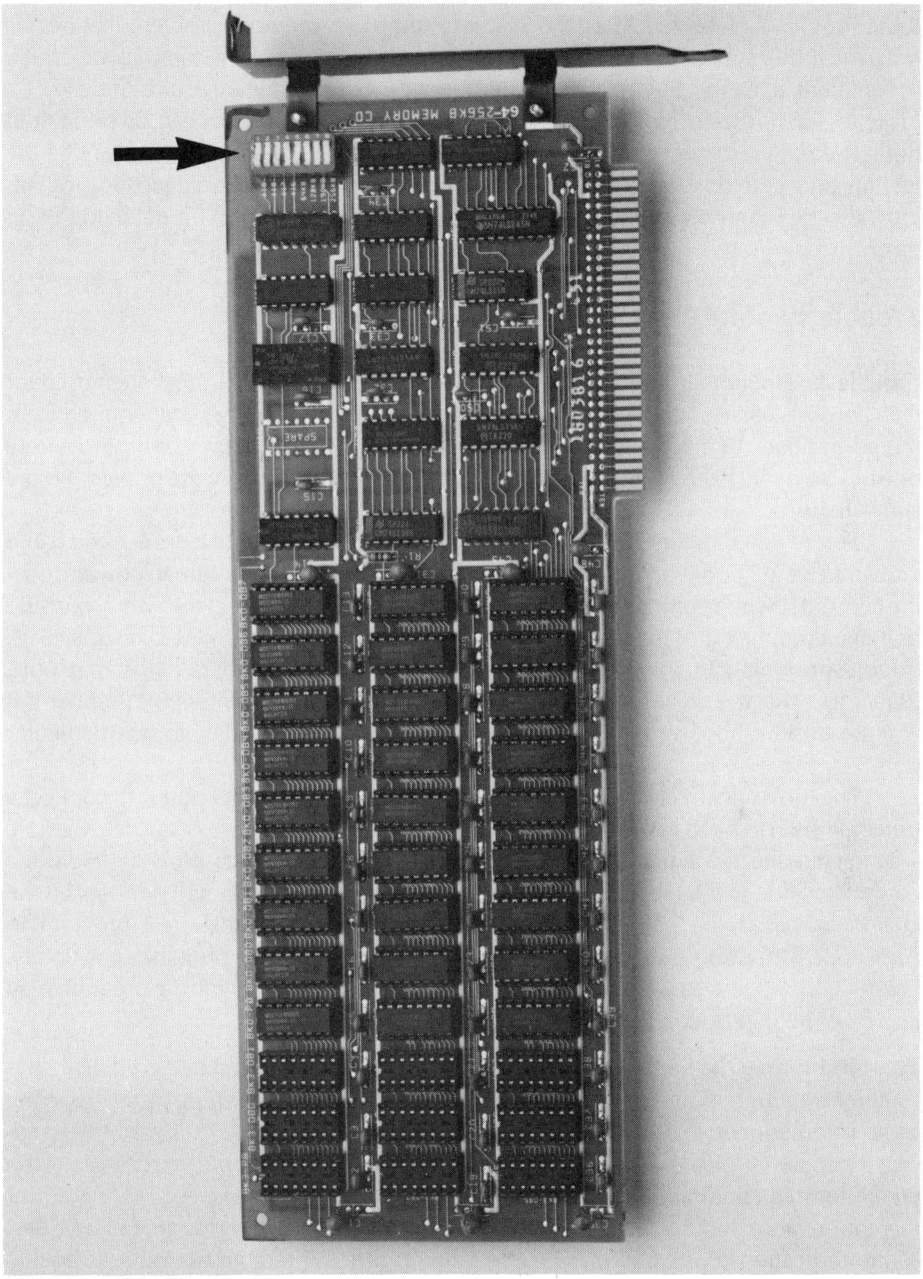

Figure 7.31 Use the memory-bank disabling switches to eliminate and thereby confirm the defective bank of RAM chips. (Courtesy of IBM)

RAM Problems Detected After the System Prompt. A memory problem that occurs only after the system is in operation for a time is probably a thermal or erratic intermittent, covered in Chapter 3. Intermittent RAM problems require the use of a diskette diagnostics program to find the problem. These problems can be difficult to find. The diagnostics program should be put into a loop to test forever, leaving the technician free to do other jobs while the computer tests itself. The diagnostic program may also be manipulated to signal the technician with a beep upon detection of an error.

Troubleshooting Computer External I/O Ports

Troubleshooting the Parallel Port. The Centronics parallel port is most often used for data transmission out of the computer to a printer. Only a few lines are required from the printer back to the computer for handshake purposes. In many applications only one or two handshake lines are used, depending on the features of the printer and the software used.

Before you diagnose the parallel port as defective, substitute a printer *and cable* known to be in good working condition and try the port again. Be sure to power-down the computer when connecting and disconnecting cables to protect the circuitry inside both the computer and the printer. Once the printer port is confirmed to be defective, troubleshooting can be done by the diskette diagnostic program for that port. Remember that the default parallel port is called LPT1 for line printer port number 1. If you are troubleshooting LPT2 or LPT3 you will have to direct data to that particular port.

The most effective way to troubleshoot the Centronics output port is to connect a printer known to be in good working condition and attempt to print out a file. A simple way to spot-check the printer is to toggle the printer on with a control—P. (Hold the control key down and tap the P key.) When this is done the printer will print out all the characters typed on the computer keyboard. The BASIC printer test program in Appendix B may be used to automatically cycle through the printable characters. Figure 7.32 shows a sample schematic for a parallel port. The diagnostic program may also be of help in troubleshooting the parallel port.

Troubleshooting the Serial Port. The serial port can also be tested using a diagnostics routine. Although it can be tested without using a special jumper plug installed on the serial port connector, use of this plug is recommended because it checks the handshake capability of the circuitry. To trace signals in the serial port circuits, put the computer in a continuous diagnostics loop testing the serial port (see Figure 7.35 for the connections required on this plug). Serial ports are usually designated as COM (Communications Port), COM1, or COM2. See Figure 7.33 for an example. Note that the ports have been marked by the servicing technician for future reference.

If the serial port being investigated for problems is used to drive a serial printer, the printer *and the cable* should be changed for a printer and cable in known good condition. Again, be sure to turn off the computer before disconnecting or connecting any cables to the computer.

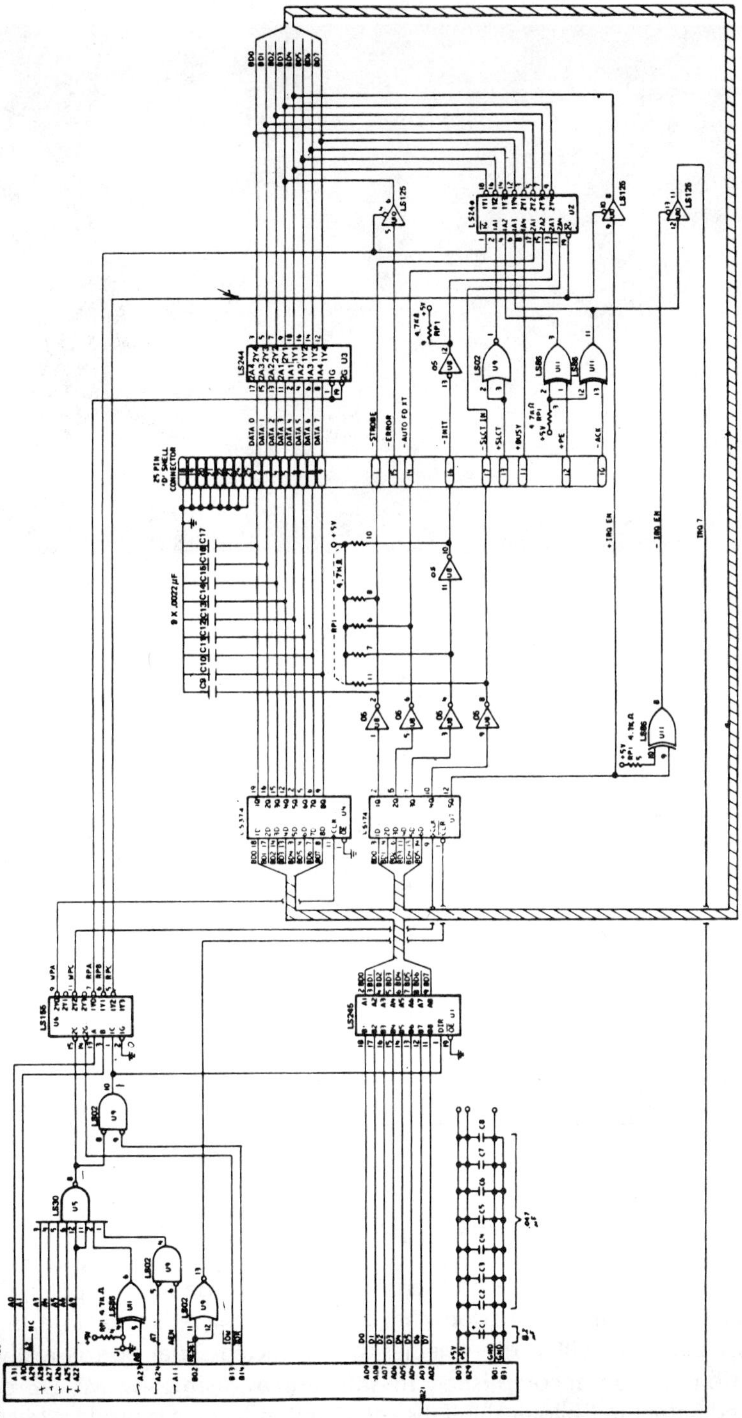

Figure 7.32 Representative schematic of a parallel (printer) port (Courtesy of IBM)

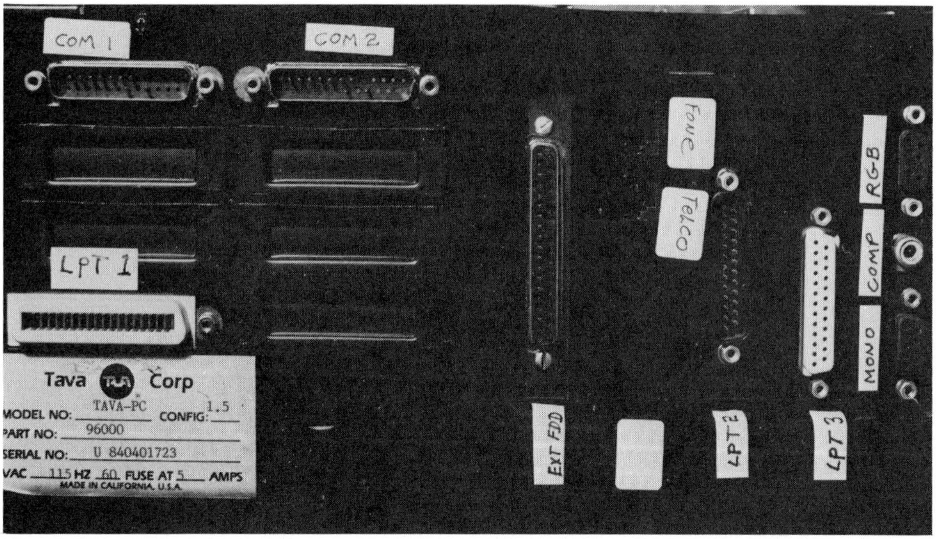

Figure 7.33 Labeling the ports of a computer is a big help for future servicing. (Abbey Enterprises)

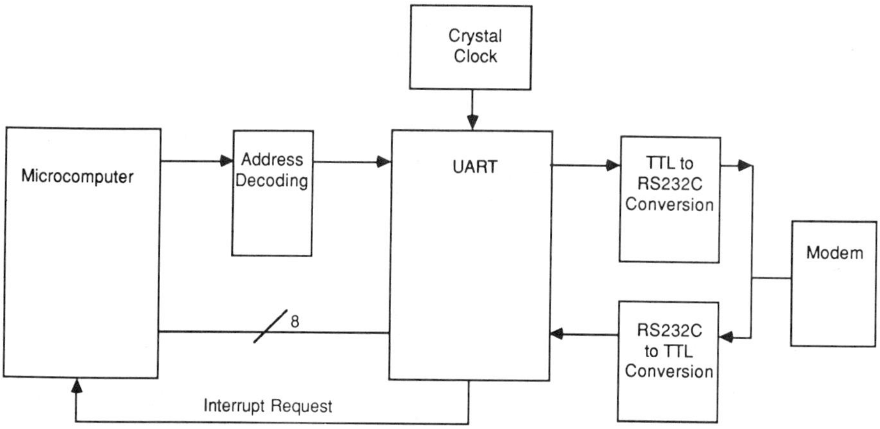

Figure 7.34 Block diagram of the serial (RS-232) port.

In the event there is a second serial port available on the computer, the printer cable can be moved from one to the other and information redirected from the first port to the second. This will verify whether the suspected serial port is really at fault. Redirection can be accomplished in software by using the MODE command (explained further in Chapter 15). If the suspected serial port is used to drive modem, another modem and interconnecting cable can be tried. Figure 7.34 shows a typical block diagram for a serial port.

The diagnostic program can be used to help troubleshoot the serial port. Options are available for troubleshooting it with the diagnostics with or without the loopback plug of Figure 7.35.

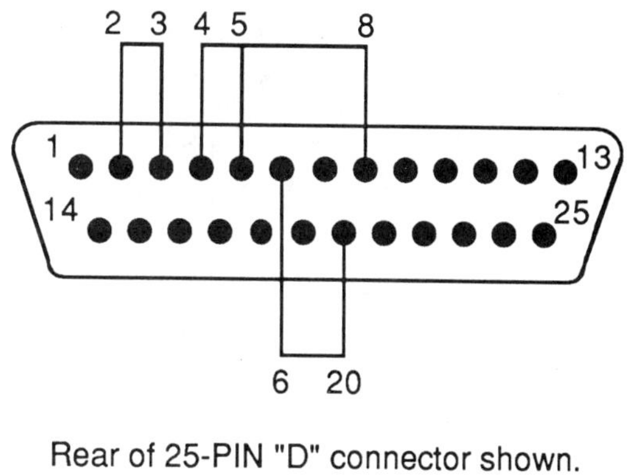

Figure 7.35 Schematic of a serial port jumper plug.

The serial port initializes data before operation. The serial port must be initialized for the proper data rate (Baud rate), number of data bits, even or odd parity checking, and number of stop bits. Table 7.1 lists the possible combinations. The MODE program is used to set these parameters.

Table 7.1 Possible combinations of bit values for serial data transmission.

Data Bits	Parity Bit	Stop Bits	Data Bits	Parity Bit	Stop Bits
5	ODD	1	7	ODD	2
5	ODD	1.5	7	EVEN	1
5	EVEN	1	7	EVEN	2
5	EVEN	1.5	7	NONE	1
5	NONE	1	7	NONE	2
5	NONE	1.5	8	ODD	1
6	ODD	1	8	ODD	2
6	ODD	2	8	EVEN	1
6	EVEN	1	8	EVEN	2
6	EVEN	2	8	NONE	1
6	NONE	1	8	NONE	2
6	NONE	2			
7	ODD	1			

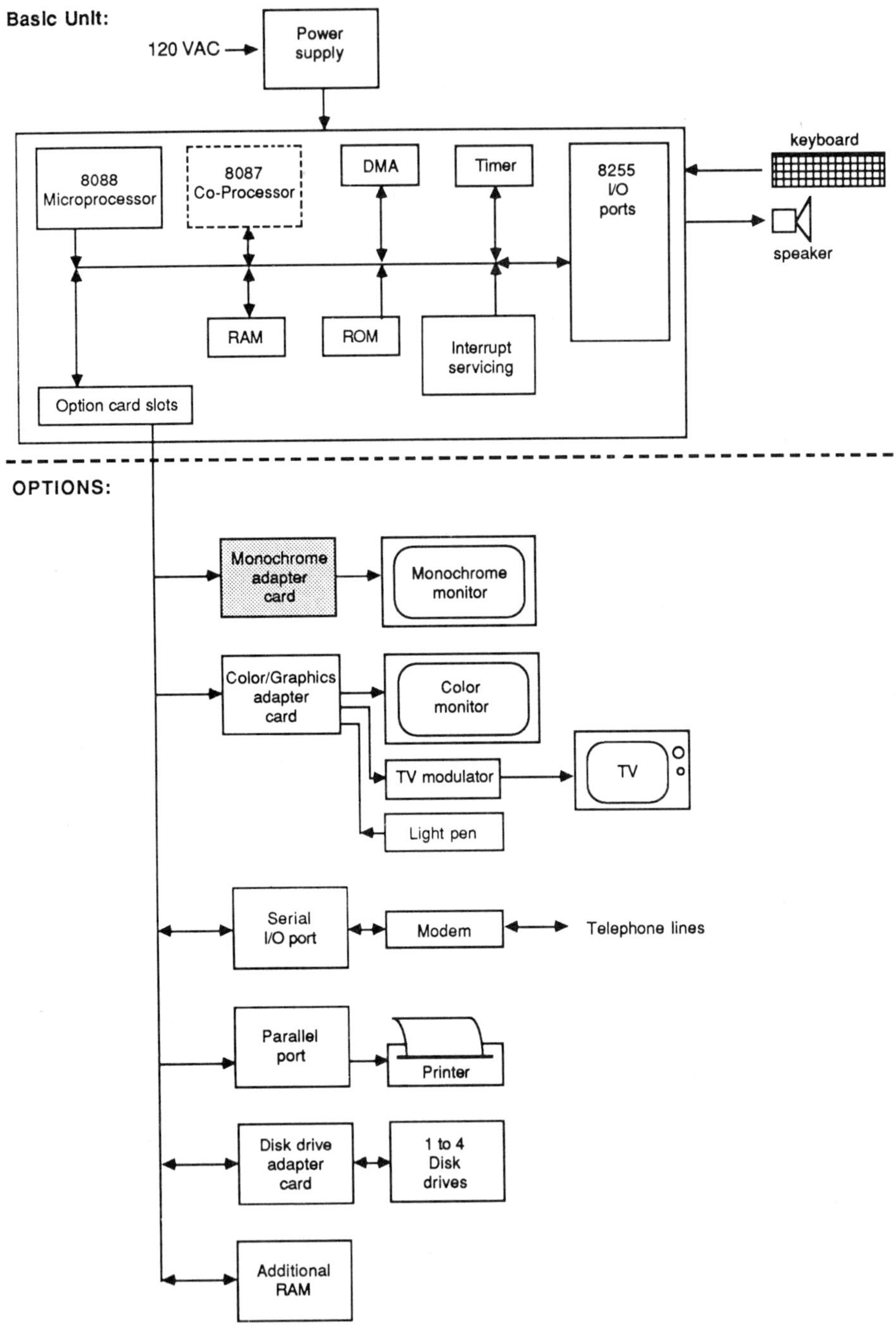

Figure 7.36 The monochrome monitor adapter card is necessary in text processing applications.

Troubleshooting Video Option Cards

Troubleshooting the Monochrome Monitor Adapter. Before troubleshooting a monochrome monitor adapter card, shown in Figure 7.36, it is important to eliminate the monitor itself as the problem. The most effective way of doing this is to substitute another monitor known to be in good condition. If both monitors are giving similar symptoms, the adapter card or possibly the system board is at fault. The possibility of the system board causing the problem can be confirmed by substituting a good adapter card. The monochrome monitor adapter contains the video memory and the support chips necessary to put the data from the memory bits on the cathode ray tube (CRT) screen. See Figure 7.37.

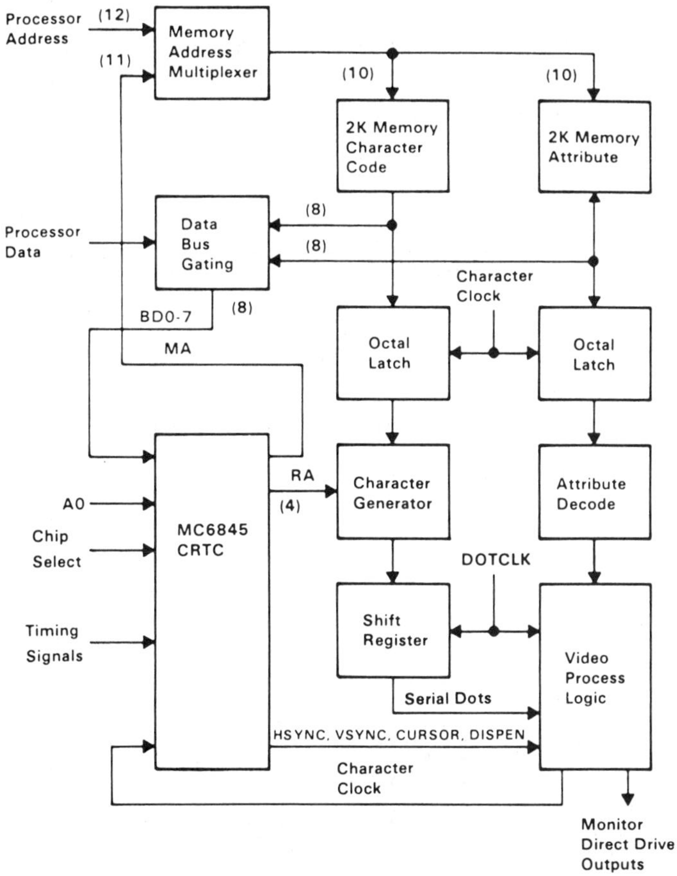

Figure 7.37 Block diagram of Monochrome Video Adapter

The video memory is, so far as the computer is concerned, a block in main memory RAM. The monochrome monitor adapter uses 4K of this RAM. The computer's CPU places data into the video memory and the CRTC (cathode ray tube controller) reads that data and passes it to the monitor. In addition to passing the data to the CRT, the controller also generates the vertical and horizontal synchronization pulses. The data taken from memory in bytes is always converted to characters or symbols according to a character-generator ROM. Each byte of data is converted thereby into bits of on-off data for the CRT to display, one line at a time. See Figure 7.38.

Most of the monitor circuits can be exercised for troubleshooting by using the diskette diagnostics program.

Troubleshooting the Color Monitor Adapter. As for the monochrome monitor, it is important to eliminate the color monitor itself as possibly causing the problem. Substitute another good monitor: if both monitors are giving similar symptoms, the adapter card or the system board is at fault. In this case, substitute another color adapter card and try the system again to determine whether or not the problem is in the adapter card. The color card is generally also designed to run graphics and is therefore often called a color/graphics card. The color adapter typically contains 16K of color video memory and the support chips necessary to put the data from these memory bits onto the CRT screen. See Figure 7.39

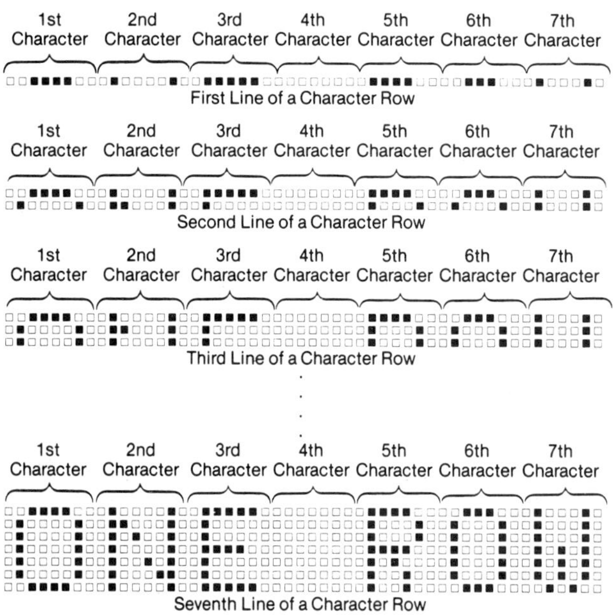

Figure 7.38 Generating text characters on a cathode ray tube, row by row (Courtesy of the Western Digital Corp.)

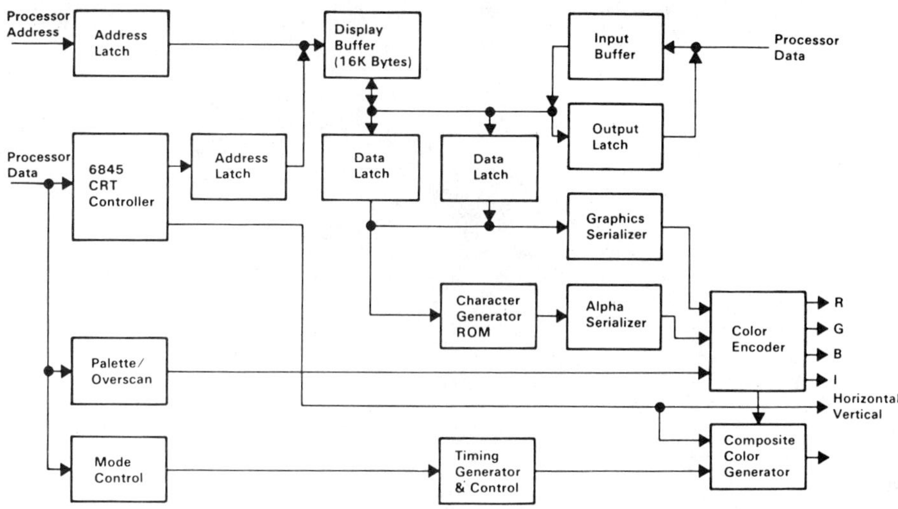

Figure 7.39 The color monitor adapter contains more circuitry than that of the monochrome monitor adapter. (Courtesy of IBM)

Several diskette diagnostics routines are available to assist in troubleshooting the color video card and the color monitor, including various color bars and intensity patterns.

The color graphics card can display text or the very fine resolution of a graphics display, all under software control. Because of the complexity of this card it is almost always better to refer any repairs to the manufacturer. Seldom will a technician have the detailed documentation or theory of operation necessary to do component-level troubleshooting on these cards.

Troubleshooting the RF Modulator

The RF modulator is a small unit that takes composite video signals produced by the computer and modulates an oscillator tuned to a television channel. This approach allows video to be sent through a relatively inexpensive television set without modifications of any kind to the TV. Although this seems like an inexpensive way to get color video, the resolution (the ability to discern small, sharp details) suffers greatly over that of a true color monitor.

The computer must first produce a composite video signal. Such a signal might look like that of Figure 12.4 when viewed with an oscilloscope. RF modulators usually have an output for TV channels 2 or 3. Some models have a switch to choose between these channels. They may or may not come with their own power supply. See Figure 7.40. The internal workings of the RF modulator consist of those circuits necessary to

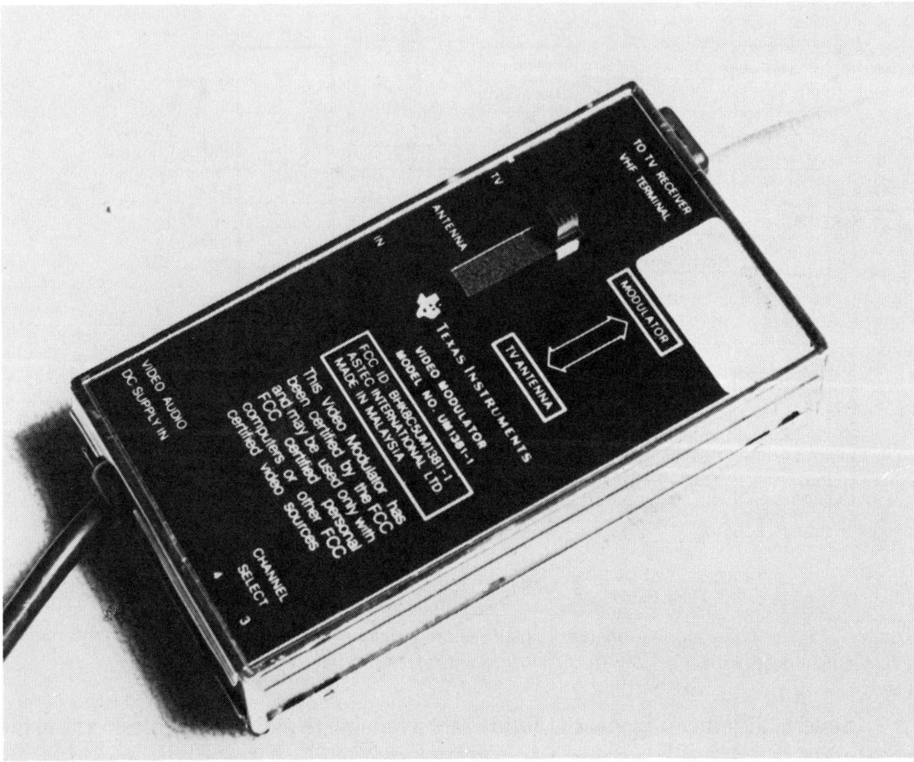

Figure 7.40 A typical RF modulator to convert computer video to a TV channel to feed a standard television set (Abbey Enterprises)

generate the TV channel signal and amplitude-modulate that signal with the video information. See Figure 7.41.

Work inside the RF modulator may require the use of expensive instruments such as an RF signal generator, RF probe or high-frequency oscilloscope (about 100-MHz frequency response or better), and tuning tools. With the current cost of these modulators below about $35, it is probably much cheaper simply to discard a defective unit unless the internal problem is one that can be identified visually, such as bad solder joints, broken wires, or the like.

Troubleshooting the Time-of-Day and Date Clock

If the computer keeps good time and date during power-on operation but fails to load the correct time from the option card's battery-powered circuitry, be sure that the option card clock is set correctly by using the special software supplied with the card. This software places the correct time and date into the battery-sustained memory of the option card (see Figure 7.42).

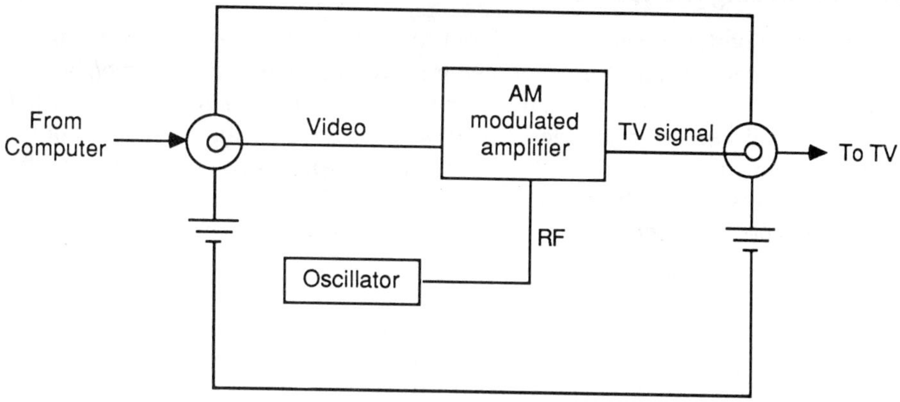

Figure 7.41 Block diagram of an RF modulator

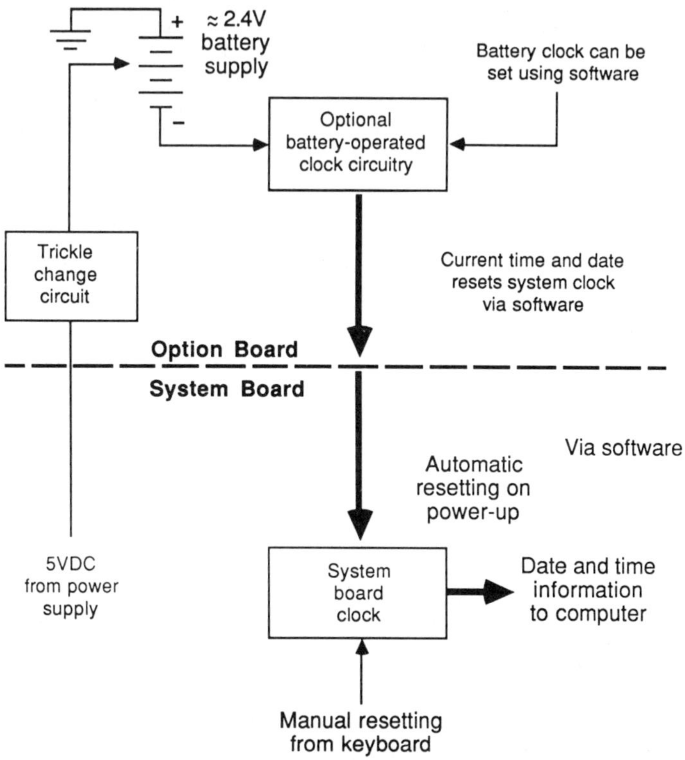

Figure 7.42 The battery-operated clock option can automatically load the system clock with the correct time of day and date each time the computer is turned on.

Troubleshooting the Game Port

The game port is provided to read four resistance values, each from 0 to about 100K ohms, from four external potentiometers into digital signals that can then be read by the computer's software. These four resistive inputs are often paired up in a joystick arrangement with two potentiometers to each joystick to detect the two dimensions of the stick movement. (See Figure 7.43.) Four analog-to-digital converters provide the conversion necessary. See the block diagram of Figure 7.44.

The diagnostics program may also be used to assist in the testing of the game port.

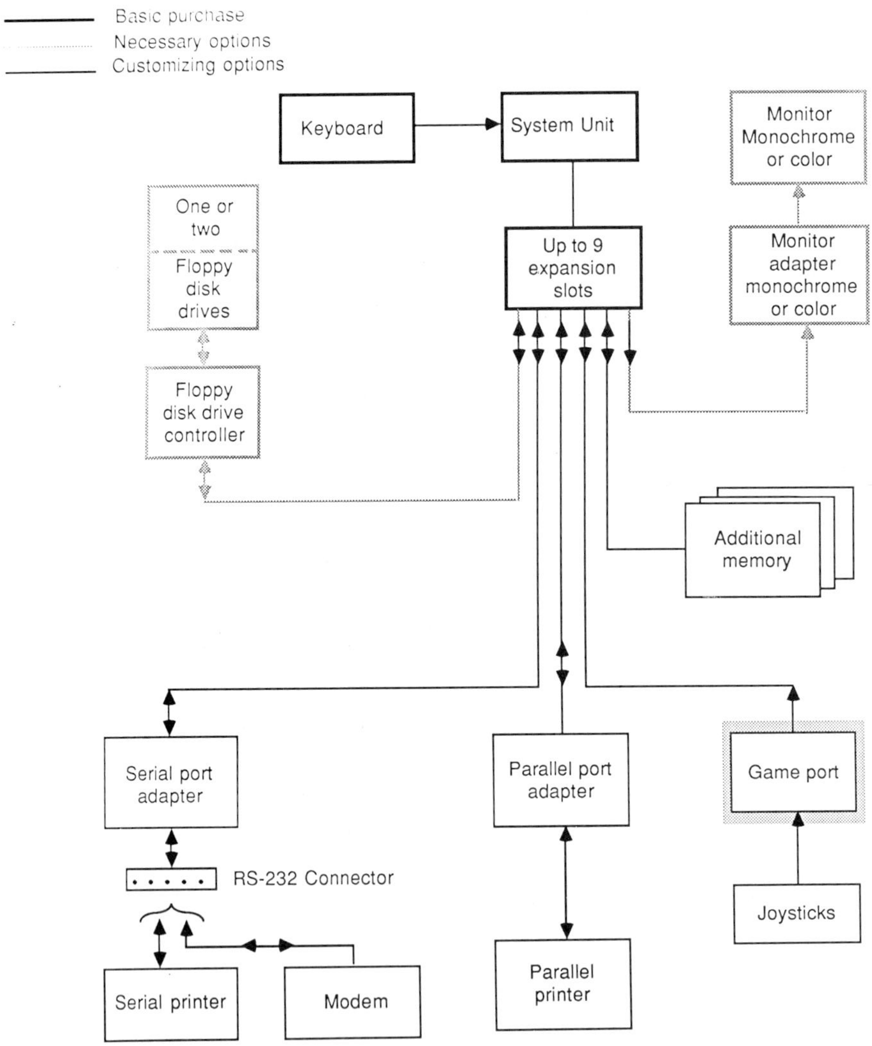

Figure 7.43 The game port allows four analog inputs and four digital inputs to the computer. (Courtesy of IBM)

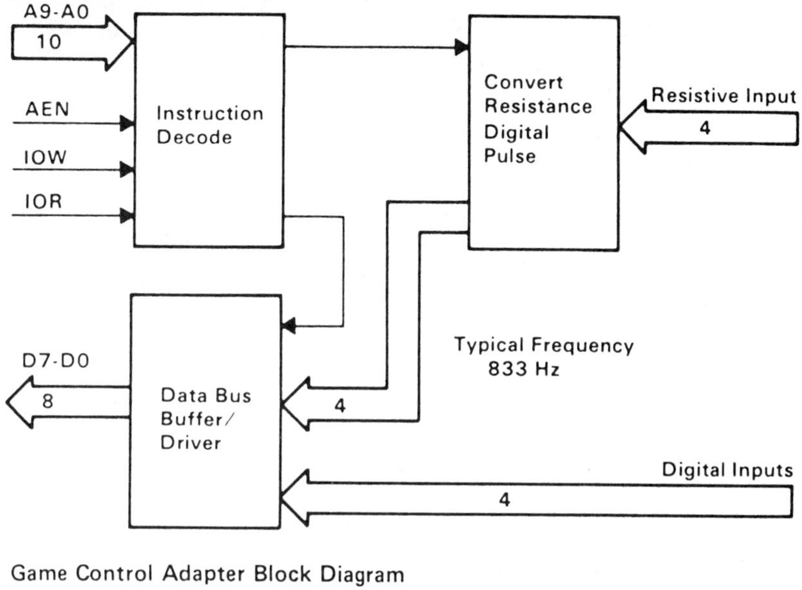

Figure 7.44 The game port interface into the computer circuitry (Courtesy of IBM)

Troubleshooting the Light Pen Circuits

The light pen is used to identify a specific point on the CRT face. When the CRT beam passes in front of the light pen, the pen produces a pulse that is decoded by the CRT controller chip to identify exactly where the pen is touching the screen. This information is used by appropriate software to select items from menus or for other program use.

The diagnostics software is a principal troubleshooting tool to be used if substituting another good light pen does not correct the problem. Problems with light pens usually amount to a problem with the pen's cable to the computer. This cable takes considerable punishment because it is being constantly flexed during use of the light pen.

Troubleshooting Modems

Modem problems are usually software and cabling problems. The cable from the computer to the modem should first be checked by substitution. The telephone line should also be checked with a standard telephone instrument to be sure that there is a dial tone. A call to a friend's house or to get the local time with the telephone will effectively test the line. It is also quite possible that the software used with the modem may have been damaged. Try using a backup copy of the communicating software to eliminate this as a possibility. As a last resort, use a different, good modem as a substitute to see if the trouble symptoms are no longer present.

CHAPTER SUMMARY

This chapter focused on the basics of troubleshooting some of the problems associated with option cards. With proper documentation—specifically the block, layout, and schematic diagrams and the theory of operation for a particular card—at hand, the technician can attempt these repairs with confidence.

REVIEW QUESTIONS

1. What is the most probable cause of problems that occur after the installation of an option card?
2. What is the purpose of the jumpers provided on a card added to provide an additional I/O port?
3. What software program might be used to redirect the output of the parallel port to that of the serial port?
4. What printer standard is often used, usually in part, for the connection of a parallel printer?
5. What is the primary purpose of the IEEE-488 port?
6. Name two equipments often connected to a serial port from a microcomputer.
7. What is the acronym for the chip used in serial communications?
8. Telephone lines can be used for digital data transmission only if a _______ is used.
9. A high on an RS-232C data line to a modem is _______ voltage.
10. A high on an RS-232C control signal to a modem is _______ voltage.
11. A DTE normally has a _______ DB-25 connector.
12. Connecting a DTE to a DTE or a DCE to a DCE with direct wires requires that the wiring be crossed over in some cases. This is called a _______ modem hookup.
13. What principle of troubleshooting could be used to find the defective bank of memory chips on an option card?
14. Before a serial port can be used, it must be initialized for what parameters?
15. What is the typical amount of memory used for the monochrome display?
16. Setting of the computer's internal clock from a battery-oriented clock requires _______.

chapter eight

Troubleshooting the System Board

CHAPTER OVERVIEW

This chapter discusses failures on the system board and troubleshooting them. Block diagrams of typical microcomputers indicate where a problem might be in any specific situation. The use of the diagnostic routines is emphasized in helping to diagnose problems and during troubleshooting. The importance of properly setting the system parameter switches is discussed in detail. Due to the complexity of this board, the alternative of replacing the entire board is explored.

BLOCK DIAGRAM OF THE SYSTEM BOARD

Taken as a whole, the block diagram of the system board of a microcomputer in Figure 8.1 is complex. Even so, the servicing technician should keep in mind that, although this may seem overwhelming, the board divides into specific blocks that are used during particular operations.

The system board usually has everything necessary for fundamental computer operations except: (1) A video processor, video memory, and the necessary support chips. (2) A means of loading a program from a floppy diskette. At least one floppy diskette drive is needed. The IBM Personal Computer does not absolutely require such an interface, since it will revert to its lowest level of operation by loading IBM BASIC from its internal ROM chips. The IBM is also capable of loading a program from a cassette recorder, but this is very seldom done as it is a time-consuming way of loading a program and awkward for routine use.

The system board will probably have a minimal amount of RAM memory installed, perhaps 64K or 128K. These memory chips are often soldered into the system board, making their replacement difficult. This amount of memory can be extended by adding additional memory chips in banks of eight or nine chips, depending upon whether or not RAM parity checking is used by the computer. Chapter 14 covers this subject in more detail. The remainder of this chapter will break down the system board

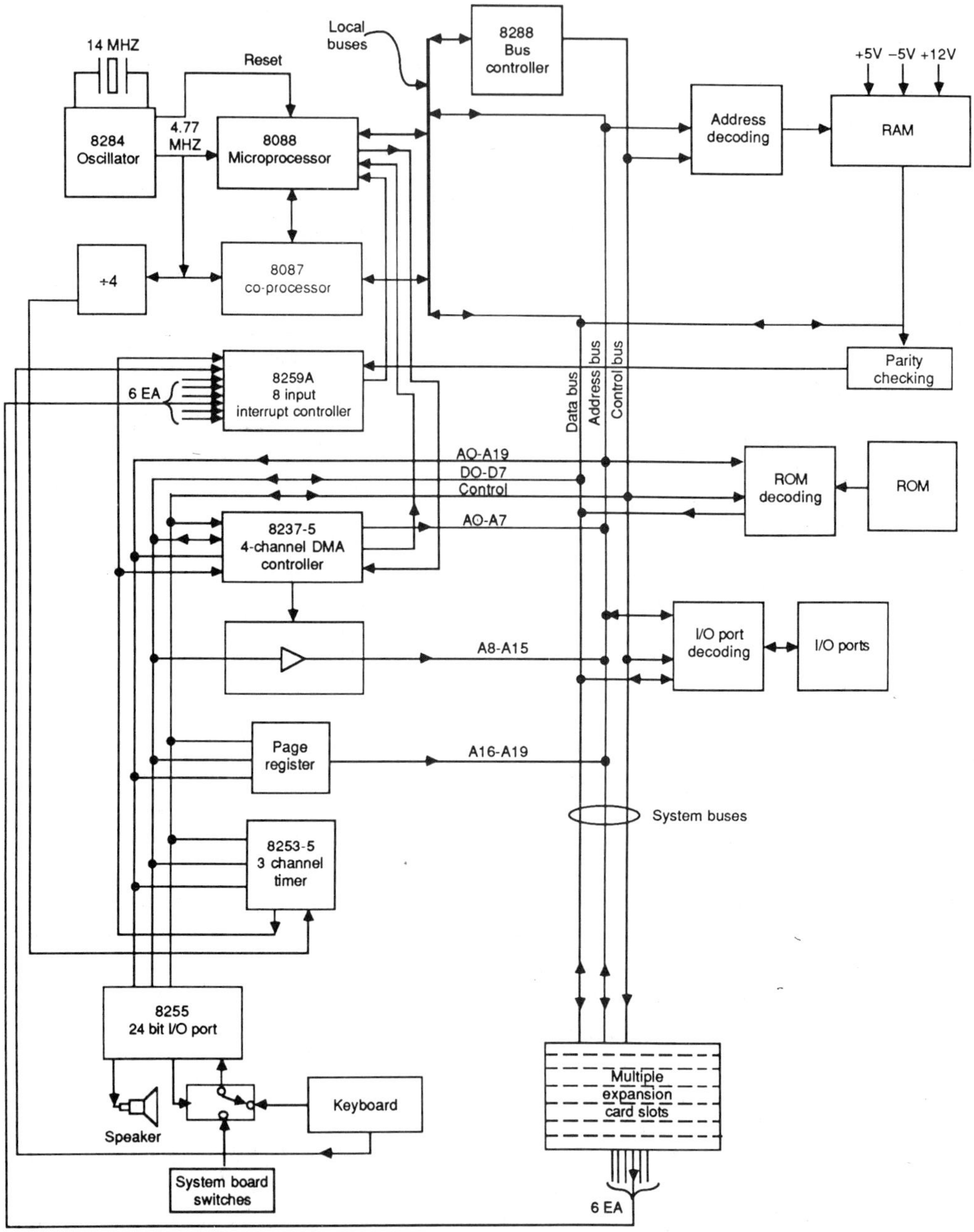

Figure 8.1 The overall block diagram of the system board is complex. (Stephanie Enterprises)

into the blocks that are used during specific operations of the computer. This will help you to visualize which chips are involved in the following specific operations:

1. System reset
2. Chip address decoding
3. Reading a program from ROM
4. Initializing the LSI chips of the system board
5. Getting system parameters from the DIP switches
6. Reading the keyboard
7. Getting data into and out of RAM
8. The system timer chip
9. Getting data from a diskette drive
10. Operation of the system serial port
11. Operation of the system parallel port
12. DMA data transfers

System Reset

When a computer is first turned on, the microprocessor starts at a specific address looking for a program. The 16-bit 8088 microprocessor goes to memory location FFFF0H. Eight-bit microprocessors start at memory location 0000H. In the event of a computer crash, the complete reset of the computer is the only way to get the computer working again. A cold reboot is the same action as turning off the computer for a few moments and then reapplying power. This starts the computer all over again from the very beginning. ROM diagnostics again checks memory, and all LSI chips are reinitialized. Some computers provide a pushbutton switch to accomplish the system reset. Other computers, notably the IBM PC, require that the computer be shut off for a few seconds, then turned on again. Figure 8.2 shows the blocks that are involved in rebooting a system from a cold start.

Chip Address Decoding

The system memory of a computer is normally laid out in a manner very similar to Table 8.1. Each of the chips that performs memory functions must be selected from all the others by an address decoding scheme. Each location must be unique, none being accessed by the same binary address. These addresses are generated by the microprocessor chip in its normal-operation reading and writing of data. The decoding of specific addresses as it applies to the function under discussion is covered in the following paragraphs.

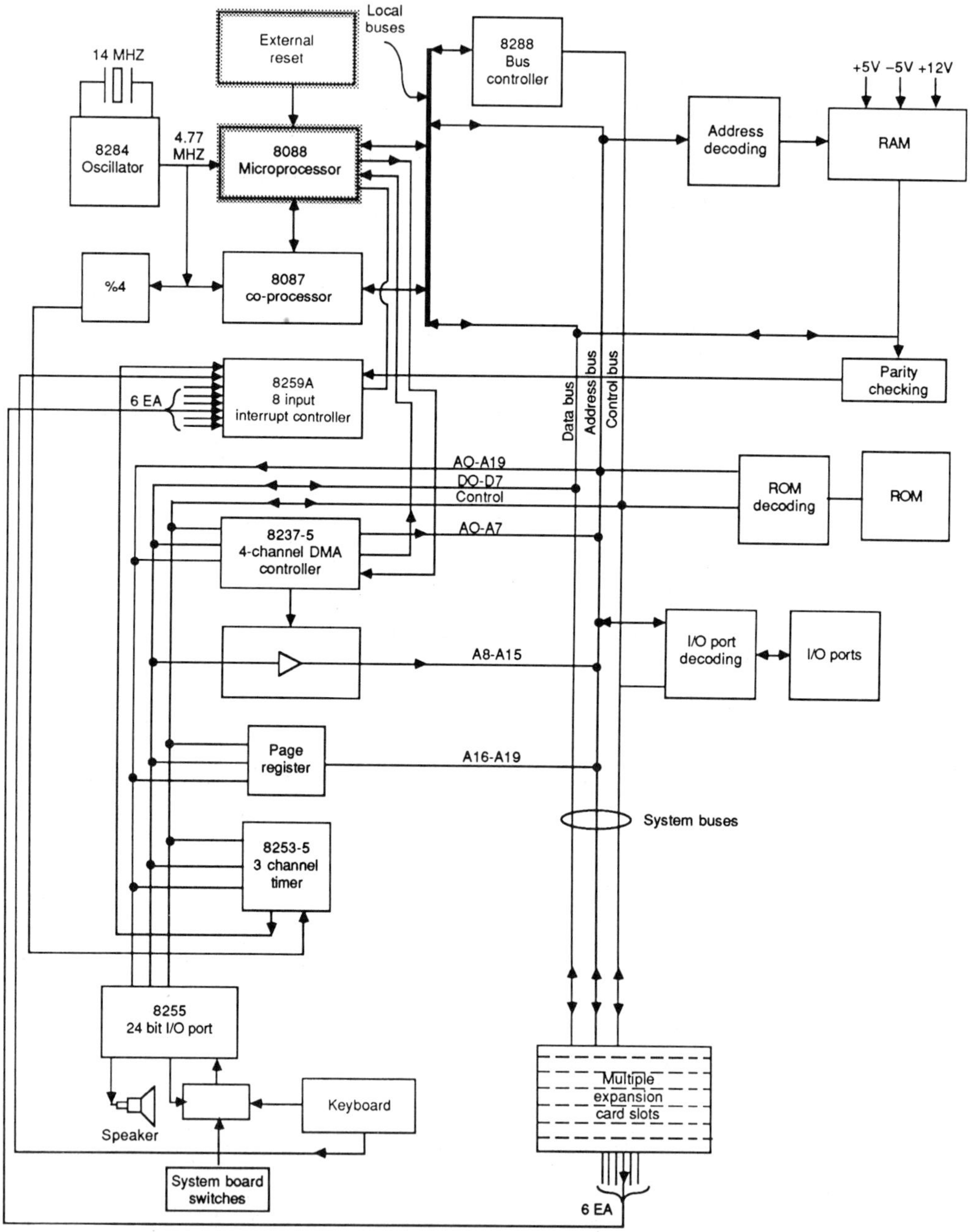

Figure 8.2 The system is reset from a cold start using these circuits. (Stephanie Enterprises)

Table 8.1 Typical Microcomputer Memory Map

Hex Address	Decimal "K" of main memory
FFFFF	1024K
F0000	960K
E0000	896K
D0000	832K
C0000	768K
B0000	704K
A0000	640K
90000	576K
80000	512K
70000	448K
60000	384K
50000	320K
40000	256K
30000	192K
20000	128K
10000	64K
00000	0

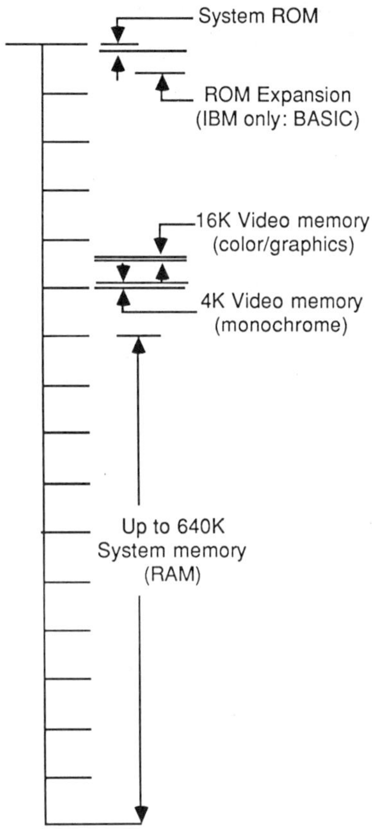

Reading a Program from ROM

The ROM (Read Only Memory) holds the permanent instructions for the computer. When the computer is turned on it uses the program in the ROM to further load more advanced programs from storage media, usually a floppy diskette drive. Figure 8.3 shows the blocks necessary to accomplish a read of the ROM instructions.

Initializing the LSI Chips of the System Board

One of the first operations that are performed by the microprocessor is to initialize the programmable chips of the computer. Programmable chips are thus told how to operate in the microcomputer system. These chips have several ways of operating, only one of which is appropriate for getting the system up and running. The

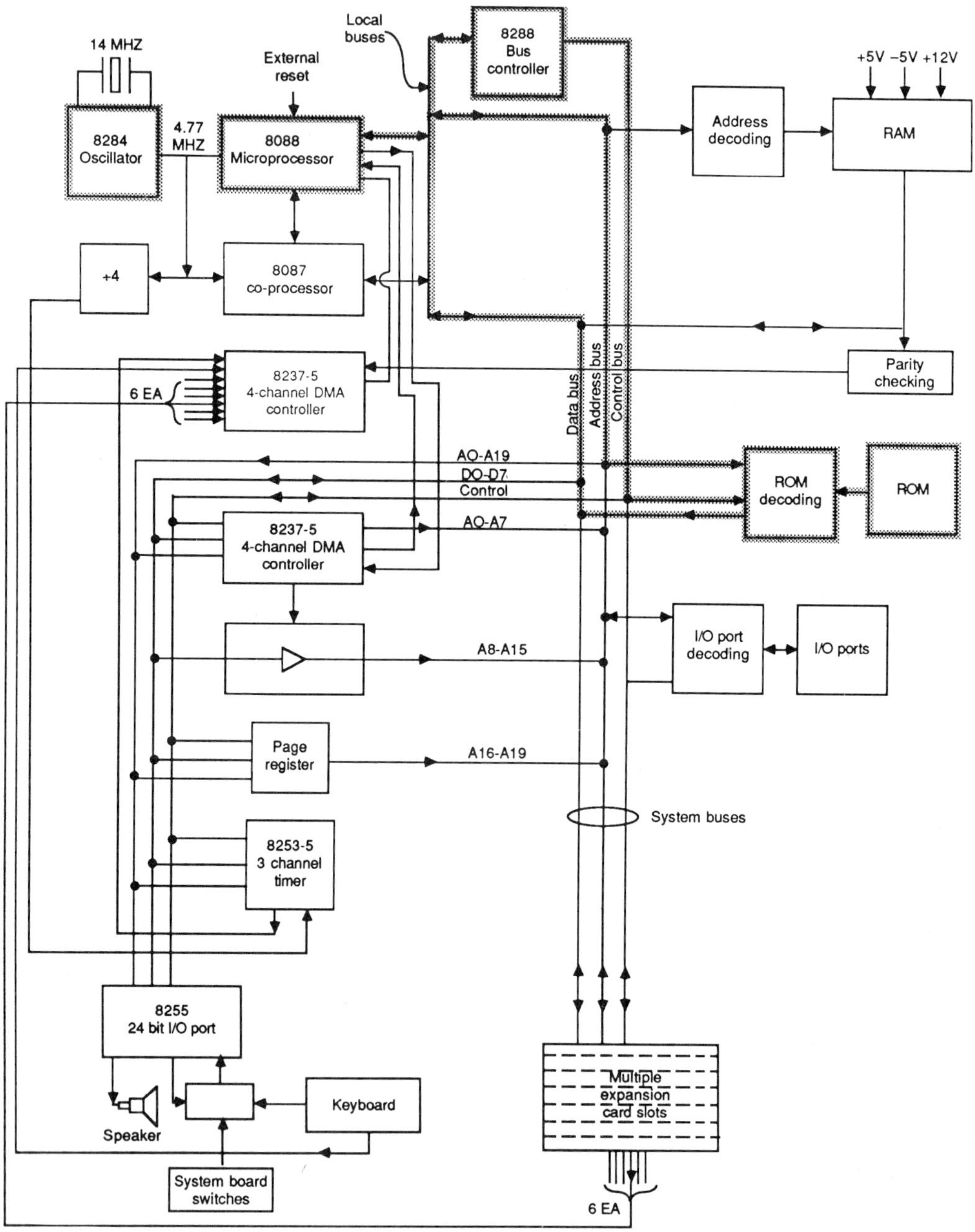

Figure 8.3 Blocks used during a read operation from the system ROM. (Stephanie Enterprises)

following LSI chips are programmable and must get instructions from the microprocessor during system initializing:

Parallel I/O chip, 8255

Diskette drive controllers (FDC), PD765

Cathode ray tube controllers (CRTC), 6845

DMA controller, 8237-5

UART, 8251

System timer chip, 8253-5

Interrupt controller, 8259A

Problems with initialized chips may be traceable to the system ROM chip, where the initializing instructions originate. Since the ROM chip is usually a plug-in chip, it can be changed for another ROM rather easily to verify this as the possible cause of the problem. Be sure to use another ROM having the same version number: different versions of the ROM chip may act entirely different in the same computer. Other versions may not even work in a given computer because of hardware differences. See Figure 8.4.

Getting System Parameters from the DIP Switches

Most microcomputers must be "told" what resources are available, something usually done by setting a series of tiny switches to appropriate positions. These switches are then read during the system power-up. For instance, the computer must know how many diskette drives are installed, since it would do no good to attempt storing data on a nonexistent drive.

It is important to realize that any changes made in the system switch settings are *not* read unless the system comes up from a cold reboot. As an example, if the system switches showing the amount of memory installed are changed, the computer will not read the new switch settings without a cold reboot. The computer must be turned off or manually reset to a cold start for the new settings to be used; a warm reboot (CONTROL-ALT-DEL) will not suffice. Figure 8.5 shows an example of a computer's system switches, often called simply system DIP switches in a microcomputer. Trouble with the system switch settings is almost always the result of technician or operator error. The switches themselves are very reliable, but a less than thorough understanding of the switch functions leads to errors in setting them. These switches are read through one of the I/O chips, typically an 8255 chip. See Figure 8.6 for a block diagram of this switch- reading operation.

As an aid in understanding the functions of these switches, the example of switch settings that follows may help. Sample system board switch settings for an IBM PC II with 640K of total memory, two floppy diskette drives, no 8087 co-processor, and a monochrome display. Note that the switches here are reversed with an off as a Yes, and

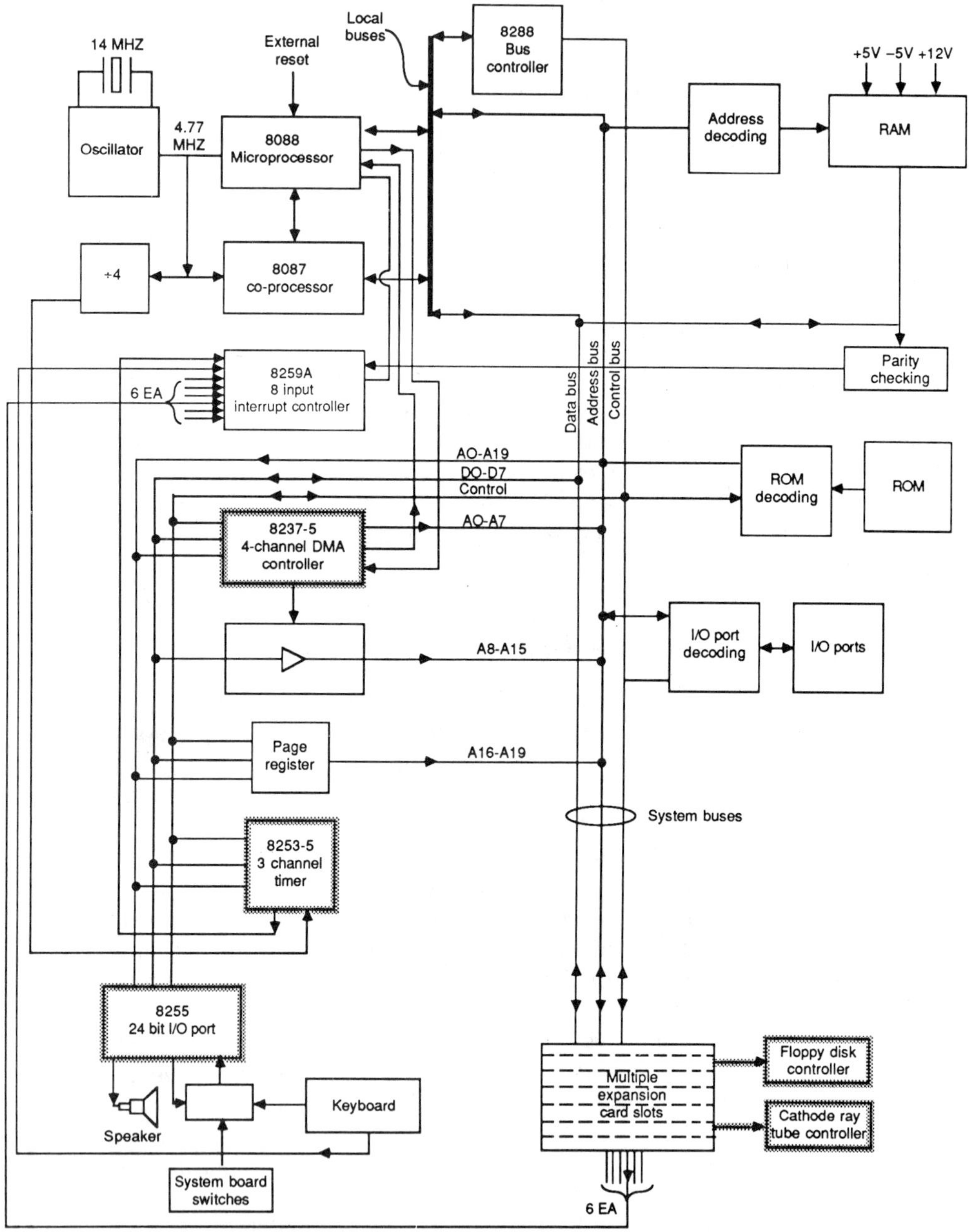

Figure 8.4 Blocks needing system initialization at power-up. (Stephanie Enterprises)

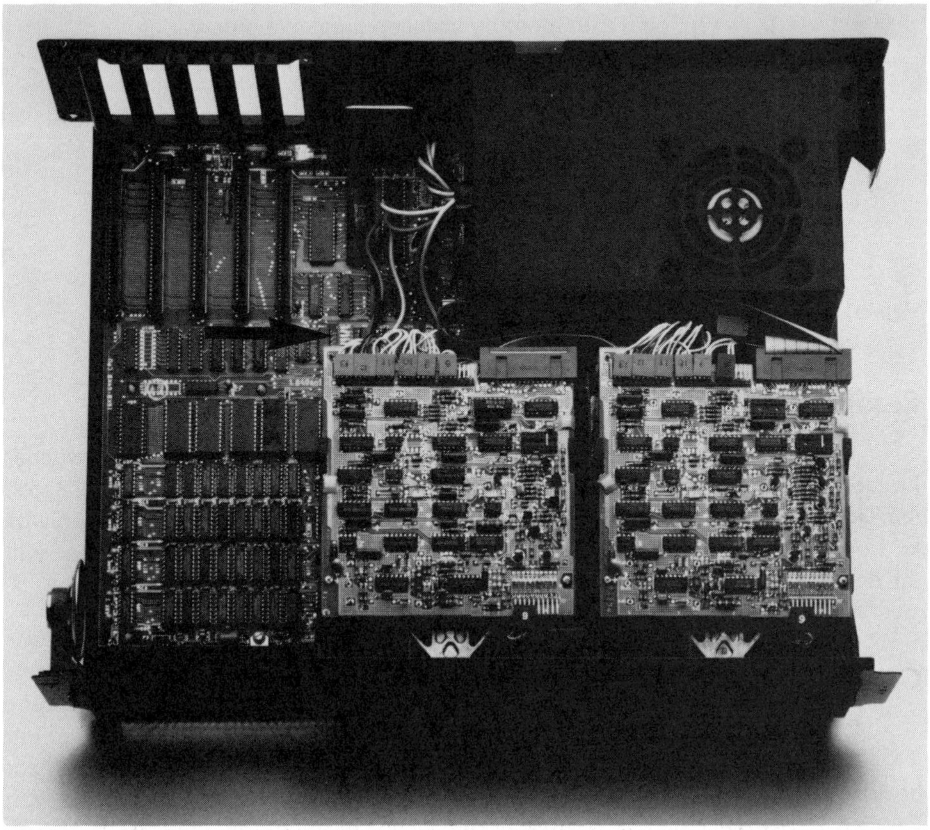

Figure 8.5 System parameter switches tell the computer what resources are available. (Courtesy of IBM)

an on as a No. Details of how the switches are set may be obtained from the computer operations manual.

SW1:

0		1	Existence of floppies (example: yes)
	1	2	8087 co-processor (example: none)
0		3	Binary count, memory on system board (example: full)
0		4	Binary count, memory on system board (example: full)
0		5	Display (example: monochrome)
0		6	Display (example: monochrome)
0		7	Number of floppies (example: 2)
	1	8	Number of floppies (example: 2)

SW2:

Off	On	Switch	Description
	1	1	Optional card memory installed (negative binary logic)
0		2	Optional card memory installed (negative binary logic)
	1	3	Optional card memory installed (negative binary logic)
	1	4	Optional card memory installed (negative binary logic)
0		5	Optional card memory installed (negative binary logic)
0		6	This switch is always off.
0		7	This switch is always off.
0		8	This switch is always off.

Note: 0 indicates switch is off, 1 is on.

Reading the Keyboard

The keyboard uses the same I/O lines as those used to read the system switches. Problems involving both the system switches and the keyboard may indicate a problem in the blocks, as shown in Figure 8.6. Once the computer is booted up, only the keyboard is read by this I/O port. Troubleshooting of the keyboard can be done with the diskette diagnostics program and by tracing signals through the circuitry.

Getting Data Into and Out of RAM

Programs are executed directly from the system RAM. Programs are loaded into RAM and then the microprocessor goes to the beginning of the program in RAM and begins executing the instructions. The blocks involved in using RAM are shown in Figure 8.7. The mechanics of troubleshooting RAM problems are covered in detail in Chapters 4, 7, and 8.

The memory used in a microcomputer is of the dynamic type and must be read frequently to maintain its retention of data. This requirement is met through the systems timer chip and one of the interrupt lines to the CPU. Failure of this memory refresh function will result in the complete failure of all of RAM.

The System Timer Chip

The major use of the timer chip is to generate the necessary signals to perform the dynamic RAM refresh cycling mentioned above (see Figure 8.8). The system timer chip is one of the chips that must be properly initialized during system power up. The system timer chip carries on several operations independent of the microprocessor, taking care of some housekeeping chores, thus freeing the microprocessor to do other tasks. The system timer chip has three internal timers. One of the timers generates periodic interrupts to the microprocessor to serve as time-markers for the computers clock. See Figure 8.9. Troubleshooting the timer chip is best done by signal tracing of the waveforms that it originates.

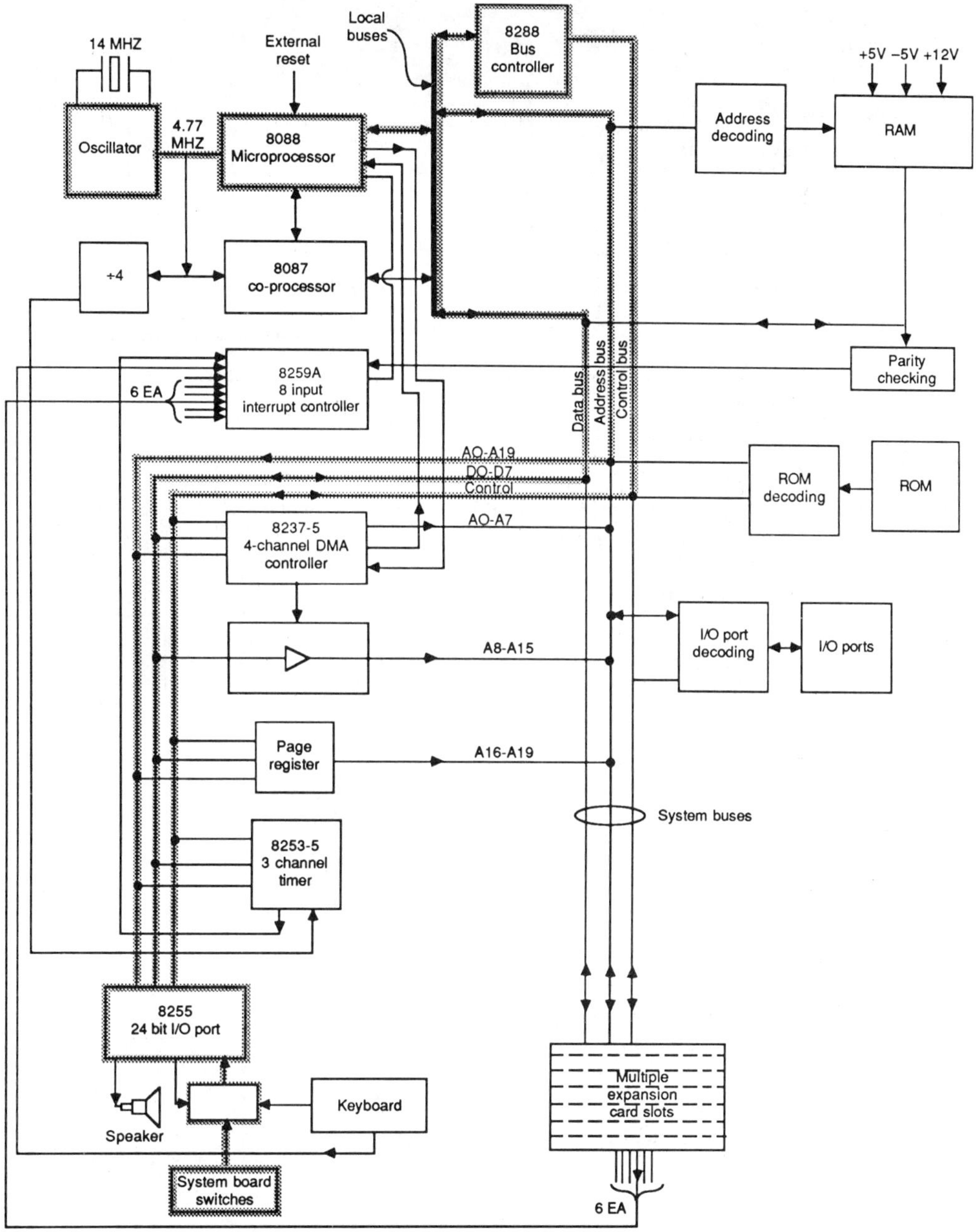

Figure 8.6 Block diagram of blocks needed to read the system parameter switch settings. (Stephanie Enterprise)

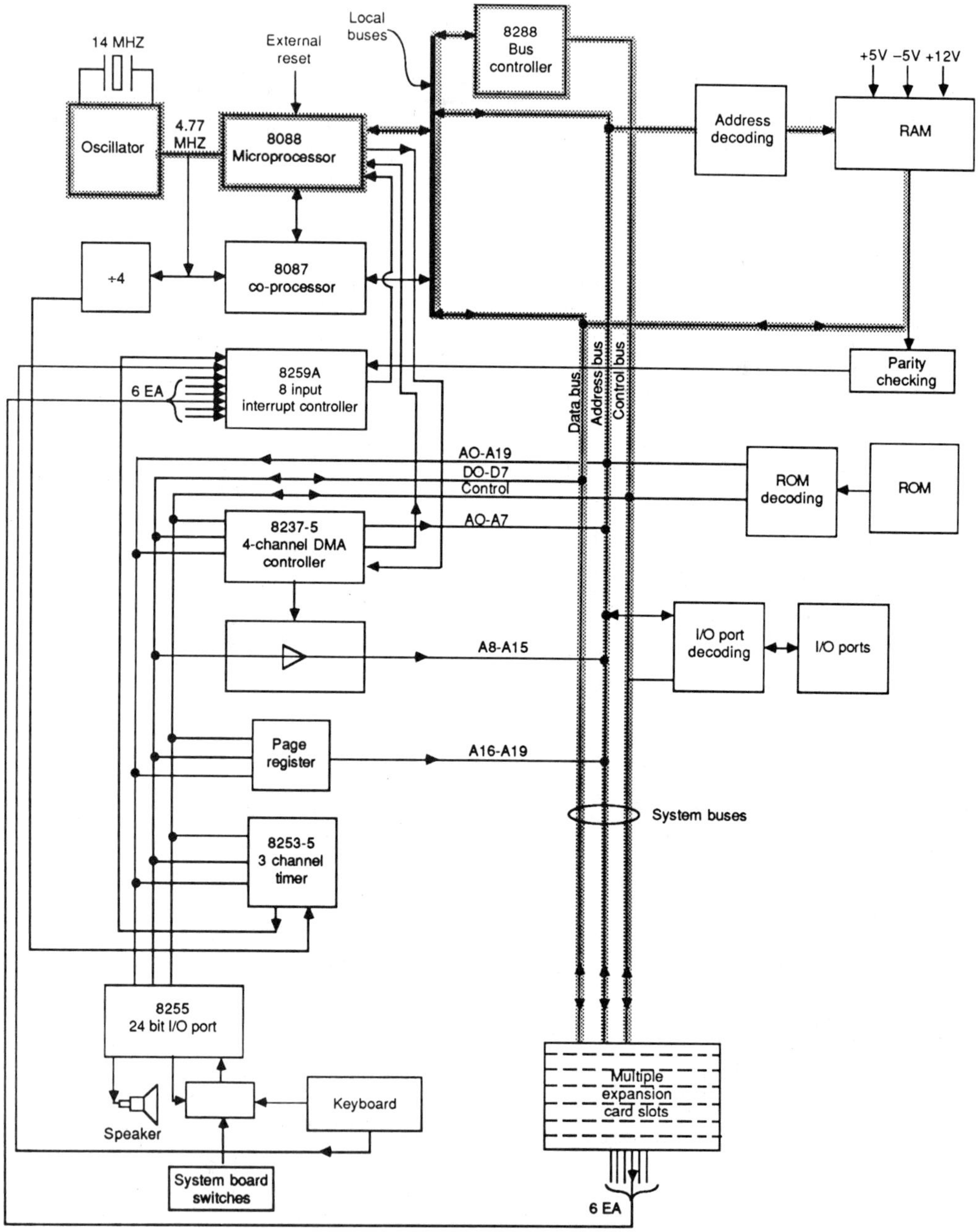

Figure 8.7 Block diagram of blocks involved in a RAM read operation. (Stephanie Enterprises)

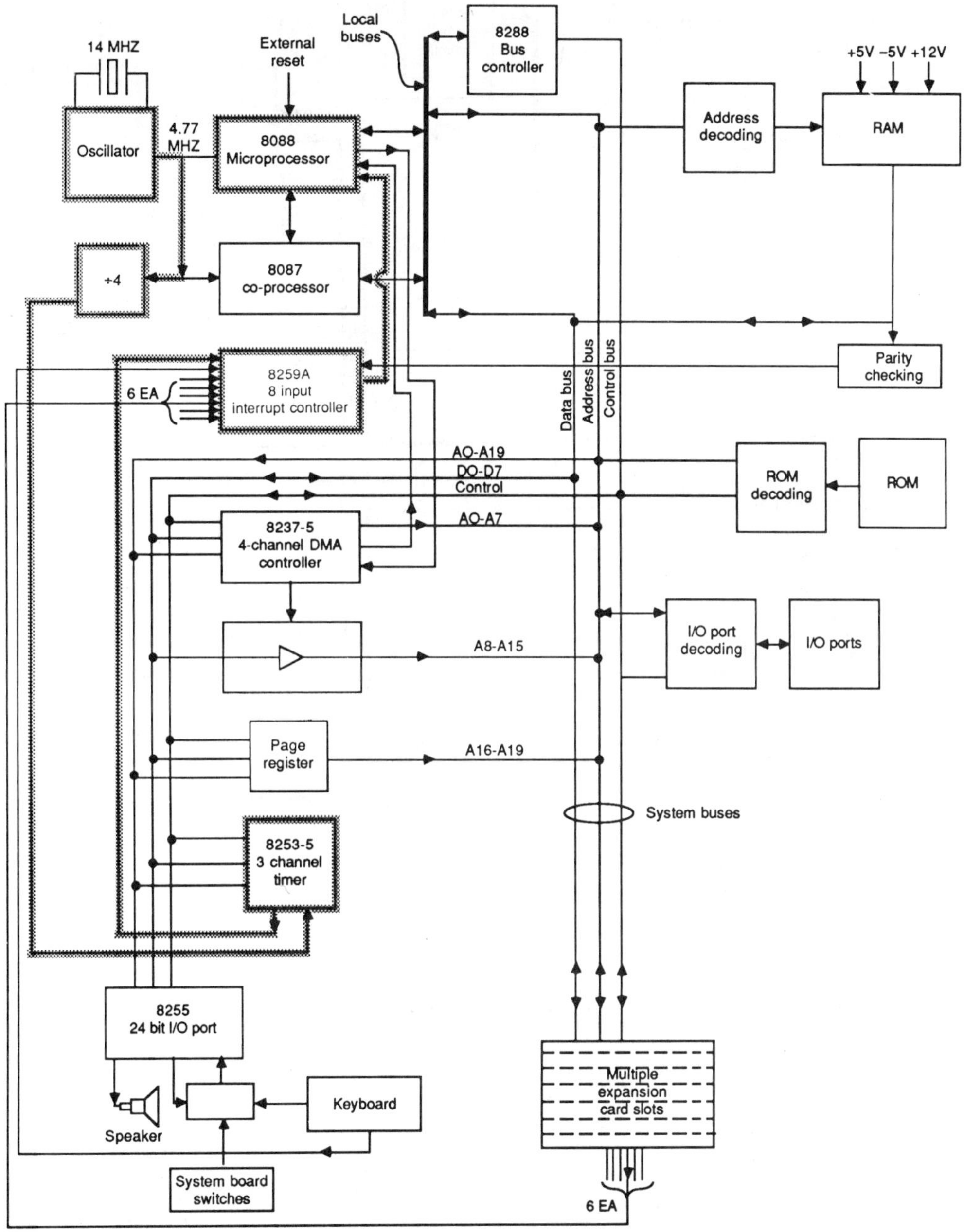

Figure 8.8 The system timer is responsible for generating the dynamic RAM refresh cycling. (Stephanie Enterprises)

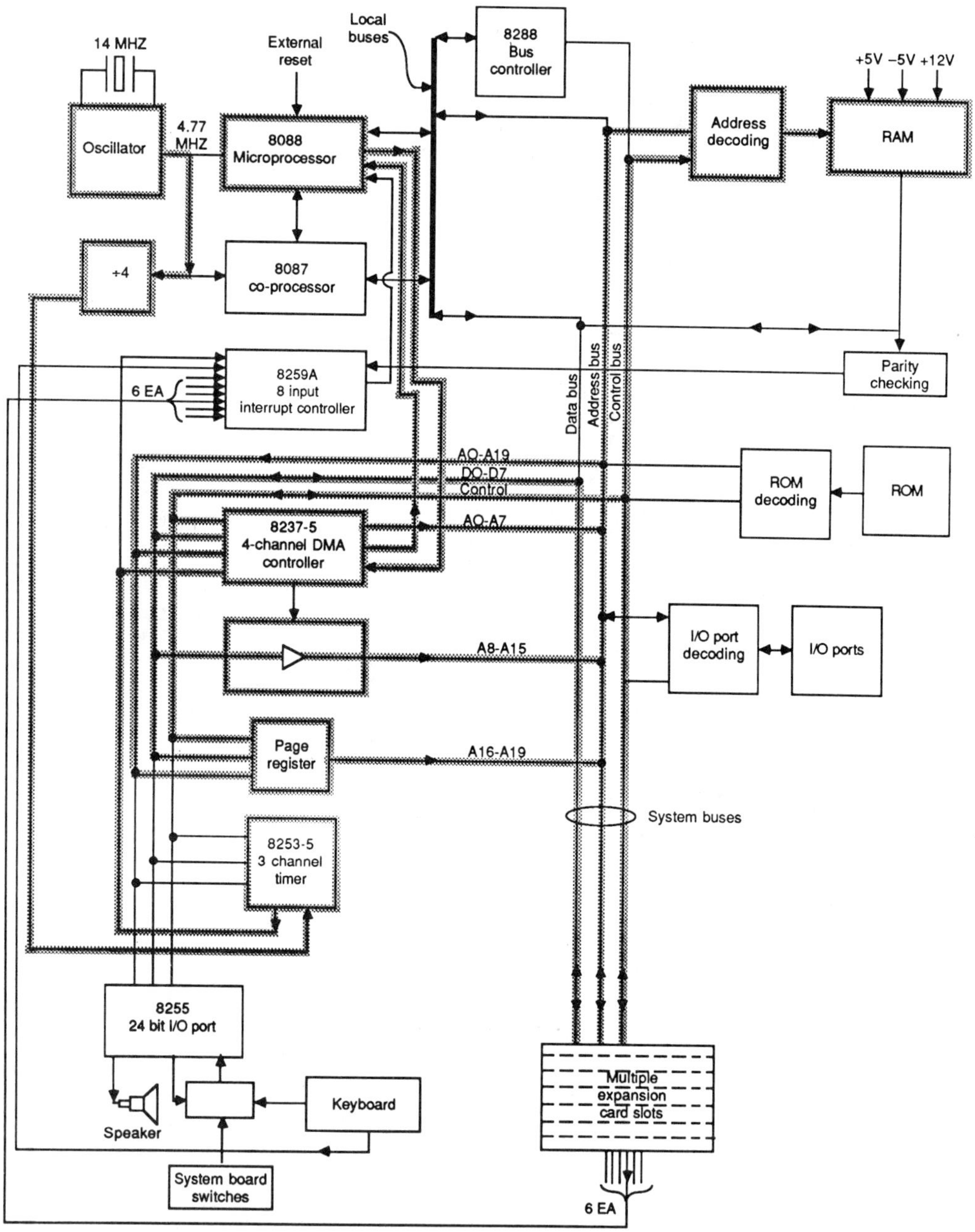

Figure 8.9 One of the purposes of the timer chip is to interrupt the microprocessor periodically to accomplish the time-of-day function of the computer. (Stephanie Enterprises)

The third channel of the timer chip generates the signals for the system speaker. A programmable square wave is sent to the speaker to produce tones. Figure 8.10 shows the blocks involved.

Getting Data From a Diskette Drive

One of the primary signal paths is to read and write data to the diskette drives connected to the computer system. The diskette drives (up to four of them) are controlled by a single floppy diskette controller (FDC). This controller is usually an option card, plugged into one of the system expansion slots. Troubleshooting these signal paths is best accomplished by substituting of the FDC board and/or the drives themselves to localize the problem, then putting the system into a diagnostic loop to further trace signals. Figure 8.11 shows the signal paths to and from the drive controller card.

Operation of the System Serial Port

The computer is able to send data to and from the "outside world" via serial ports. Some computers include one or two of these ports on the system board, while other computers have no serial port on the system board at all, requiring an option card for this capability. The heart of the serial port is the universal asynchronous receiver-transmitter (UART). See Figure 8.12. The CPU parallel-loads bytes of data into the UART, which outputs them at preprogramed rates, one bit at a time, with special bits added in. The UART is another chip that must be initialized before it can be used.

Troubleshooting the serial port is accomplished by putting the computer into a diagnostics loop, constantly testing the port while tracing signals. It will be necessary to make up a jumper plug (Figure 8.13) to test the serial port properly. To test the serial port with advanced diagnostics, make up a connector with three jumpers. This will make the serial port "think" there is a normal load connected to it, and that it is appropriate to send more data. See Figure 7.37 for the wiring to make up this test connector.

Operation of the System Parallel Port

Most microcomputers provide at least one parallel output port on the system board since this is the primary means of communicating with a printer. The port provides 8 bits of data on eight lines, along with several controlling lines to and from the printer. Details of the pinouts of the parallel port are covered in Appendix A. The blocks involved in reading or writing to a parallel port on the system board are shown in Figure 8.14. The parallel port not only decodes its address but also adjusts its direction of data flow according to the read and write signals that come from the microprocessor. Signals may be traced through the parallel port circuitry by putting the computer into a looped diagnostics routine involving the port.

DMA Data Transfers

Direct memory access (DMA) uses the blocks as shown in Figure 8.15. Up to four external devices can access memory without directly involving the microprocessor during the data transfer. This enables higher-speed data access. Direct memory access may also be used for data acquisition for video display, diskette drive operations, and for external devices such as hard disk drive operations.

A malfunction of the DMA circuitry will probably require the use of a logic analyzer and a good deal of time to pinpoint the problem. Replacement of the system board will probably be the most efficient means of repairing DMA problems.

THE EXPANSION SLOTS

The following is a listing of the signals provided at the expansion card sockets of a professional computer. Note that the socket has two sides, A and B, each of which is further numbered:

Signal Name	Expansion Slot		Signal Name
GROUND	B1	A1	−I/O CHECK
+RESET	B2	A2	+D7
+5V	B3	A3	+D6
+IRQ2	B4	A4	+D5
−5V	B5	A5	+D4
+DRQ2	B6	A6	+D3
−12V	B7	A7	+D2
−HRQ I/O	B8	A8	+D1
+12V	B9	A9	+D0
GROUND	B10	A10	+I/O READY
−MEMW	B11	A11	+AEN
−MEMR	B12	A12	+A19
−IOW	B13	A13	+A18
−IOR	B14	A14	+A17
−DACK3	B15	A15	+A16
+DRQ3	B16	A16	+A15
−DACK1	B17	A17	+A14
+DRQ1	B18	A18	+A13
+DACK	B19	A19	+A12
+CLOCK	B20	A20	+A11

+IRQ7	B21	A21	+A10
+IRQ6	B22	A22	+A9
+IRQ5	B23	A23	+A8
+IRQ4	B24	A24	+A7
+IRQ3	B25	A25	+A6
−DACK2	B26	A26	+A5
+T/C	B27	A27	+A4
+ALE	B28	A28	+A3
+5V	B29	A29	+A2
+OSC	B30	A30	+A1
GROUND	B30	A30	+A0

Notes:

Reset = Output signal resets the computer system

+IRQ2 to +IRQ7 = Interrupt input request lines. #2 has the highest priority, #7 the lowest. Signal is held high until acknowledged by the service routine.

+DRQ1 to +DRQ3 = Input DMA request lines. #1 is highest, #3 lowest priority. Line held high until corresponding DACK received.

−DACK0 to −DACK3 = DMA acknowledge output lines. −DACK0 reserved for refresh. Refresh cycle indicated by −DACK0 and −MEMR.

+T/C = Terminal count output of the DMA channel.

−MEMW = Write output to memory

−MEMR = Read output from memory

−IOW = Write output to an I/O

−IOR = Read output from an I/O

+I/O READY = Input, when low memory or I/O cycle will be extended in multiples of 210 ns. Never more than 2.1 us.

+CLOCK = 14.3 Mhz Clock output.

+OSC = 4.77 Mhz system clock, 30% duty cycle.

+AEN = When high, this output means the DMA chip has bus control.

−I/O CHECK = Input to indicate an error on expansion slot. CPU receives as an NMI.

+ALE = Output to indicate address bus valid. Addresses latched on trailing edge of this signal.

+DO TO +D7 = Input/output data bus.

+A0 to +A19 = Address bus. (I/O uses only +A0 to +A7)

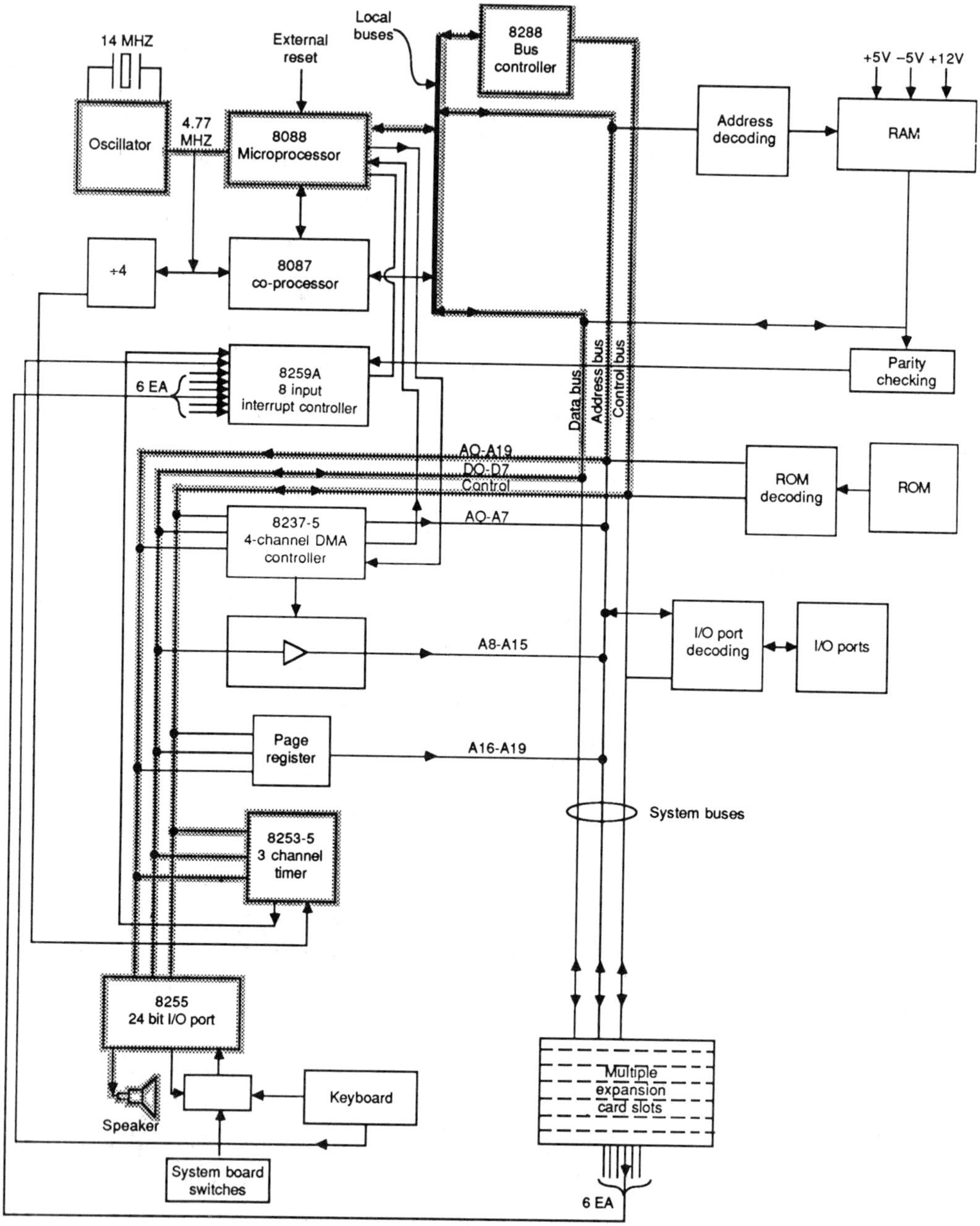

Figure 8.10 One use of the system timer is to produce sound from the system speaker. (Stephanie Enterprises)

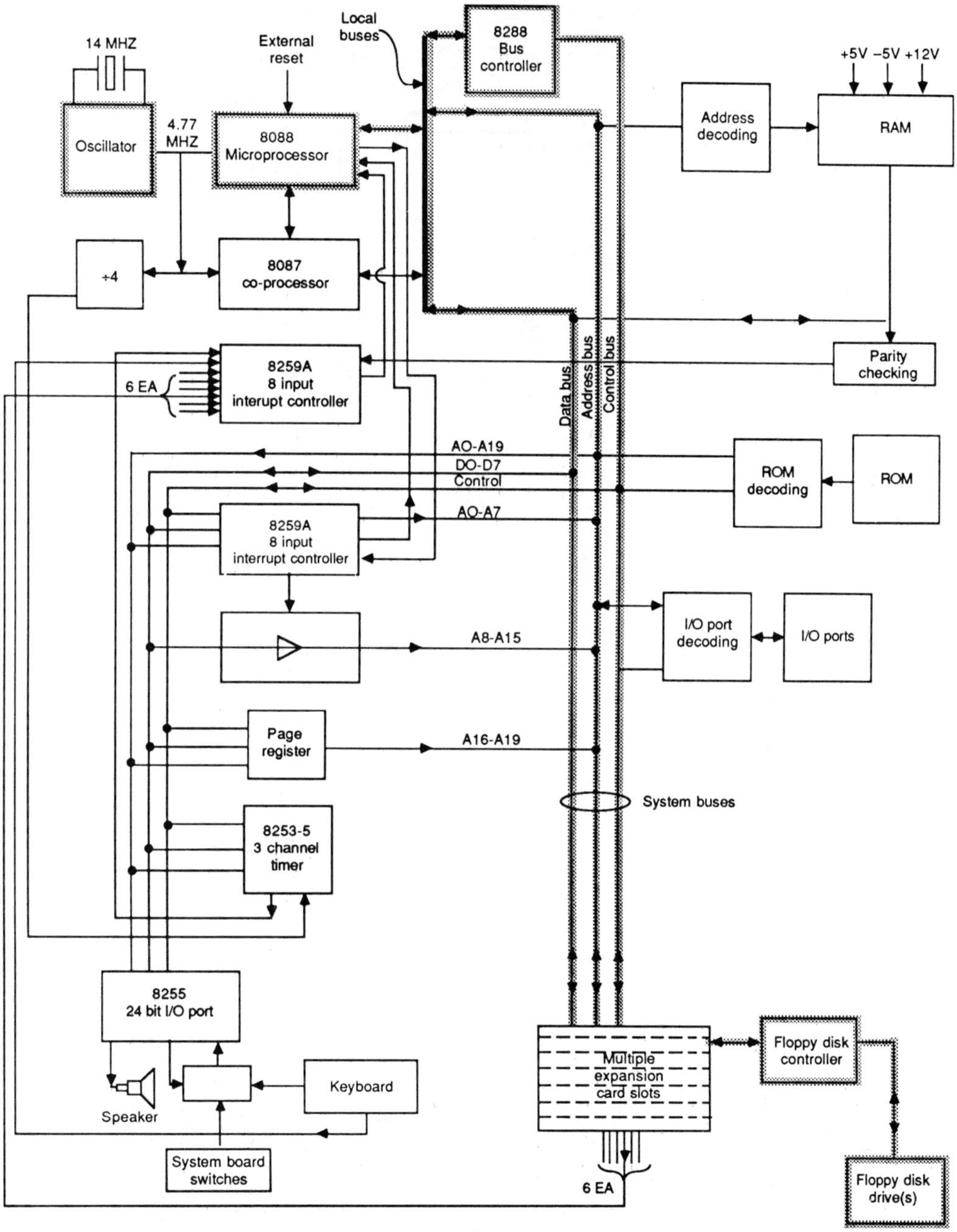

Figure 8.11 Most of the complexities of the diskette drive are handled by the floppy diskette controller (FDC) chip, located on the controller board. (Stephanie Enterprises)

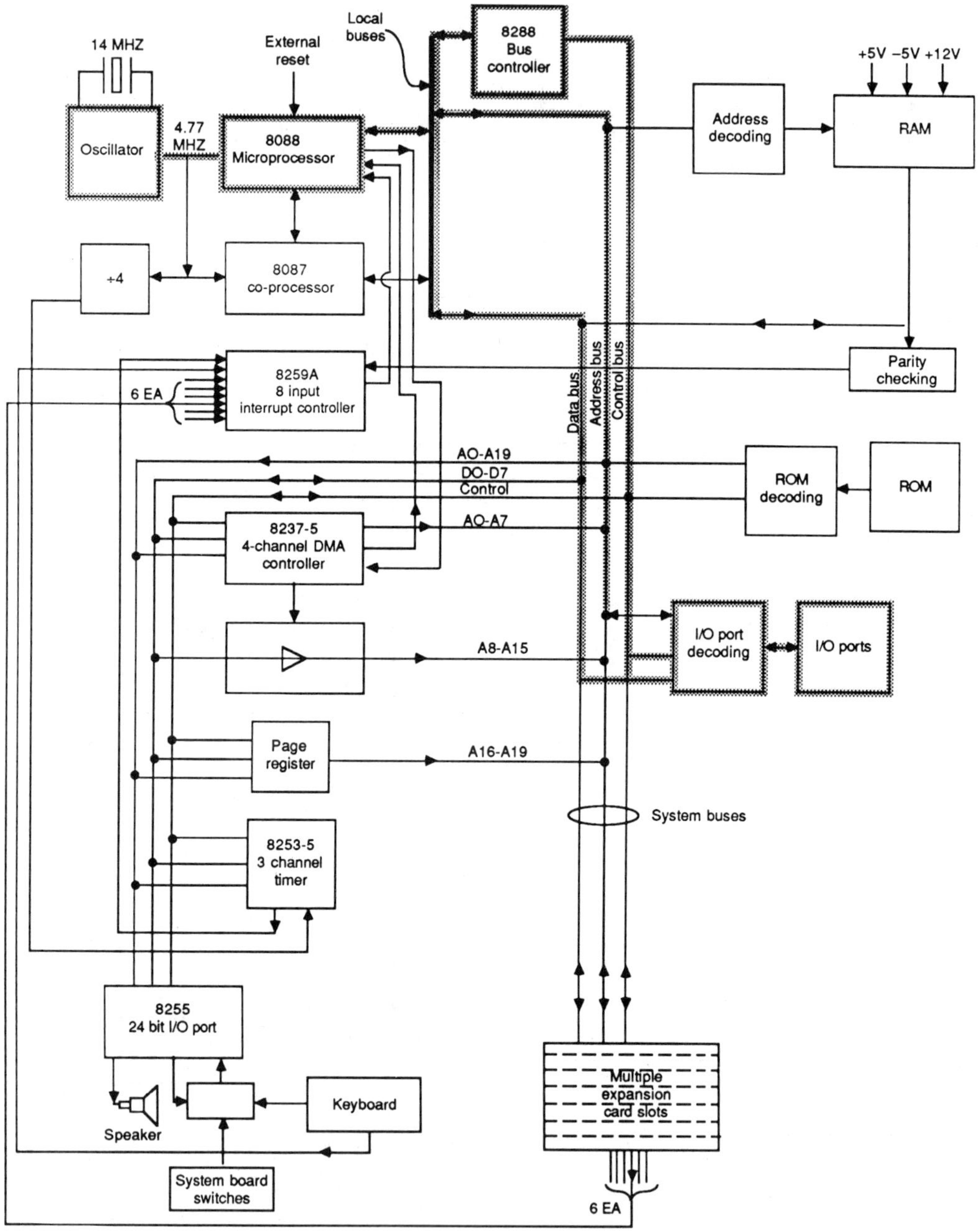

Figure 8.12 Block diagram of the serial output port and blocks used during its use (Stephanie Enterprises)

Figure 8.13 A serial port jumper plug such as this should be used with the diskette diagnostics program to test and troubleshoot the serial port. (Abbey Enterprises)

REPLACING THE SYSTEM BOARD

You may have to replace the system board of the computer if the problem cannot be solved in a reasonable length of time. Removal of the system board should be done carefully, in a static-free work area. Unplug all the option cards and all cabling to the board, noting the location and orientation of all of the plugs. Be careful to remove all of them, including the speaker leads, which are sometimes forgotten in the process of board removal. Install the new board and reconnect everything in reverse order of its removal. Install appropriate chips if necessary, including the system ROM and RAM chips. Carefully inspect the final installation before applying power. A few moments of care can avoid a costly mistake. It is a good idea to check each plug-in chip to be sure that it is installed with proper orientation, too.

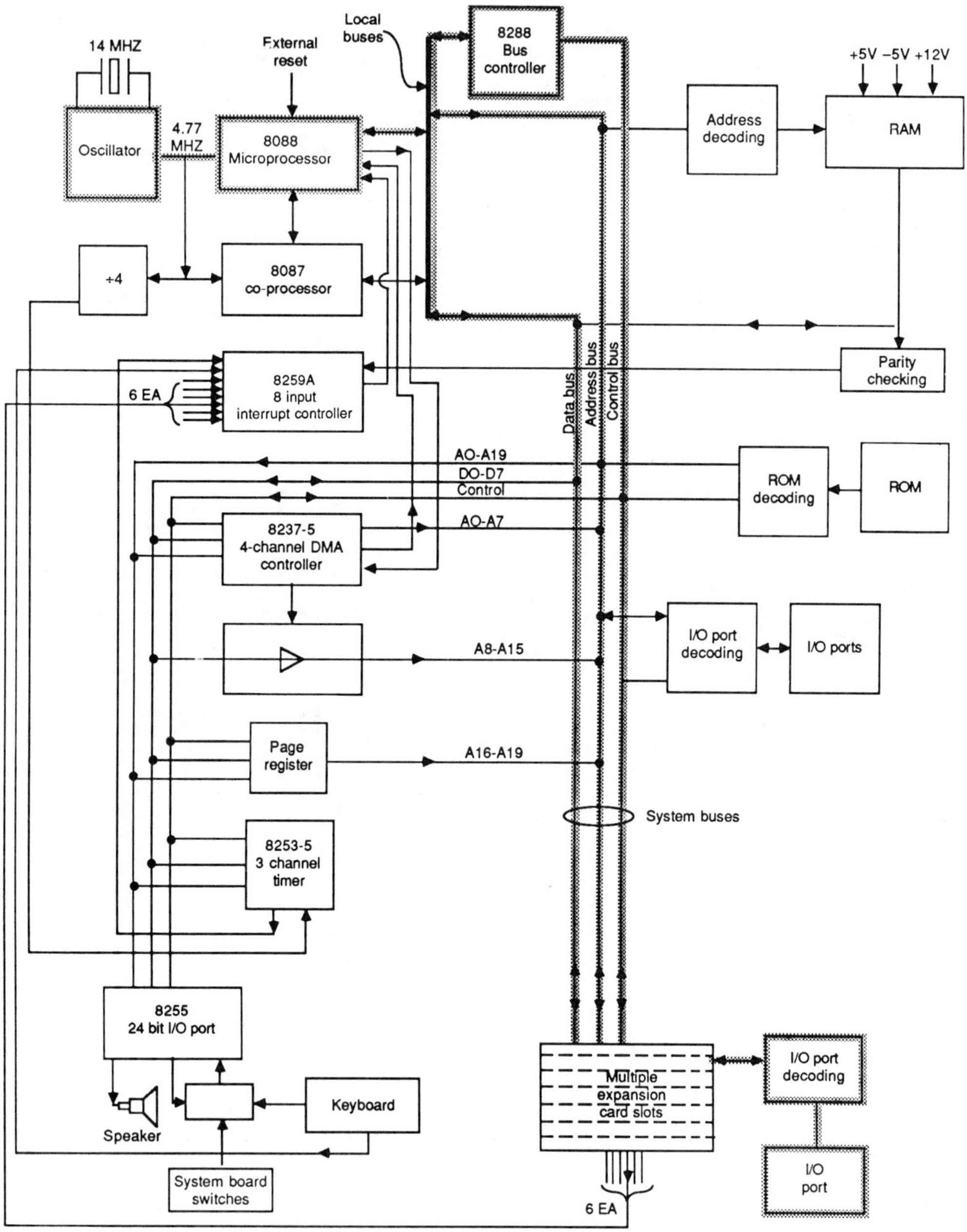

Figure 8.14 Blocks involved in reading or writing to the system boards parallel port (Stephanie Enterprises)

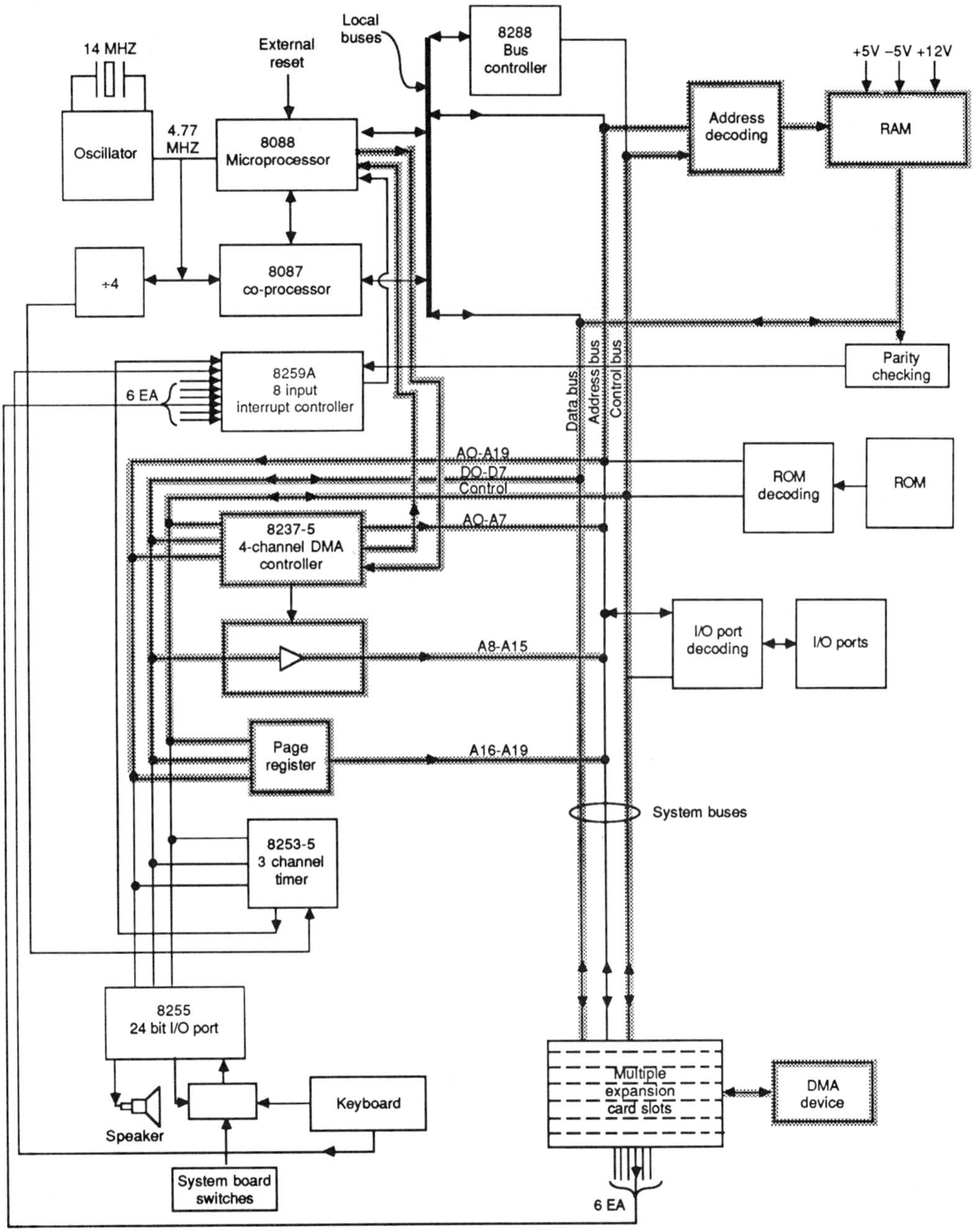

Figure 8.15 Direct memory access uses these blocks for rapid data access. (Stephanie Enterprises)

CHAPTER SUMMARY

This chapter has provided guidance for the technician to troubleshoot the most complex board of the computer, the system board. Troubleshooting has been taken only to the block diagram level because of the variations in system boards from different manufacturers.

REVIEW QUESTIONS

1. When, and only when, are the system board switches read into the computer?
2. Name the two system uses for the timer chip.
3. What is the major IC used in setting information to and from the diskette drives?
4. What chip adds the start and stop bits to a serial communication link?
5. When is a jumper plug attached to the serial port?

chapter nine

Troubleshooting the Keyboard

CHAPTER OVERVIEW

Keyboard troubleshooting is one of the more common problems of microcomputers. This chapter will help you quickly correct the problem by proper diagnosis of the problem and replacement of the entire unit or the connecting cable. You are cautioned not to disassemble a keyboard on-site because of the possibility of losing parts.

THE KEYBOARD CABLE

Keyboard Problems

While some keyboards are part of a computer or monitor cabinet, most are separate units (see Figure 9.1).

Figure 9.1 The keyboard must be integrated into a CRT cabinet or a separate unit. (Courtesy of the Keytronic Corp.)

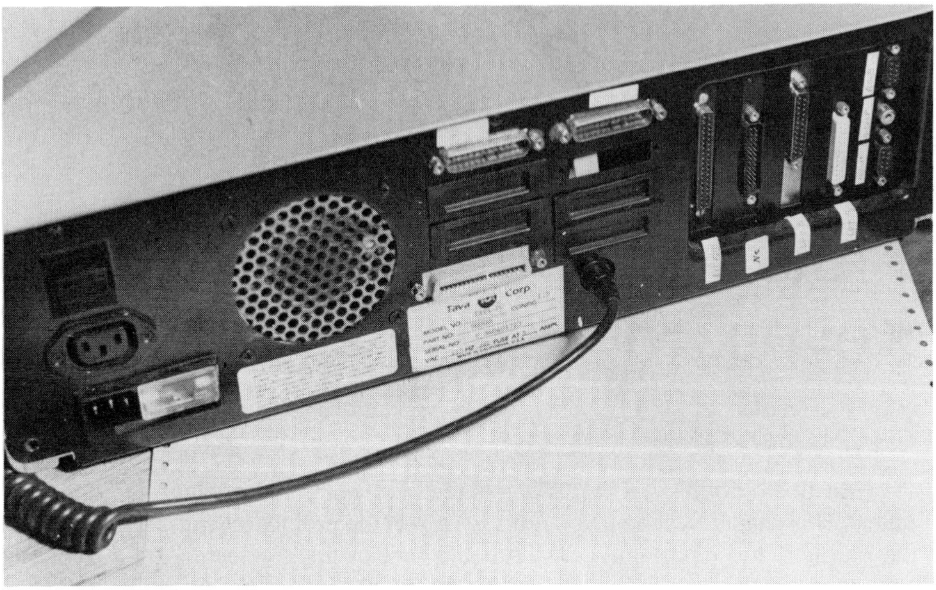

Figure 9.2 The stress on the keyboard cable connector at the back of the computer makes this a common trouble spot. (Abbey Enterprises)

Intermittent keyboard cables are a common problem. The cable to the keyboard is constantly being stretched. The wires to the components at the keyboard end of the cable are not often a problem because the cable is usually firmly attached to the keyboard and there is no stress on the individual wires where they attach. The computer end of the cable is where most problems occur. Here is where a connector is often used on the cable. Normal pulling on the keyboard subjects the wires inside to a 90° stress from the connector. Many intermittent connections are found inside the wiring where the cable goes into the plug at this point. See Figure 9.2.

Replacement of the cable to the keyboard is a possibility. Before assuming that the cable is defective, however, use an ohmmeter and check the lead from where it contacts the circuitry inside the bottom of the keyboard out to the corresponding pin at the connector on the other end.

Another common keyboard problem is the intermittent connector mounted on the system board at the back of the computer. Microcomputers often use a system board-mounted connector whose contacts are soldered to the fragile printed circuit traces. Stressing the keyboard connector back and forth where it enters the rear of the computer is a good way to damage the system board traces. If the intermittent problem is dependent upon the angle at which the connector is pulled against the system board, this specific problem is identified. Repair will probably require complete disassembly of the computer to gain access to the bottom of the system board connector.

One of the most important replacement items a field servicing technician can carry is a spare keyboard complete with a good cable. This allows the customer to get the computer back into operation quickly. Replacements for the cable alone are also good items to carry along.

The Keyboard Connector

The keyboard connector often has the pinout shown in Table 9.1.

Table 9.1 Pinout of the typical keyboard connector

Pin 1	=	TTL clock pulses to the keyboard
Pin 2	=	Scanning code bytes (synchronous serial) from the keyboard
Pin 3	=	Reset TTL level to the keyboard (resets keyboard, normally high)
Pin 4	=	Ground for the keyboard
Pin 5	=	+5VDC source for the keyboard

USING A KEYBOARD DIAGNOSTICS PROGRAM

Keyboard problems can be diagnosed quickly and easily with the diskette diagnostics program. This program produces a likeness of the keyboard on the computer screen. Testing for reliable keyboard response and the automatic repeating feature (called Typematic™ by IBM) is easy. When the keyboard pattern is shown on the monitor screen during the diagnostics program, pressing the keys results in the corresponding patterns on the screen responding with the appropriate letter, number, or symbol. Intermittent cabling can be detected by holding down a suspected malfunctioning key and at the same time gently stressing or flexing the cable over its full length and particularly near the ends.

KINDS OF KEYBOARDS IN COMMON USE

Keyboard Mechanics

Keyboard Functions. A computer is capable of interpreting a great many keys. Besides the normal response of showing a character on the screen when a key is pressed, there are many controlling possibilities. Control functions vary with the software in use, but examples of control functions typed into the keyboard might be:

Save this file on disk

Go to the bottom of this file

Move the cursor to the right

Stop the scrolling of the screen

In order to use a keyboard with some 85 keys or so, some of the keys can be made to do double or triple duty and thereby provide many additional functions. The use of the familiar shift key is a good example of the character keys giving either of two kinds of characters, upper- (capital) or lowercase letters. Holding down another key called the control key allows the keys to assume a third duty, that of controlling various functions within the computer. Still another key, the ALT key, is used to provide another way of providing even more functions.

The Function Keys. Function keys are available on many computers. These keys provide single-stroke controls instead of several keystrokes and are a great convenience to the operator. They are also often changeable in their use through SETUP or INSTALL programs. Using this capability, the function keys can be customized for special purposes. The software used with the computer often specifies the use of these keys. As an example, a word-processing program might assign the function keys to change a disk drive with a single keystroke or to print a file.

The Auxiliary Keys. Auxiliary keys such as a numeric keypad are sometimes provided. These keys may also be used to control the cursor.

Types of Key Closures

There are four common types of keyboard mechanisms in general use:

Hard key contact closure (switches)

Reed switch contact closure (sealed reed switches)

Switching by the hall effect (no mechanical closure)

Switching by capacitive increase (no mechanical closure)

Each type of keyboard will have unique circuitry necessary to accomplish the purpose of the keyboard, to provide the primary input to the computer. Each type also has its advantages and disadvantages. The hard key closure is the simplest but is prone to the usual failures of switches: dirty contacts, intermittent operation, and breaking of the switch springs or contacts. Reed switches are an improvement over open-air switches in that they are sealed from oxygen, which helps prevent their oxidation; they can also be made with very close tolerances, thus making a shorter-stroke switch that does not fatigue as easily. Special electronics makes the use of the hall effect possible for keyboard input. This method involves no mechanical contact either, and is very reliable.

A magnet brought close to a hall effect wafer through which a current is flowing will cause a voltage to be produced at right angles to them both (see Figure 9.3). This principle can be used to cause a logic circuit to close, thus reducing failures due to wear and eliminating entirely the problems of dirty contacts.

The capacitive keyboard places two adjacent PC board pads near each other on a printed circuit board. One of the pads is energized with RF, and the other is the detector pad. Normally there is insufficient RF coupled to the detector pad to close a circuit attached to the detector pad. If a metallic paddle such as the kind used in the IBM keyboard, is brought near to the surfaces of both the RF and detector pads, the paddle

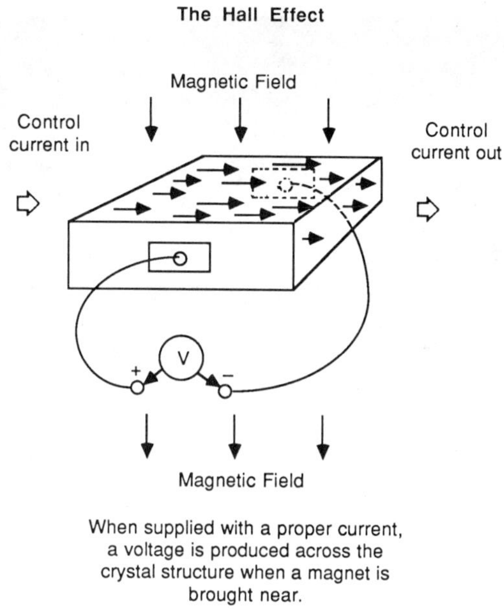

Figure 9.3 The hall effect is sometimes used to produce circuit closure without physical contacts.

couples RF to the detector pad and the detector circuit senses this and closes a logic circuit. This type of key closure is also very reliable, not depending upon a hard switch closure.

GETTING AT THE KEY MECHANISMS

Sticking keys can sometimes be repaired in the field with the use of a key-puller (Figure 9.4).

Once the key cap is removed, some of the internal workings of the switch may be exposed, depending upon the make of the keyboard. The IBM PC keyboard will have only a small spring and a metal paddle under the key, as mentioned in the discussion of capacitive keyboards. The electronics of this type of keyboard are entirely accessible only from the bottom. Gentle cleaning of the mechanism under the keycap using a cotton swab and some denatured alcohol may clear the problem. If this approach is not successful, the keyboard may have to be replaced for the customer and later disassembled in the shop for more extensive cleaning. Familiarity with the specific kind of keyboard in use will quickly enable the technician to clear most mechanical keyboard problems. See Figure 9.5.

Repairs in the field should be restricted to the replacement of the entire keyboard if at all possible. Dismantling a keyboard, sometimes a necessity, should not be attempted in the field unless unusual circumstances dictate otherwise. A keyboard may be so constructed that releasing the retaining screws will cause it literally to fall apart.

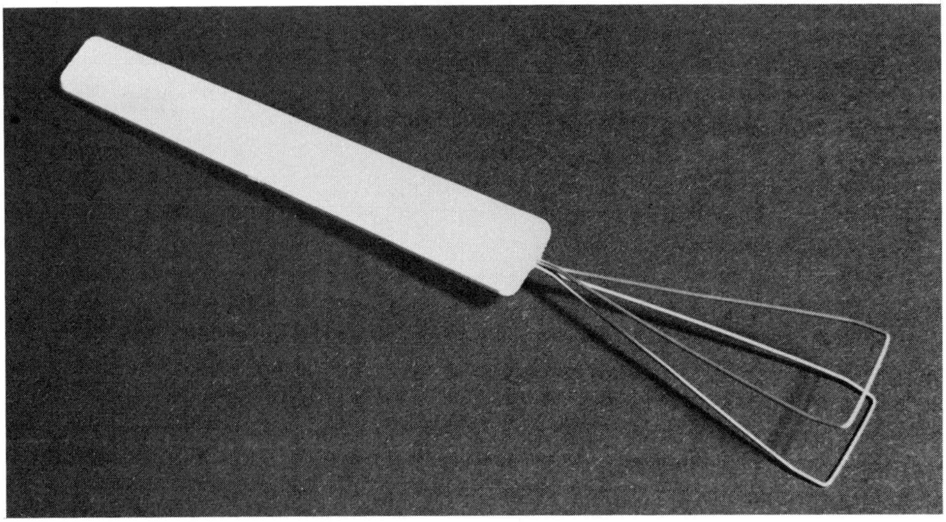

Figure 9.4 This strange-looking tool is used to pull key caps off for maintenance. (Abbey Enterprises)

Figure 9.5 Some keyboards have hard switch closures that may be cleaned easily after the key is removed. (Abbey Enterprises)

Springs, capacity plates, and other miscellaneous hardware can become so easily lost on the floor, particularly in a rug, that it makes sense to reserve such drastic repairs at least until a shop is available. The electronic support circuitry in the keyboard is sufficiently complex (having its own processor, an 8048) that component-level troubleshooting is seldom cost-effective. The keyboard is generally a throwaway item.

CHAPTER SUMMARY

Replacement of a defective keyboard is the most efficient method of curing a keyboard problem. Troubleshooting to the component level will seldom be warranted due to the low cost of the entire assembly.

REVIEW QUESTIONS

1. What is the fastest way to cure a problem in a separate keyboard unit?
2. Name two of the four ways a key closure might be accomplished.
3. Field repairs to keyboards should be restricted to simple _______ if at all possible.
4. The hall effect results in the production of a voltage when a _______ is brought near the semiconductor material.

part three

Making Repairs and Changes

chapter ten

After the Defective Part is Identified

CHAPTER OVERVIEW

By the time you are familiar with the contents of this chapter, working on the components of a printed circuit board will hold no mystery. Tricks of the trade and precautions to keep in mind are given to enable you to do a repair quickly and with minimal disturbance to the circuit card. There are even some cautions to observe when packing microcomputers and peripherals, and preventive maintenance is discussed.

WORKING ON THE PRINTED CIRCUIT BOARD

Static Precautions

Of the two digital families of integrated circuits—transistor-transistor logic (TTL) and complementary metal oxide semiconductors (CMOS)—the latter is the more susceptible to damage from mishandling. The input circuits of CMOS chips are theoretically open as a result of an extremely thin layer of insulation within the chip. The smallest static discharge is more than sufficient to puncture this insulation, however, ruining the chip. There are a few rules that, followed carefully, will reduce the chances of damaging the internal circuits of computers.

Establish a static-free environment for working on computers. This will mean grounded benches (if they are metal), static-free floor covering (no synthetic rugs, please!), and leather-soled shoes, to name a few cautions.

When packing or unpacking IC chips, use the original static-free containers or foam packing material. Do *not* use styrofoam materials to pack any computer circuitry!

Whenever the computer boards are removed or replaced, be certain that the power to the computer is off (Figure 10.1). This is a fundamental rule that *must* be observed by all servicing technicians and that cannot be overemphasized. Whenever ICs are passed from one person to another, be sure that the people touch each other first, before both of them contact the IC at the same time. In other words, reach out and touch the other person, then while touching, offer the IC (see Figure 10.2).

Observance of these rules must become second nature to technicians who work with these static-sensitive devices.

Figure 10.1 Always turn off the power before removing or installing circuitry in a computer. (Abbey Enterprises)

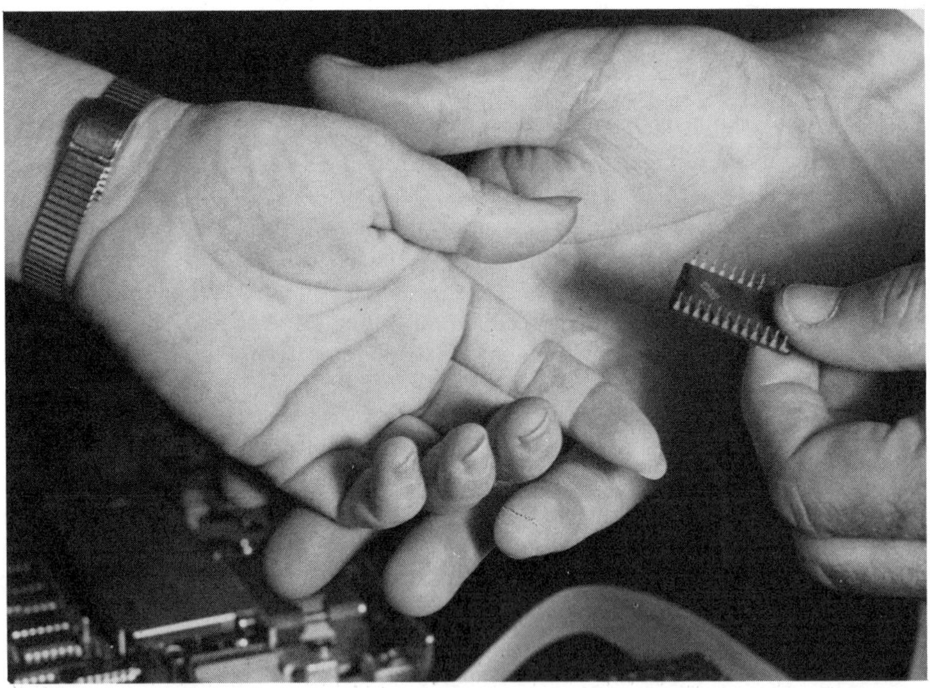

Figure 10.2 Touch the other technician to discharge possible static before reaching for an offered IC. (Abbey Enterprises)

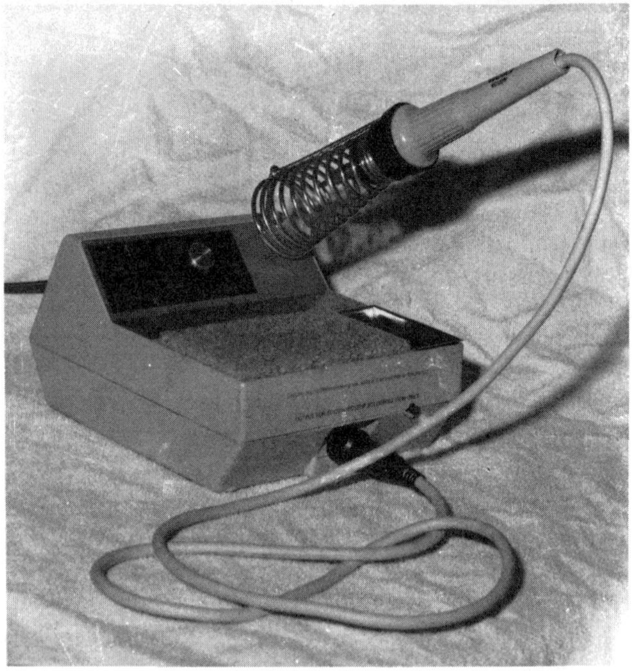

Figure 10.3 This temperature-controlled iron is particularly well suited for PC board work. It applies far less heat than a conventional iron and produces no transient voltages that could damage sensitive components. (Courtesy of the Cooper Group-Weller Plant)

Board Soldering

Soldering on computer printed circuit boards should be done only with a temperature-controlled iron if damage to the board is to be minimized. One such iron is shown in Figure 10.3. A temperature-controlled iron reaches operating temperature much faster than an iron that has no temperature sensing and must therefore operate at much higher temperatures to be useful. The lower temperature of the sensing iron is much less likely to cause damage to a printed circuit board because of excessive heat. A typical soldering operation should take five seconds or less to prevent damage to the board.

This iron is particularly well suited to working on critical circuitry. Not only is it temperature-controlled through a sensor at the tip of the iron, it also regulates power to the heating element in such a way that the power is turned on and off when the power-line cycle is passing through zero. This prevents any possible small transient voltages that could damage critical circuits. The exact temperature desired can also be dialed into this particular model, allowing circuits to be worked on with the minimum amount of heat. Several different tip sizes and shapes are available for specialized jobs.

Never solder on a board with power applied to the board! The tips of many irons, such as that pictured in Figure 10.3, are connected directly to the power-line ground.

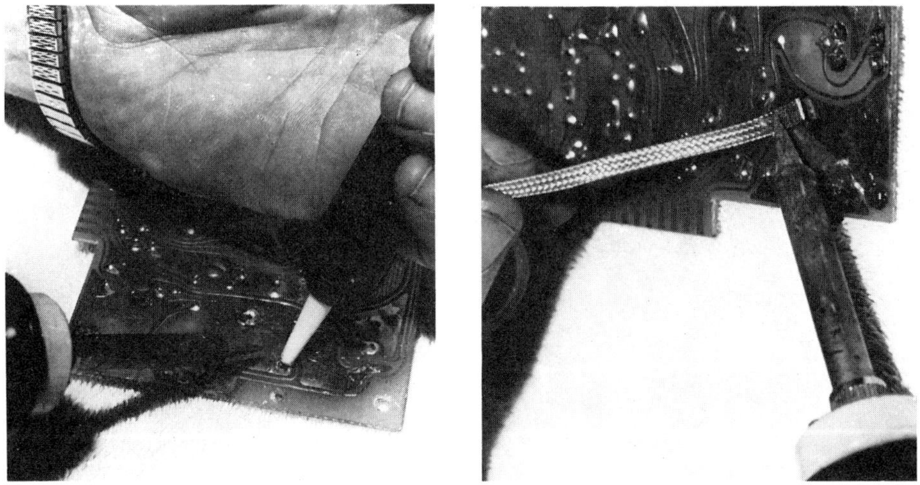

Figure 10.4 Two common methods of solder removal are the vacuum and wick methods. (Abbey Enterprises)

Working on a "hot" board could cause a great deal of damage from accidental grounding of the circuit.

Replacing Parts on Printed Circuit Boards

Getting the Part Out of the Board. Integrated circuits must be removed by taking away as much of the solder as possible before wiggling the leads loose one at a time. Two methods are popular for removing solder, the wick and the vacuum (see Figure 10.4). After the solder is removed, each component lead should be pressed from side to side in the board hole until it is free of solder. In many cases this is accompanied by a small click as the lead is broken free of the last bit of solder. Scratching the pins of an IC that have been broken free of solder produces a sound distinctly different from one that is still being held by solder on the other side of the board.

Components with only two or three leads may often be removed by heating the connection on the bottom of the board and gently rocking and pulling the component from the top. As each lead is heated in turn, the lead is pulled farther from the board with each rock.

Still another way to remove ICs and other multipinned components is to clip off the leads (Figure 10.5) at the component body, then remove each of the "stubs" left in the board one at a time with a pair of hemostats and the iron. Be careful not to pull on the tips remaining in the board until the solder has melted completely through the board (in the case of plated-through holes). It is very easy to pull a trace right off the board if too much pull is applied.

Be sure to look carefully at both sides of the circuit board when removing components. The top sides of some components are often soldered to the board, too. It will be necessary to remove the solder from both sides of such components.

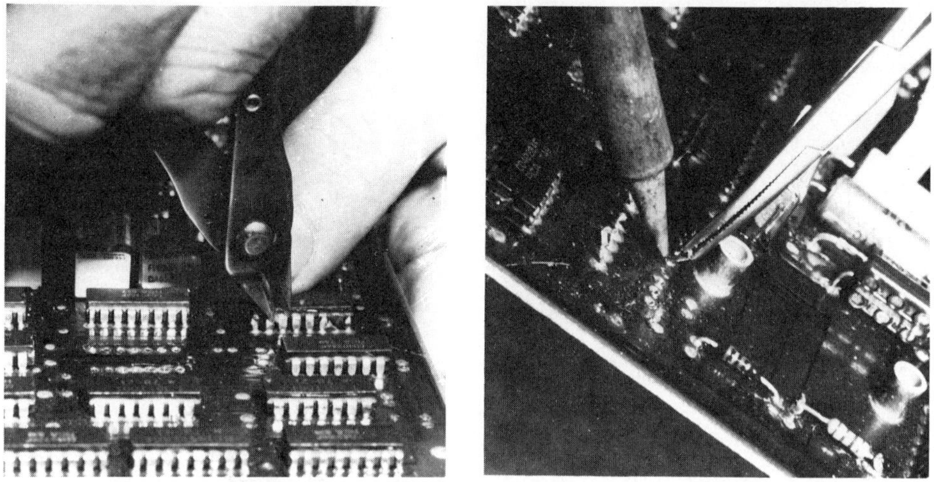

Figure 10.5 ICs can be removed by clipping off all the legs, then removing each stub separately from the board.

Cleaning and Repairing Damaged Microcomputer Board Traces. Work on printed boards requires a few special tools to make the job easier. A pair of small side-cutters that has accurate mating of the jaws right to the very tip are important. These can be used to cut off component leads close to the printed circuit board. If possible, one side should be without a sharpening bevel. This will enable more accurate placement of the cut for precise trimming of component leads and a flush cut rather than a tapered, sharp component lead. See Figure 10.6.

Medium and small screwdrivers of both the (Phillips) (+) and (straight) (-) blade types are also needed. A two-in-one screwdriver is useful especially for a technician's small field toolbox.

For benchwork a good magnifying glass is a useful item. The projection lens from an old 35mm projector is ideal because it does not distort toward the edges of the field of vision. A magnifier is used to inspect PC boards closely and for reading the ultrasmall lettering on some components.

Dental tools are also very handy for working on the small components of a computer. Try to get an explorer, a pointed instrument good for scratching and probing about on the boards. The most useful tool is a pair of small hemostats. They are extremely useful in handling and manipulating tiny components. Still another useful tool is the miniature chisel, used to make temporary breaks in board traces. See Figure 10.7.

When the old component has been removed, the board should be cleaned carefully with denatured alcohol to allow a very close inspection of the connections. Look for lifted traces and damage caused by previous work on the board or the desoldering operation. Lifted traces and open circuits can be repaired with short lengths of bare wire. Damage can be minimized by using a temperature-controlled

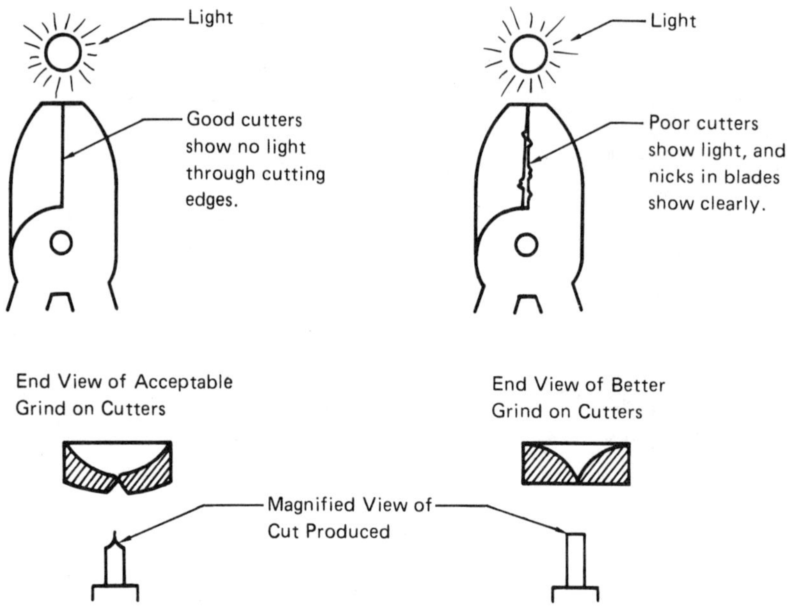

Figure 10.6 Select good-quality wire cutters without a bevel on one side. These are called flush cutting diagonal wire cutters. (Abbey Enterprises)

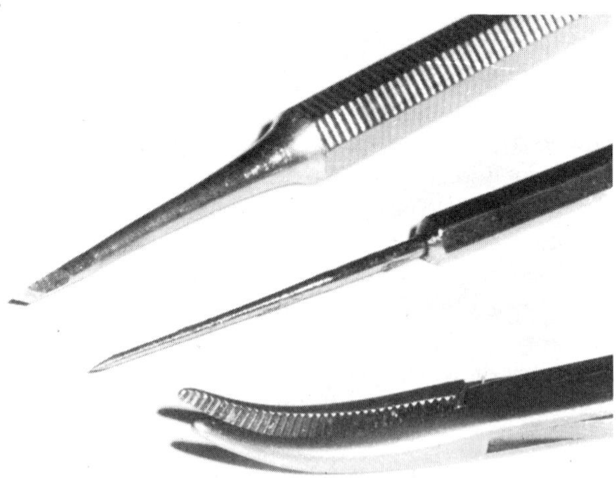

Figure 10.7 These dental tools are very useful in working on printed circuit boards. (Abbey Enterprises)

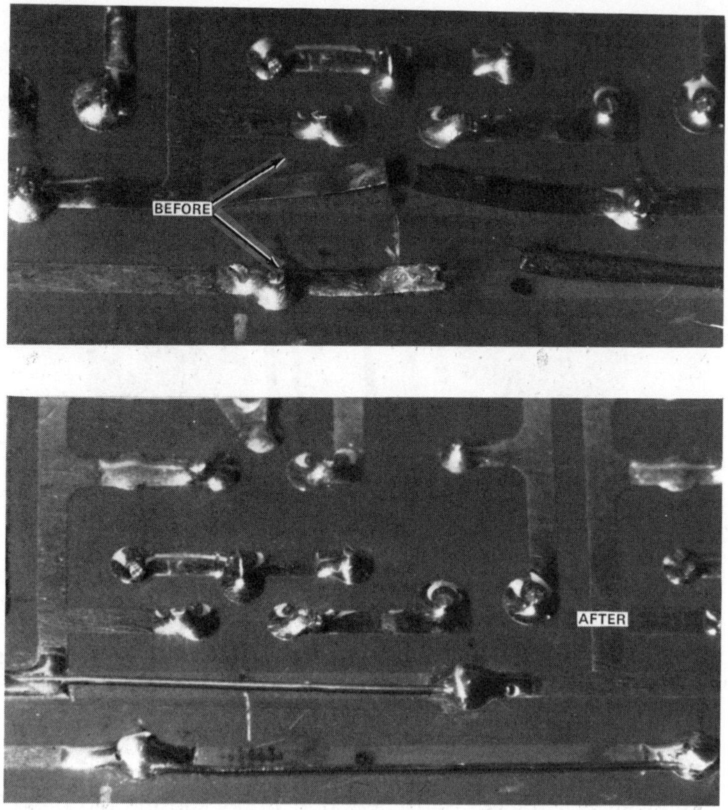

Figure 10.8 Damaged board traces can be repaired. This kind of damage is the result of using a non-temperature-controlled iron and leaving the iron in contact with the board too long. (Abbey Enterprises)

iron and making connections and desoldering operations as quickly as possible, consistent with quality work (see Figure 10.8).

Installing New Parts. Components such as resistors can be damaged if their wire leads are bent too close to the body of the part. Transistors have glass seals that can also be damaged by bending too closely. A broken seal will allow the component to absorb moisture and may eventually cause a failure. When replacing power transistors and diodes in the computer power supply, be sure to use a special heat-conducting grease such as silicon grease to help conduct away the normal operating heat of the component to the chassis or heatsink. This conducting grease has the consistency of a light lubricating grease and does not conduct electricity. It is sold in small tubes at electronic supply houses as transistor heatsink compound. A small amount of the grease spread over the mounting surface of a large transistor will greatly increase the life of the component because the component will not get as hot as it would without the compound.

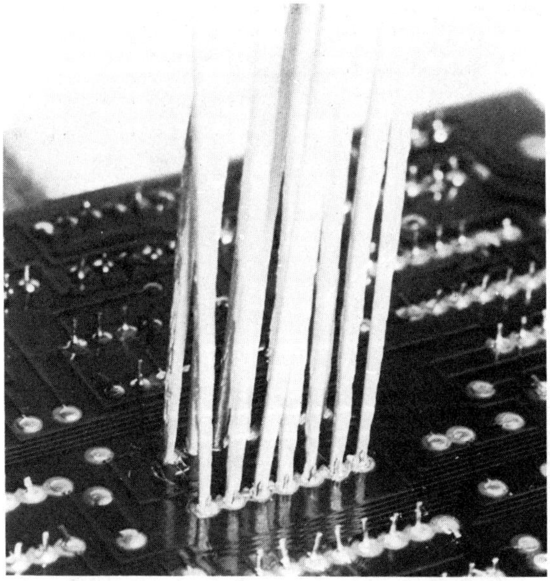

Figure 10.9 Toothpicking an IC into a circuit allows a test of a new IC without soldering it into the circuit. (Abbey Enterprises)

The final test of whether a component is good or bad is to substitute a known good component in its place. If the new one works and the old one did not, the evidence is pretty conclusive that the old one was defective. To temporarily test an IC in the circuit without soldering it in, you must ensure good contact of each of the pins before applying power. This can be done by "toothpicking." Get the new IC into the circuit the right way! Beware of getting it turned around and probably ruining it by forcing the supply current through it the wrong way. The IC is placed down against the board and the toothpicks are inserted gently from the opposite side of the board into the holes alongside the pins, forcing them into solid contact with the sides of the holes (see Figure 10.9). This method will work well only with microcomputer boards that have through-plated holes, however. With single-sided boards the IC will probably have to be soldered in for a valid test.

Where to Get Parts

Replacement computer parts should be obtained from reliable sources (Figure 10.10). Hundreds of reputable manufacturers are represented at electronic distributors across the country. These distributors may be found in the local telephone directory listed under Electronic Equipment and Supplies. These distributors often give discounts for purchasing in quantity and will ship COD to established customers.

Figure 10.10 Get replacement computer parts from a reputable dealer. (Radar Electric Co.)

Checking Out the Final Job

Final Tests. You must conduct final tests on equipment that has been repaired to assure that all of the faults have been corrected. Perform the same tests that verified that the computer was repaired, as discussed above. Be very thorough in the check-out procedure. If the original problem was an intermittent, run the appropriate diagnostics program in a loop for a while to be sure the computer is repaired.

Use of Solvents for Cleaning. When using any cleaner other than mild soap and a damp rag, possibility of damage from the solvent is present. Plastics are susceptible to immediate and long-term damage from solvents. Denatured alcohol seems to be about the safest solvent to use, but should be used on plastics only as a last resort, and then after use on a test spot.

Final Precautions

Reassembling the Equipment. There isn't much to putting things back together if you're the person who took them apart. If someone else took the equipment apart some time ago, don't be surprised if the bolts are not there or other small hardware is missing. And beware of putting long bolts into holes not intended for them. This can sometimes cause problems if the bolt is long enough to contact parts of the circuit board. Also beware of pinching wiring when tightening cover screws.

Another professional touch that can impress the customer very favorably is to give the cabinet a bath. Equipment returned looking strikingly cleaner than when it came into the shop helps customer relations immensely. Common household cleaners will work fine, a favorite being "409." Be sure to use only a little—and only on the outside of the cabinet.

A repaired computer should be operated to be certain that the repair is effective. It is not unusual to find that another problem has arisen, a problem which may or may not be directly related to the original. Merely working on the internal circuits of a computer may have stressed one or more of the ICs with a static discharge, or a break may have been caused in the circuit board by the process of replacing a part.

Once the computer cabinet is reinstalled, run the diagnostic program or other appropriate software to be sure that the computer does work as it should. It is not unheard of for replacement of the cabinet to have resulted in a broken or pinched wire that now prevents the equipment from working normally. The usual ways to test a computer are to run either the software that originally gave the problem's symptoms or a diagnostics program to ensure that the computer is again in normal operation.

Shipping Cardboard for Disk Drives. The recording and read head of a single-sided diskette drive has a felt pad that presses the diskette into contact with the head from the opposite side of the diskette. If the drive door is closed on such a drive, the head is touching the felt pad—which presents no problem. Such is not the case with a double-sided drive. Each side of the diskette had a head in contact with the diskette during normal operation, and when there is no diskette in the drive the heads are separated by the door mechanism. Problems arise when the door of a double-sided drive is closed without any diskette or a cardboard shipping disk inserted into the drive. The heads are then forced into direct contact with each other. The heads are constructed of a glass-like material that can be ruined if they are jarred while in this touching position. Make it a practice *never* to close the door of a double-sided drive without something inserted to prevent the heads from touching each other.

When originally purchased, the double-sided diskette drives were probably furnished with a cardboard insert to prevent chipping the heads during transportation of the drive (Figure 10.11). These cardboard shipping diskettes are usually lost once the computer is installed in the workplace. A technician transporting a computer or shipping it via any mode of transportation must be sure to insert either a cardboard diskette or a scratch diskette (one that has failed in use and is no longer usable for data storage).

NECESSARY PAPERWORK

Although the majority of employers do not require one, it is a good idea for the technician to keep his or her personal log of equipment worked on. These logs can be very handy when questions arise weeks later with reference to a specific job. Minimum information is all that is needed, date, equipment type, problem, and (particularly) serial numbers. Since it is a personal log, it is also a good place to make other notes, such as symptoms and cures.

Figure 10.11 These cardboard shipping diskettes can prevent costly damage to the double-sided read/write heads during transportation.

Shop policies concerning how the customer is to be billed should be established. The time spent on the repair and the part numbers of the parts used should be noted at the completion of each job. A piece of paper with this information may be handed to the company clerk, who handles it from this point. In some cases the technician makes out a job order sheet with this information and this document is used to bill the customer. Ask your shop supervisor how the paperwork for billing is to be handled.

ORDERING PARTS TO REPLACE THOSE USED FROM STOCK

When a repair uses parts from stock, that stock must be replaced. The procedures consist of using the part number and quantity and contacting the parts supplier. The supplier can be a local generic parts distributor or the manufacturer for the proprietary parts. Proprietary parts will not be available anywhere but through the manufacturer. The manufacturer either makes these parts for its equipment or procures generic parts and removes the identification, affixing its own. In this way the manufacturer will get your return business for parts, priced at what the market will bear. Often an identical part could be obtained at a parts distributor for a fraction of the manufacturer's price.

In any case, the shop stock must be kept up so that future repairs can be made without undue delay. This inventory of parts may be kept manually or, as in some of the more progressive shops, on computer data-base programs. The later method is the best. It is sure and accurate *as long as the stock changes are given to the computer!* A single omission of information makes the inventory system that much weaker.

Shop policy should also be established for those occasions when the technician wants to borrow a part for a few minutes for a quick check, then return it to stock.

PACKING FOR SHIPMENT

Pack electronic equipment for shipment with care. Almost any packing that will cushion the equipment may be used except any of the styrofoam packing materials that are now in common use. These are very static-producing and should not be used with equipment having CMOS chips. This is very important to note when packing printed circuit cards, which have many input and output leads coming to the edge of the card without additional protection.

Wrap the equipment and tape the wrapping in place. Place the bundle into a suitable cardboard box along with any paperwork required to be inside the box, and seal it with nylon tape. Attach the mailing label and any shipping documents to the outside of the box as indicated by shop procedures. Don't forget to keep a log that records the shipping of the item in case there are later inquiries as to the date and destination.

PREVENTIVE MAINTENANCE OF COMPUTERS

Working inside computers poses hazards to them. Wiring is pulled, circuits are probed with test leads, and circuits bumped around. Failures can be caused in the very process of trying to prevent failures. In fact, serious thought should be given to doing nothing with digital equipment that is working. If it is performing as it should, leave it alone.

Some computers are outfitted with internal blowers that are supposed to ensure an adequate supply of air circulating inside the computer to keep internal temperatures at safe levels. Suction from blowers that draw air into the computer at the back can pick up papers, which will completely block the flow of air. Keep all papers away from blower grills. Be sure that the computer has a few inches of free space around the rear of the cabinet, where the blowers are most often located. And keep liquids off the top of electronic equipment! Coffee cups are a common potential danger around electronics (Figure 10-12). A coffee spill, particularly if well sugared, can make quite a mess on a circuit board.

Figure 10.12 Liquids should be ruled out within a dozen feet of the computer. (Abbey Enterprises)

CHAPTER SUMMARY

Professional workmanship is an absolute must when working on the dense circuitry of a microcomputer board. Even though finding the part might be done efficiently, sloppy work while replacing the part can cause additional problems and reflects badly upon the technician. Use the right tools, the right procedures, and use only quality parts. In addition, pack the equipment well and include all the proper paperwork. Prevent damage by pointing out computer hazards in the workplace such as pointed out in this chapter.

REVIEW QUESTIONS

1. What logic IC family is most sensitive to static damage?
2. What fundamental rule must be observed when removing and inserting printed circuits?
3. What type of iron is most suitable for working on PC boards to minimize circuit damage?
4. What is the danger of soldering on energized circuits?
5. Name two general methods of solder removal.
6. What is the final test of whether a suspected component is good or bad?
7. What special precaution must be taken when installing ICs?
8. What should be done after a computer is repaired, the cabinet reinstalled, and all nuts and bolts replaced?
9. Lacking a cardboard shipping diskette or an old damaged diskette for use as a shipping precaution in a diskette drive, what can be done to prevent head damage during a short-haul transport of a computer?
10. What material should not be used to pack computer equipment?

chapter eleven

Troubleshooting and Repairing Floppy Diskette Drives

CHAPTER OVERVIEW

This chapter introduces the terminology of maintaining floppy diskette drives, the most common means of storing data for microcomputers. Specialized-equipment use is covered, along with the right and wrong indications these instruments give when testing and aligning the drives. Although practice with aligning drives is important in maintaining them, understanding why and how is a prerequisite to troubleshooting drive problems.

FDD HARDWARE OVERVIEW

The floppy diskette drive is a very popular method of data storage, both for programs and for the data used with them. Figure 11.1 shows the relationship of the diskette drive to the entire computer system.

Some cautions are in order here to help the technician prevent further damage to the drives and the diskettes used in them.

1. Never close the door on a dual-sided diskette drive without a diskette in the drive. To do so puts the ceramic heads on the top and bottom sides of the diskette in direct contact with each other, which invites chipping. A chipped head can instantly ruin a diskette rotated in the drive. Transporting a drive without the protection of a diskette or a cardboard protector is especially dangerous because of the vibration and bumping of normal transportation.

2. When inserting diskettes into the drives, insert the diskette slowly and carefully, all the way in. Close the drive latch or door carefully too. Inserting the diskette and clamping it when the drive motor is running will assist greatly in properly seating the drive spindle into the hole with less stress on the edges of the diskette hole. Some drives are designed to rotate while the diskette is clamped.

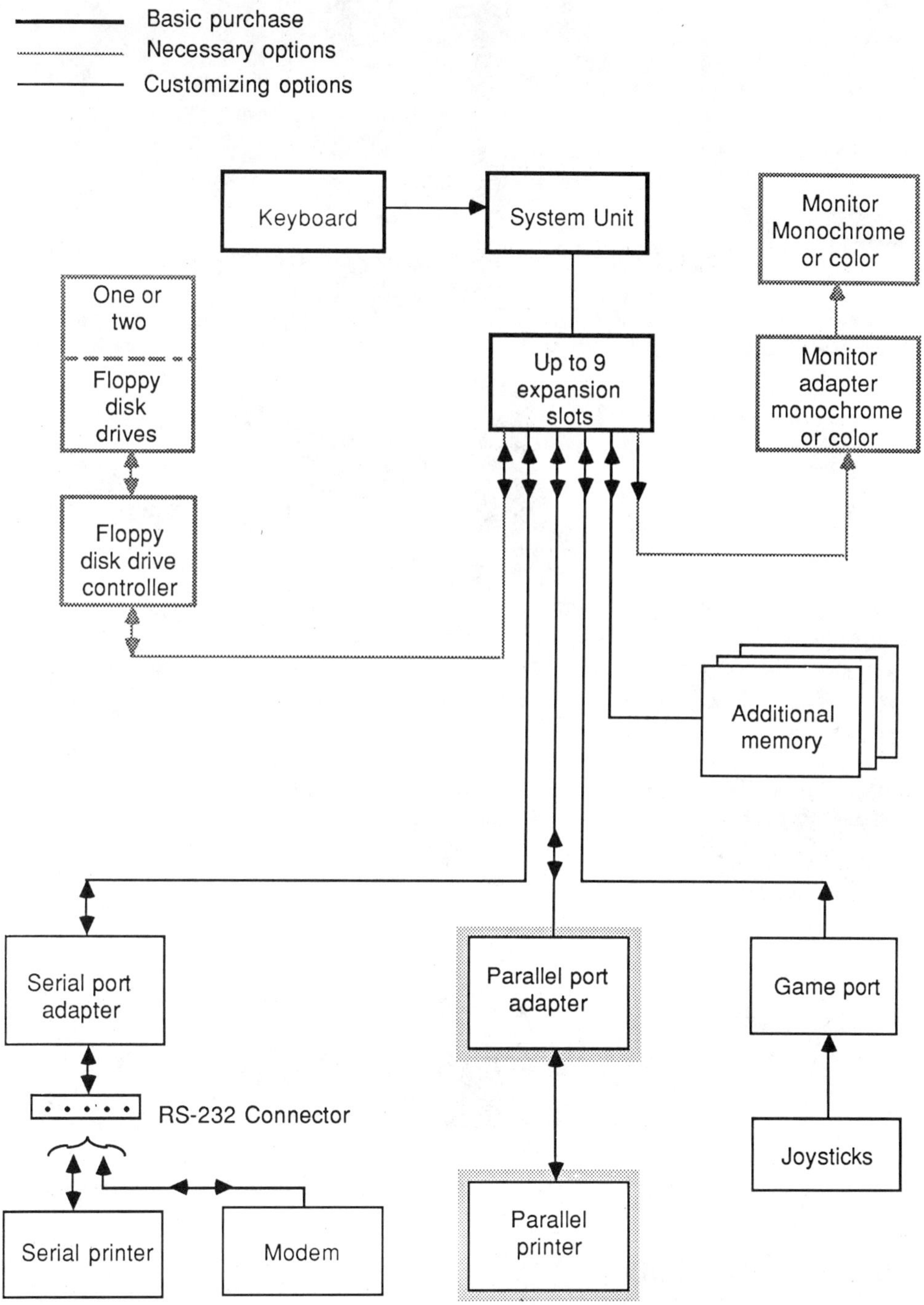

Figure 11.1 The floppy diskette drive is a major part of most microcomputer systems.

Figure 11.2 The machinery of a floppy diskette drive is manufactured with a great deal of precision but is not complex. (Abbey Enterprises)

Mechanics of the FDD

For all the electronic complexity of the diskette drive, the mechanical portion of the drive is not complicated. It consists of a motor drive to rotate the spindle at a precise

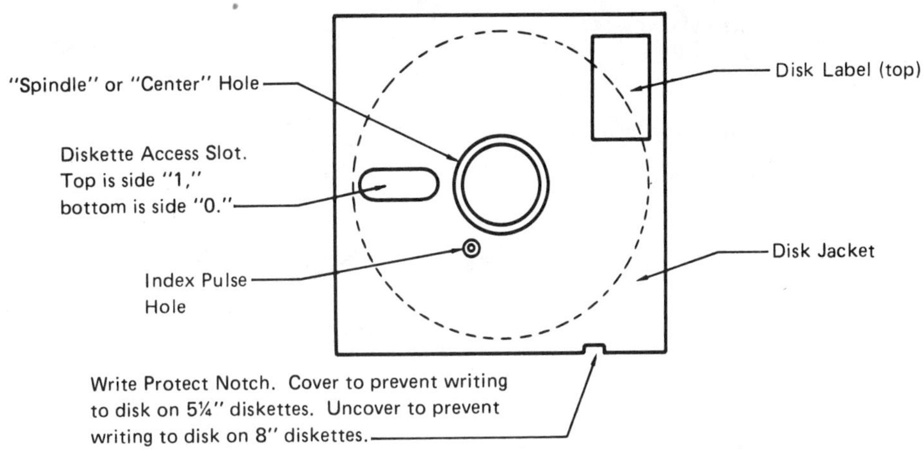

Figure 11.3 The parts of the floppy diskette

rate of speed, the read/write heads sliding along a radial track and in detectors to read the passage of the index hole and one to read the status of the write-protect notch in the diskette jacket (see Figure 11.2). Each time the drive is accessed by the computer the motor for the drive is turned on and the read/write head is moved along a radial path until the appropriate track is encountered. The data is then read by the computer.

The use of floppy diskettes has given rise to some special terms:

- **Centering.** Centering of a diskette on the drive spindle is critical. Any off-centering causes all of the tracks to wander in radial alignment—much like trying to play one of the old 45 rpm records (with its large center hole) on a standard, small-spindle turntable. Where the turntable arm might follow the grooves of a record, the read/write head of the diskette drive is fixed in one position and the tracks would wander back and forth past them.
- **Rotational Speed.** The 5 1/4-inch floppy diskette turns at precisely 300 rpm: exactly 200.0 milliseconds per revolution. Software that checks for rotational speed often reads out the period of the speed rather than the rpm, 2000 rather than the proper 200.0.
- **Index Width.** The most popular diskette is the soft-sectored diskette. The soft-sectored diskette has a single index hole, the hard-sectored multiple index holes. (The index hole is visible through the diskette jacket, near the center; see Figure 11.3.) The signal derived from the index hole is also used to indicate to the computer that there is a diskette in the drive and that the drive is turning. The index hole is about 4000 microseconds wide at the proper rotational speed of 300 rpm. The exact width of the electronic index pulse derived from the index hole of a rotating disk may be anywhere from 2000μs to 5000μs.
- **Radial Alignment.** The tracks on a diskette, 40 of them on each side of a 5 1/4-inch diskette, are concentric. These tracks begin at the outside of the diskette with

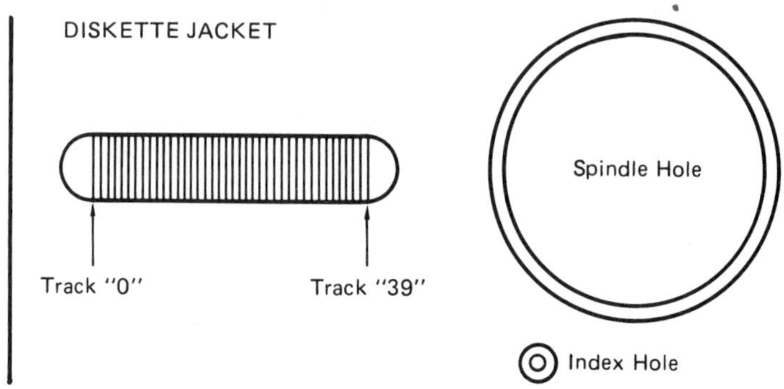

Figure 11.4 Floppy diskette tracks begin from the outside, track 0.

track 0 and number inward toward track 39, near the center hole (see Figure 11.4). Thirty-five-track diskettes have been used in the past but are now obsolete. Be aware that using an old 35-track diskette in a 40-track drive can cause the head to run into the end of the shorter disk-access slot and cause alignment problems.

The read/write heads of a disk drive are usually moved from track to track by a stepper motor. The stepper motor moves a precise amount at each phase increase of the electronic circuits driving it. From the home position, track 0, the stepper moves a precise amount to each given track. There is no means on the standard floppy drive to lock onto a track: the stepper motor is "blind" and goes a certain distance. If the track is where it is supposed to be on the diskette and the head moves the right amount, the two coincide and everything works well. But, as sometimes happens, the stepper motor puts the read/write heads slightly off from the center line of a track. Once out of true alignment position on a track, the drive has no way of finding it again. This can happen, for instance, if the head mechanism is friction-clamped to the stepper motor shaft by a coupling that can loosen and slip. See Figure 11.5.

This misalignment can be corrected by loosening the coupling and putting the head back on the proper track, then retightening the clamp securely. An alternative way to realign slight misalignment problems is to move the entire head and stepper motor assembly slightly with a cam-head screw. The method of alignment adjustment depends upon the drive concerned. Some disk drives change the relationship of the head by turning the entire stepper motor in its mounting if no other means of adjustment is evident. Radial alignment is monitored using data read from an alignment diskette by the *bottom* or 0 head. Radial alignment of the top, 1, head is seldom worth attempting but must be performed only after the bottom head is accurately in alignment.

Azimuth Checks. The heads of a diskette drive must meet the data at precisely a 90-degree angle. Looking directly down on a drive, any rotation of the head about its center is a misalignment of that head's azimuth (see Figure 11.6). The

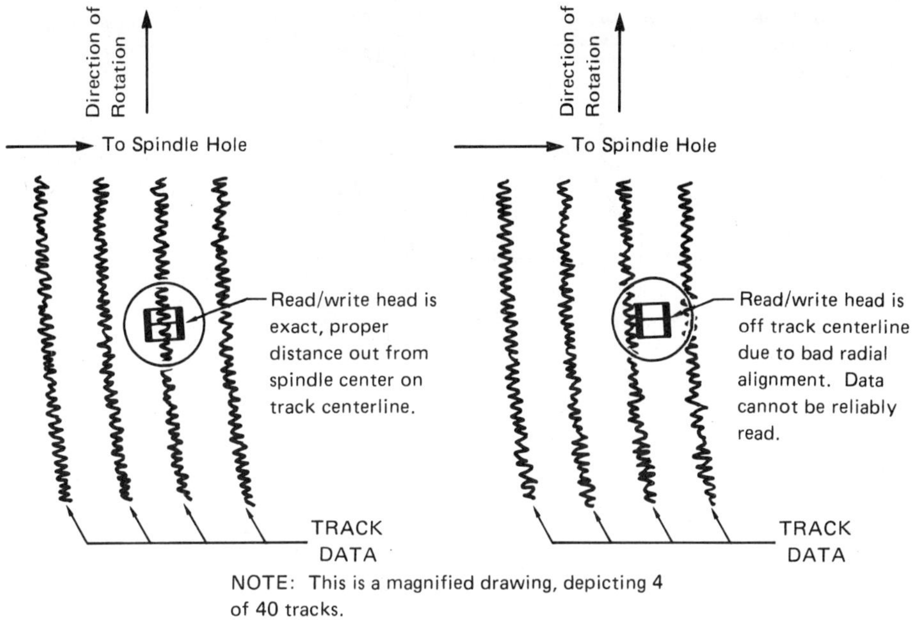

Figure 11.5 If the read/write head is not on track center, data may be inaccessible.

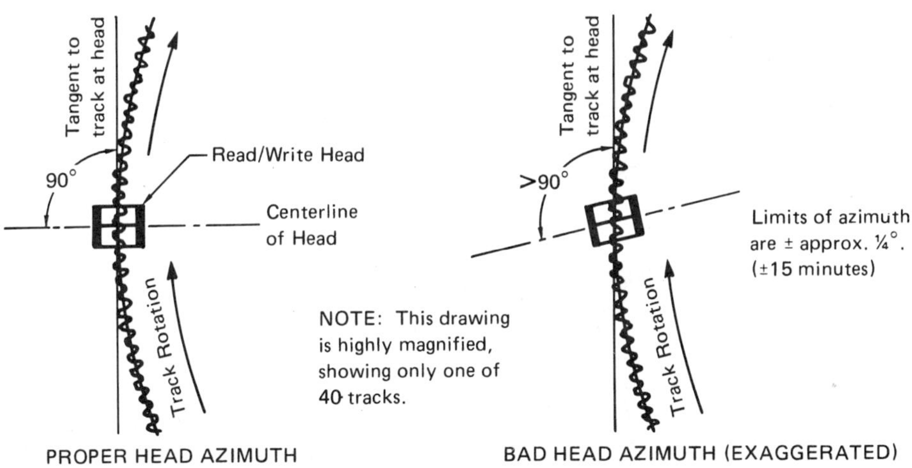

Figure 11.6 Data must come into the read/write head at 90°, ± 18 minutes.

bottom head of a double-sided drive (the only head of a single-sided drive) cannot be changed in azimuth because these heads are usually set into epoxy and are therefore not adjustable.

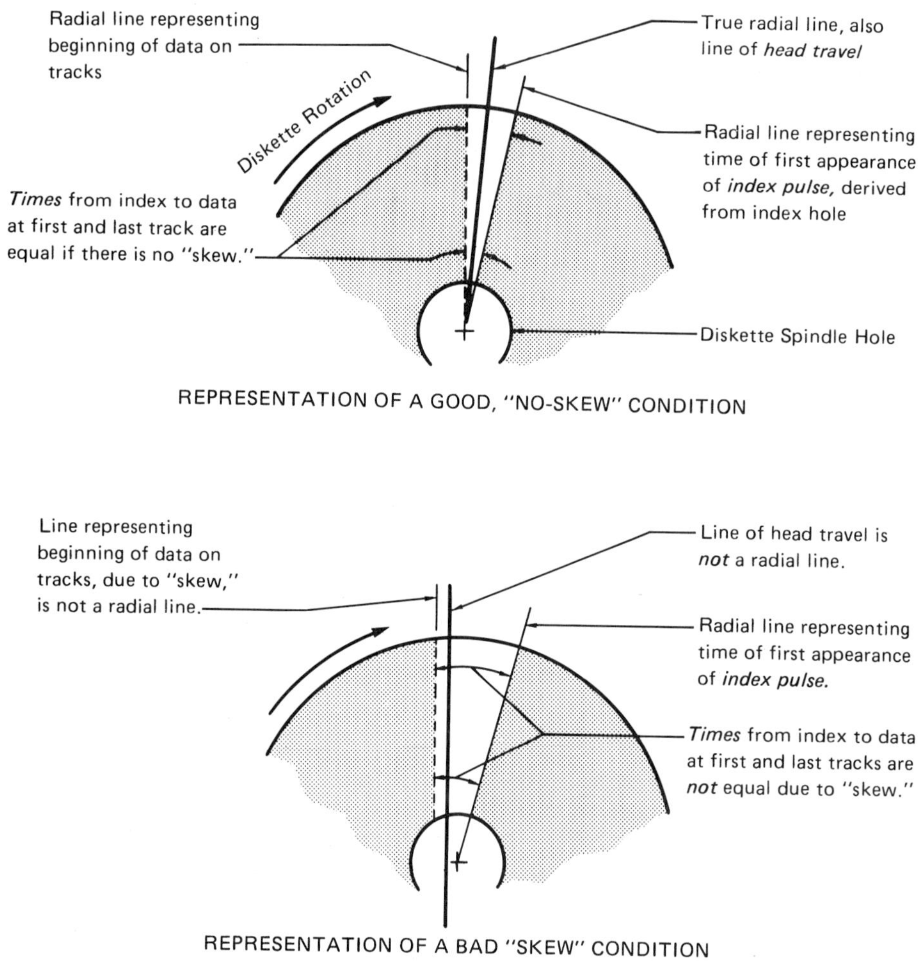

Figure 11.7 Skew is a measure of how far the read/write heads departs from a true radial line to the center of the diskette.

- **Index-to-Data Timing Check (Skew).** Skew is a measure of the amount by which the head, in moving from the outside to the inside of the diskette, departs from a true radial course straight to the center of the diskette (Figure 11.7). Skew can be measured by noting the time between the beginning of the index pulse and the first reading of data from an alignment diskette. If there is no skew, the time between these two events will remain the same whether the drive is reading track 0 or track 34 (Figure 11.8).

To give you a feel for the specifications of a representative floppy diskette drive, the technical specifications for a Tandon drive appear in Table 11.1.

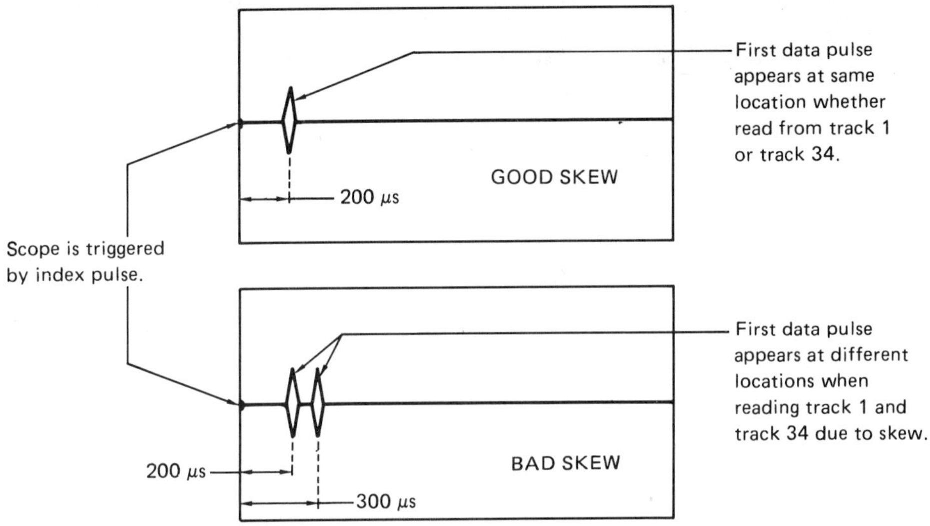

Figure 11.8 Oscilloscope patterns showing an unacceptable skew condition

Details of the Floppy Diskette

Floppy diskettes in the 5 1/4-inch diameter come in two basic capabilities, single- and double-sided. Single-sided diskettes often have one side that cannot pass the manufacturer's quality tests. The good side is placed down in the jacket and used there by single-sided drives. Diskettes that pass tests on both sides are placed into the jacket without special regard to one side or the other, since both the bottom and top surfaces can be used.

The operating system used in microcomputers requires that the data on the diskettes be placed in very well-defined areas on the diskette surface. This is done electronically by recording sectors on the diskette, eight or nine of them on each of the 40 tracks. DOS 2.1 uses nine sectors and previous versions use eight. Each sector is apportioned as in Figure 11.9.

Diskettes have varying capabilities for holding data, depending upon the number of sides and the number of sectors:

Single-sided, 8-sectored diskette: 160,256 bytes of storage space

Single-sided, 9-sectored diskette: 179,712 bytes of storage space

Double-sided, 8-sectored diskette: 322,560 bytes of storage space

Double-sided, 9-sectored diskette: 362,496 bytes of storage space

Single-sided diskettes use only the bottom of the diskette for recording data. The bottom of the diskette is the one opposite the side that has the diskette label and is called side 0 in some technical literature. The top or label side is called side 1. Data is

Table 11.1 Typical Specifications for a Floppy Diskette Drive

Media	ANSI-compatible, 5-1/4-inch diskette
Media Life (for reference only)	4 x 10^6 passes per track
Tracks Per Inch	48 TPI, both drives
Tracks Per Drive	
TM50-1	40 Tracks
TM50-2	80 Tracks
Track Spacing	0.529 millimeters, 20.8 millinches
Head Life	20,000 media contact hours
Disk Rotational Speed	300 RPM ±1.5 percent
Average Rotational Latency	100 milliseconds
Instantaneous Speed Variation (ISV)	±3 percent
Motor Start Time	One second, maximum
Seek Time, Track to Track	20 milliseconds
Fast Step Motor (Optional)	6 milliseconds
Head Settling Time	20 milliseconds
Fast Step Motor (Optional)	15 milliseconds
Average Track Access Time, including head settling time	287 milliseconds
Fast Step Motor (Optional)	95 milliseconds
Typical Recording Modes	FM, MFM, MMFM
Data Transfer Rate	250,000 bits per second, double density

recorded on the diskette in a manner similar to that used to record voice on magnetic tape. A tiny electromagnet with a microscopic gap in the head magnetizes the diskette spot directly in contact with the head (see Figure 11.10).

A diskette can be read without modifying the data on the diskette. Writing, however, destroys all data written over by the recording head. To prevent expensive programs from possible accidental erasure, the jacket of a 5 1/4-inch diskette has cut

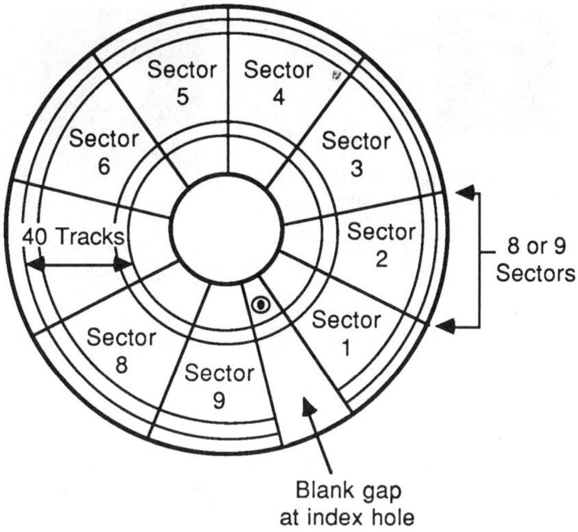

Figure 11.9 Each sector of a diskete has its own code for positive identification.

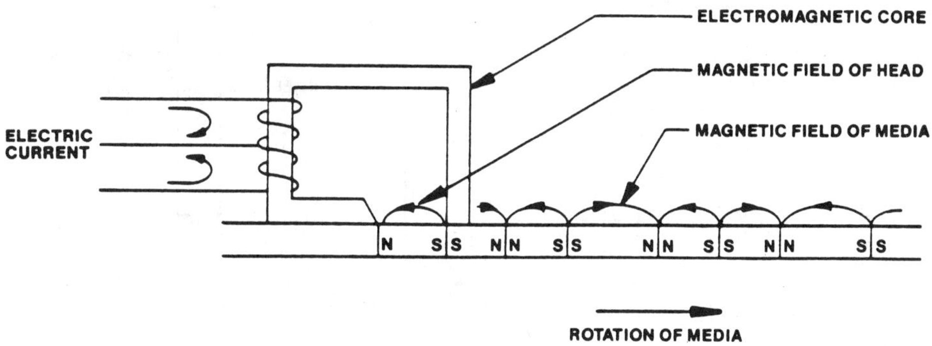

Figure 11.10 A tiny coil produces a magnetic field which is concentrated into a microscopic gap that magnetizes a spot on the diskette. (Courtesy of the Tandon Corp.)

into it a notch that, if blocked by opaque tape, will prevent any writing to that diskette (Figure 11.11). A few program diskettes are provided without a write-protect notch to prevent their ever being written onto.

Eight-inch diskettes also have the write-protect notch, but its use is reversed. Blocking the write-protect notch will enable writing to the diskette.

The Controller Chip and the FDC Card

The electronic circuits necessary for the operation of the floppy diskette drives are split between two boards (see Figure 11.12). The more complex operations are

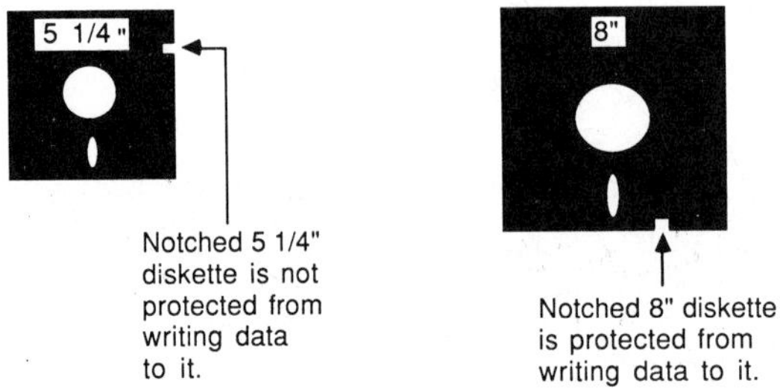

Figure 11.11 The write-protect notch will prevent accidental writing on a protected diskette by disabling the writing circuitry of the diskette drive.

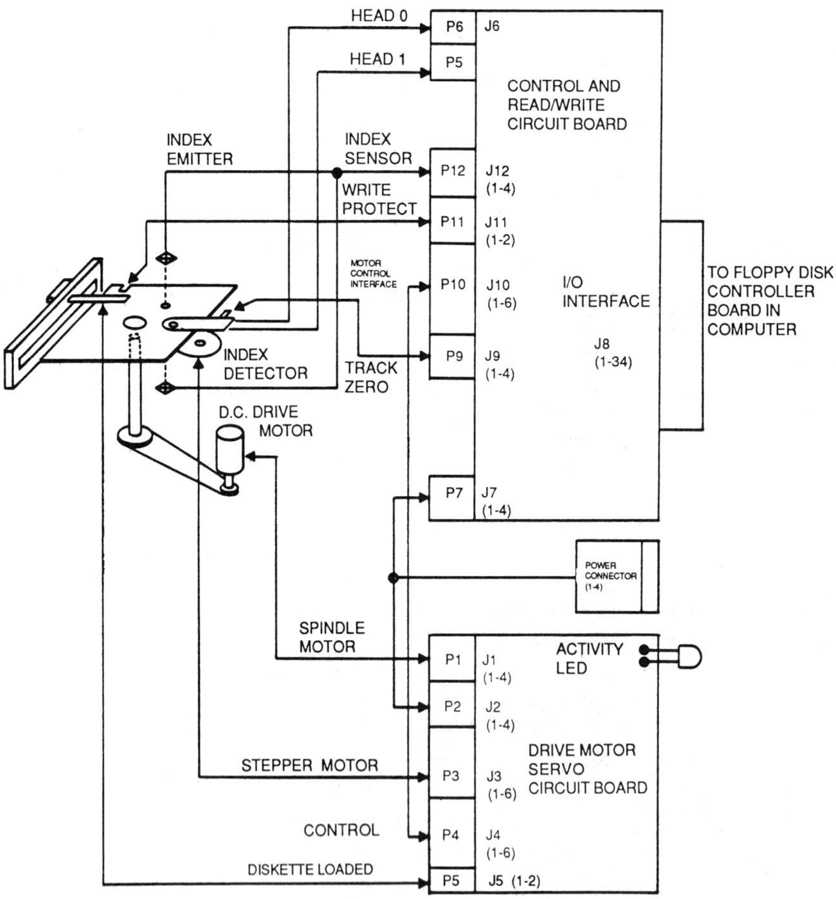

Figure 11.12 The diskette drive electronics system is divided between two units, that of the board which usually plugs into the system expansion slot and that attached to the diskette drive unit. (Courtesy of the Tandon Corp.)

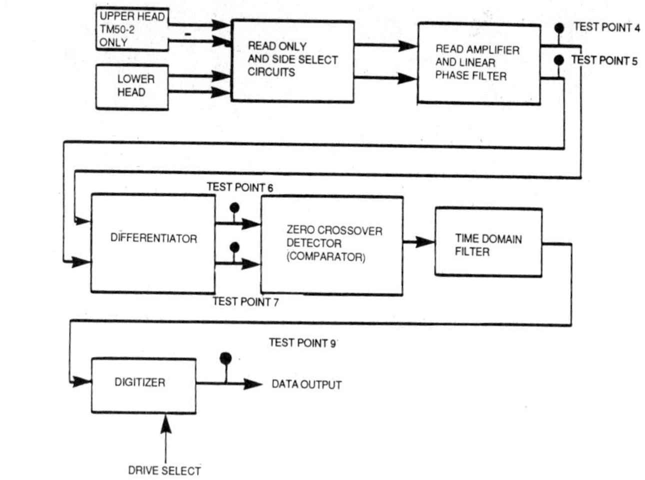

Figure 11.13 These shaded blocks of the floppy diskette controller card are involved in a read operation from the diskette. (Courtesy of Tandon Corp.)

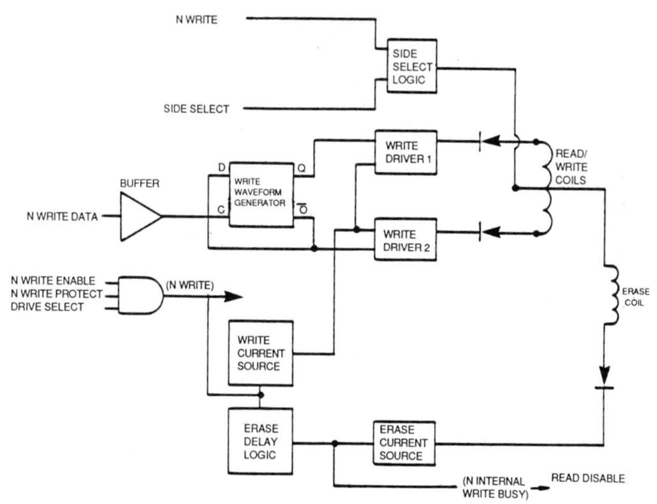

Figure 11.14 The write operation involves the shaded circuits of the FDC. (Courtesy of the Tandon Corp.)

carried out within the floppy diskette controller, a card which is usually installed in one of the expansion slots. Both the card and the major controller chip on it are sometimes called the Floppy Disk Controller.

Block diagrams show the circuits involved in a read and write operation of the disk drive electronics board. (Figures 11.13 and 11.14).

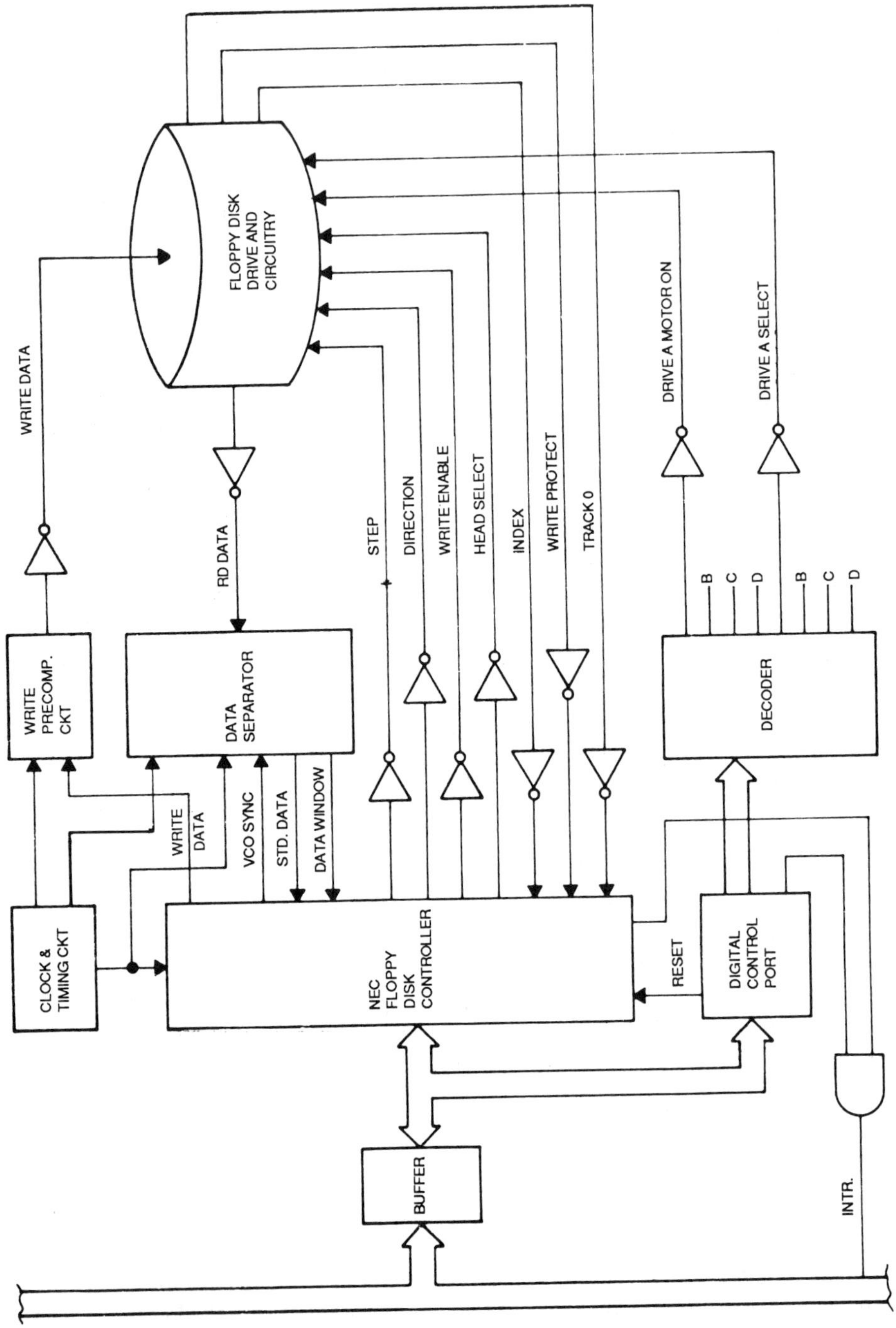

Figure 11.15 Block diagram of floppy diskette drive controller and interface circuits. (Courtesy of IBM)

The floppy diskette controller is a complex chip, generating the necessary drive signals and processing data streams to accomplish the task of reading and writing to the diskette. The signals generated by the floppy diskette controller (FDC) card then drive the interface board, which is attached to the diskette drive itself. The block diagram of a floppy disk controller and the interface card are shown in Figure 11.15.

The first step in isolating a problem within the diskette drives is to eliminate the drive and the interface electronics mounted to it. Since a failure is most likely a mechanical one, substitute another drive. Often simply switching control cabling with another drive connected to the same computer is the best step to take. Switching drives is a matter of exchanging the control line plugs between the two units. The old A drive becomes the new B drive and vice versa. Figure 4.4 shows how the two control cables can be easily switched. If this procedure is used the computer will boot up on the opposite drive from normal. If the problem switches *with* the drive, the problem is either in the floppy diskette controller card although, of course, a bad diskette can also cause these symptoms. Substitution of another controller card can verify that the old card was causing the problem.

If exchanging the drive control cables results in the problem remaining with the originally suspected drive, that drive should be examined further to see if the cure is a simple one. It is possible that the electronics mounted to the diskette drive are causing the problem. Some diskette drives offer easy removal of the boards, in which case substituting a known good board on the drive can be done. Other drives have more complicated connections between the mechanical and electronic units and substitution of another board may not be so attractive an option (see Figure 11.16).

If the problem has been localized to the mechanisms on the drive, the following section covers further pursuit of a mechanical problem.

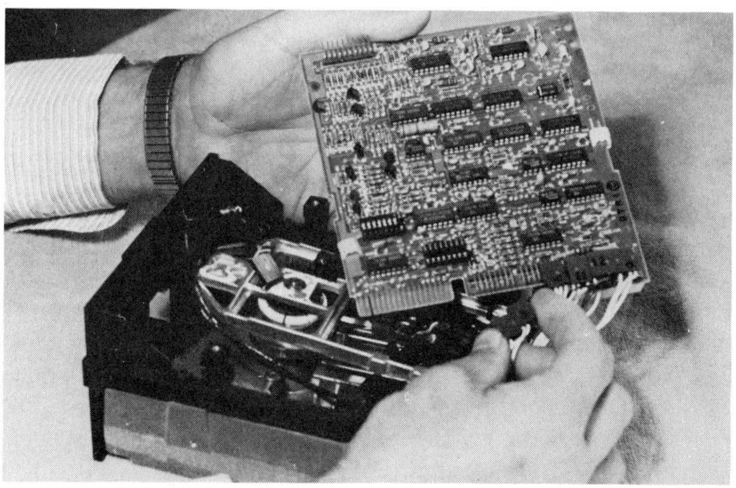

Figure 11.16 Circuit boards on some drives are easier to substitute and therefore eliminated as the possible cause of the problem. (Abbey Enterprises)

TESTING DRIVE ALIGNMENT WHILE OPERATING THE MICROCOMPUTER

Using a Digital Diagnostics Diskette

A diskette drive can be checked for alignment without taking the cover off a computer if the computer can be booted up. This is often the case when the B drive is suspect. A special diskette is available from Dysan that puts the read/write heads of a drive through their paces in reading the specially recorded data on the diskette. This digital diagnostic diskette, or DDD, is used with an interrogator program. When using the DDD diskette, keep in mind that the drives can be switched as noted above for troubleshooting, but this will mean that the computer must be opened up.

The Dysan DDD diskette 508-400 is used with the interrogator software to examine double-sided, double-density drives. Separate test diskettes for single-sided and single-density drives are also available. The following important tests are among those available:

1. Radial alignment
2. Azimuth alignment
3. Skew
4. Index pulse width
5. Index-to-data timing

In order to use the DDD diskette, the computer must be able to load and execute a program with at least one drive, the one into which the interrogator diskette is inserted. The principal use of this method of testing drives provides the computer operator an excellent way to monitor gradual changes in drive efficiency, thus helping prevent sudden failures of the drive.

Using a Diskette Diagnostics Program

Another option open to the technician is to load and run the diskette diagnostic program to check a diskette drive. It is a very good idea to run the diagnostic tests on known good drives to become familiar with the program prompts used, and the results obtained from good drives builds confidence in the diagnostics programs. The diskette drive portion of the diagnostic program is used along with at least one diskette (often two, to test two drives at the same time) specially formatted and used as a "scratch diskette." This diskette exercises the writing and reading capabilities of the drive or drives under test. Be sure that whatever diskette you designate as scratch is indeed that—a scratch diskette. The formatting process wipes out any data that might be on the diskette before formatting. Of course, the diskette must be able to record data; it cannot be a damaged diskette. Once you have the scratch diskettes formatted and ready to go, choose option 6 from the diagnostics program menu and follow the prompts. There are four tests that can be run with the program. Following are the tests, what they do, and some of the error codes with accompanying probable causes for the errors.

Diskette Diagnostic Tests Available. The *random seek* test is a read-only operation with a quick look at side 1 at the end.

The *verify* test is a read-only operation with eight sweeps of each side, side 0 first.

The *sequential seek* test is a read-only operation with eight sweeps of head 0, and a quick look at side 1 at the end.

The *speed check* is just that, but the readout is in tens of milliseconds. A readout of 2005 is actually a measured 200.5 milliseconds per revolution. 200.0 is the best reading.

Possible Diskette Diagnostic Error Codes Returned. Common error codes returned during use of a diagnostic program may have the following causes:

> Time Out. Close the drive door. Check the index pulse circuitry. As far as the diagnostics program is concerned, the diskette is not turning.
>
> Bad Adr Mark. Either R/W is not reading for some reason or you are using a damaged scratch diskette. Try reformatting the diskette with the DFORMAT.COM program on a good drive.
>
> Bad CRC. Failure to read or write. Check scratch diskette. Reformat the scratch diskette on a good drive.
>
> Rec not Fnd. Either head not reading. (Connect head control lead?). Reformat the scratch diskette on a good drive.
>
> Bad Cntl-Seek. Track 0 sensing is bad. Either the switch/LED or the end stop is out of adjustment. Sometimes accompanied by a rattle of the stepper as it tries to go beyond the end stop.

THE CLASSIC SYMPTOMS OF A MALFUNCTIONING FLOPPY DISKETTE DRIVE

A diskette drive that is slightly out of mechanical alignment may very well read a diskette it has itself written upon. The written path and the reading path are the same, so the signal is retrieved without problems. Such a drive, however, could be totally unable to read diskettes written on by other drives that *are* in proper alignment. In other words, absence of interchangeability of disks from one drive to another is a good indication of alignment problems. This problem can be localized to one drive if a known good diskette will not read properly on that drive. A known good diskette is one that has been written by a drive known to be in good condition or one of the special alignment diskettes such as the Dysan DDD diskette.

If the drive door of the booting drive is left open or the drive is not providing normal reading of data from the diskette during booting up, the computer will do one of three things: (1) show only a blinking cursor on an otherwise blank screen, (2) in the case of IBM computers, BASIC will load from the IBM ROMs in the computer and the prompt will be the standard BASIC logging on information and the BASIC prompt OK, or (3) an appropriate "use a system diskette" message appears on the monitor. If the drive access light of the booting drive comes on for a few moments, then goes off without providing the normal data required to boot the computer, a problem is certainly indicated.

ALIGNING A FLOPPY DISKETTE DRIVE

There are three levels of pursuing a diskette drive problem:

1. Merely obtain information about the present state of a drive using the computer and special software
2. Realign or otherwise repair a known defective drive using a computer to send commands to the drive and an analog alignment diskette
3. Analyze problems of a drive *and* correct them using specialized test equipment

Level 1, simply getting the status of a drive, can be done with a digital diagnostic diskette, as discussed previously. Load the special software called the interrogator and place the digital diagnostic diskette in the drive under test. Following the prompts of the program the condition of the drives can be very accurately ascertained. Records kept of these tests can provide warnings of deteriorating drive performance and possibly avert the loss of data in the future if corrective action is initiated in time. This program and the DDD are indicators and are not used for the actual alignment of a faulty drive.

Level 2 involves a computer, an analog alignment diskette (AAD), and some BASIC software to put a drive back into alignment. (Appendix B contains these BASIC programs.) These programs can be typed into a computer and kept as a permanent part of your troubleshooting software. Load and run MENU.BAS and follow the prompts. See below for the details of using the computer's drive B cables as a source of power and drive commands (Figure 11.17).

Level 3 is available to those fortunate enough to have access to a specialized diskette drive exerciser such as the one shown in Figure 11.18. An hour or so learning to use the performance and alignment tester will enable the technician to analyze, with the help of a DDD diskette, nearly any problem a diskette drive can develop. Using the AAD, this tester can be used to generate the drive commands necessary to realign a drive. See below for detailed explanations of the use of an instrument such as this and for details of the digital diagnostics diskette. Once a drive is put back into alignment, the exerciser should be used with the DDD diskette to verify that the drive is back to specifications.

Alignment Using a Computer, an Alignment Diskette, and a Scope

It will be necessary to apply power to the drive under alignment and supply the proper electronic commands to control the drive. An oscilloscope will be required to monitor the signals picked up by the read heads. A source for these power and command signals may be a computer. Remove or disconnect the computer's B drive. Bring out both the power cable and the command signal cable with cable extensions. The extensions shown in Figure 11.19 are required to work on the drive conveniently and to have access to either side of the drive while the drive is operating. The drive head will need to be positioned to specific test diskette tracks during the alignment procedures. To use a computer, the BASIC program of Appendix B can be used on most

Figure 11.17 As a minimum of equipment necessary to align a driver, the analog alignment diskette and an oscilloscope are required, plus a source for commands to the drive. The computer can be used with a simple BASIC program for these commands. (Abbey Enterprises)

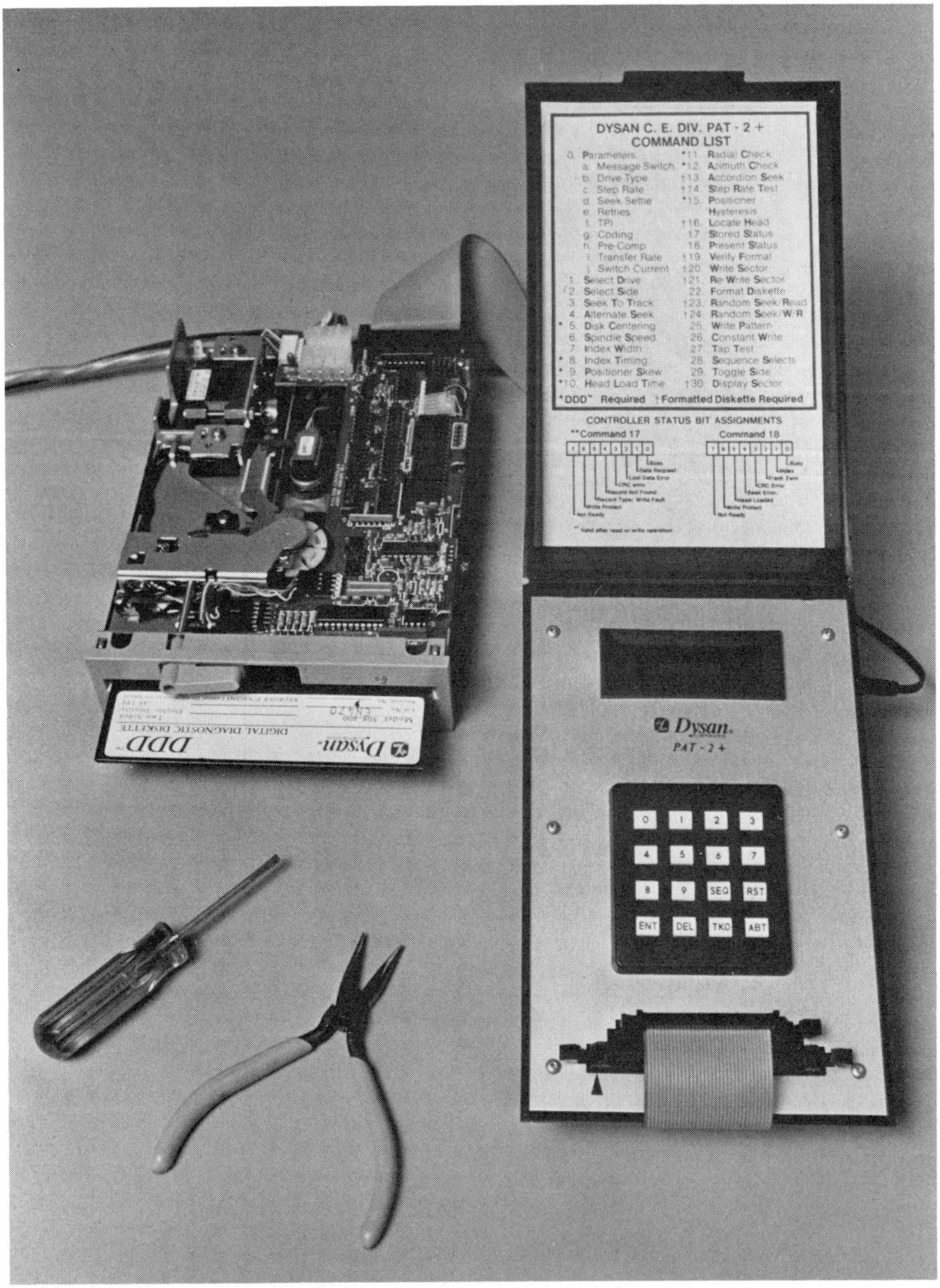

Figure 11.18 The combination of this exerciser and special diskettes for analysis and alignment are powerful troubleshooting tools for diskette drive problems. (Courtesy of the Dysan Corporation)

Figure 11.19 Extensions for the power and drive cables are necessary to use the computer's drive B for aligning a drive. (Abbey Enterprises)

microcomputers. It may be modified if necessary to run other computers. To use the program, load BASIC, all three programs, run MENU.BAS, and follow the prompts.

Note: Both of the special diskettes mentioned, the AAD and the DDD, are made by special recording instruments. They *cannot* be duplicated. The tracks are recorded by deliberately offsetting them by varying degrees well outside of the normal limits of the tracks. For this reason, they should *never* be placed in a drive that might have a writing problem because of the possible destruction of these precision tracks.

The alignment of a floppy diskette drive should progress in logical steps:

1. Radial check and possible realignment of head 0, the lower head
2. Azimuth check of head 0
3. Index-to-data check of head 0
4. Radial check of head 1, the upper head
5. Index-to-data check of head 1
6. Resolution check of both heads
7. Skew check of both heads
8. Check index pulse width
9. Check data stream output
10. Check write-protect circuitry

To accomplish these tests you must understand the principles involved in using the analog alignment diskette. Dysan's analog alignment diskette 224/2A is precisely recorded to test double-sided diskette drives and to put them back into alignment. Diskette 224A is used for single-sided drives.

The tracks of the double-sided AAD are recorded *on both sides* as follows:

Track	**Content**
00	125 KHz, full revolution
01	Index timing data burst
16	Radial alignment lobes
32	62.5 KHz full revolution
33	125 KHz full revolution
34	Index timing data burst and azimuth bursts
39	125 KHz full revolution

Summary of track use:
Radial alignment uses track 16.
Azimuth checks use track 34.
Index-to-data uses tracks 34 and 01
Resolution uses the comparison in amplitude read from tracks 32 and 33.
Skew uses tracks 1 and 34.

Be sure to use the index pulse to trigger the scope during tests.

The most common mechanical adjustment that will be made on a diskette drive is that of putting it back into radial alignment. The read/write heads must be positioned directly over the proper diskette location to read or write data properly. The heads are unable to tell if the data is directly under them or off to one side. The radial realignment process amounts to taking the reading head to what should be the midpoint of the radial alignment track, track 16. Small corrections are made mechanically to ensure that the head reads down the center of the track. This track is recorded with the spindle off center so that the read head will read a continuous signal first from the inside of the proper track and then from the outside. If the head is reading down the middle of the proper track, the wobble of the recorded data will produce a pattern as shown in Figure 11.20.

To realign the drive, begin by positioning the read head over track 16 of the analog alignment diskette. Attach an oscilloscope to read the data coming from the read head on side 0, the bottom head; details of where and how to attach the oscilloscope should be contained in the disk drive alignment maintenance manual. On

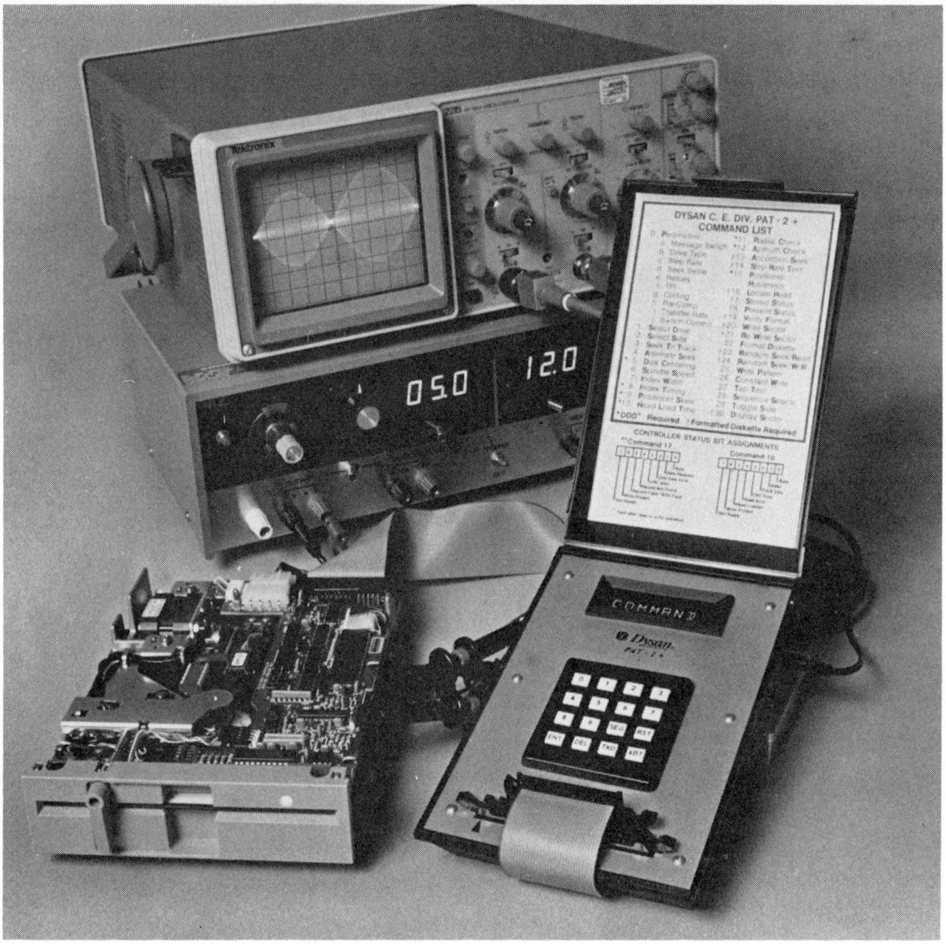

Figure 11.20 The cat's-eye pattern is used to align the reading head directly over the proper location for track 16. (Courtesy of the Dysan Corporation)

many diskette drives, these signals are available on test points labeled 1 or 2. The symmetrical pattern of Figure 11.20 indicates that the head is reading down. The schematic of a typical drive's electronic board may look similar to Figure 11.21.

If the check on track 16 shows patterns such as those in Figure 11.22, the drive is out of alignment. Adjustments that must be made to place a drive back into radial alignment vary with the manufacturer of the drive. Basically, the radial alignment adjustment moves the location of the head assembly with respect to the frame of the drive (see Figure 11.23).

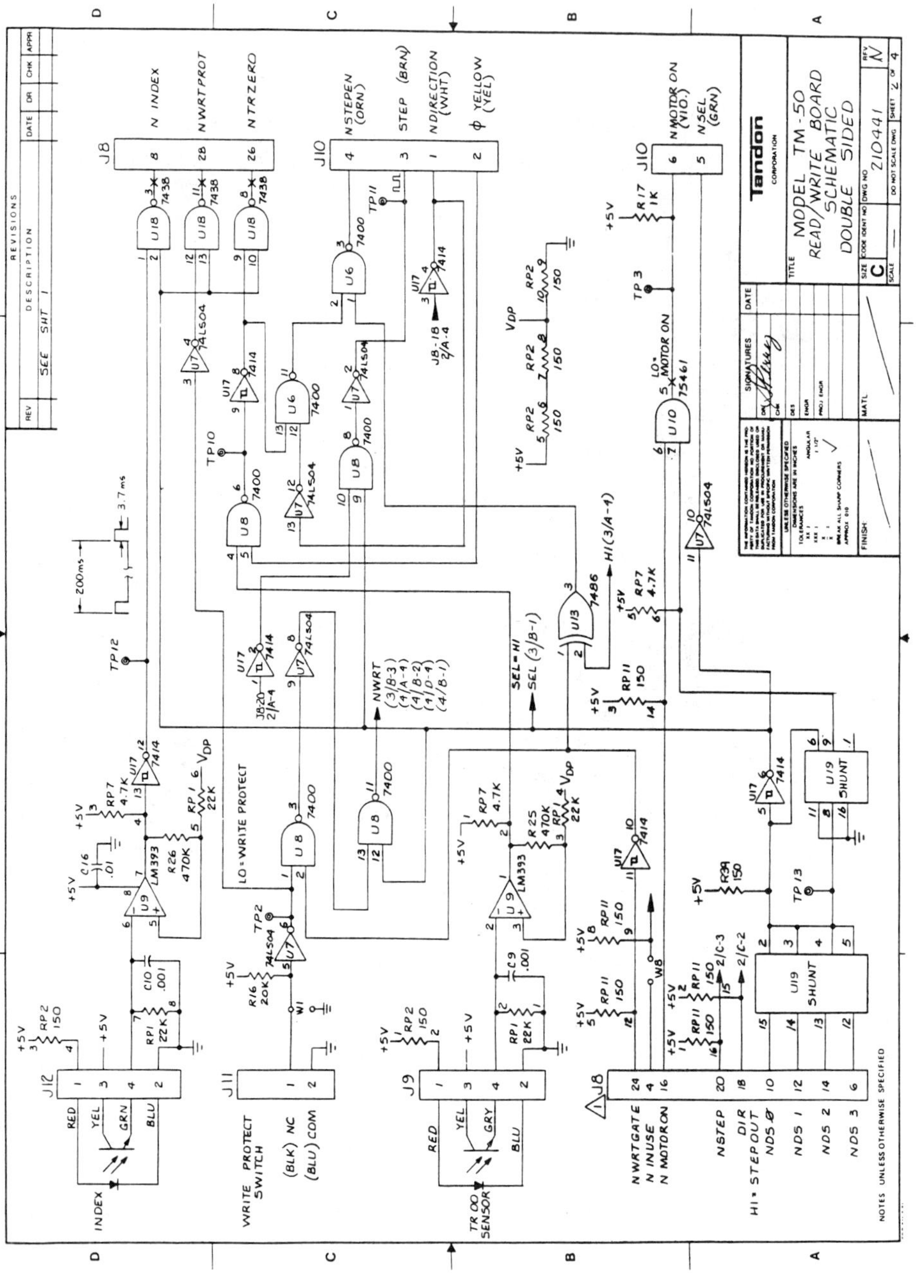

Figure 11.21A Typical schematic of diskette drive electronic board, indicating test points for analog signals, read data output, index pulse, trk 00 signal, write-protect, motor on gate. (Courtesy of the Tandon Corp.)

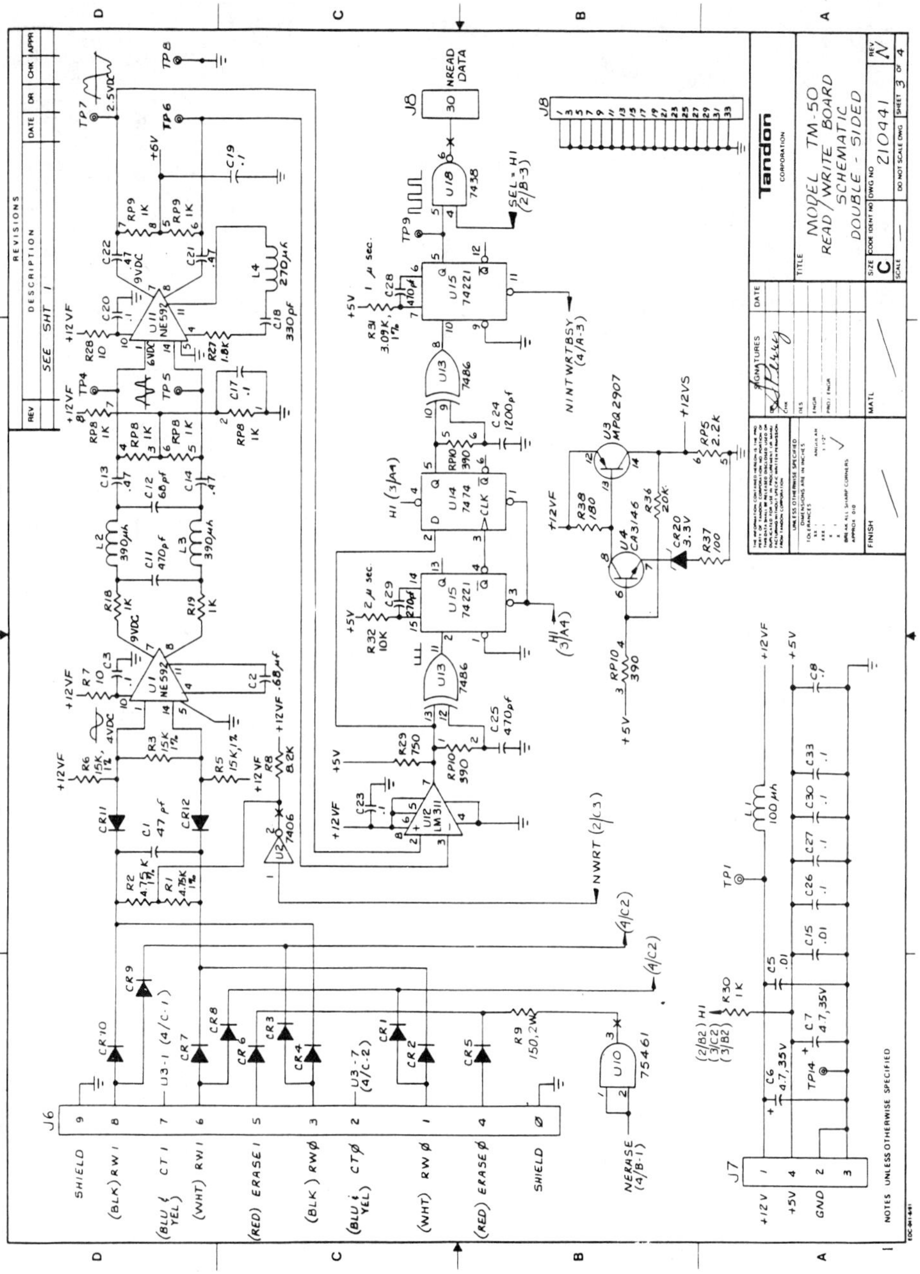

Figure 11.21B (Courtesy of the Tandon Corp.)

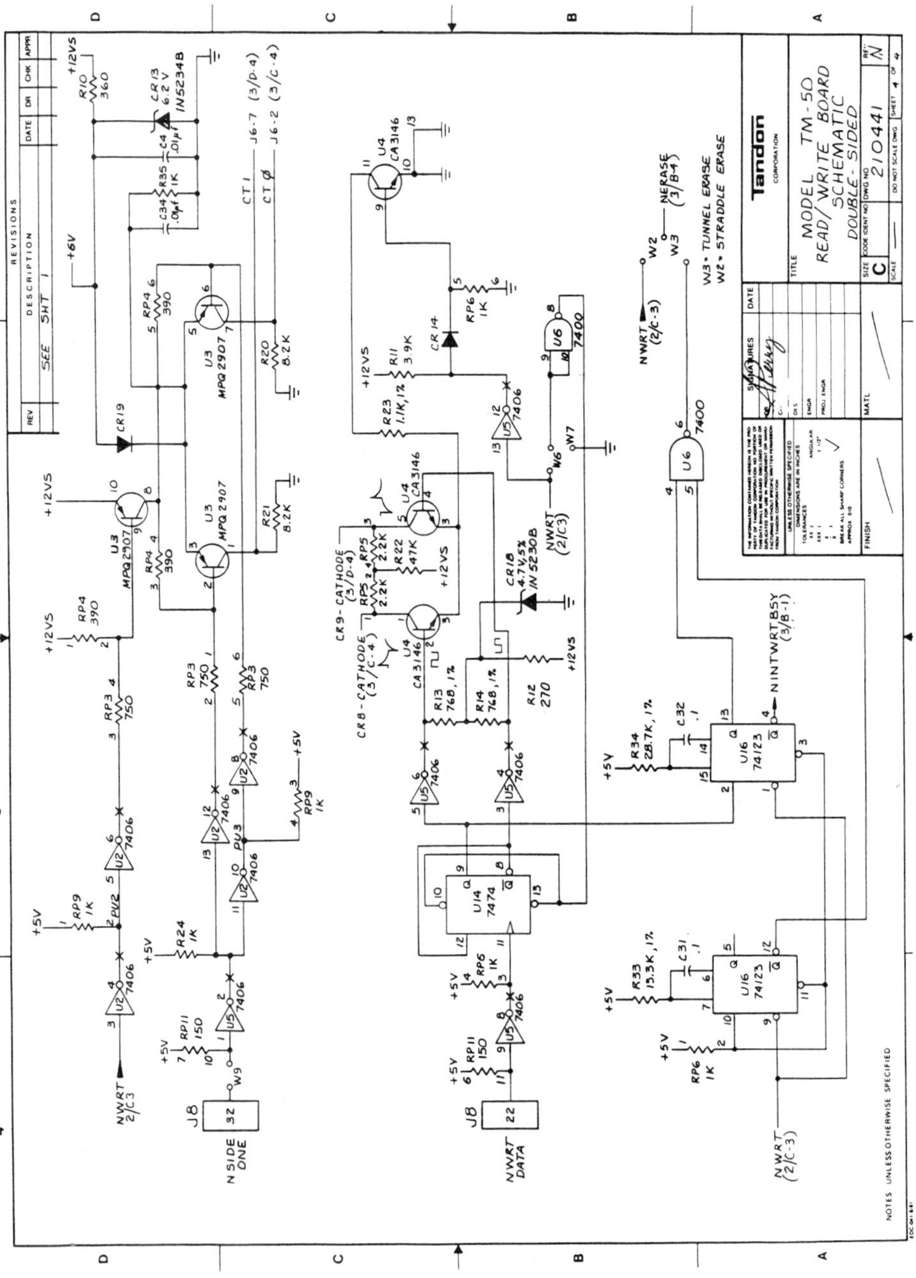

Figure 11.21C (Courtesy of the Tandon Corp.)

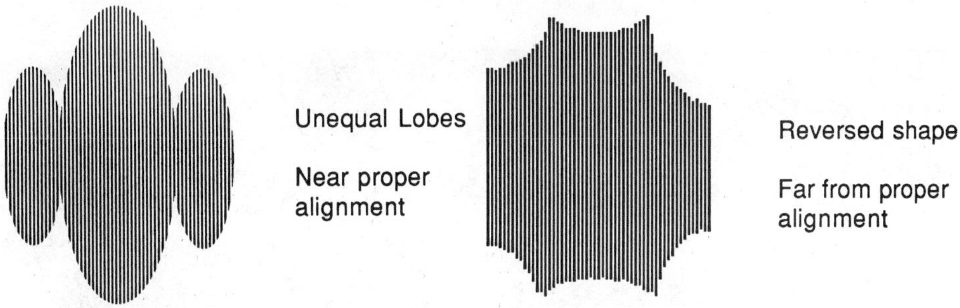

Figure 11.22 Unacceptable patterns produced by a drive out of radial alignment.

Figure 11.23 The location and method of putting the heads back into radial alignment will vary with the manufacturer of the drive. (Abbey Enterprises)

Figure 11.24 Some drives need to have the stepper motor clamp retightened after alignment. (Abbey Enterprises)

Once the heads are back in alignment the locking screws should be tightened to lock the heads in the proper adjustment position. It is a good idea to put a spot of fingernail polish on these screws to help prevent their loosening again. Some diskette drives depend upon a small clamp and friction to hold them in alignment. These drives can be helped considerably in maintaining their radial accuracy if this coupling is checked for tightness before the drive is realigned. See Figure 11.24.

After the bottom head is in alignment, there is not much that the technician can do to further align the drive. Many checks can be made, however, to ensure that the drive is meeting proper specifications.

The azimuth of a read/write head is a critical item. Good azimuth of a head means that the data from the media is moving at exactly right angles to the microscopic gap of the head. See Figure 11.7 for a sketch explaining azimuth alignment. The analog alignment diskette provides a track that tests the azimuth of a head. If the head is within specifications, the pattern observed will be as shown in Figure 11.25. The oscilloscope is attached to the same test point as in the radial checks above. This test may be made, but out-of-specification drives must be taken out of service. The lower head is set into epoxy or is otherwise not adjustable in azimuth.

For the following tests the oscilloscope should be set for triggered operation (not "auto") and triggered from the drive's index pulse. This is often brought out to a convenient test point, sometimes marked TP7. The width of this pulse is one of the times to check; it will usually be about 4000 microseconds. This is not a critical timing waveform and may be acceptable, depending upon the drive specifications, anywhere from 2000 to 5000 microseconds. No adjustment is provided for this reading.

The next test is that of the index-to-data timing of the lower head. Move the read head over track 34 on the AAD. With the oscilloscope triggered by the index timing pulse and using a fast sweep, look for the data pulse shown in Figure 11.26. Measure the elapsed time from the beginning of the sweep to the beginning of the data pulse. This is the index-to-data timing. This timing specification is typically 200 microseconds, with actual readings of 100 to 300 generally acceptable. Drives not meeting this specification should be adjusted, which is done by varying the position of the index pulse detector. The index pulse detector may be adjustable in a manner similar to that shown in Figure 11.27. The same test should then be made using track 01 of the AAD. It may be necessary to switch between the tracks 34 and 01 and to make a compromise adjustment of the index pulse detector to make both tracks within the 100-to-300 microsecond range.

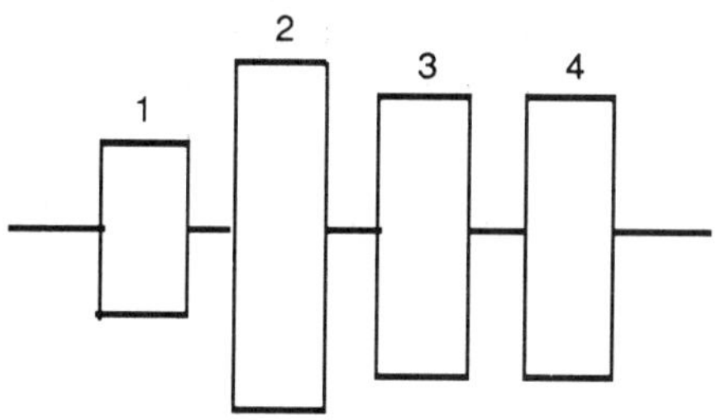

Figure 11.25 These patterns check for proper head azimuth and are found on track 34 of the Dysan analog alignment diskette.

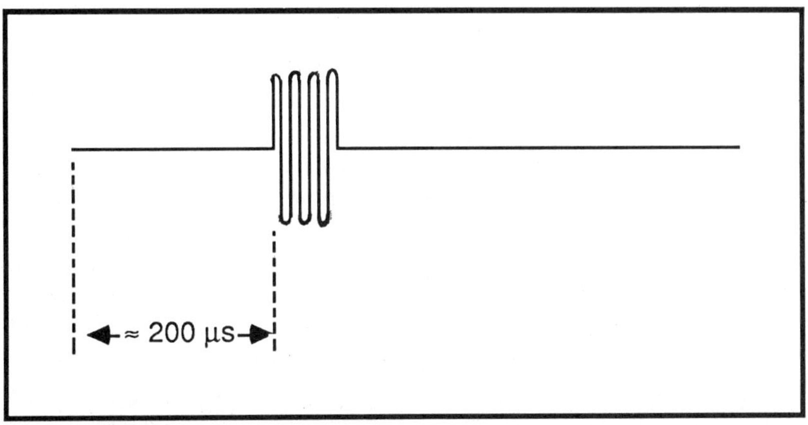

Figure 11.26 The data pulse as seen on the oscilloscope. Measure the time from the beginning of the trace (the falling edge of the index pulse) to the data pulse.

Figure 11.27 Changing the adjustment of the index pulse detector changes the timing between the index pulse and the beginning of data. (Abbey Enterprises)

The next test to make is a check of the radial alignment of the upper head. Switch to the upper head with the appropriate command and make the same radial alignment checks as covered above. If the radial alignment of the top head is not acceptable, consider setting the drive aside and installing a new drive. Attempting to adjust the top head is a very time-consuming job. Although it can be done, realignment of a top head is extremely difficult. Simple radial alignment is not the only issue; the head must simultaneously satisfy the critical requirements of radial, azimuth, and index-to-data alignment. Add to this possible head damage resulting from manual pushing and pulling back and forth a great many times, only to have it break something in the process, and the futility of this attempt becomes obvious. If the upper head passes the radial alignment test, check the azimuth and index-to-data checks as explained above.

A test should then be made of the amount of skew the drive might have. A skew check is made by noting the index-to-data timing of the lower head while using track 34 and then taking the same reading on track 01 and finding the difference between them. For instance, if the index-to-data reading on track 34 was 150 microseconds and on track 01 it was 200, the amount of skew would be 50 microseconds, the difference between the two readings.

The resolution test can now be made. This test gives a rough indication of the high-frequency capability of the heads. Monitor the analog output of both heads (one at a time) while switching from track 32 to track 33. The track 33 higher-frequency 125 KHz signal should be almost as high in amplitude as the track 32 62.5 KHz signals.

While the oscilloscope is available, the digital output data stream can also be checked. This is often marked as test point 5. Put a good data diskette in the drive and move the read head over several of the tracks. A good data output stream should be seen.

Also check the write-protect circuitry to ensure that if a write-protected diskette is inserted no data can be written upon it. This test is simple. Using a scratch diskette, cover the write-protect notch with an opaque tape made for the purpose and monitor the write-protect circuitry for a change when the diskette is inserted into the drive. This test point is sometimes marked TP9. The state of the voltage at this test point should be different if a diskette without the tape is then installed.

Some problems in diskette drives involve the track 00 detection circuits. These circuits can be tested by driving the head with an appropriate command to track 00. At the same time watch the signal at what is often marked TP8, the track 00 signal. This signal is used to verify to the diskette controller chip that the read/write head has actually reached track 0, or home position. If this circuitry is not working properly the heads may attempt to go beyond the stops at either end of travel. A typical malfunction of this circuit may result in the head stepper motor rattling as it tries to continue stepping after reaching the end of travel. At the other extreme, it may never be able to get to track 00, falling short by several (often four) tracks. Adjustment of the track 00 detector varies with the drive manufacturer and model. Again, refer to the appropriate maintenance manual for specifics.

Alignment Using a Drive Exerciser Such as the PAT – 2 +

The Dysan performance and alignment tester takes the place of the computer and the BASIC program as used in the preceding paragraphs. The tester generates the appropriate commands for the diskette drive under test. This instrument was designed not only to provide the proper commands for aligning a drive but, in conjunction with the digital diagnostic diskette (DDD), to read and analyze drive performance to a great depth. Using this instrument and an analog alignment diskette, the only other equipment needed for 5 1/4-inch diskette drive alignment is an oscilloscope and a power supply capable of 5VDC at 500MA and 12VDC at about 1.5 amperes (see Figure 11.28).

When the PAT2 + is first turned on it goes through a memory check and signifies successful conclusion of the test with a MEM OK message flashed on the LED readout. This is followed by a short identification message that can be aborted by touching the CMD key. The tester responds with a command query, awaiting your selection of the test to be made. The test assumes certain default values that will apply to most drives. By entering a 0 command and pressing ENT, the default values are shown, stepping through them one by one with the ENT key. These defaults may be changed if necessary to operate different drives.

Although this instrument makes many tests possible, routine alignment of a drive uses only a few of them. Among the most used are the commands listed below and their meaning:

1. SELECT DRIVE. Must be set up to match the drive number of the drive under test. Usually 1 or 2, corresponding to drive A or B. Some microcomputers such

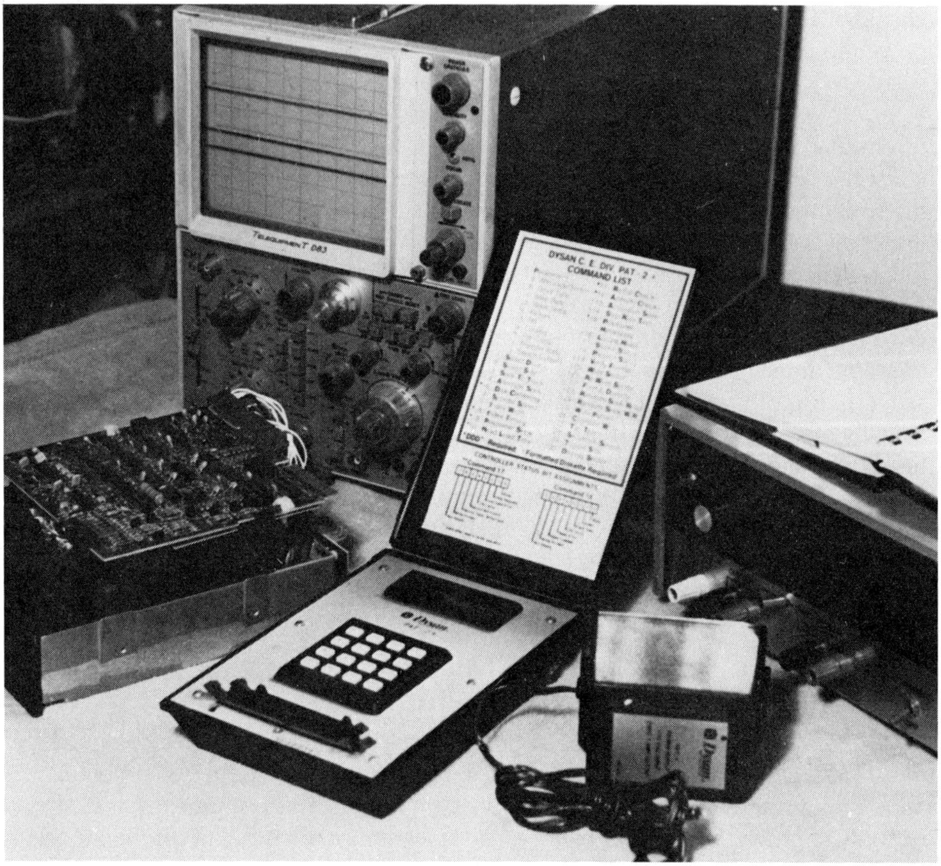

Figure 11.28 Equipment needed for drive alignment when a computer is not used. (Abbey Enterprises)

as the IBM use a designation of drive 1 for both drives, the actual selection being the result of twisting part of the control cable on drive B.

2. HEAD SELECT. Select 0 for the bottom and 1 for the upper head. Most tests begin with head 0.
3. SELECT TO TRACK. Select the track you wish the head to move to—track 16 for radial alignment or checks, for instance.

With these three commands it is possible to run all of the alignment checks using the oscilloscope presentations shown earlier in this chapter.

The real use of the PAT2+ is with the DDD diskette. After an alignment is done, the DDD should be inserted into the drive and tests run with the PAT2+. The documentation provided with the tester details the many tests that can then be made and the results you should obtain. There are some small differences in the labeling of the tracks on the digital diagnostics diskette diskette compared to those on the analog alignment diskette. The documentation provided with the 508-400 DDD refers to the radial alignment tracks as progressive offset tracks where the analog diskette calls them radial alignment lobes. Tests for skew use tracks 0 and 34, called index format tracks by the DDD while the analog diskette refers to similar tracks as index timing tracks. These differences between track names may not be immediately evident from reading the accompanying information.

INSTALLING A NEW DISKETTE DRIVE

When installing a new diskette drive there are two items to which the technician should pay particular attention. These are the presence or absence of the *terminating resistor* and the selection of the proper *option jumpers*.

The terminating resistor is usually a DIP resistor pack, installed only on the last of a string of two or more floppy drives. Its purpose is to provide a proper terminating resistance for each of the signals of the signal interconnecting cable. This resistor prevents reflections of the signals and data errors that could result from them. (See Figure 11.29). Some drives use a terminating resistor pack with individual resistors inside while others use a resistor pack with a single common connection for all the resistors. For this reason be sure that the resistor pack used is the proper one for the drive, and be sure that the pack is oriented properly when installed in the socket.

Diskette drives may also come with one socket as a programming socket for some of the options that may be built into the drive (Figure 11.30).

For many microcomputers only the third position from the rear or from the side of the diskette drive need be jumpered (shorted). All other positions should be open-circuited.

Figure 11.29 Only the last of a string of drives supplied by a single cable has a terminating resistor. (Abbey Enterprises)

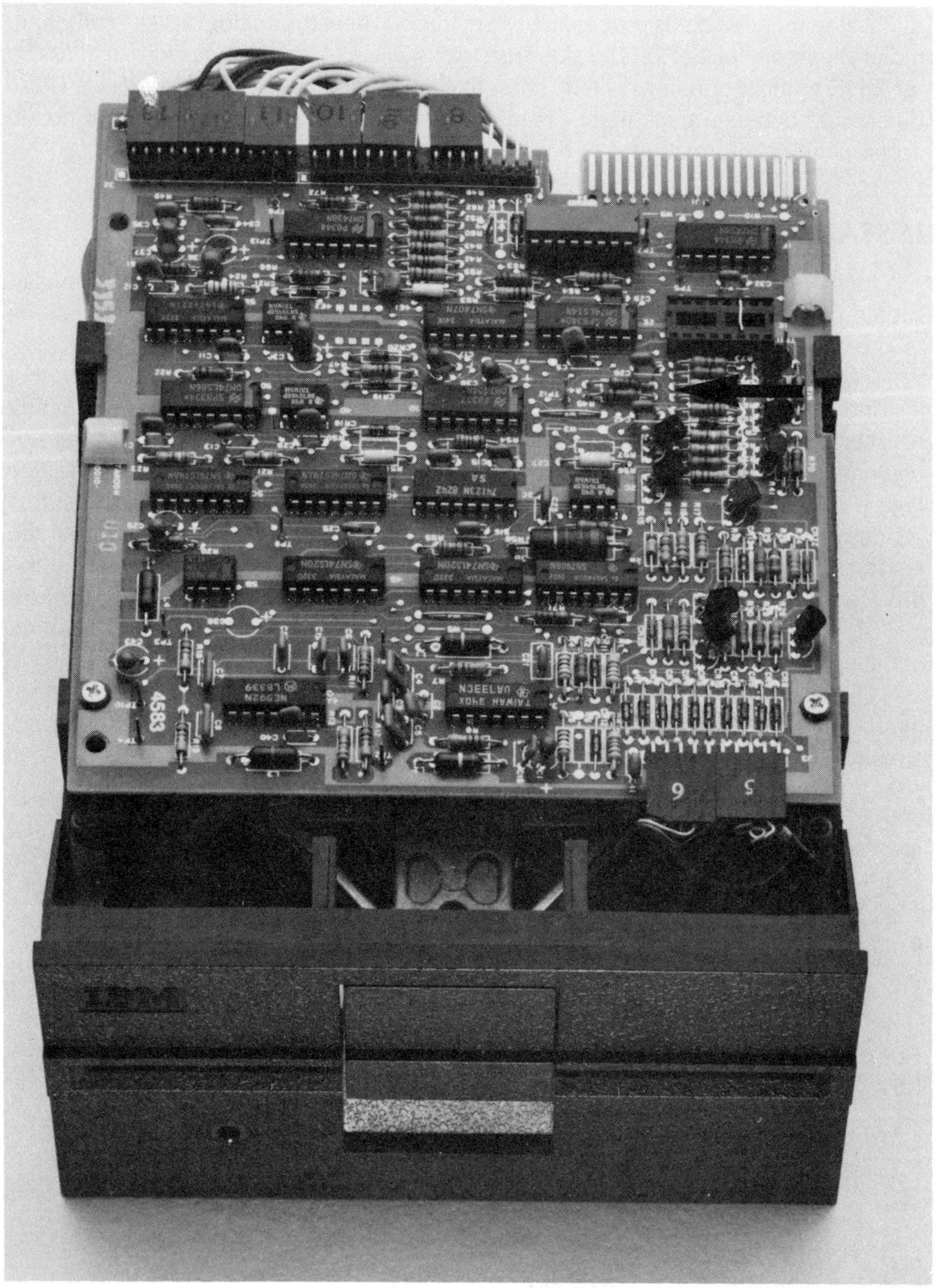

Figure 11.30 Most 5 1/4 drives come with a possibility of several options that have been built into the drive to make them compatible with different computers. (Courtesy of IBM)

CHAPTER SUMMARY

This chapter has introduced you to the details of analyzing both electronic and mechanical diskette drive problems and correcting them. These tests and alignment procedures should enable you to correct the majority of diskette drive problems, simple mechanical misadjustments. Once the principles are understood a technician can move on to the repair of 8-inch diskette drives using the necessary alignment diskettes required for larger drives. The principles of radial alignment and other tests apply equally well to other sizes of floppy diskette drives.

REVIEW QUESTIONS

1. If the diagnostic program for a diskette drive reports a reading of 2003 on a speed check, what is the time required for the diskette to turn one revolution?
2. What is an average duration for the index pulse?
3. Where is track 0 of a diskette located on the diskette?
4. How many tracks does a 5 1/4-inch diskette have on one side?
5. What is the designation for the first track of a diskette?
6. Which of the read/write heads, the top or the bottom, is called the 0 head?
7. Skew is a measure of how far the read/write heads depart from a true ______ line to the center of the diskette.
8. Is it possible for a software routine to overcome the write-protect tab on a diskette and write onto a protected diskette?
9. What is the purpose of a digital diagnostic diskette?
10. What is the purpose of an alignment diskette?
11. What is used to trigger the oscilloscope during alignment tests?
12. What is the cat's-eye pattern used for?
13. What does the radial alignment adjustment do to adjust the placement of the read/write heads? In other words, what relationship is changed to accomplish the realignment?
14. What adjustment is made to change the timing between the index pulse and the beginning of data?
15. What two items must be checked during the installation of a new diskette drive?

chapter twelve

Repairing Computer Monitors

CHAPTER OVERVIEW

Since computer monitors involve high voltages and circuits that use non-sinusoidal voltages, special troubleshooting techniques are necessary so that the servicing technician will have no trouble doing routine shop maintenance on them. Troubleshooting monitor circuits is quite different from troubleshooting digital circuits because of effects such as rectification, magnetic field collapse, and time constants. This chapter presents those points in some detail to prepare you for servicing these special circuits.

A MONITOR OVERVIEW

The monitor displays the data contained in the video memory. This information may be ASCII characters or graphics symbols in the case of a monochrome text monitor or, in the case of a color graphics monitor, colored bit patterns generated by special software. Either kind of monitor displays information as a series of tiny dots on the screen. Note, however, that the video processing takes place not only in the monitor, but in a special option card provided for that specific purpose.

Monitor problems can be caused by either the monitor or the video adapter card. Since the monitor is usually connected to the computer with a cable that is relatively easy to disconnect, it is easy to substitute a good monitor to localize the problem to the monitor or the video card. After checking the obvious problems of power switches left off and brightness and contrast controls turned down, this is the next test that the technician should make to be certain of where the problem lies. If the problem is still evident after replacing the monitor, the adapter card is probably defective. Replacing the card will verify this. Two different kinds of video cards are used: monochrome (black-and-white) and color (Figure 12.1).

The Block Diagram of a Video Adapter Card

The Monochrome Video Adapter Card. A monochrome video adapter card's function is to take the binary data in RAM memory and to convert that data to characters and

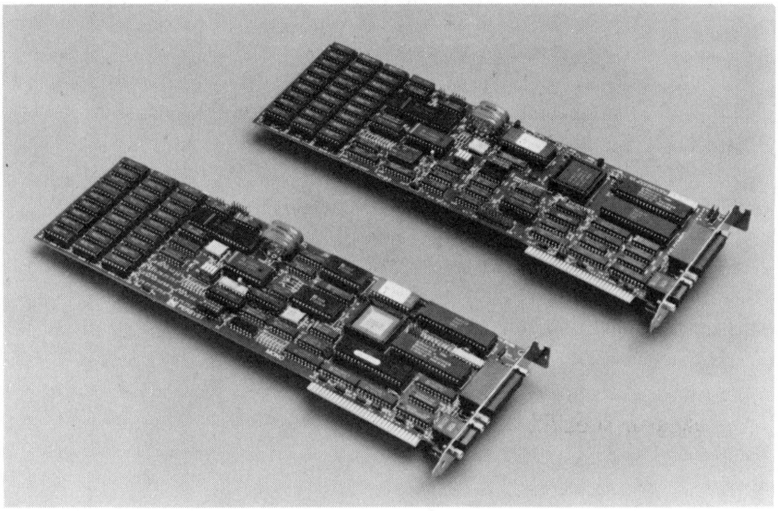

Figure 12.1 Examples of monochrome and color video adapter cards. Note the slightly more complex color card as compared to the monochrome. (Courtesy of the Emulex Corp.)

symbols in a dot-matrix format. The output circuits of this card provide these necessary signals:

Synchronization of the CRT horizontal and vertical sweeps

Video on/off data for the CRT screen

Intensity information (full intensity or half intensity)

Two methods may be used for passing this information to the monitor. The first is to provide separate lines for each of these signals. The most common method of passing these signals is to use a small 9-pin D connector, similar in appearance to but smaller than the 25-pin D connector used with the serial output port of the computer (see Figure 12.2).

The second method of passing information to the monitor is by using a single coaxial cable. The signal is called a composite signal. This method uses what is commonly called an RCA jack and a small coaxial cable (Figure 12.3.) This signal is an analog signal that contains the synchronizing signals, intensity signal, and the video information all in one signal. See Figure 12.4 for a graphic representation.

The Color Graphics Adapter Card. The function of the color graphics card is similar to that of the monochrome card—to take the binary data from RAM and convert that data to the appropriate dot patterns for the

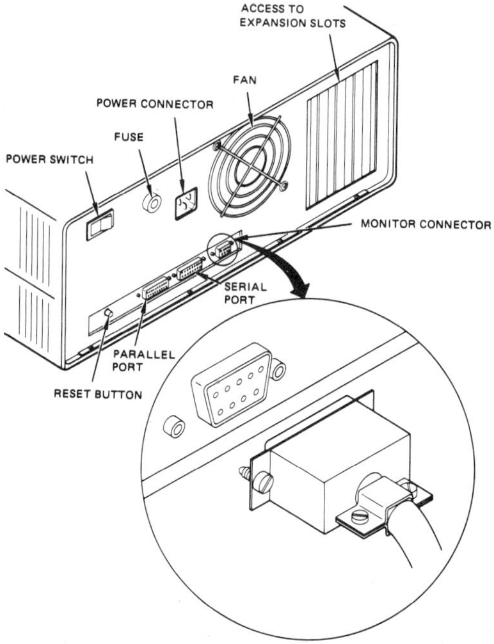

Figure 12.2 This connector is commonly used for connecting a monochrome or color monitor to a microcomputer. (Courtesy of Corona Data Systems, Inc.)

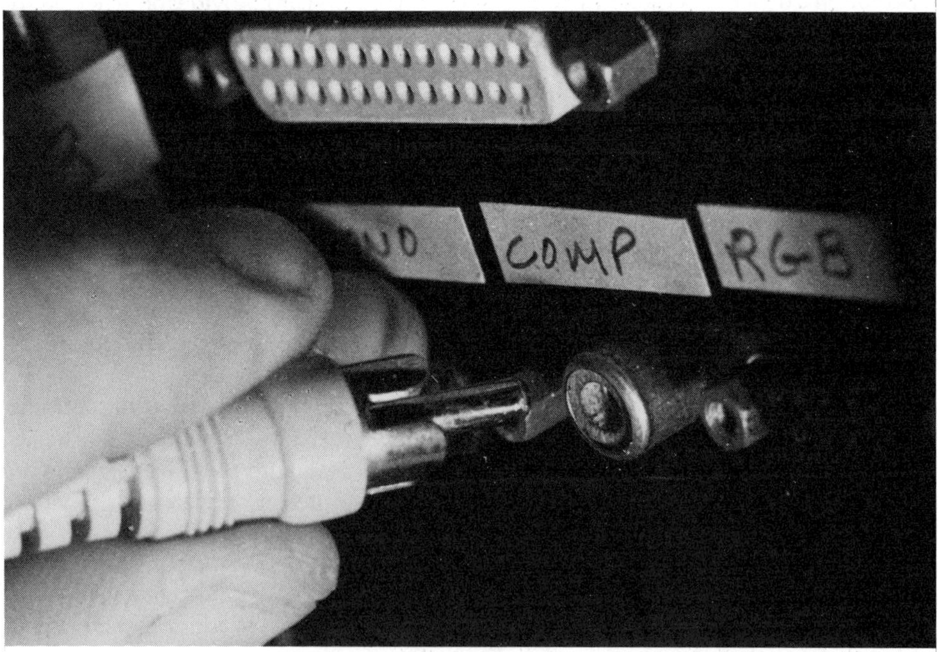

Figure 12.3 The use of the RCA jack enables the monitor to get all the necessary signals through a small coaxial cable.

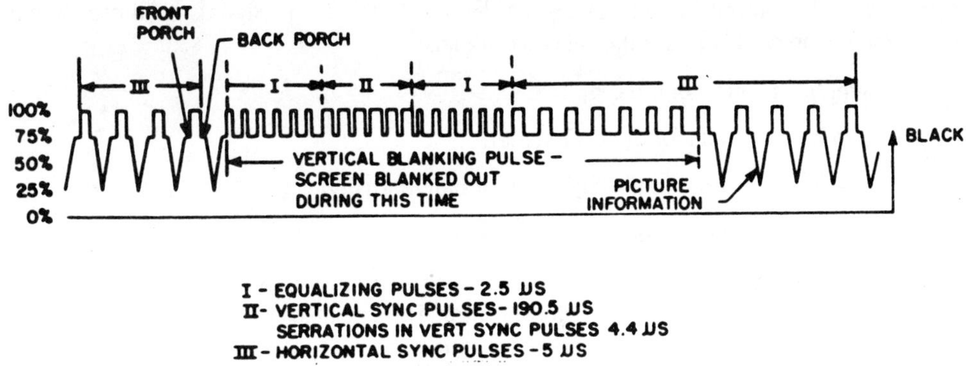

Figure 12.4 The composite video signal contains all the signals needed by the monitor.

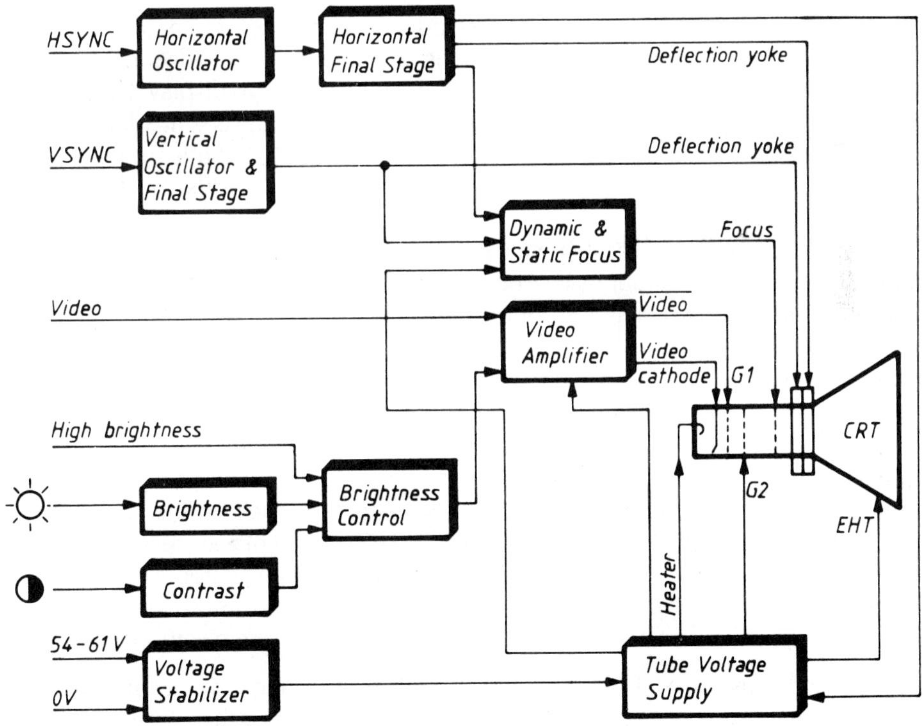

Figure 12.5 Block diagram of a monochrome video adapter card (Courtesy of Ericsson Information Systems)

monitor. The output circuits of the card provide the same signals as those of the monochrome card with additional color signals:

Synchronization of the CRT sweep

Video on/off data for the CRT screen

Intensity information (full intensity or half intensity)

Three color signals: red, green and blue

The same two signal transmission methods as used for monochrome may also be used to pass video information to the color monitor. The first is to provide separate lines for each of these signals. One method of passing these signals is to use the 9-pin D connector. See Appendix B for the pinout of this plug. Using this connector for a color monitor identifies it as an RGB, (red-green-blue,) monitor, since each of these primary colors is passed individually to the monitor. The second method of passing information to the color monitor is by using a composite signal similar to that used in the monochrome signal. This is also an analog signal, but the color information is also multiplexed on the video signal and separated within the monitor.

The CRTC. The heart of the video adapter card is the complex CRT controller (CRTC). This large-scale integrated circuit converts the character bytes in video RAM into the proper video, brightness, and sweep timing signals necessary to display those characters on the screen of the monitor. Microcomputers set aside a specific block of RAM memory for video information. This usually starts at B0000H and is 4K bytes wide. Color and graphics memory begins at B8000H and is 16K bytes wide. The CRTC reads the character information from RAM. This is converted into the proper dot patterns by the internal character generator if characters are being displayed and passed to the monitor on the video output lead. At the same time, the CRTC generates the proper drive-synchronization signals and controls the brightness of the CRT electron beam.

Internal Analysis of Monitors

Block Diagrams. Figures 12.5, 12.6, and 12.7 show block diagrams of the several monitors and their methods of providing the monitor circuitry with the proper signals from the computer's video adapter card. Note that in each of the monitors the horizontal signal is also used to generate the very high voltage necessary for the operation of the cathode ray tube. Many monitors combine electronic functions into large-scale integrated circuits rather than deal with numerous discrete components. Only the high-voltage and high-power stages of some are discrete components.

The Cathode Ray Tube. The CRT cathode produces the electrons that are eventually splashed onto the front screen, where they produce light. The electrons exit the cathode area through a hole in the cylindrical CRT grid (Figure 12.8). Video monitors usually operate the cathodes near ground potential since the input to these CRTs

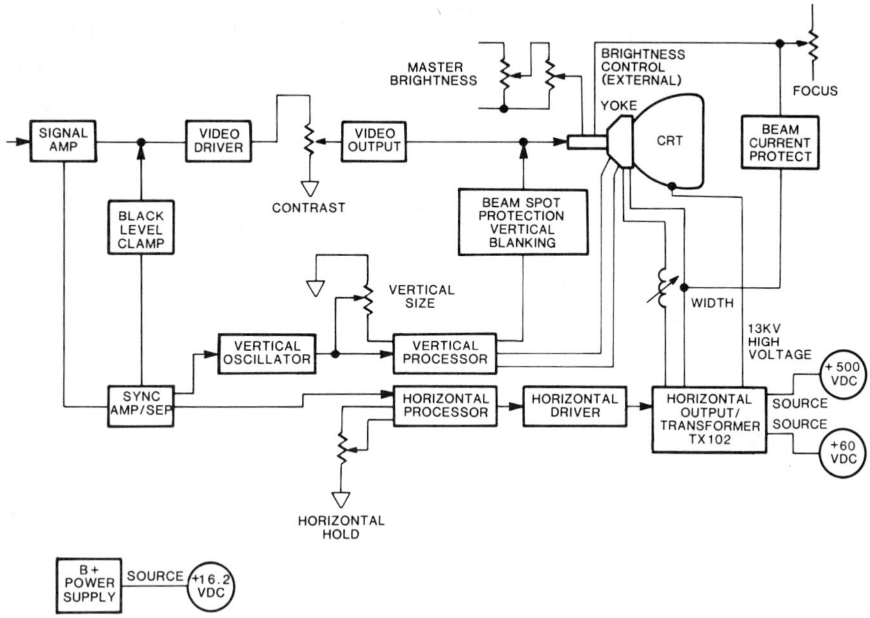

Figure 12.6 Block diagram of a composite video monitor (Courtesy of Zenith)

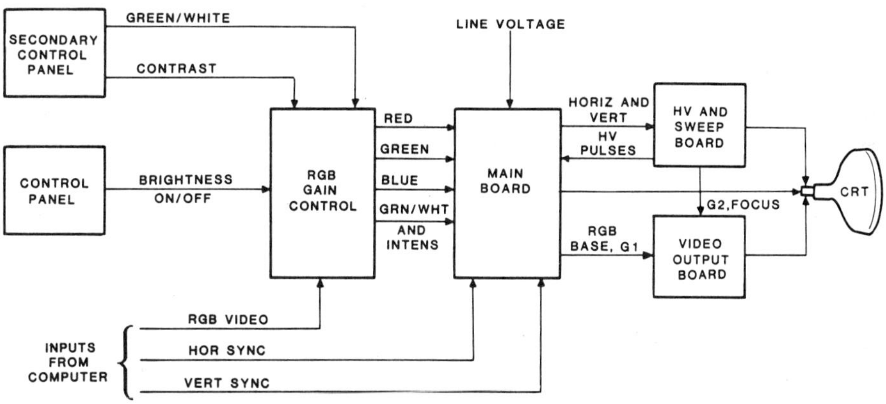

Figure 12.7 Block diagram of RGB color monitor. Note use of several incoming lines. (Courtesy of Zenith)

involves putting the video signal into the grid or cathode circuit to turn the CRT beam on and off. The accelerating anodes are operated at very high positive voltages with respect to ground.

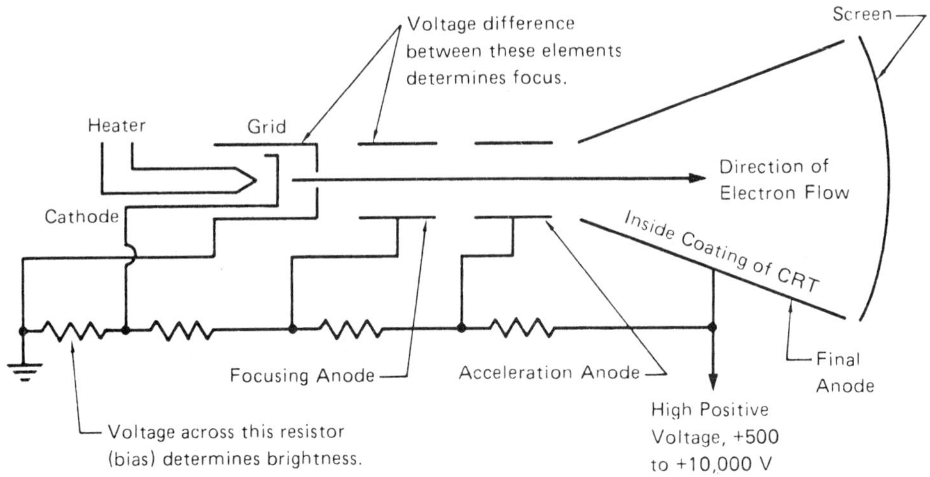

Figure 12.8 Internal structure of the cathode ray tube

Normal CRT voltages require that the tube-element voltages increase in positive steps from the cathode to the screen with the exception of the grid—which is held at a negative voltage with respect to the cathode. This negative voltage is made adjustable to control the intensity of the spot on the screen through a brightness control.

The voltage difference between the focusing and the accelerating elements determines the focus of the spot. Troubleshooting focusing problems begins with measuring these two voltages. CRT circuits may have regulators on several voltage sources to hold critical ones constant. Failures of these regulator circuits can cause brightness fluctuations and focusing instability of the spot. The higher the final accelerating voltage, the brighter the spot. If the spot on a CRT is dim and unfocused, the high-voltage supply should immediately be suspected as being too low. This may also be confirmed by the fact that the CRT shows images too large. Below-normal final accelerating voltage makes the image larger because the electron beam is moving more slowly and is more easily deflected.

Be careful when measuring the voltages associated with these tubes. Read the following information carefully before proceeding with any voltage measurement: high voltages may be present where they are not expected. Cathode ray tubes require the use of voltages much higher than those used with semiconductors. Familiarity with the following safety rules will help avoid a shock hazard.

1. When using a voltmeter on high voltages be sure to attach the ground lead to the chassis or common point before checking voltages. Failure to do this first may produce a hot negative lead that can be dangerous if touched.
2. When measuring voltages up to perhaps 200V, remove any metal jewelry and keep your left hand (assuming you are right-handed) in your back pocket. This helps avoid the possibility of accidental current flow through the chest.

3. In addition to the rules above, when measuring voltages higher than about 200V, other precautions become prudent. Turn off the equipment, discharge the filter capacitors, attach the meter, then turn on the power and take the reading. Do not touch the meter or the leads until the power is again turned off and the capacitors are discharged.
4. Electrical-insulating rubber matting on the floor in front of the bench to stand on is also advisable.

TYPICAL MONITOR PROBLEMS AND SYMPTOMS

High-Voltage Loss Problems

The horizontal oscillator and amplifier circuits eventually provide the horizontal sweep current for the horizontal deflection yoke and also provide a very high DC voltage for the CRT (see Figure 12.9). When measuring the high-voltage DC produced by this circuit, a special very-high-voltage probe must be used. Since this circuit can produce in excess of 25,000 volts, a standard meter will be damaged if not provided

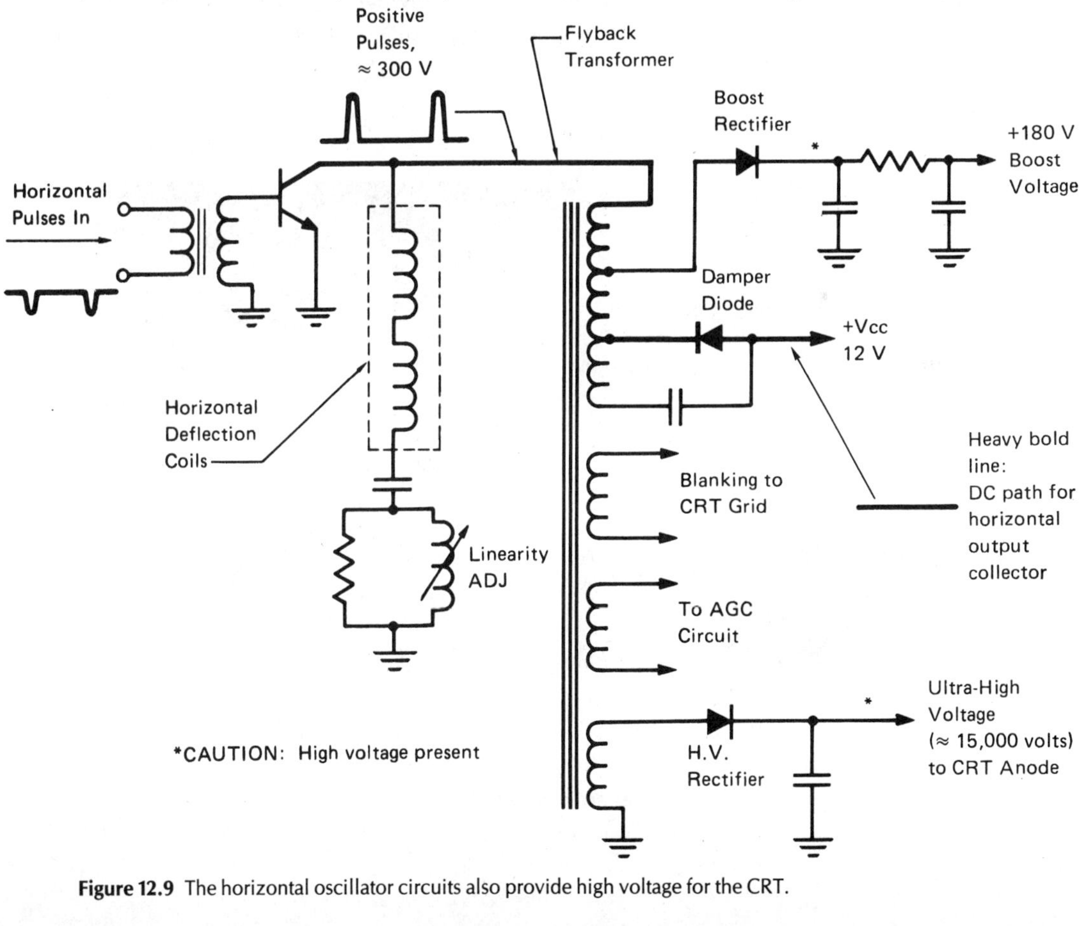

Figure 12.9 The horizontal oscillator circuits also provide high voltage for the CRT.

with additional multiplier resistance. Figure 12.10 shows a probe designed specifically for measuring these ultra-high voltages.

Synchronization Problems

Synchronization problems produce picture flipping and tearing. Some of these problems can be cured with a simple adjustment, but the monitor may require disassembly and further troubleshooting to get it working properly again. Adjustment of the horizontal hold or horizontal oscillator adjustment will often cure horizontal tearing or jitter. This situation occurs when the monitor ages and component values drift enough to cause the oscillator to drop out of synchronism. Whenever an adjustment is made to stabilize either the horizontal oscillator or the vertical oscillator, the adjustment should be left in the middle of the range, where normal locking occurs.

Because of the dependence upon the horizontal oscillator to produce the high voltage for the CRT, lack of horizontal oscillations will cause the screen to be blank. Simple lack of synchronizing pulses will not, however, prevent the horizontal oscillator from still functioning, producing the high voltage. In other words, the screen should have a raster with or without a horizontal synchronizing pulse from the computer.

Figure 12.10 A high-voltage probe is necessary to measure the CRT high voltages.

The controls that should be familiar to the technician include the vertical hold, height, and the vertical linearity adjustments. These three all interact to some extent. When the characters at the top of the monitor are taller than those at the bottom, the vertical linearity should be adjusted until they are the same height. Adjust the height control until the characters are just inside the top and bottom of the screen. Seldom will these technical adjustments be out where the usual operator of the monitor can adjust them. They are usually placed inside the monitor, out of the reach of tinkering fingers. The only two controls routinely accessible to the operator are the contrast and brightness controls.

VIDEO PROBLEMS

Common Problems That can Occur in Monochrome or Color Monitors

If either the left or right edge of the monitor is apparently obscuring a character or two, the mode command can be used to correct the problem. The same situation may also be handled through a BASIC statement. More severe cases of off-centering (see Figure 12.11) will require the technician to adjust the centering magnets on the rear of the CRT (Figure 12.12). If the entire picture is tilted, the deflection yoke clamp must be loosened and the yoke assembly rotated until the picture is again straight. (Figure 12.13). The yoke clamp should then be snugged down but *not* clamped tightly. The neck of a CRT is fragile and can be easily broken.

Unique Color Monitor Problems

Before assuming that a color problem is in the monitor, be sure to substitute either the monitor or the color video adapter card. Color and synchronization problems can be located in either. Color video problems can get a bit more complicated than monochrome. Each of three electron guns in the CRT must be adjusted to work together for the screen to produce the sharpness and purity of color that the CRT is capable of producing.

Adjustment of the color guns and the convergence adjustments is beyond the scope of this book. If there is sufficient need for this information, a good text on color TV repair will detail the steps and additional test equipment required to perform these adjustments to bring the monitor back into alignment. If such adjustment is to be attempted, the monitor manufacturer's service documentation must be obtained and followed very closely.

PICTURE TILTED

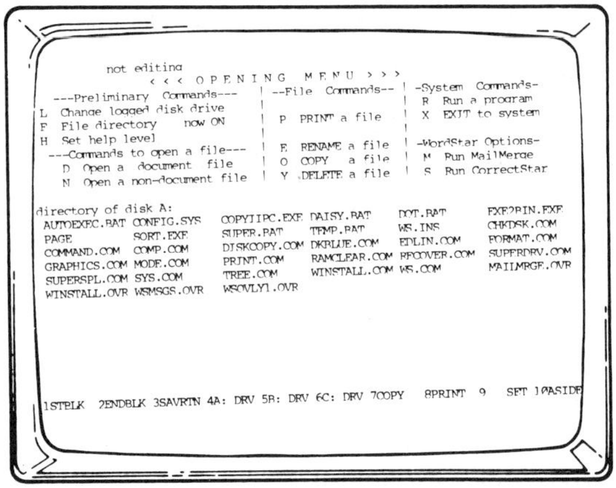

PICTURE TOO FAR LEFT

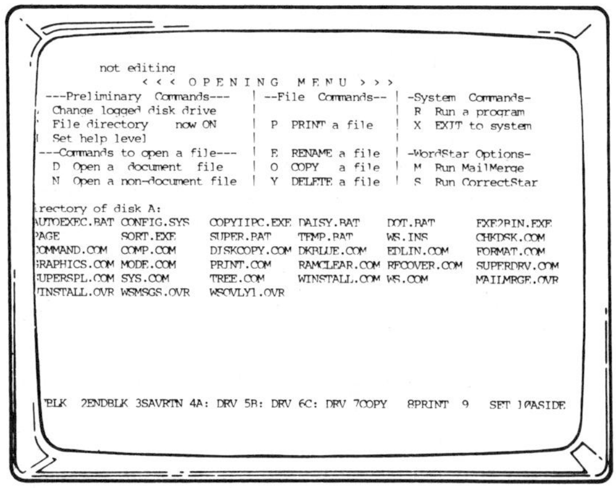

PICTURE TOO HIGH

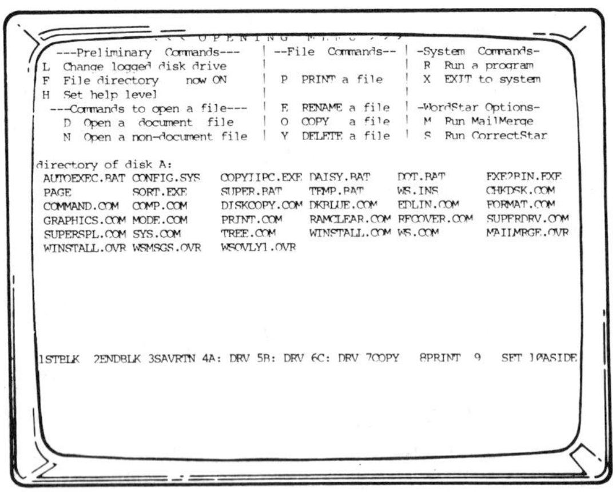

Figure 12.11 Horizontal oscillator and synchronization problems

Figure 12.12 The centering magnets are two rings, each with an adjusting tab. Their relationship to each other and as a unit determine the centering of the raster. (Abbey Enterprises)

Figure 12.13 Turning the yoke after loosening the clamp allows the picture to be adjusted straight on the screen. (Abbey Enterprises)

Troubleshooting TV Monitors Used with RF Modulators

One of the alternatives to buying a color monitor for computer use is to adapt a standard color television to computer use. This is usually done in the interest of reducing the computer system investment. Although this approach can be used, the quality of the video shown on a TV is inferior to the image seen on a good color monitor. The conversion of the monitor signals to TV modulation signals and back down again to the TV screen results in a considerable loss of resolution on the screen. The TV modulator used on the computer takes the composite video signal from the computer and puts it onto a tiny transmitter within the TV modulator. See Figure 7.40 for a picture of a TV modulator.

If the TV modulator is not working, check to be sure that the modulator and the television are both on the same channel. Some modulators are switch-selectable for either channel 2 or 3. This switch is provided in case there is local interference on one of the channels. Some modulators hide this switch internally. The TV must also be fine-tuned to exactly the right channel for the best picture. If the TV still does not work with the modulator, substitute another modulator or TV if one is available. Be sure to check the condition of the interconnecting cables, too, as they often cause problems.

The TV modulator must have power to operate. Check to be sure that the wall outlet supplying power to the modulator's transformer is supplying 120VAC. If the modulator runs on DC from the computer, the Vcc line should be checked to be sure that power is available from that source.

SPECIAL TROUBLESHOOTING THEORY FOR MONITOR CIRCUITRY

Diagnostic Program Troubleshooting

The diskette diagnostics has excellent software to assist in troubleshooting monitor problems. A full set of characters and color patterns is available. All the technician has to do is load the diagnostics program and call up those routines. The output of the computer will continuously put out the necessary synchronization and video signals needed for monitor repairs.

Special Pulse Definitions

Troubleshooting to the component level in a monitor requires understanding of some additional definitions:

- **Duty cycle** is a term used frequently in dealing with pulsed circuits. The duty cycle of a pulse waveform is the time that the signal is on divided by the time of the whole cycle, expressed as a percentage. See Figure 12.14.

The names of various pulse parameters given in Figure 12.15 should be familiar to the servicing technician.

Another point peculiar to pulse circuits is the polarity indicator on sine transformers used in these circuits. When the marked lead of a transformer primary has a specified polarity applied, the same polarity will appear at a marked lead of the secondary. The mark is a small dot or other coding on both the schematic and the transformer (Figure 12.16). This marking of the leads is necessary to properly phase the transformers in the circuits.

Biasing in Pulsed Circuits

Pulsed circuits almost always operate class C. As such, they have no output current flow in the absence of an input signal. Bipolar transistors by their nature are cut off until driven into conduction, so no special bias supply is necessary. Troubleshooting in monitors begins as it does for any other equipment—check the power supply voltages to be sure they are correct. When a defective stage is identified, check right at the stage to be sure it is receiving proper operating voltages.

An input signal to a class C stage must be sufficiently high in amplitude and have enough current capability to bring the stage into full conduction. Remember that it takes 0.7V of forward bias to make a bipolar transistor conduct. Watch for this as a possible problem and note input pulse amplitudes as compared to the bias of the stages.

Test Instruments Needed for Monitor Servicing

The Computer as a Monitor Troubleshooting Signal Source. A computer can be used to generate all the video and synchronizing signals required for troubleshooting a monitor problem. The diskette diagnostics program will supply a test pattern. In invoking this program it may be necessary temporarily to use another monitor to set up the proper monitor output for testing, then switch the monitors to the bad one.

Using the Oscilloscope. The oscilloscope probe must be considered as it relates to monitor circuits. Some monitor circuits generate hundreds of volts because of the nature of pulsed circuits. Oscilloscope probes have voltage limitations, commonly 500 volts maximum. Maximum means the peak value that the probe can withstand without damage. Be sure that the circuit you are working on will not damage a probe before

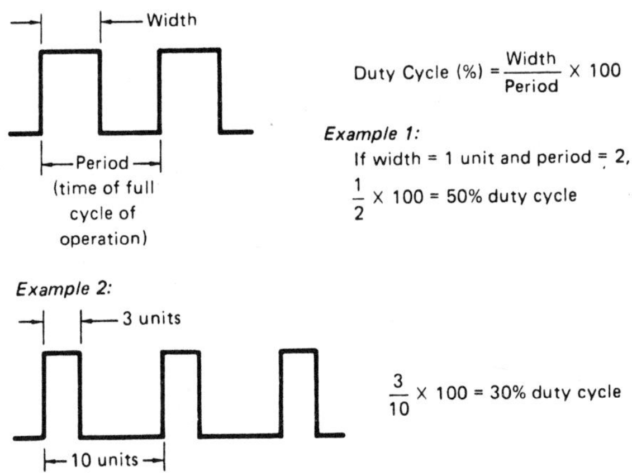

Figure 12.14 The term *duty cycle* is often used in pulse applications.

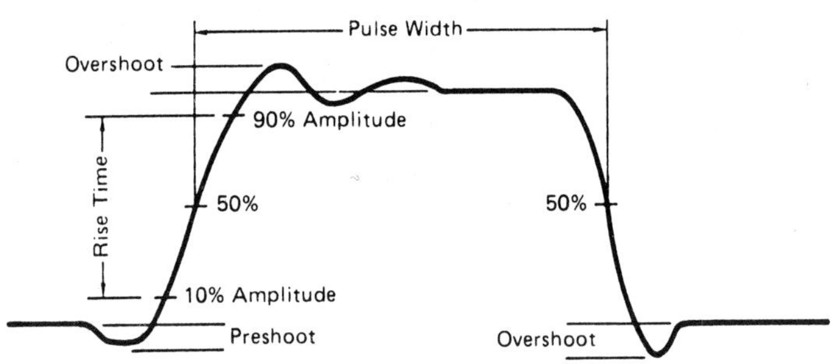

Figure 12.15 Names and definitions of various measurements of a pulse.

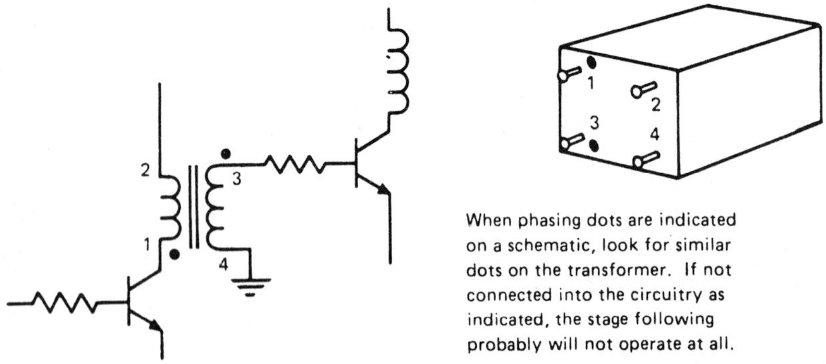

Figure 12.16 Dots on a transformer or on a schematic indicate instantaneous polarity.

using one. Surprisingly high voltages can be produced from low-voltage sources in pulsed circuits.

Whenever an oscilloscope is used for any application where the vertical amplitude of the signal is of importance, the probe must be compensated for use with the oscilloscope's input circuit. This is done by placing the probe tip on the oscilloscopes calibrator output and adjusting the probe (the adjustment may be at either end of the probe cable) for a proper square wave. This was covered in detail in Chapter 6.

How Signals Change in Pulse Circuits

Capacitors and inductors can cause drastic changes in pulse waveforms as signals progress through the circuitry.

DC Level Changing. A capacitor can be used to remove, add, or change a DC component. A common example is the output stage of an RC coupled transistor amplifier. The capacitor is used to remove the DC component of the signal because that component would upset the normal functioning of the following stage. And, of course, the capacitor can be used to change from one level of DC component to another (see Figure 12.17).

Signal Rectification. When AC signals or pulses are coupled into a bipolar transistor, diode, or other rectifying element through a series capacitor, a special effect occurs. This effect is best known as producing a driving level. See Figure 12.18.

When the incoming signal goes into the positive half of the cycle (for this type of transistor) the voltage at the base cannot exceed about 0.7 volts, due to the clamping action base-emitter junction. Additional voltage must be dropped across the capacitor. Upon reversal of the input signal, the charge on the capacitor adds to that of the signal, producing a very negative voltage at the base of the transistor. This voltage provides a good indication of the amount of input signal voltage. A DC voltmeter can be used in this case to monitor the amount of RF driving the stage. This fact is often used by manufacturers, providing special test points at circuit inputs for this purpose.

Knowing that signals can be converted in some inputs to a DC voltage, it should come as no surprise when a large pulse signal fed into a transistor base suddenly becomes a large negative voltage with apparently no direct source. The input to the horizontal output transistor of a monitor is a good example of this circuit.

CHAPTER SUMMARY

Monitor problems found during service calls are best solved by the replacement of a good monitor and the defective one taken to the shop for repair. The repair of monitors requires some additional training in pulse techniques. The cost of a monochrome monitor is low enough that technician time must be held to a minimum. Color monitors, particularly high-resolution ones, are worth more repair time because of their higher replacement costs.

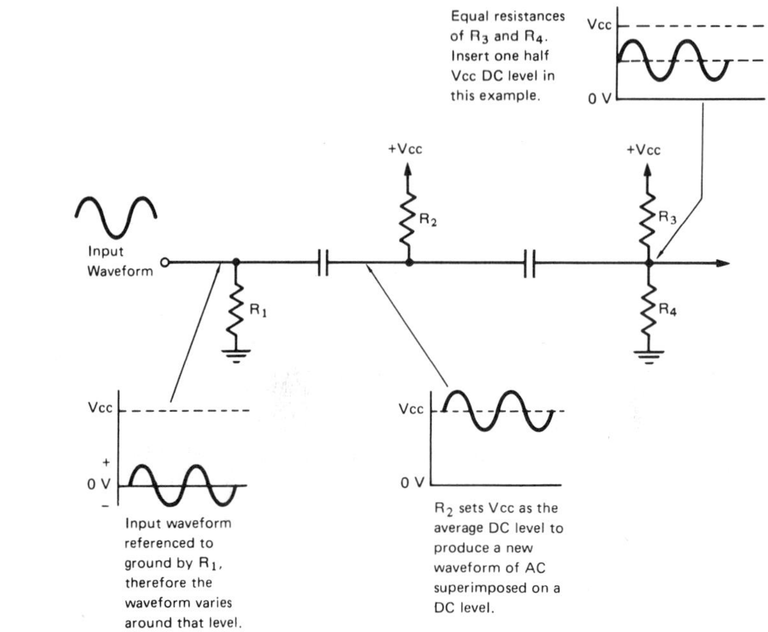

Figure 12.17 The output capacitor prevents coupling the collector DC into the following stage.

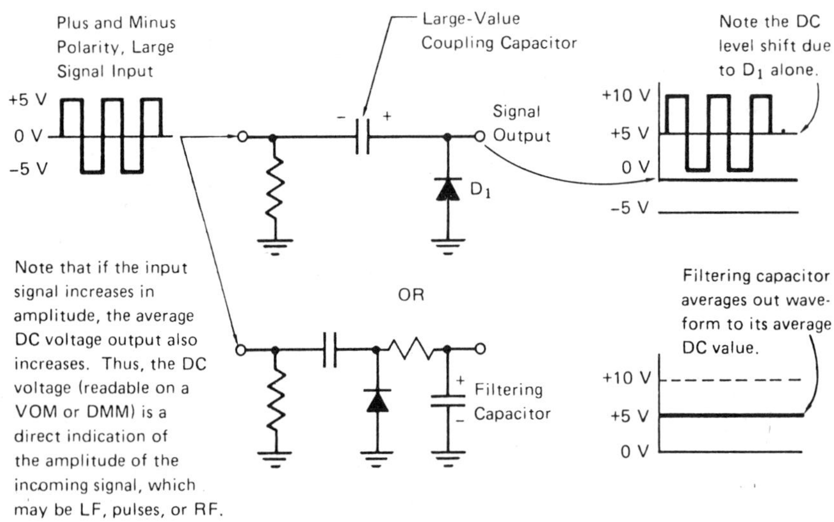

Figure 12.18 Changing DC levels can be easily accomplished using a capacitor.

REVIEW QUESTIONS

1. What is the first troubleshooting step to be performed when a bad monitor is suspected?
2. What danger is there in servicing cathode ray tubes?
3. In what circuits would you look for problems described as "tearing" or "flipping" of the CRT picture?
4. What could you adjust to put a monitor picture on the screen straight, instead of slanted to one side?
5. What could you adjust to center the picture on a monitor if it is too high or off a bit to one side?
6. What does the TV modulator do for the computer video output?
7. Can the diagnostics diskette be used to advantage in troubleshooting a monitor?
8. What are the small dots sometimes used on pulse transformers and pulse schematics for?
9. Circuits used in pulsed applications are most often biased as class ____ amplifiers.
10. What is the most logical signal generator for testing a monitor?
11. What is the common voltage limitation for a typical 10X oscilloscope probe?

chapter thirteen

Repairing Printers

CHAPTER OVERVIEW

The computer printer is perhaps the most abused piece of hardware in a microcomputer installation. Even at the highest speeds of operation, there are times the operator wishes it could go faster. Because of the push for ever-higher printing speeds, the mechanisms of the printer are subjected to more and more punishment and fail often. This chapter will prepare you to diagnose and repair most printer problems by familiarizing you with how they work electrically and mechanically in general terms.

WHY A PRINTER?

The Printer as a Secondary Computer Output

The basic computer system requires the system unit, a keyboard for input to the computer, and a monitor screen to output information to the operator. A minimal system such as this is capable of many useful tasks, but a most important peripheral unit is missing: the printer. The printer is used to make permanent records (called *hard copy*) of the information generated by the computer. A printer may be a small unit, relatively slow but effective in its job (Figure 13.1). At the other end of the printer spectrum is the commercial printer, capable of printing at high speeds and for long periods to produce the records generated by large computers (Figure 13.2). The subject of this chapter is microcomputer printers ranging in price from less than $300 to perhaps $1200.

The printing of a dot-matrix printer (shown in Figure 13.3) is actually made up of tiny dots strung together to give the impression of characters (Figure 13.4). Characters are "scanned" from left to right and, in the case of a bidirectional printer, also from right to left. The speed of any printer, dot-matrix or fully formed-character, is enhanced if the printer is also able to print a line from either direction, left to right or "backwards" from right to left. Reversed-direction printing saves some time ordinarily taken for the carriage to return to the left between lines.

In an effort to make dot-matrix printing more attractive and easier to read, special techniques may be used to fill in between the dots making up the dot-matrix characters. This entails at least two passes along a line of print and a very slight position shift of either the paper or the printhead (see Figure 13.5).

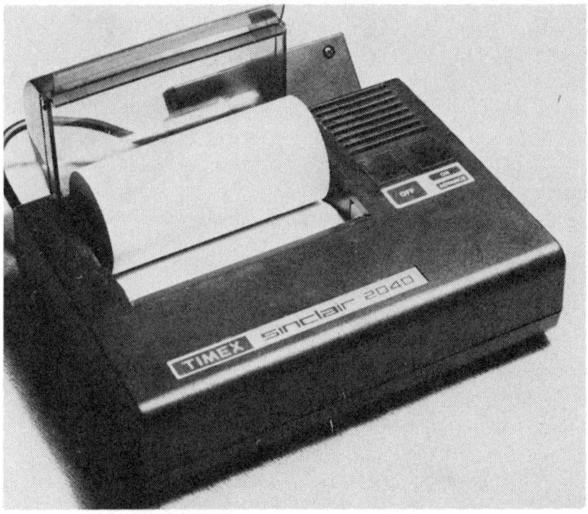

Figure 13.1 Even a very small printer offers all the necessary functions to provide hard copy. (Abbey Enterprises)

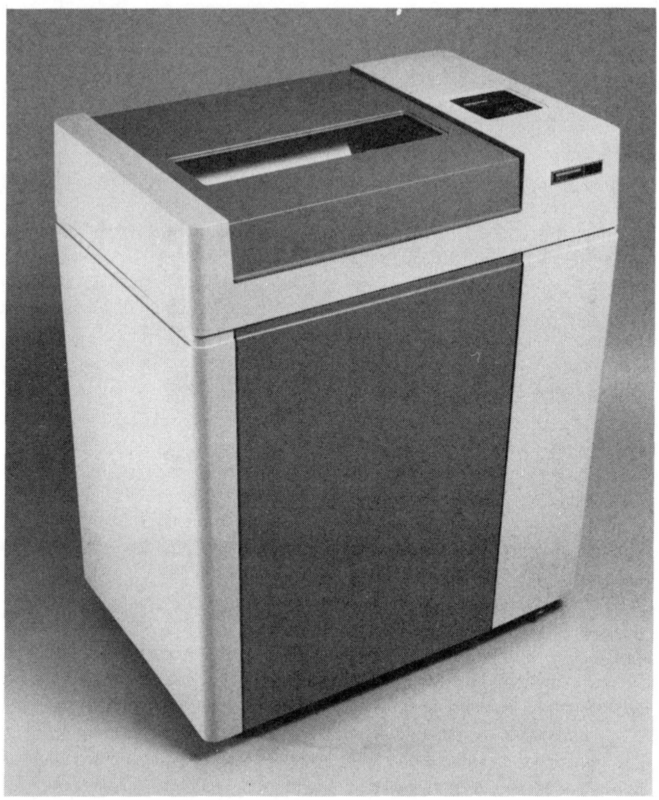

Figure 13.2 A commercial printer such as this is used with mainframe computers in applications requiring the printing of large volumes of data. (Mannesmann Tally)

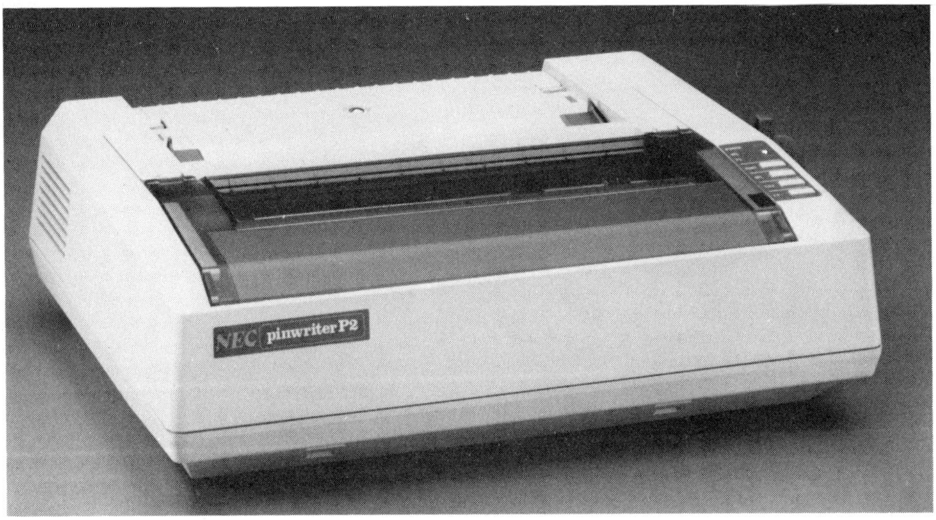

Figure 13.3 A typical dot-matrix printer used with a microcomputer (Courtesy of NEC Information Systems, Inc.)

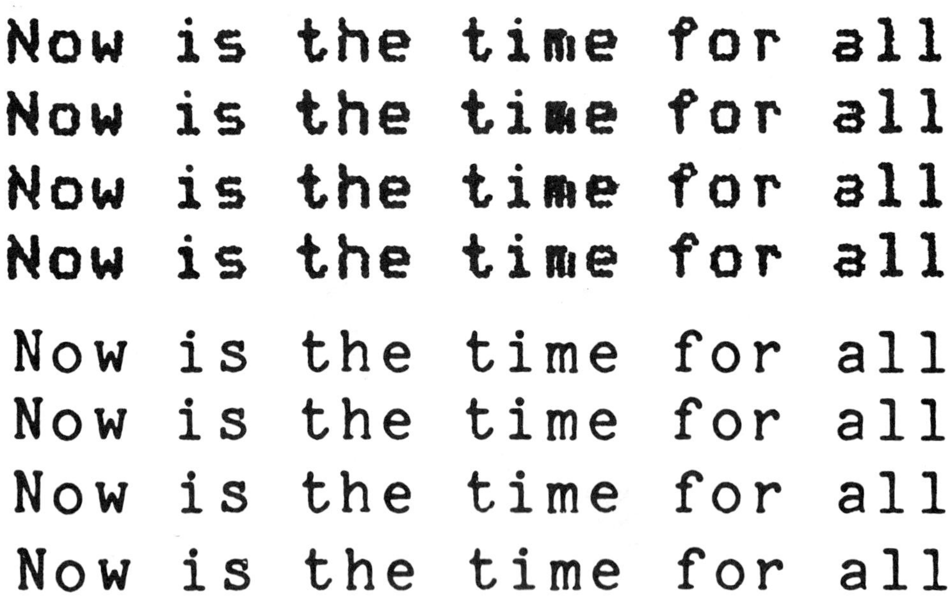

Figure 13.4 Dot-matrix printing is not as easy to read as that of a fully formed character printer.

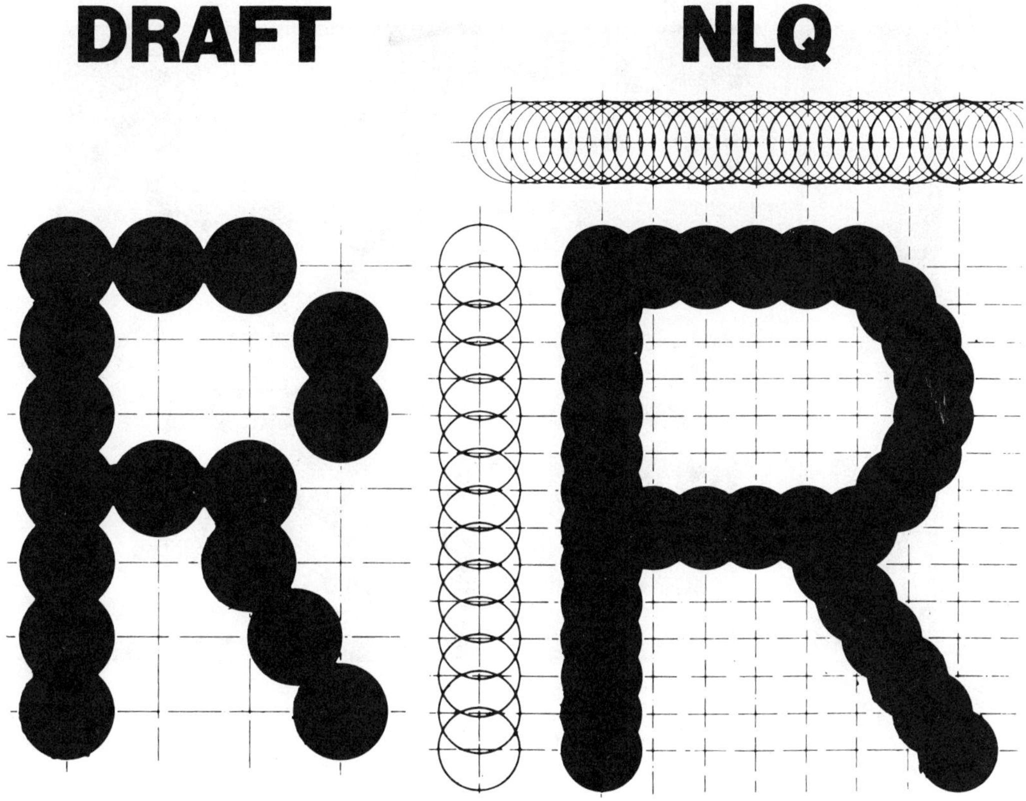

Figure 13.5 Multiple-passes of a dot-matrix pattern in a slightly different location produce a much more attractive dot-matrix copy. The resulting copy is called NL, for near-letter-quality or correspondence quality printing. (Mannesmann Tally)

Figure 13.6 shows a typewriter capable of operation from its own keyboard. With an internal add-on circuit board this machine can also be used as a computer printer. There are printers available that use the fully formed-character principle but do not have a keyboard, their only purpose being computer printers (Figure 13.7).

The Two Most Popular Types of Printers

The Dot-Matrix Printer. The dot-matrix printer in Figure 13.3 is representative of a great many brands now on the market. Its operation consists of "firing" the ends of print wires against a ribbon that carries ink onto the paper behind it (see Figure 13.8). By the proper selection of possible dot positions in a 5 × 7 matrix, uppercase letters may be formed. A 7 × 9 or 9 × 9 matrix can be used to form all upper- and lowercase letters. The speed of operation of the dot-matrix printer is limited by the time taken for the wires to fire, make the impression, and recover, ready for the next row of dots.

Figure 13.6 With an appropriate add-on circuit board, this daisy-wheel typewriter does double duty as a typewriter or as a computer printer. (Abbey Enterprises)

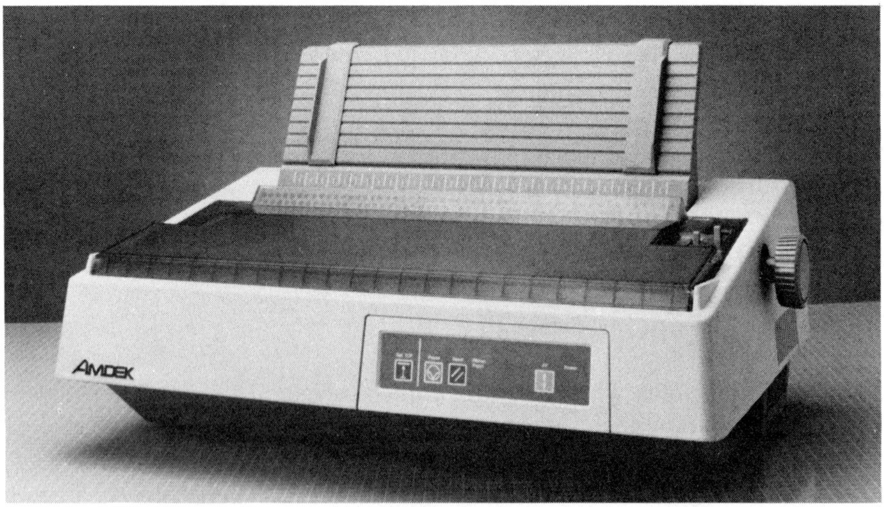

Figure 13.7 Fully formed-character printer without keyboard (Courtesy of Amdek)

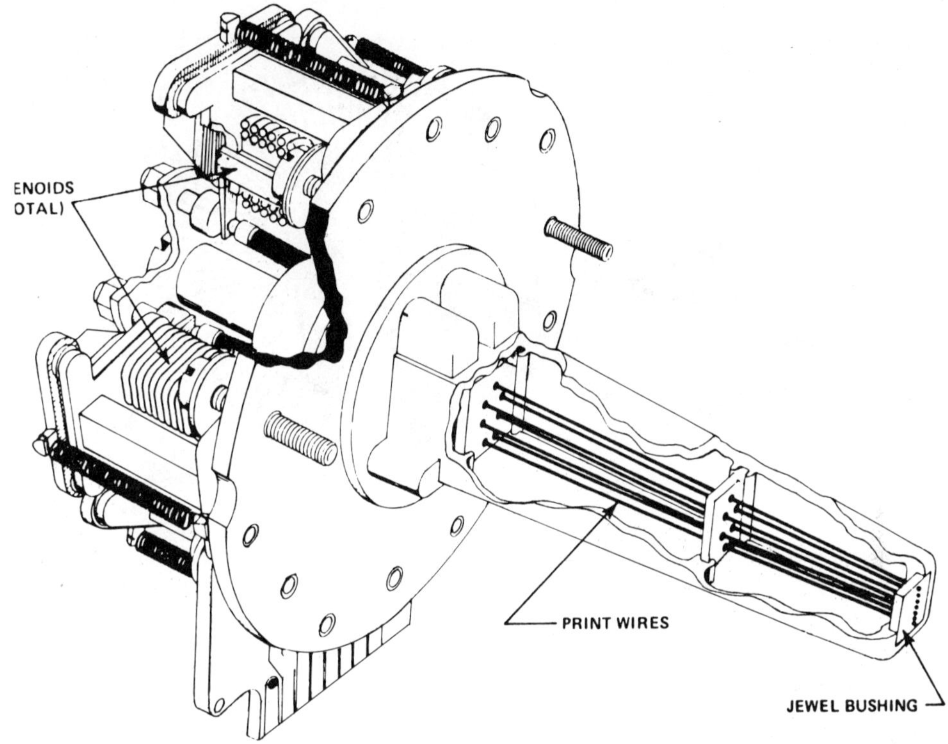

Figure 13.8 The dot-matrix printer head momentarily fires printing wires against the ribbon and paper, thereby leaving a printed impression. (Courtesy of Texas Instruments, Inc.)

The Fully Formed Character Printer

The fully formed-character printers are usually of the daisy-wheel or thimble types (Figure 13.9). The daisy-wheel printhead is very popular and will be the principal fully formed-character printhead under discussion.

The speed of operation of fully formed-character printheads is limited by the speed in which the next character can be brought into position under the striking solenoid. In an effort to minimize the time taken for this task the microprocessor chip in the printer notes the present location of the printhead and the location of the next character, then determines the shortest direction to rotate the print wheel to bring the next character into proper position.

The principal advantage of the fully formed-character printer is that the printed characters are fully formed and pleasing to read. Because of the attractive print quality these printers produce what is commonly called letter-quality printing. Special-character wheels can be used to change the type font, producing different printing effects (see Figure 13.10). The major disadvantage of the fully formed-character printer is that it is slower than a dot-matrix printer. A fully formed-character printer may type as fast as 100 words per minute, not much faster than a fast typist.

Figure 13.9 Several methods of fully-formed character printing involve the daisy wheel or the golfball-style printheads. (Abbey Enterprises)

Table 13.1 summarizes advantages and drawbacks of the two most frequently used printers.

Table 13.1 Relative merits of the dot-matrix fully formed.

Dot-Matrix Printer	**Fully formed-character Printer**
Fast*	Slow
Hard to Read*	Attractive printing
Flexible type fonts	Restricted type fonts
Graphics capability	No graphics

*Except in the special near-letter-quality mode which is slower in operation but easier to read

Less Popular Printer Types Used with Professional Computers. Other kinds of printers are available for use with computers, but for various reasons they are not as popular as the two types mentioned above. They include:

Band printers

Line printers

Inkjet printers

Thermal printers

Electrostatic printers

Laser printers

EXTENDED PRINT
ABCDEFGHIJKLMNOPQRSTUVWXYZ abcdefghijklmnopqrstuvwxyz 1234567890
!"#$%&'():*-=;+,<.>/?

PICA (DRAFT)
ABCDEFGHIJKLMNOPQRSTUVWXYZ abcdefghijklmnopqrstuvwxyz 1234567890
!"#$%&'():*-=;+,<.>/?

ELITE (DRAFT)
ABCDEFGHIJKLMNOPQRSTUVWXYZ abcdefghijklmnopqrstuvwxyz 1234567890
!"#$%&'():*-=;+,<.>/?

SEMICONDENSED
ABCDEFGHIJKLMNOPQRSTUVWXYZ abcdefghijklmnopqrstuvwxyz 1234567890
!"#$%&'():*-=;+,<.>/?

ULTRACONDENSED
ABCDEFGHIJKLMNOPQRSTUVWXYZ abcdefghijklmnopqrstuvwxyz 1234567890
!"#$%&'():*-=;+,<.>/?

HEADLINE
ABCDEFGHIJKLMNOPQRSTUVWXYZ abcdefghijklmnopqrstuvwxyz 1234567890
!"#$%&'():*-=;+,<.>/?

PICA PROPORTIONAL (DRAFT)
ABCDEFGHIJKLMNOPQRSTUVWXYZ abcdefghijklmnopqrstuvwxyz 1234567890
!"#$%&'():*-=;+,<.>/?

ELITE PROPORTIONAL (DRAFT)
ABCDEFGHIJKLMNOPQRSTUVWXYZ abcdefghijklmnopqrstuvwxyz 1234567890
!"#$%&'():*-=;+,<.>/?

PICA (NLQ)
ABCDEFGHIJKLMNOPQRSTUVWXYZ abcdefghijklmnopqrstuvwxyz 1234567890
!"#$%&'():*-=;+,<.>/?

ELITE (NLQ)
ABCDEFGHIJKLMNOPQRSTUVWXYZ abcdefghijklmnopqrstuvwxyz 1234567890
!"#$%&'():*-=;+,<.>/?

PICA PROPORTIONAL (NLQ)
ABCDEFGHIJKLMNOPQRSTUVWXYZ abcdefghijklmnopqrstuvwxyz 1234567890
!"#$%&'():*-=;+,<.>/?

ELITE PROPORTIONAL (NLQ)
ABCDEFGHIJKLMNOPQRSTUVWXYZ abcdefghijklmnopqrstuvwxyz 1234567890
!"#$%&'():*-=;+,<.>/?

Figure 13.10 A fully-formed character printer type font can often be changed by simply changing the print wheel.

Band printers are used on very high-speed printers used with larger computers where a great volume of material must be printed in a short time. Line printers such as the one shown in Figure 13.2 are capable of very high-speed operation: this one operates at 600 *lines* (about nine pages of solid text) per minute. The text is printed in horizontal rows, not unlike the scanning of a video monitor, from the top of the page down. This printer uses 66 print wires similar to those of a dot-matrix printer. Each print wire covers the space occupied by two matrix spaces. Thus, as a particular print wire passes down through a line, it prints two adjacent characters. All the 66 print wires operate simultaneously, which enables very high printing speeds.

The inkjet printer has the advantage of being very quiet in operation in contrast to both the dot-matrix and fully formed-character printers. Its principle of operation is to force a minute amount of ink directly onto the paper from tiny nozzles. This kind of printer is relatively new and not yet in widespread use.

Thermal printers heat the special paper used with them, making a dark mark on the paper. Although quiet, the fact that the thermal printer cannot be used with standard paper is its principal disadvantage. The electrostatic printhead places a mark on special metalized paper. Like the thermal printer, this printer is relatively quiet but also requires special paper, again a major disadvantage.

PRINTER ELECTRONICS

A basic block diagram of a printer is given in Figure 13.11.

The On-Line/Off-Line Switch

Since there is a need for local adjustments to the printer, some means must be available to take the printer away from computer control. An example would be a need to reposition the paper in the printer. To accomplish this there should be an on-line/off-line switch on the printer. Some printers call this the select/deselect switch. Leaving this switch in the off-line position will result, of course, in the inability of the computer to operate the printer. This is a very common operator error, although one is usually caught by the operator early in the learning process. Even so, occasionally the servicing technician may find that this switch is the only problem with the system! See Figure 13.12.

Parallel and Serial Data Communications

Two types of communications are used for driving printers, the serial and the parallel methods. Serial communications make use of the computer's RS-232C port. Parallel operation uses the Centronics output port. The type of interface may be determined by simple inspection. The standard 36-pin Centronics connector (Amphenol 57-40360) and a flat cable with a dozen or more wires indicates the use of a parallel output port. On the other hand, a small cable with only three to five wires and a DB-25 connector indicates the use of the RS-232C serial communications port. (See Figure 7.8 for photos of these two connectors.)

Block Diagrams of Typical Printers

The purpose of the I/O circuitry is to obtain the input characters in binary byte format and to store a limited number of these characters in a temporary RAM storage space called a buffer. When the buffer is full of input characters, the host computer is told to stop sending characters until the buffer is empty and ready for another load of characters. This action frees the computer to do tasks other than printing.

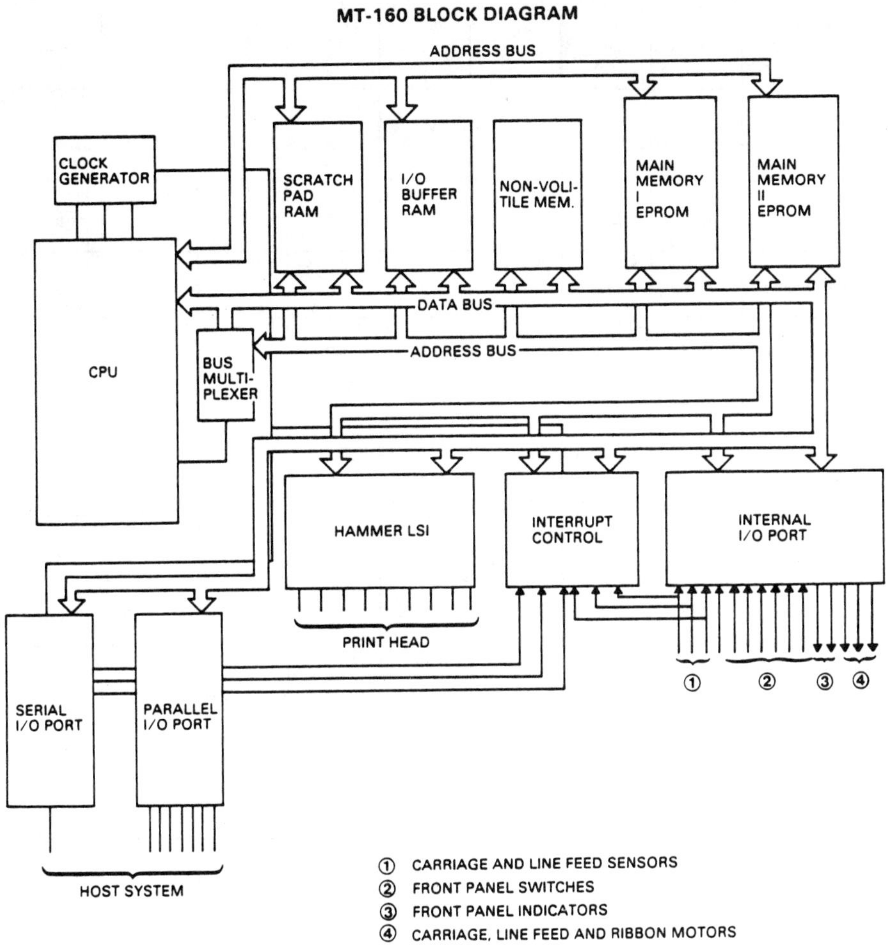

Figure 13.11 Basic block diagram of a printer's electronic circuit (Mannesmann Tally)

Characters are usually sent to the printer in a standardized format called ASCII code. In addition to the standard letters and numbers, control codes are also sent. These control codes, if applicable to the printer in question, can ring a bell on the printer, return the carriage to the left margin, feed the paper through the printer, allow super- and subscripts, underlining, and so forth. A copy of the standard ASCII code appears in Table 13.2. A more thorough explanation of the ASCII code may be found in Appendix C.

The CPU board is the intelligence of the printer. Using the incoming character and control codes, the CPU has many tasks to perform. The incoming binary data must

Table 13.2

BITS D6 D5 D4	0 0 0	0 0 1	0 1 0	0 1 1	1 0 0	1 0 1	1 1 0	1 1 1
D3 D2 D1 D0	CONTROL		NUMBERS SYMBOLS		UPPER CASE		LOWER CASE	
0 0 0 0	0 NUL 0 0	20 DLE 10 16	40 SP 20 32	60 0 30 48	100 @ 40 64	120 P 50 80	140 ' 60 96	160 p 70 112
0 0 0 1	1 GTL SOH 1 1	21 LLO DC1 11 17	41 ! 21 33	61 1 31 49	101 A 41 65	121 Q 51 81	141 a 61 97	161 q 71 113
0 0 1 0	2 STX 2 2	22 DC2 12 18	42 " 22 34	62 2 32 50	102 B 42 66	122 R 52 82	142 b 62 98	162 r 72 114
0 0 1 1	3 ETX 3 3	23 DC3 13 19	43 # 23 35	63 3 33 51	103 C 43 67	123 S 53 83	143 c 63 99	163 s 73 115
0 1 0 0	4 SDC EOT 4 4	24 DCL DC4 14 20	44 $ 24 36	64 4 34 52	104 D 44 68	124 T 54 84	144 d 64 100	164 t 74 116
0 1 0 1	5 PPC ENQ 5 5	25 PPU NAK 15 21	45 % 25 37	65 5 35 53	105 E 45 69	125 U 55 85	145 e 65 101	165 u 75 117
0 1 1 0	6 ACK 6 6	26 SYN 16 22	46 & 26 38	66 6 36 54	106 F 46 70	126 V 56 86	146 f 66 102	166 v 76 118
0 1 1 1	7 BEL 7 7	27 ETB 17 23	47 27 39	67 7 37 55	107 G 47 71	127 W 57 87	147 g 67 103	167 w 77 119
1 0 0 0	10 GET BS 8 8	30 SPE CAN 18 24	50 (28 40	70 8 38 56	110 H 48 72	130 X 58 88	150 h 68 104	170 x 78 120
1 0 0 1	11 TCT HT 9 9	31 SPD EM 19 25	51) 29 41	71 9 39 57	111 I 49 73	131 Y 59 89	151 i 69 105	171 y 79 121
1 0 1 0	12 LF A 10	32 SUB 1A 26	52 * 2A 42	72 : 3A 58	112 J 4A 74	132 Z 5A 90	152 j 6A 106	172 z 7A 122
1 0 1 1	13 VT B 11	33 ESC 1B 27	53 + 2B 43	73 ; 3B 59	113 K 4B 75	133 [5B 91	153 k 6B 107	173 7B 123
1 1 0 0	14 FF C 12	34 FS 1C 28	54 , 2C 44	74 < 3C 60	114 L 4C 76	134 \ 5C 92	154 l 6C 108	174 ¦ 7C 124
1 1 0 1	15 CR D 13	35 GS 1D 29	55 – 2D 45	75 = 3D 61	115 M 4D 77	135] 5D 93	155 m 6D 109	175 } 7D 125
1 1 1 0	16 SO E 14	36 RS 1E 30	56 . 2E 46	76 > 3E 62	116 N 4E 78	136 ∧ 5E 94	156 n 6E 110	176 ~ 7E 126
1 1 1 1	17 SI F 15	37 US 1F 31	57 / 2F 47	77 UNL ? 3F 63	117 O 4F 79	137 UNT — 5F 111	157 o 6F 111	177 RUBOUT (DEL) 7F 127
	Addressed Commands	Universal Commands	Listen Addresses		Talk Addresses		Secondary Addresses Or Commands	

octal	25 PPU	GPIB code
	NAK	ASCII character
hex	15 21	decimal

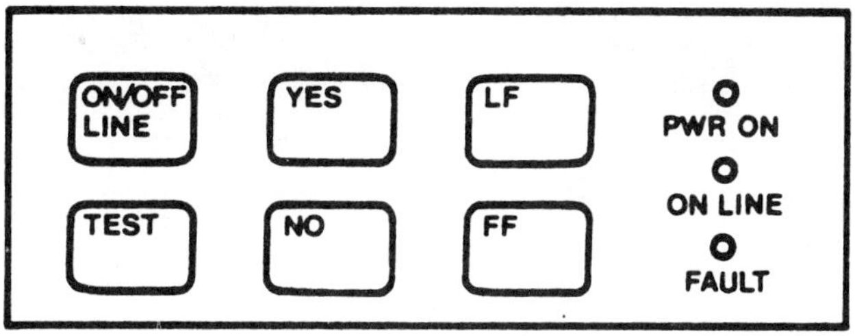

Figure 13.12 The on-line/off-line switch is necessary to make mechanical adjustments to the printer such as paper positioning. (Mannesmann Tally)

be converted into meaningful signals for the printhead. When printing text, the incoming binary ASCII codes must be decoded into a letter to be printed during the sweep of the printhead across the paper.

The dot-matrix printer prints text by converting ASCII bytes into dot patterns placed into a memory buffer as bits. These bits are then printed by the printhead as it scans horizontally across the paper. In the graphics mode of the dot-matrix printer, ASCII is not used. Each bit of binary information represents a specific location for a dot. The binary patterns are placed into the memory buffer, which is scanned and printed bit by bit.

The fully formed-character printer, on the other hand, requires an entirely different approach to putting the characters on the paper. ASCII bytes are decoded into print wheel locations for those characters and placed into a memory buffer. The current character position of the print wheel is noted, the location of the next character calculated, then the CPU determines which direction the printwheel must turn to bring the next character under the strike solenoid to travel the shortest distance. In addition to all this activity, the overall density of each character may be coded so that the striking solenoid will strike the character with varying force. For instance, the period (.) will require minimal force to make an impression whereas the character W will require maximum force to make a similar-appearing density of printed character.

With either kind of printer the CPU directs the printing machinery through the use of drivers which are often power transistors. These drivers convert the low-power signals coming to them to high-powered pulses suitable for driving the various mechanisms to which they are attached. Figure 13.13 shows the drivers required for a typical dot-matrix printer head.

Ribbon drives are those mechanisms required to keep the ribbon changing position from one spool to another while traveling in front of the printhead. These drives sometimes parasite energy from the mechanism driving the carriage across the paper or use the reversal of a paper-feed motor in a printer which does not allow reversal of the forward direction of paper. They have dedicated drive mechanisms to accomplish this task. Spooled fabric ribbons often have a ribbon-reversing mechanism that recycles the ribbon back and forth until the ink is depleted. Ribbon cartridges,

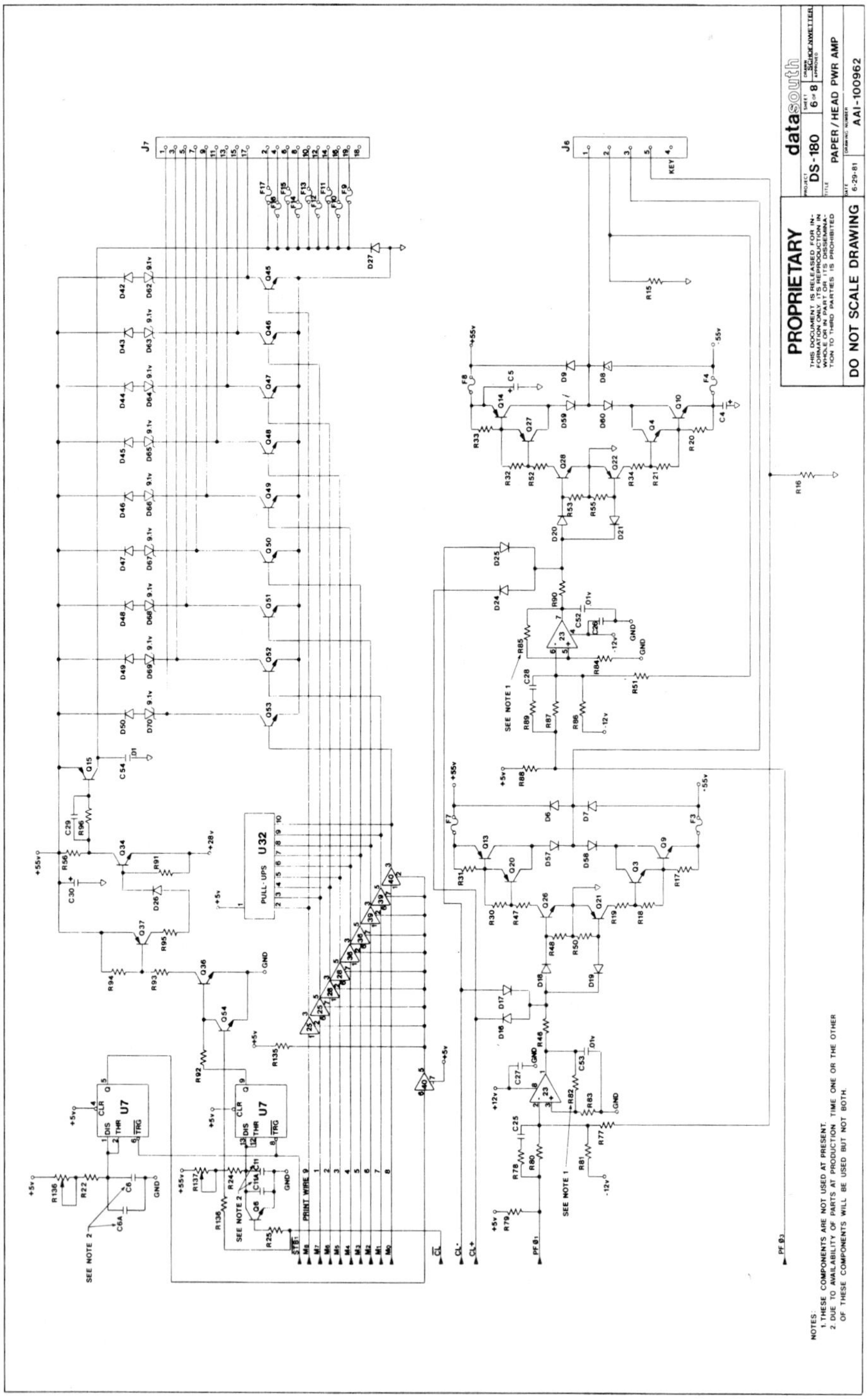

Figure 13.13 Dot-matrix drivers and their outputs (Courtesy of Datasouth Computer Corp.)

particularly the carbon lift-off (erasable) types, can be used only once past the printhead.

Initializing a Printer for Use

When a printer is connected to a microcomputer, the printer and the computer must both be set up so that data will be present at the proper port for the printer, the data is in the proper format to be used, and the printer is able to control the incoming data to prevent receiving characters too fast to print them.

Parallel Printer Communications Considerations. The proper output port of the computer must be used for data transfer. Parallel printers are connected to the port called LPT1. LPT2, the second parallel port, is also available on some computers for an alternate or secondary printer. LPT3 may be available on a few computers. Software programs may or may not control the port in use for the printer. When setting up new software, a new port from the computer or a new printer, the setup or install program for the software should be used to configure the new system. (See Chapter 15 for tips on installation of computer software.) The setup procedure will ensure that the printer is able to temporarily halt or otherwise control the incoming rate of information to prevent overflow and consequent missing of data.

Serial Printer Communications Considerations. In addition to the software setup requirements discussed above for parallel printer outputs, the serial printer will require that data coming from the computer arrives at the proper speed, or baud rate. Many standard speed choices are available, only a few of which may be usable on the printer in question (see Table 13.3).

Table 13.3 Standard baud rates of serial data transmission.

50*	600*
75*	1200<
110*	1800
134	2400
150	4800
200	7200
300<	9600<

*These speeds commonly use 2 stop bits, the remainder use 1 stop bit.
<Most commonly used baud rates.

Besides the baud rate requirement, the printer may require special software-control codes called protocols. If no control protocols are used, the computer should send data slowly enough to prevent the possibility of overrunning the printer. Without protocols, paper faults or other printer problems may cause data loss. These include the XON/XOFF and other protocols that establish data flow control as the printing job progresses. Using XON/XOFF protocol, the computer sends binary data until the printer sends an XOFF code byte (a control S or DC3 or 13H or 00010011 binary byte, these items being all the same thing), at which time the computer stops sending data. When the printer is again ready it will send an XON byte (control Q, DCI, 11H, or 00010001 binary). The ENQ/ACK codes for data control require that the computer periodically send an inquiry code of ENQ to the printer. ENQ is a control E, 5H, or 00000101 binary). If the printer is ready for more data, the printer returns an ACK code (control F, 06H, or 000001100 binary). Otherwise, the computer sends no more data until the printer returns the ACK byte. The ETX/ACK code is the same as the ENQ/ACK except that the computer uses a different inquiry code of ETX (control C, 03H, or 00000011 binary) instead of an ENQ code.

The ACK/NAK protocol differs in that the printer sends an ACK after each line of data if no error was detected. The computer can immediately send another line of data. If the printer sends a NAK (control U, 15H, or 00010101 binary), the computer is thereby requested to repeat a line sent in error.

Although not a true protocol, the ready/busy line may be used as a simple handshaking line to control the flow of data from the computer to the printer. In any particular application this line may mean ready when high or low (busy of course; the opposite state). This line may be switch-software-, or jumper-selectable at the printer.

In order to print, the printer must be on-line. If a fault occurs or if the operator takes the printer off-line for any reason, the printer will send the proper code to the computer to halt the incoming data.

Printer Initialization. Printers may offer special programmable options, some of them noted in the paragraphs that follow. These selections may be made with software, switches, or jumpers.

1. Bidirectional printing is a method used to speed the printing of documents by reducing the carriage-return time. Instead of always returning the carriage to the left margin after the printing of each line, the distance to the nearest end of the following line is computed and the carriage is then taken to that end of the following line, either right or left. According to which end of the line the head is moved, the data for the line is then read into the printhead a character at a time from the proper end of the data. Thus, if the printhead is returned to the right end of the following line rather than its normal left end, the characters are fed into the printhead in a reversed order and the printhead prints "backward" across the paper from right to left.

2. Another feature that is often programmable at the printer is whether the printer should automatically insert a line feed (take the paper up one line) whenever the printer receives a carriage return. If the printer overprints each line without running up the paper at the end of each line, this switch may be changed at the printer or the software can be changed, possibly through a setup or install program, to insert the proper line feeds. On the other hand, if the printer always double-spaces, the printer should probably be changed to eliminate the automatic insertion of a line feed.

3. Serial printers will require additional settings for selecting the proper baud rate and for selecting the parity error-detecting options available for serial data transmission. Common baud rates for printers are 300 and 1200 baud. Faster and slower rates are also available, as seen in Table 13.2, but these rates are less commonly used.

The programming options of a printer are often set with the use of small switches commonly called DIP switches. These switches are read only during power up; if changed, the printer must be turned off and then turned on again to reread the switches.

The connections required to connect a printer of either the serial or parallel types to the computer are shown in Appendix A. Problems commonly occur in the interunit cabling because of the mechanical stresses the cables are subjected to in the normal course of moving equipment around. Printer problems should prompt the technician to check the printer cable and replace it with a good cable if there is any doubt as to its condition. Figure 13.14 shows two of the common intercabling connections—for a serial and for a parallel printer. The actual connections for a specific printer may vary considerably from these diagrams, but these give the simplest versions of interconnection.

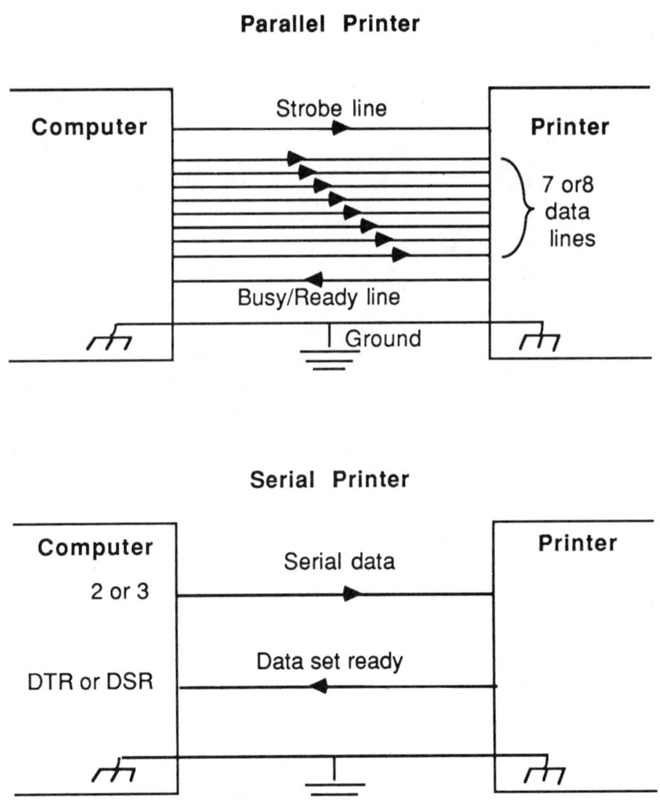

Figure 13.14 Typical serial and parallel printer cabling connections for a microcomputer.

Figure 13.15 The interlock switch is a common cause of service call due to failure or misadjustment. (Abbey Enterprise)

Interlock switches are often provided so that operators cannot get their fingers, ties, or hair caught in the mechanisms. Some of the carriage-return and paper-feed mechanisms are quite powerful and could cause injury. When the interlock switches are open, indicating the presence of a human in the works, the printer cannot operate. A common problem causing service calls is the misadjustment or failure of this interlock switch (see Figure 13.15).

THE MECHANICS OF PRINTERS

The mechanical side of printers consists of four major functions:

The printhead mechanism

The paper-feed mechanism

The carriage-movement mechanism

The ribbon-feed mechanism

While the carriage mechanism moves across the width of the paper, the printhead puts characters on to the paper. At the end of each line, when the carriage prepares to begin another line, the line feed mechanism moves the paper up one or more lines. During the actual printing, the ribbon-feed mechanism moves the ribbon to ensure fresh ink for the next character.

Printheads

Careless operation can cause damage to printheads. Operating a printer without paper and/or ribbon can damage the print wires of a dot-matrix printhead. The wires can mushroom at the tip, causing them to jam and to make poor characters —particularly where the printhead fires against a metal platen or bar. The daisy wheel, too, should have the cushioning of the paper and a ribbon. Any kind of printer should be kept clean of ribbon and paper debris, dust and dirt. A small amount of denatured alcohol applied with a cotton swab makes a good cleaning tool.

The Daisy Wheel. Probably the most common problem the daisy wheel causes is the missing character. This occurs when the wheel has a broken "petal" and no character is present to be struck against the paper. The only cure is, of course, replacement of the daisy wheel itself. A related problem is one or more characters out of horizontal position, caused by a bent petal. The printing of scrambled letters can have at least two causes: if a daisy-wheel printer, the wheel has lost track of where it is due to a paper jam or the serial data (baud) rate of a serial printer is incorrect. If the printer has worked well and the serial data rate has not been changed, the head has likely lost track of where it is and the printer must be reinitialized by turning it off and back on again. If, however, the printer has never worked with that particular computer and/or software, the software should be suspected first as being improper. If a serial printer, check the printer parity selection switches and the number of data bits being sent by the computer.

Another problem that is common with a daisy-wheel printer is the printing of the same character at each strike of the strike solenoid, regardless of the character sent. This is caused by the failure of the daisy wheel to turn. This in turn is often caused by a mechanical jamming of the wheel that prevents its turning or the failure of the driving mechanism for the daisy-wheel stepper motor.

If the printhead seems to be working but little or no impression is being made on the paper, the head-to-paper distance may be too great. Check the printer instruction book for details of setting this adjustment. A failure such as binding of the strike solenoid can also cause these symptoms.

The Dot-Matrix Printhead. The dot-matrix printhead may run quite hot in normal operation due to the high speed and continuous use of the driving solenoids. Common problems include missing or broken print wires, evident by the broken wires, evident by a missing horizontal row of dots. The defect is easiest to identify if a repeating series of diagonals are printed: / / / / / / / / / / / / /. Another cause for missing dots in the matrix might be a binding solenoid or defective driving circuitry for that wire. Another cause could be a binding drive solenoid, or the driving circuitry for a solenoid could be defective.

Paper Feeds

One of the common problems that arises with printers is improper paper feed. This could be the result of gearing caused by the operator. Since the paper feed is often driven by a stepper motor that in turn is often geared down a great deal, the stepper motor is not only able to turn the platen with great torque but also takes a great deal more torque than normal applied by an operator to force. For this reason, operators of printers should be aware of this potential damage to the printer and be trained in to how to avoid it. Sometimes this means turning off the printer before turning the platen; at other times it is necessary only to disengage the stepper mechanically by pressing inward or pulling outward on the platen knob.

The printhead must have something against which to strike, behind the paper. This is often a rubber roller for a friction-feed system similar to that of a typewriter. Such paper feeds systems are used when the paper has no holes along the edge. See Figure 13.16.

Dot-matrix printers most often have a paper-feed system that feeds the paper precisely according to the advancement of the holes along each side of the paper. See Figure 13.17.

Some printers offer the option of using either method of paper feed: friction for more letter-quality printing on single sheets of paper and tractor paper feed for long strings of data printing using paper with holes along the edge. Some operators have problems with these printers because either one or the other of these methods should be used, but not both at the same time. If friction and tractor feeds are used together, the paper will eventually wrinkle and pull from the tractors, thus jamming the printer. See Figure 13.18.

Typical problems with the paper-feed mechanism include the usual out-of-paper error message and jamming of the paper in the printer. Jamming can cause the printhead of a daisy-wheel printer to go out of synchronization and will require reinitializing the printer by turning it off and back on after the jam is cleared. Damage can occur to the paper feed, carriage, and printhead mechanisms if the printer is not cared for. Turn off the power, clear the jam, and turn the printer on again. Remember not to turn the printer on without paper feeding into it as the printer may begin typing against the bare platen and cause printhead damage.

Another cause of paper-feed problems is too much drag on the paper for the printer to pull against. Such a problem might be caused by the printer sitting on the paper, for instance.

Figure 13.16 The friction paper feed is used with paper that has no holes along its edges, such as ordinary typing paper. (Abbey Enterprises)

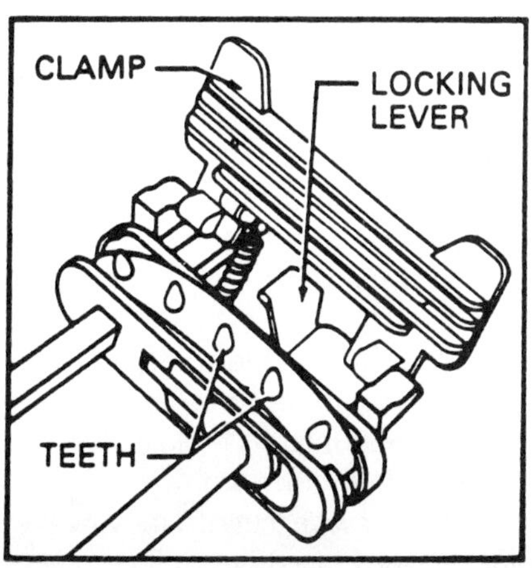

Figure 13.17 Tractor feeds make automatic feeding of long strings of paper precise and trouble-free. (Mannesmann Tally)

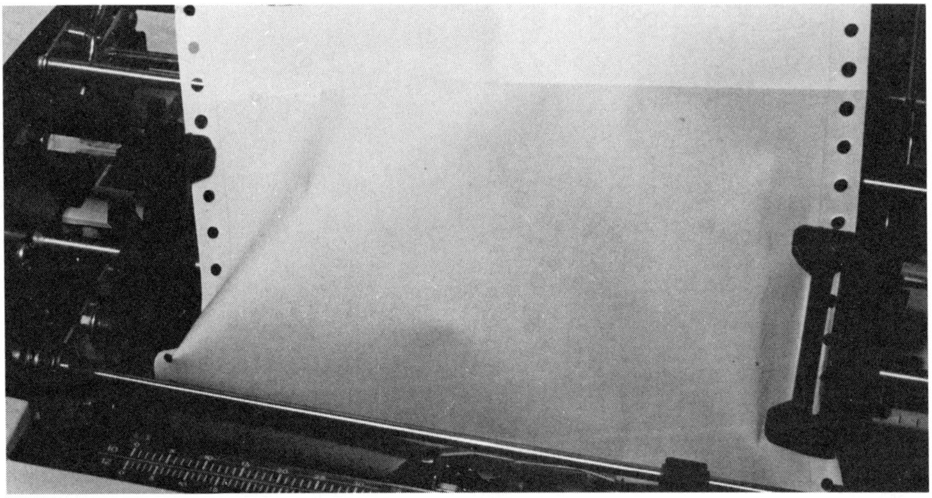

Figure 13.18 Do not use both the friction and tractor paper feeds at the same time. (Abbey Enterprises)

Carriage Mechanisms

The carriage mechanism of a printer is built to very close tolerances. The carriage must go across the width of the paper without play or backlash for the printed characters to be in their proper places. The suspension bars in particular are carefully machined.

The carriage is moved across the paper by one of several methods. A lead screw, toothed belt, and cable are common methods. In many cases, the motor that does the work of moving the carriage is a stepper motor. When the printer is first turned on, the carriage is brought to the left end of the carriage and its presence there detected by a switch or a photo-coupled device. This is then the starting position from which all further movement is calculated.

The horizontal spacing of the printer is sometimes programmable, commonly occurring in steps of 10, 12, or 15 characters per inch. Other printers, called microspacing printers, offer customizing of the horizontal carriage movement in increments as small as 1/120th of an inch for special uses. Sophisticated printers are also available which determine the horizontal spacing according to the width of the individual letters. For instance, an *i* would occupy less horizontal spacing than a *w*. This is called proportional spacing of letters.

Common problems with carriage movement mechanisms include the buildup of sticky residue on the carriage suspension bars from careless lubrication of the suspension shaft and the dust from the paper feeding through the printer. A broken cable or toothed belt or one that has come off one of the pulleys is another problem that can occur with some regularity. A more subtle problem is the carriage that isn't moving the distance it should consistently because of a slipping setscrew in a drive pulley.

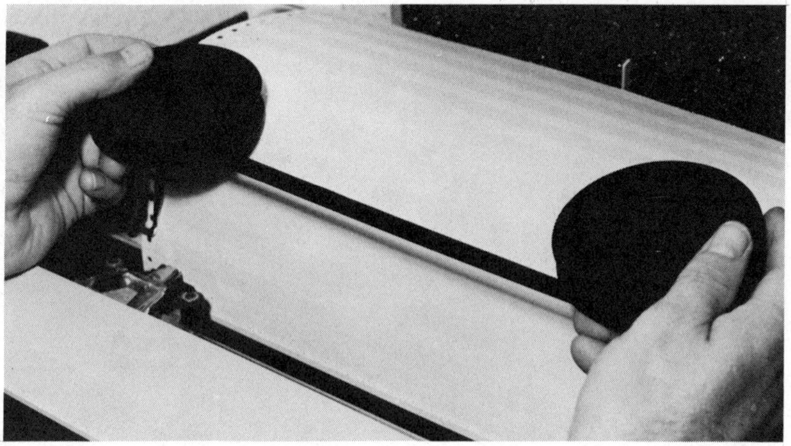

Figure 13.19 The fabric ribbon is rugged and often used in dot-matrix printers. (Abbey Enterprises)

Ribbon Feeds

There are two basic kinds of ribbons in common use for dot-matrix and fully formed-character printers, the fabric ribbon and the carbon ribbon. The fabric ribbon in Figure 13.19 is rugged and can be used many times through the printing-head mechanism. As the ribbon is used the printed characters become progressively lighter and more difficult to read. This is the most common ribbon used with dot-matrix printers because of their heavy and high-speed use for draft copies and large amounts of data.

The carbon ribbon in Figure 13.20 is sometimes used in typewriters that double as printers. These machines are fully formed-character machines and used mostly for typing of formal correspondence. The carbon ribbon can be used only once since the carbon is completely removed from its plastic backing and placed upon the paper at each strike of the printhead. The advantage of this ribbon is that the printed character can be easily removed from the paper using a special sticky tape. This type ribbon is sometimes called a correctable ribbon.

There are two common methods of installing ribbons. One is to package them in cartridges and replace them as a unit. This makes them quick, clean, and easy to replace by nontechnical personnel. The other alternative is the older method of providing the ribbons on individual spools. These require more work in replacing the ribbons, since they must be fed through the printing mechanism by hand and threaded onto a takeup spool at the opposite end. See Figure 13.21.

Common problems relating to the ribbon mechanism include jamming of the ribbon mechanism and running out of ribbon. Jamming of the mechanism will eventually cause all of the ink on the ribbon in one spot to be depleted. In severe cases, there may be a hole in the ribbon because of the constant pounding of the printhead. This is usually a mechanical problem in the feed mechanism, but occasionally a ribbon that is binding can cause such a problem.

Figure 13.20 The carbon ribbon is often used in fully formed-character printers that double as typewriters. (Abbey Enterprises)

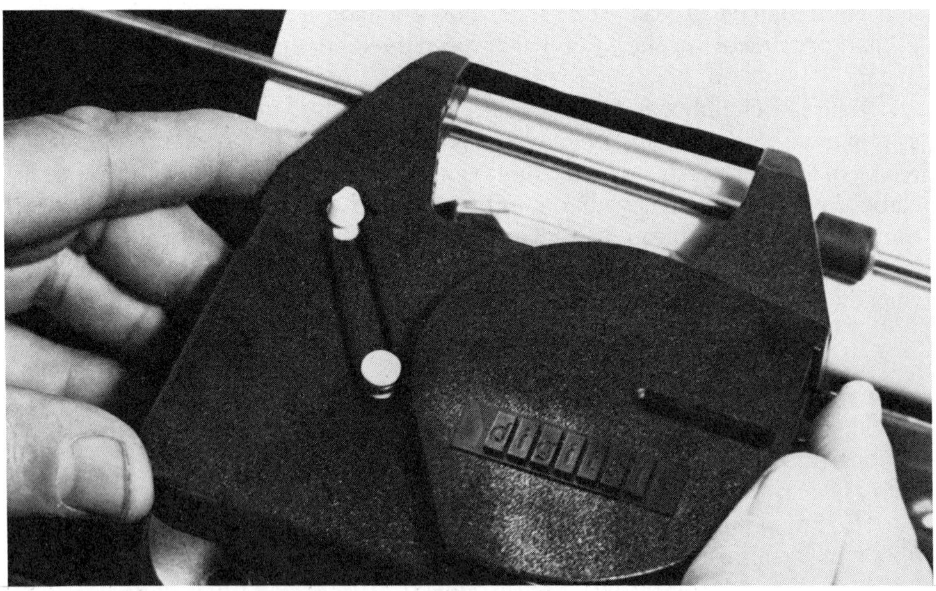

Figure 13.21 The ribbon cartridge is more convenient but often more expensive than the spool-to-spool ribbon mechanism. (Abbey Enterprises)

PRINTER TESTING

Internal Printer Tests

Computer printers have a considerable amount of electronics within them to orchestrate their action. They have special ROM chips that contain the program necessary for the printer to interpret the incoming information from the computer and convert it to the proper responses to print on the paper. Since these elements of a computer are already in the printer it is a simple matter to include a self-diagnostic routine that will greatly assist the servicing technician in determining where a problem might lie. Invoking these diagnostic routines vary from one printer to another, but a common entry method is to hold down a specific key on the keyboard while turning on the power to the printer.

To be sure there is no problem external to the printer, the cable to the computer can be disconnected entirely for these internal tests. Typical problems that might be disclosed by internal tests include missing print wires, a bad solenoid or driver on a dot-matrix printhead, and missing characters on a daisy-wheel printer. Ribbon-feed and paper-feed problems will show up with either type printer through these tests.

Computer Tests of the Printer Port

The printer port of a computer can be tested using diskette diagnostics. The serial port can be tested without anything connected to it, but a more meaningful and thorough test should be made using a special shorting plug installed on the serial port (see Chapter 7). This shorting plug has a jumper from pin 2 to 3, 4, a jumper from 4 to 5 to 8, and another 6 to 20. These jumpers cause the computer to acknowledge its own handshaking requirements and also to read the data it transmits. The servicing technician may use the BASIC program of Appendix B, which will cause the printer to output all of the characters the printer is capable of producing in a long string down the left edge of the paper.

If Computer and Printer are OK. If a printer passes the internal diagnostics tests but refuses to operate with the computer, several possibilities should be considered:

1. Check that the serial baud (bit) rate is the same on both the printer and the computer. Baud rates of 300 and 1200 are the most common, but rates of from 50 to 9600 are possible. In addition to the baud rate, the printer and the computer must agree on the same number of stop bits being sent and the kind of parity, even or odd. Only proper documentation for the equipment involved will enable the technician to verify these parameters.

   Some software, for example word-processing programs, takes over much of the work of sending data to the printer. As a result, these programs must be initially set up for the proper kind of printer and for all of the variables listed above. An install or setup program probably will be necessary to check or change these parameters within the application program.
2. Check that the printer is connected to the proper connector on the back of the computer. Most microcomputers are able to work with up to three parallel

output ports and a pair of serial ports. It is easy to connect the printer to the wrong port. Applications programs mentioned above can also select the type of printer and therefore affect the actual connector in use. The operating system can test a printer easily. Toggle the printer on with a control P and type anything on the keyboard of the computer. The printer should echo any ASCII characters typed.

3. Failure of a printer that has worked until very recently may be caused by a cabling problem. The wires within some connectors are not physically supported sufficiently well to withstand daily abuse and may break. Be particularly watchful for this kind of problem in a working situation where nothing has changed in the equipment or software for a relatively long time.

PRINTER PREVENTIVE MAINTENANCE

Printer maintenance is mainly a matter of keeping the printer clean, inside and out. The keyboard of a printer, if it has one, can be cleaned with a soft brush, taking care to brush lint and dust away from the keys as much as possible rather than pushing it down between and under the keys.

The interior of the printer can usually be reached only partially without dismantling the cabinet. A thorough job of cleaning can be accomplished by removing the cabinet and vacuuming out the interior with a small vacuum cleaner. Be careful not to damage any small mechanisms such as levers and cables. Take it slow and easy, and do not move around too quickly inside the printer. The printhead can be cleaned using a small cotton swab and denatured alcohol. The mechanisms of the printer such as the carriage rails should *only* be lubricated in accordance with the manufacturer's instructions. Use of improper lubricants can result in these rails and mechanisms becoming contaminated with sticky residue, countering any good intentions of the service technician by creating more problems than would have resulted if there were no lubrication applied in the first place. Remember too, that the printhead of some printers may be hot if the printer has been in recent full high-speed service. It may be wise to wait for a while for the head to cool off.

CHAPTER SUMMARY

This chapter has given the overall computer-printer servicing techniques at the disposal of the technician. Specifics of servicing routines must depend on the instructions of the printer manufacturers, so only general guidelines have been possible here. The chapter has also made you aware of the possibilities of internal printer diagnostics and intercabling problems and how to troubleshoot typical problems most effectively.

REVIEW QUESTIONS

1. What is hard copy?
2. What kind of printer can have full capability as a graphics printer?

3. What kind of printer has the easiest-to-read type?
4. What type of printer, dot-matrix or fully formed-character, is the fastest?
5. What printer control besides the power on/off is most likely to be the cause of complete printer inoperation due to operator error?
6. How many bits are usually used to transmit data to a printer?
7. What is the purpose of having control of a daisy-wheel printer's hammer energy?
8. Name two common baud rates for serial data transmission to a printer.
9. What binary value is the XON control byte?
10. What is meant by a printer having bidirectional capability?
11. What can operation of a dot-matrix printer without ribbon and paper do to damage the printer?
12. Name two causes for a daisy-wheel printer printing garbage.
13. Is there an occasion when both friction feed and tractor feed might be used at the same time in a printer?
14. Name the two general types of ribbons.

chapter fourteen

Installing Memory Chips or a Co-Processor

CHAPTER OVERVIEW

Installation of memory chips and numerical co-processors is only one of the many tasks the technician must be prepared to accomplish. This chapter points out the how-to and the possible problems that can arise during the installation of these common chips.

WORKING INSIDE THE COMPUTER

There is always a risk of damaging a computer when opening it. Be sure to turn off *all* power before removing the computer cabinet. This is mostly to prevent accidental shorting of the circuitry inside but also to prevent the small possibility of electric shock. It is especially important to turn off the power before connecting or disconnecting anything within the computer. This chapter deals with the installation of chips and boards—and every installation and removal of either a chip or a board *must* be done while the circuit is off.

Installing Memory Chips in System Board Sockets

Professional computers are purchased with only a minimum of memory, much like a new automobile bought without such options as power steering or power brakes, and it will often be necessary for a technician to install additional memory. This job is quite simple: just plug in the new memory chips into the sockets on the printed circuit board. A few things must be kept in mind while performing this task, however:

1. Keep the new memory chips to be installed in their original packaging until actually needed. This helps prevent static damage to the chip.
2. Work in a static-free place. This will mean that carpeting, particularly of the synthetic type, must not be allowed in the shop. Leather soles are preferable to rubber-soled shoes. Touch the computer frame with your free hand while installing chips to ground any possible charge you may have generated while moving around.

3. Be absolutely certain you are installing the chips with the 1 pin in proper orientation to the socket. Manufacturers are quite careful about labeling the sockets for 1-pin placement, but sometimes the chips themselves are less than obviously marked (see Figure 14.1). The printed circuit may be marked to indicate the end of the socket where the 1 pin of the IC should be installed (Figure 14.2).

New chips will come with their leads bent slightly outward and may not fit easily into the sockets. The leads should be bent slightly inward until the leads line up properly with the socket before they are pressed into place. One way to do this is to grasp the IC as in Figure 14.3 and gently bend all of the pins on one side together, reverse the IC, and bend the leads on the other side. A bit of practice will be necessary to get the right amount of bend the first time around. Try to get all the pins at exactly right angles to the chip.

One of the more popular memory chips is the 4164. This is a dynamic RAM chip containing 64K memory cells. Each chip is used as a single bit of storage at 64K different addresses. Since a data byte is 8 bits wide, at least eight of these chips are required to install a new bank of 64K bytes of memory. Some of the first microcomputers used 16K-bit memory chips, where each additional bank of memory added an additional 16K bytes.

Data bytes read from the memory of most microcomputers are individually checked to detect errors each time they are read. The type of error detection used is parity checking. Since each byte of memory may need an extra bit to make the parity consistent, a ninth bit is necessary. Therefore each additional bank of memory may require nine chips rather than the expected eight chips. The average cost of these chips at the time of this writing is about a dollar each, or a total of $9 for a bank of nine ICs.

Memory chips of this variety are available with different speeds of operation, 150, 200, 250, 300, and 450 nanoseconds being representative of the speeds available for

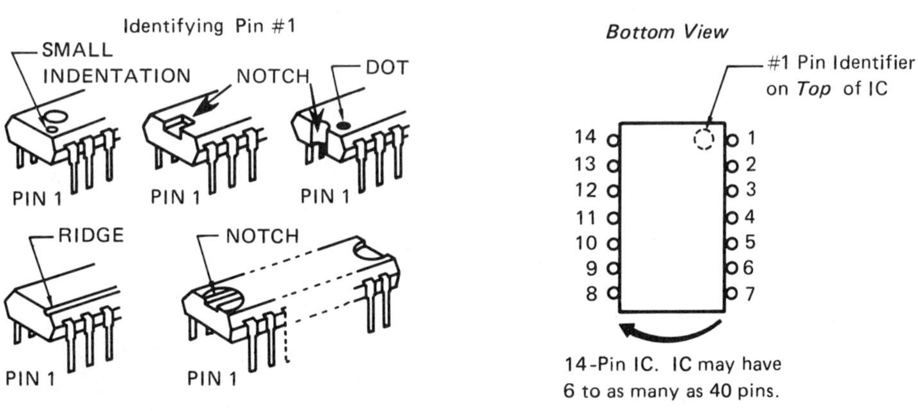

Figure 14.1 How to identify the 1 pin of an IC.

Figure 14.2 Be sure the IC #1 is properly inserted. (Abbey Enterprises)

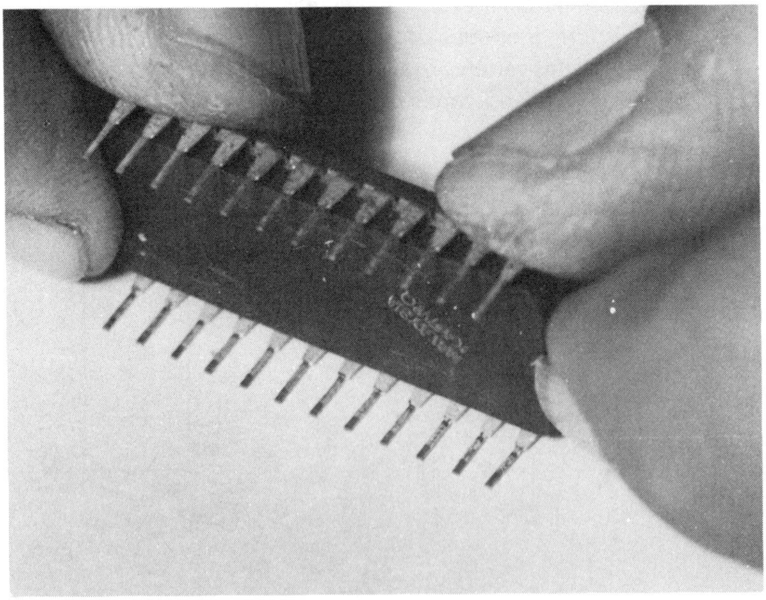

Figure 14.3 Carefully bend the IC leads so that they line up with the socket. (Abbey Enterprises)

this use. Although some brands of computer seem to work well with any of these speeds, even intermixed within the same computer, other brands of computer are very selective as to the speeds required for operation of the memory chips. Some computers may even balk at using the same speed of chip manufactured by a different company than those already installed. It is a good idea to carefully match the speeds and manufacturers of these memory chips as much as possible. The memory chip manufacturers have many different ways of coding the speed of their chips, so the manufacturer's data is necessary to decode the numbers on the chip in determining the speed of the chips.

INSTALLING MEMORY EXPANSION ON THE SYSTEM BOARD

Additional memory must be installed in such a way that the total memory has no holes in it. In other words, the proper bank of sockets must be selected to install the next bank of memory chips. Some computers have a logical physical layout of the memory chips, and installation presents no problem. In any event, the instruction book for the computer will give the necessary information as to which sockets should be filled first. The first banks of memory will probably be installed close to the factory-installed chips. The factory memory chips are often soldered into the board (see Figure 14.4).

Figure 14.4 Many computer manufacturers solder the initial memory chips into the system board. (Abbey Enterprises)

Setting the System Board Switches

In order for a microcomputer to know how memory is installed, most of them must read a set of DIP (dual in-line plastic) switches to determine how much memory is installed in the computer. These switches are read during the booting up of the system. When additional memory or option cards are added to the system board, the system board switches must be reset to indicate the new total amount of memory (Figure 14.5). The operations manual provided with each computer will give detailed information as to how these switches must be set for the different amounts of additional memory. Generally speaking, a few of these switches—usually three or four of them—will be set in a binary pattern to indicate the number of 64K banks of total memory. The following listing is representative of the way computers code the memory amount using DIP switches:

64K Banks Installed	Total Memory	Binary DIP Switch Coding
1	64K	0001
2	128K	0010
3	192K	0011
4	256K	0100
5	320K	0101
6	384K	0110
7	448K	0111
8	512K	1000
9	576K	1001
10	640K	1010

Sometimes the system memory switches are used to indicate only the amount of 64K segments in addition to the factory-installed memory. In this case, the following table would be appropriate to working on those computers that have 128K of memory factory-installed:

64K Banks Installed	Total Memory	Binary DIP Switch Coding
1	64K	0000
2	128K	0001
3	192K	0010
4	256K	0011
5	320K	0100
6	384K	0101
7	448K	0110
8	512K	0111
9	576K	1000
10	640K	1001

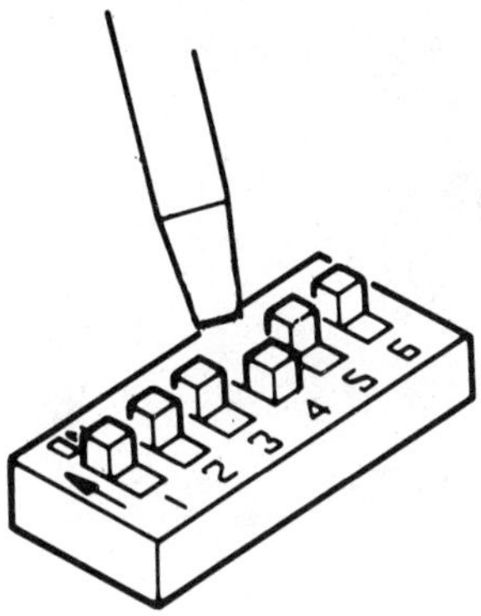

Figure 14.5 The system board switches must be set properly to use any additional memory chips installed. (Courtesy of Corona Data Systems)

In this example, a computer might have 64K of initial factory memory, and the installation of an additional four banks of 64K of memory (320K total) would result in a binary count of 0100 on the switches. Note that the four corresponds directly to the 0100 binary setting.

About the time the technician is comfortable with this method of memory identification, a computer that reverses the switch settings shows up. An example like the one above would use switch settings of 1011 rather than 0100.

After memory chips are installed they must test it. Be sure that the chips are installed all the way into their sockets and turn on the computer. Watch the monitor carefully. If there are any bad memory chips you may have a computer that will give a numerical code for a moment at the top left of the screen before an error appears, such as:

PARITY CHECK ONE

This error code would indicate a problem in the memory just installed on the system board. The numerical code indicates the bank in error. Consult the computer instruction book for the interpretation of the codes. Additional checking of the memory is advisable using the diskette diagnostics program. Put the program into a "forever" loop and run continuous checks of the memory for a half-hour or more if practical.

Installing Memory Expansion Chips on an Option Board

The instruction manual for the option card must be read and understood in detail before installing an option card into a computer. Option cards that allow the addition of six or more banks of 64K memory chips are available (see Figure 14.6). Installing memory chips in these cards is similar to the methods described earlier in this chapter. Install them in the proper order of banks, ensuring that the memory will be continuous in addressing. The information booklet supplied with the option card will specify

Figure 14.6 A memory-expansion option board that allows for multiple banks of 64K bytes of memory. (Abbey Enterprises)

which banks must be filled first. Be sure that the system board switches are set for the proper amount of memory according to the number of banks added. When installing memory on an option board, there is another set of switches on the option board that require setting. These switches set the starting address of the memory banks on the card—necessary because the manufacturer of the card has no way of knowing how much memory will have been installed on the system board of a specific computer or how many other option boards might be used in addresses ahead of the card in question.

The proper setting of the switches on the option card is not limited to the memory-starting address alone. Some card manufacturers offer the option of bypassing the parity-check feature of the card. This decision is one that must be made by the user of the card. True, it can cause a computer crash if an error is detected by the parity-checking circuitry, but some business users would rather that happen, with a possible loss of data, than have the smallest possibility of an error creeping undetected into important data. Additional switch settings must be set on the option card to determine the addressing of any serial or parallel ports that may also be offered on the card.

Once the option card is ready for installation look for a card guide in the box the option card came in (see Figure 7.21). The card guide provides some support on the far end of the option card and helps prevent the boards flexing during shipment.

Multiple function cards that offer several options on a single board may not have enough room on the end of the card for all of the necessary connectors to the outside world. Additional external connectors from the option card may be installed in the rear panel area adjacent to unused expansion slots. See Figure 14.7.

Memory tests should be made after installing option card memory, too. ROM diagnostics will catch most memory errors, as indicated earlier in this chapter. The

Figure 14.7 Mounting an external connector in place of another card. (Abbey Enterprises)

error message for an error on an option card is different from that of a system board memory error:

PARITY CHECK TWO

but is not preceded by an error location. See Chapter 7 for further details of locating memory problems on an option board.

INSTALLING AN 8087 MATH CO-PROCESSOR

Although the 8088 microprocessor used in the majority of microcomputers is far more capable of mathematics calculations than its predecessors, another large-scale integrated circuit called the 8087 is now available to do the math operations. This chip is optimized for calculating speed and for doing higher-math operations, such as trigonometry.

Installation of the chip requires a bit more care than a memory chip, since this single chip can cost as much as $250. It is a 40-pin IC and looks very much like the 8088. Installation consists of carefully bending the pins to align with the socket and gently pressing it into place. Be careful, of course, that you do *not* get it in backwards, which could be a very costly mistake. Look for its socket next to the CPU chip, the 8088.

CHAPTER SUMMARY

This chapter has pointed the way to successful addition of optional memory to the computer. The necessity and methods of setting the system and option card switches were discussed. Also covered was the procedure for installing the 8087 math co-processor, required for efficient operation of some advanced mathematical applications programs.

REVIEW QUESTIONS

1. Beside turning off power before installing new additional memory chips in a computer, what must you do before turning on power to utilize these new chips?
2. Can memory be added to an option board before the system board memory sockets are filled?
3. What is an 8087 chip?
4. What three precautions must be observed when installing an 8087?

part four

Troubleshooting Computer Software Problems

chapter fifteen

Troubleshooting Computer Software Problems

CHAPTER OVERVIEW

This chapter is among the most important of this book. Even if you are highly qualified to handle the hardware and electronics portions of a repair job, the overall impression given a customer is pretty weak if you cannot help resolve routine software problems—or worse yet, fail to recognize them! This chapter will help in analyzing problems that are entirely related to the programs used with a computer, problems that may make the computer seem defective when it really isn't at all.

RANDOM ACCESS MEMORY: THE HEART OF A COMPUTER

Computers interpret instructions and manipulate data only while it is resident in RAM. Since RAM has a limited length, other means are used to store the massive number of bytes that represent programs and data. Floppy and hard disk drives are common examples of mass storage used for this purpose. When a program is executed, then, it must first be taken from such a storage media and copied into RAM. After the program is loaded into RAM, the computer then goes to the beginning of that program in RAM and begins to execute the instructions of the program there.

Programs share RAM with other information, too. Certain portions of RAM are reserved for DOS commands and jump tables, for instance. Because of this, programs to be executed must start at a specific location in memory. Available RAM can be set aside in large amounts for special purposes such as RAM disks (a program that makes a portion of RAM operate like an additional disk drive for fast and wear-free temporary storage of data), and print spoolers (which load data to be printed into a section of RAM), thus through the use of direct memory access (DMA) freeing the CPU for other tasks while printing.

Generally speaking, the A or first floppy drive of the computer will be used to store the programs that will be executed on the computer, perhaps word-processing or electronic spreadsheet programs. If the computer is supplied with a second or B drive, that will usually be the one into which is put a diskette which stores the data generated and used by the program in the A drive.

Booting Up the Computer

The computer is usually set up to boot from the A diskette drive. In other words, it will look at the A drive diskette to have the operating system. There are two special programs that must be on the booting diskette of a microcomputer in order for it to operate: BIOS.COM and DOS.COM files. Without them, you will get an error message:

```
Non-System Disk or Disk Error
Replace and strike any key when ready
```

These error messages mean that one or both of these programs cannot be read or are missing. The files BIO.COM and DOS.COM are called IBMBIO.COM and IBMDOS.COM on IBM software. These two files and the VOLUME NAME are unique among normal files in that they are hidden files, and as such they will not appear on a normal readout of a diskette directory. To verify if they are listed, use the utility program called CHKDSK. Insert the questionable disk in the B drive and load the CHKDSK program (probably on your utilities diskette) into the A drive. Type CHKDSK B: when the DOS prompt A> appears. A readout such as the following might appear:

```
A>CHKDSK B:

   362496 bytes total disk space
    22528 bytes in 3 hidden files   <......(This is the entry to look for.)
   168960 bytes in 12 user files
   171008 bytes available on disk

301056 bytes total memory
275936 bytes free
```

The three hidden files referred to by the line indicated above are the BIO.COM, DOS.COM, and VOLUME LABEL entries in the diskette directory. The computer cannot boot up from the diskette in question without the BIO.COM and the DOS.COM files. The VOLUME NAME, on the other hand, is purely optional, an electronic nametag for the diskette.

A fourth program, COMMAND.COM, is also necessary for the diskette to be completely bootable. If it alone is missing or damaged, the following error will be displayed:

```
Bad or Missing Command Interpreter
```

The COMMAND.COM file is visible in a directory listing.

The BIO.COM, DOS.COM, and COMMAND.COM files are necessary only on a diskette that will be used to boot up the computer. Data-file diskettes do not need the system files.

Data diskettes without the system installed may provide a response as follows with the CHKDSK program:

```
A>CHKDSK B:

    362496 bytes total disk space
    129024 bytes in 6 user files
    233472 bytes available on disk

301056 bytes total memory
275936 bytes free
```

Note that there are no hidden files, as required for a bootable diskette.

USING APPLICATIONS SOFTWARE THAT WORKED WELL UNTIL THE PROBLEM AROSE

The first computer commands a computer technician should become familiar with are as follows:

DIR (directory)

COPY

ERASE

RENAME

TYPE (put on the screen)

These commands are contained in the program COMMAND.COM and form the basis of looking at and manipulating files. The technician should be very familiar with how to find out what is on a disk by typing DIR, looking at a file by typing TYPE followed by the whole name of the file to be observed, erasing a file by typing ERASE and the full name of the file to be deleted, and renaming a file by typing RENAME followed by the present name and then the desired name of the file. The COPY command is very useful and is often used to copy files one wishes to manipulate. Just type the word COPY, followed by the name of the originating file and then the name of the new file. The new file name can be different, and it is usually preceded by a drive designator and a colon. For instance, a file on the A drive called TEST.BAS could be copied to the other drive under the same or a different name such as B:TEST.BAS. Details of these commands can be found in the DOS instruction manual.

When a problem arises in a system that has been working properly for some time with specific software, there are several paths that the technician can take to verify if the problem is the hardware (disk drive or other parts of the computer) or if it is a problem caused by a bad diskette. Consider the options available:

1. Try the computer using a duplicate (backup) diskette of the same software. If the duplicate software works well, the problem is verified as a bad diskette. (Further options as to what to do with the bad diskette are covered later in this chapter.) If the backup doesn't work there is probably a problem in the computer. The diskette drive is a prime suspect. See Chapter 11 for details of this type of failure.

2. Try the suspected diskette in another computer of the same type. If the diskette doesn't work in another computer, this is a good indication that the diskette has been damaged.

The addition of option cards can cause software that had previously worked just fine suddenly to crash the computer. This is most often the case when the installation is an option board that has an additional I/O port, parallel or serial. The installation of a new port that has the same address as an existing port in the computer cases a port "collision" that can cause the computer to crash. The addresses of any installed port must be verified to ensure that it is different from the ports already installed. See Chapter 7 for more information on this subject.

In any case of a suspected hardware failure, the diagnostic programs should be used to localize the problem in the computer. It is often a memory failure that causes an established program to suddenly begin crashing the computer.

USING NEW APPLICATIONS SOFTWARE

Buying new software does not mean that you will be able to put the new diskette into the computer, turn it on, and have the program execute flawlessly. To begin with, economics play a part. You have bought software that will most often be built "on top of" the DOS that came with the computer. The company you purchased your new software from cannot legally sell the diskette operating system too and must sell it without that system. Therefore you, as the software installing technician may be required to do a bit of diskette manipulation before the program will run. Problems such as operator misinterpretation of the prompts and other fine points of the new software should be clarified at this point, if possible. A familiarity with the new software will be required, of course, to answer any questions the computer operator might ask. This may or may not be expected of the field computer servicing technician and will be a matter of policy of the shop.

Here is how it is usually done. Assume that the computer is provided with two diskette drives and that the program has been provided on a diskette which the technician will now copy.

1. Put the operating system on a new, formatted diskette. Use the utility program FORMAT to prepare a diskette to receive the new program. Remember that the FORMAT command wipes *all* data from the diskette being formatted, so if a used diskette is to be reused, be certain that any data or programs on it are not valuable. To format, put the diskette with the FORMAT.COM program on it in the A drive and the diskette to be used for the new copy of your purchased program in the B drive. Be sure you have the DOS prompt, the A>, showing and then type in FORMAT B:/S, then hit

RETURN. After an access to the A drive and a few moments the prompt will appear to insert your diskette to be formatted into the B drive. Since you have already placed it there, hit the space bar. The space bar is a good one to get into the habit of hitting when invited to "Hit any key," since it probably would do the least damage in any application. At the conclusion of this formatting process you will have a diskette that has the proper programming to boot up the computer.

2. Copy-protect the original software. This step is very necessary to protect the owner's investment in the software. Since some programs cost several hundred dollars or more initially, this protection is an absolute necessity. The very first step is to install a write-protect sticker so that the new software cannot be destroyed by accident. On 5 1/4-inch diskettes, cover the write-protect with an opaque tape. On 8-inch diskettes, however, the opposite is necessary: *uncover* the write-protect notch to protect the program.

3. Copy all the new software files onto the formatted diskette. To do this, place the new software in the A drive in place of the utilities diskette you had there. Type out the command COPY *.* B: and hit RETURN. This will copy each of the files on the A diskette onto the B diskette without disturbing the system files already on the B diskette. When the computer has completed the copying of all the A diskette files you should get a report as to how many were copied, similar to this:

```
6 File(s) copied
```

There are two other ways to accomplish this task as well, but the above procedure is the surest way of getting the most space out of your diskettes.

4. Once you have copied the new software, put the original diskette in a safe place immediately! This may be a safe-deposit box, the owner's home, or any other place you desire. The storage of the backup diskettes should be at normal room temperature away from any possible magnetic fields.

5. Run the new software installation program, if any. Many programs require special options to be selected within the software. As an example, a particular program may offer special programming of the function keys of the computer for use within the new software. In order to accomplish this customizing of the software, a special program will be included with the new software. This program should be invoked by typing its name and carefully reading and following the directions and prompts that follow. It is also necessary to read the instructions! (I find myself hitting my keyboard harder while typing those words, READ THE INSTRUCTIONS. An awful lot of time can be saved by performing this simple task, in contrast with what too many people do.) Only by reading and understanding the instructions can the new software be used to its fullest benefit.

6. Run the software to be sure that it operates as it should. The details of running new software must rightfully rest with those who will be operating it on a daily basis, but the technician should attempt to operate some of the more basic functions of the software to ensure that it is, indeed, operating as expected. As a minimum, the program should load into the computer and show, perhaps, a beginning menu. If there is a

problem at this point, it is probably not the responsibility of the technician but one to be handled with the software distributor, who may be able to help.

7. Add fine touches to the new software as needed. The fine touches include setting up the AUTOEXEC.BAT file and possibly using some of the features of the MODE command to ensure that the software will load automatically and that the program outputs to the printer, if any, are successful. The AUTOEXEC.BAT file is a list of DOS directions to be executed in order automatically by the computer rather than having to enter them manually each time the computer is turned on. Here is an example of such a file, generated using a word-processing program or the EDLIN program.

```
SETCLOCK
MODE COM2:12,,7,1,P
MODE LPT1:=COM2
B:
A:WS
```

This particular example file calls for a SETCLOCK program that automatically sets the computer's internal clock to the right time and loads in the correct date, all from an option card with a battery-backup clock. Next the computer is adjusted so that any serial communications from the serial port called COM2 will send data at 1220 baud, using even parity, 7 data bits, 1 stop bit, and is designated for use as a printer output. The MODE command should be familiar to the servicing technician, particularly one who installs it is expected to connect printers to microcomputers.

Software Incompatibility Problems

The programmers who write software write it with certain suppositions in mind. The addresses for the video memory and the address for the I/O ports are some of these assumptions. When a program is run in a machine for which the addresses do not coincide, the program crashes. Another problem may arise from the fact that IBM computers have BASIC contained within special ROM chips in their computers *only*. Any program written for the IBM may depend upon these ROM chips and make program calls to routines there. A compatible machine cannot have these ROM programs because of copyright laws. For these reason, any program written primarily for an IBM should be tested first to be sure it will actually run on a compatible machine before it is purchased. For that matter, any program being purchased should be tested first.

Copy-Protected Software

Attempting to copy some programs may meet with defeat. In order to protect their investment in the software from being copied and given away without royalties, some programs are copy-protected. Attempts to copy these files cause the computer to crash, or the copy is partially or totally useless. These planned failures are done in one or more of several ways:

1. Deliberate CRC errors on the diskette sectors
2. Using an additional one or two tracks, such as 40 and 41 of a 5 1/4-inch diskette. (Only tracks 0 to 39 are legal.)
3. Manipulating or duplicating diskette sector identification
4. Burning a laser hole in the diskette
5. Providing software or hardware keys required to run the software.

Although it is a licensed owner's right to copy for archival purposes, it is difficult to copy such programs, either for backup or for everyday use. Special programs are available, none of them infallible, which may make such programs copyable. An example is the COPYII-PC or COPYWRITE programs. Some programs are truly copyable only through the use of an original diskette, but not through a copy of it. The technician must be aware that the use of such software to make illegal copies of copyright-protected material carries stiff penalties.

Possible Memory Allocation Problems

New software may require a great deal of available RAM memory. One version of the program LOTUS 1-2-3, for instance, recommends 196K bytes of memory to run the program. Running a program with a minimal amount of memory risks a computer crash and the loss of data and operator time. The technician, reading the instructions for the new program, should be ready to recommend the installation of more RAM if necessary for the software in question.

DATA LOSS PROBLEMS

Since prevention is the best cure, data loss can be minimized by two simple precautions:

Make a *backup* diskette of important programs and data.

Provide voltage-surge protection and possibly a battery power backup.

The making of a backup diskette has already been discussed in this chapter and the matter of surge and power backup systems was covered in Chapter 2. The frequency with which backup copies are made depends upon the importance of the data recorded. The more important the data, the more often backup data diskettes should be made. The same rationale applies to the use of a battery backup system for the computer. The more important the use of the computer, the more important it is to have the backup system. Remember, anything in RAM can be destroyed if there is a power fluctuation of sufficient amplitude and duration.

It is possible for data to *seem* to have been lost if the diskette drive is defective. The misalignment of a drive may not be evident if the same diskettes are used frequently in a single drive. The information may be written slightly off proper track position and reread by the same misaligned head without any problem being evident. If another diskette, properly written on the track position, is then used in this misaligned drive, the operator may assume that the diskette has been damaged when there is nothing at all wrong with it. For this reason, *never assume that the diskette is bad until you have had a chance to attempt reading the data with other drives*, preferably installed in other computers. To do so may result in losing data that could have been easily retrieved on a good drive and/or computer. The reverse of this situation is also possible: data written off proper track by a bad drive will be unreadable by a good drive. The only solution here is to read the data with the misaligned drive and then transfer the data to another drive for proper recording. When the data has been retrieved, the drive can be repaired as discussed in Chapter 11. In any case of lost data, look for the cause and correct it if at all possible. It may be something as simple as cautioning the operator not to drop scissors (probably magnetized) on the diskettes scattered about the desk. Data can also be lost by dirt or fingerprints on the diskette recording surface. Diskettes are fragile and should be treated with the greatest of care. Magnets and fingerprints are among the greatest enemies of the diskette.

Recovering Lost Data

If there is a backup diskette in existence for the program in question, by all means copy that backup and you are back in business. If not, it is still possible in some cases to retrieve damaged data. The success of the retrieval effort will depend mostly upon the amount of damage done, and in some cases the skill of the technician. There are several common ways of retrieving lost data:

1. *Use of an unerasing program.* One of the more common problems causing data loss is operator error resulting in the erasure of a diskette file, which removes part of the directory entry. The data, however, remains on the diskette and can be recovered with appropriate software. One such program is one of the Norton utilities, the UE or unerase program.

2. *Use of the* CHKDSK *program.* The CHKDSK program, used with the /F option, is able to identify and label strings of clusters of data recorded on the diskette and to prepare for their "fix". It does this by checking the directory and file allocation tables. If any are found, they can be retrieved, analyzed, and either given a meaningful name and manipulated as a normal file or simply erased. This program will assign a set of filenames such as this:

```
FILE0001.CHK
FILE0002.CHK
FILE0003.CHK
etc.
```

Each string of lost clusters will be given consecutive file numbers. This program is especially useful when a computer crash has managed to lose track of data that it would normally have written into the directory of the diskette.

3. *Use of the* RECOVER *program.* The technician might also be able to use the RECOVER utility program to recover files when the directory of the diskette has been damaged.

4. *Use of special programs for detailed diskette work or reconstruction of files.* Another option that could be used is to run a program such as Media Magician, available from Photon Software, Bellevue, Washington. This program allows a technician detailed access to any of the information on the diskette and includes the capacity to work with hard disks. Its use requires an intimate knowledge of the diskette data format. With this program a search can be made for specific chains of data and data changed, erased completely, or retrieval of records that have been deleted from the directory.

CHAPTER SUMMARY

This chapter has shown some solutions to software problems. Anyone using the use of these solutions may border on being less of a technician and more of a computer operator. The student of computer repair can benefit by having a good knowledge of DOS operations and commands available to help track and correct problems. Practice on a good working computer is of paramount importance. Confidence in repair begins with confidence in the computer and its normal operation.

REVIEW QUESTIONS

1. For which drive does a microcomputer usually boot?
2. What is a hidden file on a diskette?
3. Name the two hidden files that must be present on a diskette to make that diskette a bootable diskette.
4. Name the visible file that must be present on a diskette to make that diskette a bootable diskette.
5. What is meant by an error message of BAD OR MISSING COMMAND INTERPRETER?
6. Name a DOS utility program that enables you to see if there are hidden files on a diskette.
7. If a diskette worked properly in a computer until just recently, what two steps might be used to verify that the diskette has been damaged?
8. What can be used in a case of a suspected hardware failure to localize a problem without opening the computer?
9. What must be done to newly purchased software before it will boot and run on a microcomputer?
10. What should be done with the original diskette purchased with software recorded on them?
11. Name three programs that might be used to regain some or all of damaged or lost data.

appendix A

Interface Cabling Conventions

This appendix deals with repairing cables that carry signals from microcomputers to peripheral equipment: monitors, printers, and modems. Sufficient information is also given to allow a technician to fabricate necessary cables for many applications.

Signals passing back and forth between computer equipment will be one of three types: serial wire signals, serial coaxial cable signals, or parallel wire signals. Serial signals are digital pulses sent over a pair of wires or through a coaxial cable. Coaxial signals are high-frequency digital signals confined to coaxial cables because of their high frequency, need for shielding against external electrical noises, and need for transmission from source to destination over long distances without reflections within the cable. Parallel wire signals are multiple wires carrying digital signals. The most common connectors for these types of signals are discussed in detail.

THE RS-232C SERIAL DATA STANDARD

The RS (recommended standard) 232 (version of the standard) C (third or "C" revision) is the most widely used serial data connection between a computer and a modem. Derivations of the standard are used to provide serial communications between other equipment such as two computers.

The 25-pin D Connector Most Commonly Used for Serial Data Transmission

This connector has an outer shell that, with a stretch of the imagination, resembles a squared-off D. These connectors are often used for serial data transmission. They are usually referred to on microcomputers as COM1 or COM2 ports (see Figure 7.34). The standard pin layout for this type of connector is the RS-232C standard. Table AI.1 shows the RS-232C pinouts and their various signals.

For other applications of serial data transmission that do not use telephone line signals such as ringing, busy tones, dialing pulses, etc., only a few of the pins are used for a particular job. A serial printer, for instance, might use only three lines; DTE 2 to Printer 3, DTE 7 to Printer 7 (ground), a handshaking lead to DTE 6 from a specified

Table AI-1 RS232-C Connections

Pin		Name	Direction	Function
			DTE DCE \ /	
1	*	FG	None	Frame Ground
2	#	TD	--->	Transmitted Data
3	#	RD	<---	Received Data
4	#	RTS	--->	Request To Send
5	#	CTS	<---	Clear To Send
6	#	DSR	<---	Data Set Ready
7	#	SG	None	Signal Ground
8		DCD	<---	Data Carrier Detect
9	*		<---	Positive DC Test Voltage
10	*		<---	Negative DC Test Voltage
11		QM	<---	Equalizer Mode
12	*	(S)DCD	<---	Sec. Data Carrier Detect
13	*	(S)CTS	<---	Sec. Clear To Send
14	*	(S)TD	--->	Sec. Transmitted Data
		or NS	--->	New Sync
15		TC	<---	Transmitter Clock
16	*	(S)RD	<---	Sec. Received Data
		or DCT	<---	Divided Clock, Transmitter
17		RC	<---	Receiver Clock
18		DCR	<---	Divided Clock, Receiver
19	*	(S)RTS	--->	Sec. Request To Send
20	#	DTR	--->	Data Terminal Ready
21	*	SQ	<---	Signal Quality Detect
22		RI	<---	Ring Indicator
23			--->	Data Rate Selector
			<---	Data Rate Selector
24	*	TC	--->	Ext. Transmitter Clock
25			--->	Busy

The most important connections used with microcomputers. Other lines frequently not connected.
* Omitted connection on many computers, including the IBM PC.

lead on the printer. Software handshaking, on the other hand, might require the data flow from the DTE 2 to the printers, 3, handshaking data flow back from the Printers, 2 to the DTE 3 (cross-connecting them), and a common ground lead connecting 7 on both. In order to provide proper signals for the computer to operate such a printer, a jumper may have to be placed between terminals 4 and 5 of the DTE, eliminating this as a handshaking requirement. The software that outputs data to the connector is also responsible for monitoring which of the pins, and how many, are monitored for handshaking, the process of being sure that it is okay to send more data.

MODEM CABLES

The following is a listing of all the lines used by a Hayes Smartmodem™.

Table AI-2 Example of cable connections to a smart modem.

Pin	Signal Direction	Use
1	None	Protective Ground
2	--->	Transmit Data
3	<---	Receive Data
5	<---	Clear To Send
6	<---	Data Set Ready
7	None	Signal Ground
8	<---	Carrier Detect
12	<---	High Speed Indicator
20	--->	Data Terminal Ready
22	<---	Ring Indicator

MONITOR ADAPTER CABLES

IBM connections for the various connectors are shown in Table AI.3.

Table AI-3 Typical pinouts of the connectors found on a monitor adapter card

(Pinouts for monochrome direct drives, color direct drives, composite output, light pen, and RF modulator outputs.

Monochrome:
Pin 1 Ground
Pin 2 Ground
Pin 3 Not Used
Pin 4 Not Used
Pin 5 Not Used
Pin 6 Intensity Signal
Pin 7 Video signal
Pin 8 Horizontal Sync Pulses
Pin 9 Vertical Sync Pulses

Color:
Pin 1 Ground
Pin 2 Ground
Pin 3 Red signal
Pin 4 Green signal
Pin 5 Blue Signal
Pin 6 Intensity Signal
Pin 7 (Reserved)
Pin 8 Horizontal Sync Pulses
Pin 9 Vertical Sync Pulses

Light Pen
Pin 1 Light pen input to monitor adapter card
Pin 2 Not used, a key.
Pin 3 Light pen switch output to monitor adapter card
Pin 4 Ground
Pin 5 +5 VDC to light pen
Pin 6 +12 VDC to light pen

RF Modulator
Pin 1 +12 VDC to power modulator
Pin 2 Not used, a key.
Pin 3 Composite video to modulator
Pin 4 Ground

The direct drive monochrome monitor output connector is often a 9-pin D connector with the pinouts of Table AI.3. Note the similarities with the 9-pin D connector (same connector) used for color monitors. The signals on these lines are all TTL-compatible.

The RCA jack is the one favored for passing composite video information to the computer's monitor. *Composite* means that the video signals, including color signal when using color monitors, are sent along with the necessary pulses for both vertical and horizontal synchronization over the single coaxial cable that mates to this connector. The center is the hot lead and the outer shell is the ground. The cable attached to this connector must be shielded. The signals passed by this type cable are similar to the signals produced at the output of a video detector in a television set. Their amplitude coming from the computer should be about 1.5 volts peak to peak as viewed on an oscilloscope. These signals are shown in Figure 12.4.

The TV modulator jack is provided to power up an external modulator. It is most often located internal to the computer, somewhere near the rear of the computer on the monitor card. It is usually four pins sticking up from the board, with one of them, pin 2, missing as a key. Note that the power is +12V, not +5V as used with the ICs internal to the computer.

The light-pen connector is also usually a row of pins in the same general location as the TV modulator connector, internal to the computer and on the monitor adapter card. Pin 2 is again missing, with a total of six pins in a row to identify this connector.

PRINTER CABLES

Centronics Connectors

Centronics parallel data transmission is accomplished by the simultaneous transmission of the 8 bits making up a byte rather than one-bit-at-a-time as in serial transmission. Each byte of information is accepted by the printer before another is sent. Parallel transmission requires a separate data line for each of the bits, in addition to other lines used for handshaking.

Table AI-4 Centronics parallel printer standard

Pin	Centronics Line Name	IBM 25-pin D connections	Direction Computer Printer
1 *	Data Strobe (L)	1	--->
2 *	Data Bit 0	2	--->
3 *	Data Bit 1	3	--->
4 *	Data Bit 2	4	--->
5 *	Data Bit 3	5	--->
6 *	Data Bit 4	6	--->

(continued)

Table AI-4 (continued)

Pin	Centronics Line Name	IBM 25-pin D connections	Direction Computer Printer
7 *	Data Bit 5	7	--->
8 *	Data Bit 6	8	--->
9	Data Bit 7	9	--->
10 *	Acknowledge strobe (L)	10	<---
11 *	Busy #	11	<---
12	Paper End	12	<---
13	Select	13	<---
14	Supply Ground	14&	Special Use
15	Oscxt		Not generally used
16	Logic Ground		Special Use
17	Chassis Ground		Special Use
18	+ 5 Volts		Not generally used
19	Data Strobe Gnd		Ground
20	D0 Ground	18	Ground
21	D1 Ground	19	Ground
22	D2 Ground	20	Ground
23	D3 Ground	21	Ground
24	D4 Ground	22	Ground
25	D5 Ground	23	Ground
26	D6 Ground	24	Ground
27	D7 Ground	25	Ground
28	Acknowledge Gnd		Ground
29	Busy Gnd		Ground
30	Input Prime		Not generally used
31	Input Prime	16%	Not generally used
32	Fault (Error)	15+	<---
33	Undefined		Not generally used
34	Undefined		Not generally used
35	Undefined		Not generally used
36	Undefined	17$	Not generally used

Notes:
(L) means an active low signal. All others active high.
\# The busy signal is usually active high, but may be reversed with some printers.
* A few parallel printers will operate with only these signals.
% Centronics 16 used in IBM as INIT (L) signal.
& Centronics 14 used in IBM as AUTO FEED XT (L).
\+ Centronics 32 connected to IBM 15. Error (L) signal.
$ Centronics 36 connected to IBM 17, used as Select In, SCLT IN (L). High sent to printer on this line disables the printer.

All Centronics and IBM parallel printer voltages are TTL-compatible.

Centronics Definitions:

Data Strobe = short negative pulse sent by computer to signify data on parallel lines is stable.

Acknowledge Strobe = short negative strobe to the computer, indicating that the printer is ready for the next byte of data.

Busy = a logic high on this line indicates that the printer cannot accept more data. Sometimes called a not-ready line. Used in conjunction with the acknowledge line.

Paper End = a signal from the printer to the computer telling it that there is no more paper.

Select = May be used as a signal from the printer to inform the computer that the printer is turned on.

Fault (Error) = May be used as a signal to the computer upon any kind of printer problem, including when the operator takes the printer off-line.

AUTO FEED XT = When this line is held low by computer, printer will advance one line after printing.

INIT = Initialize the printer. Clear buffers, reinitialize printhead to starting position.

IBM uses a 25-pin D connector identical to that used for the RS-232C port for parallel printers, too. As an indication only, look for male pins on a 25-pin plug at the back of an IBM to be a serial port and the female connector to be a parallel port. Depending upon the manufacturer of the option card that may be involved with a specific port, this convention may or may not hold true.

A close inspection of the Centronics plug will show that the high-speed circuits of data strobe, data bits, and the acknowledge and busy signals are all on one side of the plug with the corresponding grounds for those signals directly across the plug nearest them. This provides grounds between these leads for shielding and isolation when using a ribbon cable or when using twisted-pair wire cables.

IEEE-488 CABLE CONNECTIONS

The IEEE 488 interfacing standard was initiated by the Institute of Electrical and Electronic Engineers (IEEE). It is also called the general purpose interface bus (GPIB) or the Hewlett-Packard Interface Bus (HP-IB), all of them having the same pinout numbers, functions, and the like. This bus was intended for short-distance computer-to-instrumentation use or other bidirectional data applications.

Many modern digital instruments are being designed with an IEEE-488 bus capability. This enables the instruments to be operated remotely by a computer, to have the instrument take data from the computer (e.g., a signal generator is told to generate a specific frequency) to obtain data from an instrument (e.g., get a voltage reading from a

Table AI.5 IEEE-488 interfacing standard

Pin	Use	Direction Cntrlr-Tlkr/Lsnr	Signal Name
1	D	<-->	D101 Data Bit 0
2	D	<-->	D102 Data Bit 1
3	D	<-->	D103 Data Bit 2
4	D	<-->	D104 Data Bit 3
5	G	--->	End or Identify (EOI) (Return Pin # 24)
6	H	--->	Data Valid (DAV) (High Valid)
7	H	<---	Not Ready for Data (NRFD) (High Ready)
8	H	<---	Not Data Accepted (NDAC) (High Accepted)
9	G	--->	Interface Clear (IFC)
10	G	<---	Service Request Line (SRQ)
11	G	--->	Attention (ATN)
12		None	Shield - Earth Ground
13	D	<-->	D105 Data Bit 4
14	D	<-->	D106 Data Bit 5
15	D	<-->	D107 Data Bit 6
16	D	<-->	D108 Data Bit 7
17	G	--->	Remote Enable (REN) (Return Pin # 24)
18		--->	DAV Ground
19		<---	NRFD Ground
20		<---	NDAC Ground
21		<---	IFC Ground
22		--->	SRQ Ground
23		--->	ATN Ground
24		<-->	Logic Ground

Use Key: D = Bidirectional Data Lines H = Handshaking Lines
G = General Interface Management Lines

digital voltmeter), or both (set an oscilloscopes operating parameters, then take a reading).

The signals used in the IEEE-488 standard are TTL-compatible. All signals are inverted such that a high is a 0 and a low is a 1. All of the line output drivers used with this standard can be three-stated to an open-circuit configuration. Up to 16 devices may be interconnected with a maximum cable length of 6 feet between each unit.

The IEEE-488 standard consists of 16 lines that connect all units of the system in parallel. All data transfer is under the supervision of one of the units called a controller. This is often a computer. The other instruments may be either talkers (which originate and send data on the data bus) or listeners (which use the data on the data bus) or both.

The IFC line (interface clear) is used by the controller to override all activity, putting the bus into an initialized state. Then is done only if something has gone wrong with the data transfer.

The REN line (remote enable) is used by the controller to take remote control of a listener instrument away from the front panel controls and force it to use the data sent by the system talker.

Data Flow on the IEEE-488 Bus

The controller initiates system operation by setting the ATN line true (low) and sending talk or listen addresses on the data lines in 7-bit ASCII code to the individual instruments connected to the system. These addresses are preset on each instrument by one of three possible means:

Permanently by the instrument manufacturer

By setting address switches on the instrument

By setting jumpers internal to the instrument

While the ATN line is pulled low by the controller, all of the other instruments in the system are forced into a listening state. This low indicates that there is controlling information on the eight system bus lines. When the ATN line goes false (high), only those instruments that have been addressed will be able to send or receive data on the bus. While any of the connected instruments can listen to the system data bus, only one talker may be active at any one time.

When a talker is designated, all other talkers are automatically disabled. The talker can then put data on the system bus lines in eight-bit bytes. The DAV (data valid) line is controlled by the system talker.

The talker begins a data transfer between itself and the system listeners by first monitoring the NRFD line. This line is ORed by all of the system listeners. Any of the listeners may pull this line true (low), indicating that they are not ready for a data transfer. The talker idles, watching this line, until all listeners have released their hold on it and it goes high (true). When this happens, the talker puts data levels on the eight data lines and two microseconds later pulls the DAV line true (low) to signify that the data is stable and ready to be read by the system listeners.

The system listeners control the NRFD (not ready for data) and NDAC (not data accepted) lines. As each listener absorbs the data presented, it then, by using an ORing arrangement with other instruments in the system, releases its individual hold on the NDAC line. When the last instrument releases this line it goes high, indicating to the talker that all data has been read and accepted.

When the talker sees that the data has been accepted by all the system listeners, it releases the low on the DAV line and changes the data to new values. Releasing the DAV line tells the listeners to pull down the NDAC line in preparation for the next byte of data.

The EOI (end or identify) line is pulled low (true) by the system talker to mark the last byte of a data transfer. It is also used with the ATN line to identify a specific device during a poll, as shown below.

Service Requests

Any device connected to the system can request service from the controller by pulling the SRQ (service request) line true (low.) Such an occasional might be that a voltmeter has obtained a reading and is now ready to put the data on the system data bus. When the controller "gets around to it," it must then find out which one of all the devices connected needs the service. Since all devices share the SRQ line in parallel, the controller cannot know which needs service without further work. This can be done in one of two ways:

The parallel poll

> If there are eight or fewer devices in the system, a parallel poll is fast and efficient. The controller begins the parallel poll by sending a low (true) on both the ATN and the EOI lines together. Each of the system devices has previously been assigned one of the 8 bits of the data bus as an identification bit. When the ATN and EOI lines are pulled low, each of the devices pulls its data line high except the requesting device which pulls it low, thereby identifying itself to the controller.

The serial poll

> The ATN line is pulled true (low) by the system controller and each system device in turn is then designated as a talker by the system controller. That device is then sent a special command on the data bus called a serial poll enable. The device responds by returning a full 8-bit status byte to the system controller. At the conclusion of this byte, the controller sends that device a serial poll disable to return it to the normal data mode, and continues on to the next system device for a poll of its status.

Each instrument on the IEEE-488 interface has within it an interface unit that performs specific functions in interpreting messages sent to it on the bus data lines. Other codes that may be used are as follows:

Code	**Abbreviation**	**Meaning**
AH	Acceptor Handshake	Form Listener Device
SH	Source Handshake	Form Talker Device
T or TE	Talker, Talker Extended	Addressing talker with 1 or 2 bytes
L or LE	Listener, Listener Extended	Addressing listener with 1 or 2 bytes
RL	Remote/local	Disabling of Front Panel Controls
PP	Parallel Polling	Up to 8 devices, each has one bit
SR	Service Request	Request Controller Service
C	Controller	Identifies Controller Device
DC	Device Clear	Device cleared
DT	Device Trigger	Start Device

appendix B

Basic Programs for Troubleshooting Microcomputers

BASIC PROGRAMS FOR DISK DRIVE ALIGNMENT ON IBM AND COMPATIBLE COMPUTERS

The following BASIC programs will enable a technician to use the hookup to the B drive of an IBM or compatible computer as a floppy disc drive exerciser. Using an alignment diskette such as that available from Dysan, any technician can perform alignment adjustments on the drive. See Chapter 15 for the details.

Enter all four programs, and begin by loading and running MENU.BAS first. This program will prompt you and will load and run the remaining programs as necessary.

```
"MENU.BAS"

5 CLS
10 PRINT:PRINT:PRINT"Select option:
15 PRINT
20 PRINT "    (1) Lock on a track"
30 PRINT "    (2) Select various tracks"
35 PRINT "    (3) Cycle between tracks"
37 PRINT "    (4) Exit to DOS
38 PRINT
40 PRINT "Select number of Option"
45 A$=INKEY$:IF A$="" THEN 45
50 IF A$="1" THEN 100
60 IF A$="2" THEN 200
65 IF A$="3" THEN 300
67 IF A$="4" THEN 400
70 CLS
80 GOTO 10
100 RUN "locktrac"
200 RUN"seltrac"
300 RUN "cycle"
400 SYSTEM
```

(continued)

"LOCKTRAC.BAS"

```
10 REM Following is initialization of drive
20 OUT &H3F2,&H25 : REM select drive
30 OUT &H3F5,&H3 : REM specify
40 OUT &H3F5,&HCC : REM step rate
50 OUT &H3F5,&H1 : REM non DMA mode
60 OUT &H3F5,&H7 : REM restore
70 OUT &H3F5,&H1 : REM in this drive
80 CLS
90 PRINT:PRINT:PRINT
100 INPUT "Which track do you wish to lock on?";TRAC
105 IF TRAC=99 THEN 300
110 IF TRAC>39 THEN 240
120 PRINT:PRINT "Locked on Track";TRAC
130 PRINT:PRINT:PRINT"To change tracks, hit any key"
140 PRINT"To return to menu, select track 99"
160 REM  Following is head positioning command
170 OUT &H3F2,&H25 : REM select drive
180 OUT &H3F5,&HF : REM seek
190 OUT &H3F5,&H1 : REM on head,drive
200 OUT &H3F5,TRAC : REM this track
210 A$=INKEY$:IF A$="" THEN 160
220 GOTO 10
230 RETURN
240 TRAC=39
250 GOTO 120
300 RUN"menu.bas"
```

"SELTRAC.BAS"

```
10 GOSUB 80
20 CLS
25 PRINT:PRINT:PRINT
30 INPUT "Track you wish?";TRAC
31 IF TRAC=99 THEN 350
32 IF TRAC>39 THEN 300
40 PRINT "Running track";TRAC
45 PRINT "  to cancel, select track 99"
50 PRINT
60 GOSUB 160
70 GOTO 30
80 OUT &H3F2,&H25 : REM select drive
90 OUT &H3F5,&H3 : REM specify
100 OUT &H3F5,&HCC : REM step rate
110 OUT &H3F5,&H1 : REM non DMA mode
120 OUT &H3F5,&H7 : REM restore
130 OUT &H3F5,&H1 : REM in this drive
140 RETURN
150 REM ================================
160 OUT &H3F2,&H25 : REM select drive
170 OUT &H3F5,&HF : REM seek
180 OUT &H3F5,&H1 : REM on head,drive
190 OUT &H3F5,TRAC : REM this track
200 RETURN
300 TRAC=39
310 GOTO 34
350 RUN "menu.bas"
```

"CYCLE.BAS"

```
10 GOSUB 180
20 CLS
30 PRINT:PRINT:PRINT
40 INPUT "LOW TRACK NUMBER?";LOW
50 INPUT "HIGH TRACK NUMBER?";HIGH
```

(continued)

```
55 PRINT "SPEED OF CYCLING IN MILLISECONDS"
56 INPUT"     ( >25Ø MS )";M
6Ø IF TRAC>39 THEN 31Ø
7Ø INPUT "HOW MANY CYCLES";NR
75 PRINT "  To terminate cycling, hit space bar":PRINT
9Ø PRINT "RUNNING FROM";LOW;"TO";HIGH
1ØØ PRINT
11Ø A=LOW
12Ø GOSUB 26Ø
124 FOR N=1 TO M:NEXT N
13Ø A=HIGH
14Ø GOSUB 26Ø
15Ø A$=INKEY$:IF A$=" " THEN 4ØØ
16Ø GOSUB 26Ø
165 FOR N=1 TO M:NEXT N
166 NR=NR-1
167 IF NR=Ø THEN 35Ø
17Ø GOTO 11Ø
18Ø OUT &H3F2,&H25 : REM select drive
19Ø OUT &H3F5,&H3 : REM specify
2ØØ OUT &H3F5,&HCØ : REM step rate
21Ø OUT &H3F5,&H1 : REM non DMA mode
22Ø OUT &H3F5,&H7 : REM restore
23Ø OUT &H3F5,&H1 : REM in this drive
24Ø RETURN
25Ø REM ================================
26Ø OUT &H3F2,&H25 : REM select drive
27Ø OUT &H3F5,&HF : REM seek
28Ø OUT &H3F5,&H1 : REM on head,drive
29Ø OUT &H3F5,A : REM this track
3ØØ RETURN
31Ø TRAC=39
32Ø GOTO 8Ø
33Ø RUN "menu.bas"
35Ø GOSUB 18Ø
36Ø GOTO 2Ø
4ØØ PRINT "HIT 1 TO CONTINUE, Ø TO EXIT TO MENU"
41Ø A$=INKEY$
42Ø IF A$="1" THEN 2Ø
43Ø IF A$="Ø" THEN 33Ø
44Ø GOTO 41Ø
```

Basic Program for Printer Troubleshooting:

```
1 '                        Printer Test Utility
2 '                           by Jim Walton
3 '                          Copyright 1985
4 '
5 '      This program may be used for personal use only.  Commercial use
6 '      strictly forbidden without the express written consent of the
7 '      author.
8 '
9 '      This utility is designed to provide a simple test of the IBM-PC
1Ø '     printer interface.  It will send characters to the printer that
11 '     will enable you to determine the functionality of your printer.
12 '
13 '     The first test is a simple barber pole test that prints all the
14 '     normal ascii characters in a rotating, barber pole, fashion.  All
15 '     characters should print without skips.
16 '
17 '     The next test is for bidirectional printers.  The printer should
18 '     print in the same position from both directions.  The margins on
19 '     this test should be straight, not jagged.
2Ø '
```

(continued)

```
21 '     The final test is only for dot matrix printers.  It uses the full
22 '     block character available on most printers.  An IBM compatable
23 '     graphics would probably use ASCII 219.  Check your printer manual
24 '     for the correct character.  Change the value in line 170.
25 '     accordingly.
26 '
27 '     While this program is written for the IBM-PC, it should work with
28 '     any machine running basic.  It may be necessary to change the
29 '     locate and color commands, but the basic program will run as is.
30 '
100 CLS:KEY OFF
101 '
102 ' This lets you set the proper printer width.  If you are only using
103 ' an 80 or 130 column printer the following three lines may be
104 ' omitted and replaced with:
105 '
106 ' 120 LINE.WIDTH=80
107 '        or
108 ' 120 LINE.WIDTH=132
109 '
110 PRINT "Input the line width of your printer"
120 PRINT "Normally this will be 80 or 132 columns"
130 INPUT "Width";LINE.WIDTH
137 '
138 ' The main program begins here
139 '
140 CLS
147 '
148 ' Boolean values
149 '
150 TRUE=-1:FALSE=0
157 '
158 ' ASCII constants
159 '
160 SPACE=32:FORM.FEED=12:BELL=7
167 '
168 ' Block value to use with print wire test
169 '
170 BLOCK=219
176 '
177 ' This value establishes the center of the printer for printing
178 ' test messages at the beginning and end of the tests.
179 '
180 CENTER=LINE.WIDTH-LINE.WIDTH/2
187 '
188 ' Error trap for printer problems
189 '
190 ON ERROR GOTO 1100
195 '
196 ' This is the program loop.  It continues indefinitely, and can only
197 ' be exitted by entering '4' from the keyboard.  The dummy variable
198 ' 'PROGRAM' will always be true.
199 '
200 PROGRAM=TRUE
210 WHILE PROGRAM
220   LOCATE 10,1
230   PRINT TAB(30);"Printer Test Utility"
240   PRINT
250   PRINT TAB(30);" 1. Barber Pole Test"
260   PRINT TAB(30);" 2. Alignment Test"
270   PRINT TAB(30);" 3. Print Wire Test"
280   PRINT TAB(30);" 4. Exit Program"
290   PRINT
```

(continued)

```
300    PRINT TAB(30);"      Select ."
306    '
307    ' The input loop will run until a valid input is entered.
308    ' Erroneous keys will be ignored.
309    '
310    INPUT.LOOP=TRUE
320    WHILE INPUT.LOOP
330      SELECTION$=INPUT$(1):SELECTION=VAL(SELECTION$)
340      LOCATE 17,42
350      IF SELECTION=4 THEN SYSTEM
360      WHILE SELECTION>0 AND SELECTION<4
367        '
368        ' A correct selection will display, others ignored
369        '
370        PRINT SELECTION:LOCATE 25,27:PRINT "Press ESC to terminate test";
380        ON SELECTION GOSUB 500,700,800
386        '
387        ' A correct selection will cause the input.loop to terminate so the
388        ' entire menu will reprint, erasing the input value.
389        '
390        INPUT.LOOP=FALSE
397        '
398        ' SELECTION is reset to exit this loop
399        '
400        SELECTION=0
410        LOCATE 25,27:PRINT SPACE$(27);
420      WEND
430    WEND
440 WEND
450 '
451 '                          Barber Pole Test
452 '
453 '    This test prints a rotating pattern on the printer.  Each line
454 '    consists of all the printable ascii characters that will fit on
455 '    the line starting with the ascii space in line one and incrementing
456 '    for each succeeding line.  The result resembles the barber pole,
457 '    thus the name.
458 '
459 '    The results should look similar to:
460 '
461 ' !"#$%&'()*+,-./0123456789:;<=>?@ABCDEFGHIJKLMNOPQRSTUVWXYZ[\]^_`abcd
462 '!"#$%&'()*+,-./0123456789:;<=>?@ABCDEFGHIJKLMNOPQRSTUVWXYZ[\]^_`abcde
463 '"#$%&'()*+,-./0123456789:;<=>?@ABCDEFGHIJKLMNOPQRSTUVWXYZ[\]^_`abcdef
464 '"$%&'()*+,-./0123456789:;<=>?@ABCDEFGHIJKLMNOPQRSTUVWXYZ[\]^_`abcdefg
465 '$%&'()*+,-./0123456789:;<=>?@ABCDEFGHIJKLMNOPQRSTUVWXYZ[\]^_`abcdefgh
466 '
500 LPRINT TAB(CENTER-8);"Barber Pole Test"
510 LPRINT
517 '
518 ' The first character is an ascii space
519 '
520 FIRST.CHARACTER=SPACE
530 FOR LINES=1 TO 55
540   CHARACTER=FIRST.CHARACTER
550   FOR COUNT=1 TO LINE.WIDTH-1
560     LPRINT CHR$(CHARACTER);
567     '
568     ' The printable ascii characters are 20 to 126
569     '
570     IF CHARACTER<127 THEN CHARACTER=CHARACTER+1 ELSE CHARACTER=SPACE
580   NEXT
590   LPRINT
595   '
```

(continued)

```
596    ' Each line begins with the next ascii character.  Since only one
597    ' page of 55 lines is printed, the maximum value will never be
598    ' exceeded.
599    '
600    FIRST.CHARACTER=FIRST.CHARACTER+1
610    IF INKEY$=CHR$(27) THEN LINES=55
620 NEXT
630 LPRINT
640 LPRINT TAB(CENTER-12);"Barber Pole Test Finished"
650 LPRINT CHR$(FORM.FEED)
660 RETURN
670 '
671 '                              Alignment Test
672 '
673 '   This test is to determine the alignment of the printing
674 '   while printing from either direction.  It is not as critical
675 '   for draft printing as it is for letter quality or graphics,
676 '   but still gives a rather ragged appearance if alignment is not
677 '   correct.
678 '
679 '   Your printer manual should have a procedure for adjusting the
680 '   alignment.  It may be a simple screwdriver adjustment, available
681 '   without removing the cover.  The goal is to have the characters
682 '   in perfect vertical alignment.  This is rarely possible, but
683 '   it should be possible to align them so the difference is not
684 '   noticeable with normal printing.
685 '
686 '   Most graphics will be printed with a single direction function
687 '   because of the difficulty of aligning the printer exactly.
688 '
689 '   Check the margin of the paper after this test.  It should be a
690 '   straight line.
691 '
700 MSG$="Alignment Test"
710 CHARACTER=ASC("H")
716 '
717 ' The printing is done with a subroutine shared with the
718 ' print wire test
719 '
720 GOSUB 900
730 RETURN
740 '
741 '                              Print Wire Test
742 '
743 '   This test is to see if all the print wires are firing.  Assuming
744 '   that the tops and bottoms of letters like Z and E are printing
745 '   normally, this test will indicate any printwires that are not
746 '   working properly.
747 '
748 '   The pattern should be a solid line across the page without obvious
749 '   blank spots.  A random blank spot could indicate a dirty printhead
750 '   that simply requires cleaning.  The same dot missing is probably
751 '   caused by a bent wire or defective solenoid.
752 '
800 MSG$="Print Wire Test"
810 CHARACTER=BLOCK
820 GOSUB 900
830 RETURN
840 '
841 '   This subroutine prints continuous lines of characters as
842 '   specified in the calling routines.  For the alignment test
843 '   the character is the letter 'H' and the print wire test
844 '   uses the BLOCK character defined at the beginning of the
```

(continued)

```
845 '   program.
846 '
900 LPRINT TAB(CENTER-LEN(MSG$));MSG$
910 LPRINT
920 FOR LINES=1 TO 55
930   FOR COUNT=1 TO LINE.WIDTH-1
940     LPRINT CHR$(CHARACTER);
950   NEXT
960   LPRINT
970   IF INKEY$=CHR$(27) THEN LINES=55
980 NEXT
990 LPRINT
1000 LPRINT TAB(CENTER-LEN(MSG$)-4);MSG$;" Finished"
1010 LPRINT CHR$(FORM.FEED)
1020 RETURN
1050 '
1051 '                          Error Trap Routine
1052 '
1053 '  If the printer is turned off, or has a fault, it will return an
1054 '  error status to the program.  If the program detects an error,
1055 '  it will beep the speaker and request that you correct the
1056 '  problem.
1057 '
1058 '  If the fault cannot be corrected, press the ESC key to abort
1059 '  the current test and return to the main menu.
1060 '
1100 LOCATE 25,32
```

```
1110 COLOR 0,15
1120 PRINT " Check  Printer ";:BEEP:BEEP
1130 COLOR 7,0
1140 FOR DELAY=1 TO 3000:NEXT
1150 LOCATE 25,32:PRINT SPACE$(16);
1160 IF INKEY$=CHR$(27) THEN RESUME 200
1170 RESUME
```

appendix C

An Explanation of the ASCII Chart

The ASCII chart as shown in the following figure shows the binary, hex, decimal, and octal equivalents for the ASCII set.

The entire set of normal, printable characters, including some symbols, punctuation, and the number set, can be done with less than 90 character combinations. This then requires only a part of the binary bytes capability of 256 different possible combinations. ASCII text requires only 7 bits of an 8-bit byte. Included within the 128 different possibilities of using 7 bits are combinations used for nonprintable characters used among other things to control printers. These controls can be used to change the operating parameters of a modern printer such as the number of lines per page, the microspacing of characters, the type font in use, and so forth. A printer is typically controlled by sending it 7-bit bytes, the eighth bit being ignored. This also means that text files sent via modem can be set for 7 data bits.

Text files originated by a word-processing program such as Wordstar™ use the eighth bit (D7) for special purposes such as a "soft" carriage return at the end of a line, the last letter of each word in the text, and special characters such as a "soft" hyphen. Such files will look strange if brought up on the monitor screen at the system level with the "type" command, but will look normal when viewed through the word-processing program. If these files are to be sent via a modem they must be sent using an 8-bit format to maintain the eighth bit special codes. If they are sent with only 7 bits, the special features built into the text will be lost.

Binary files such as a program for the CPU to execute (a .COM or .EXE file, for instance) also uses the eighth bit and must be sent on a modem without parity checking as mentioned above.

BITS D6 D5 D4	0 0 0	0 0 1	0 1 0	0 1 1	1 0 0	1 0 1	1 1 0	1 1 1
D3 D2 D1 D0	CONTROL		NUMBERS SYMBOLS		UPPER CASE		LOWER CASE	
0 0 0 0	0 NUL 0 0	20 DLE 10 16	40 SP 20 32	60 0 30 48	100 @ 40 64	120 P 50 80	140 ' 60 96	160 p 70 112
0 0 0 1	1 GTL SOH 1 1	21 LLO DC1 11 17	41 ! 21 33	61 1 31 49	101 A 41 65	121 Q 51 81	141 a 61 97	161 q 71 113
0 0 1 0	2 STX 2 2	22 DC2 12 18	42 " 22 34	62 2 32 50	102 B 42 66	122 R 52 82	142 b 62 98	162 r 72 114
0 0 1 1	3 ETX 3 3	23 DC3 13 19	43 # 23 35	63 3 33 51	103 C 43 67	123 S 53 83	143 c 63 99	163 s 73 115
0 1 0 0	4 SDC EOT 4 4	24 DCL DC4 14 20	44 $ 24 36	64 4 34 52	104 D 44 68	124 T 54 84	144 d 64 100	164 t 74 116
0 1 0 1	5 PPC ENQ 5 5	25 PPU NAK 15 21	45 % 25 37	65 5 35 53	105 E 45 69	125 U 55 85	145 e 65 101	165 u 75 117
0 1 1 0	6 ACK 6 6	26 SYN 16 22	46 & 26 38	66 6 36 54	106 F 46 70	126 V 56 86	146 f 66 102	166 v 76 118
0 1 1 1	7 BEL 7 7	27 ETB 17 23	47 ' 27 39	67 7 37 55	107 G 47 71	127 W 57 87	147 g 67 103	167 w 77 119
1 0 0 0	10 GET BS 8 8	30 SPE CAN 18 24	50 (28 40	70 8 38 56	110 H 48 72	130 X 58 88	150 h 68 104	170 x 78 120
1 0 0 1	11 TCT HT 9 9	31 SPD EM 19 25	51) 29 41	71 9 39 57	111 I 49 73	131 Y 59 89	151 i 69 105	171 y 79 121
1 0 1 0	12 LF A 10	32 SUB 1A 26	52 * 2A 42	72 : 3A 58	112 J 4A 74	132 Z 5A 90	152 j 6A 106	172 z 7A 122
1 0 1 1	13 VT B 11	33 ESC 1B 27	53 + 2B 43	73 ; 3B 59	113 K 4B 75	133 [5B 91	153 k 6B 107	173 7B 123
1 1 0 0	14 FF C 12	34 FS 1C 28	54 , 2C 44	74 < 3C 60	114 L 4C 76	134 \ 5C 92	154 l 6C 108	174 ¦ 7C 124
1 1 0 1	15 CR D 13	35 GS 1D 29	55 – 2D 45	75 = 3D 61	115 M 4D 77	135] 5D 93	155 m 6D 109	175 } 7D 125
1 1 1 0	16 SO E 14	36 RS 1E 30	56 . 2E 46	76 > 3E 62	116 N 4E 78	136 Λ 5E 94	156 n 6E 110	176 ~ 7E 126
1 1 1 1	17 SI F 15	37 US 1F 31	57 / 2F 47	77 UNL ? 3F 63	117 O 4F 79	137 UNT – 5F 111	157 o 6F 111	177 RUBOUT (DEL) 7F 127
	Addressed Commands	Universal Commands	Listen Addresses		Talk Addresses		Secondary Addresses Or Commands	

octal	25	PPU	GPIB code
	NAK		ASCII character
hex	15	21	decimal

Some of the abbreviations in the ASCII table are not obvious, so here they are in more digestible form. Note that these are really single-byte messages that can be used in communications between a computer and a modem, a printer, or other peripheral.

NUL = All zeros. Used for idle marking time without occupying buffer space.

SOH = Start of a heading

STX = Start of the text

ETX = End of the text ("End of data, did you receive it?")

EOT = End of a transmission. May be used as a turn-around for half-duplex.

ENQ = Enquiry. Solicits automatic identification from a remote terminal.

ACK = Acknowledgment ("Data has been received OK")

BEL = Bell or attention signal (nowadays a speaker "beep")

BS = Backspace or <--- key (may or may not erase on the way)

HT = Horizontal Tab or -->| key (normal keyboard Tabulator key)

LF = Line feed on a printer (paper up a line)

VT = Vertical Tab (jump lines on a page)

FF = Form Feed (go to beginning of next page)

CR = Carriage return (Return to left margin of paper)

SO = Shift out (Go to alternate character font set)

SI = Shift in (Shift back to normal character font set)

DLE = Data Link Escape. May be used prior to EOT for an automatic disconnect.

DC1 = Device Control 1 (Also called "XON," used in software handshaking)

DC2 = Device Control 2

DC3 = Device Control 3 (also called "XOFF," used in software handshaking)

DC4 = Device control 4

NAK = Negative acknowledgment

SYN = Synchronous/idle

ETB = End of transmitted block

CAN = Cancel (error in data). May be used to cancel an escape sequence.

EM = End of medium

SUB = A character used in place of a character received in error.

ESC = Escape. An introducer for an escape or control sequence.

FS = Information File Separator

GS = Information Group Separator

RS = Information Record Separator

US = Information Unit Separator

DEL = Delete (backspace and erase too)

Glossary

AAA Analog alignment diskette. Term coined by Dysan Inc. to describe its diskette intended to be used when recalibrating diskette drives.

Active low Negative logic. When the voltage is at minimum or zero the logic condition is satisfied to activate the circuit in question.

Active high Positive logic. When the voltage is at maximum or high the logic condition is satisfied to activate the circuit in question.

Adapter card A card inserted into a microcomputer to interface the systems address, data, and other lines to a specific purpose such as providing signals to and from the computer and an external port, or to put characters on a monitor screen.

Address A name, label, or number identifying a register, or location in memory.

Append Add information onto the end of an existing file. This does not alter the existing information.

Application program A program that uses the operating system to perform a specific task for an operator. Examples are word-processing and data-management programs.

ASCII American Standard Code for Information Interchange. A standard code used in transmitting text information. Upper- and lowercase letters, numbers, symbols and communications control information is represented. ASCII uses only seven of the 8 bits available in a byte.

Assembly language A means of programming a computer that is one step removed from manipulating instructions and data at the machine, or binary, level. Uses mnemonic codes to symbolize operations. Final assembly language code must be assembled by a computer program called an assembler to produce an intermediate HEX code result. This HEX code is then converted into a binary (executable) file by another computer program called a linker or a loader.

AUX Alternate name for the first serial communications port of a computer. Also called COM1.

Azimuth In floppy diskette drives, the alignment of a read/write head around its own center as one views the head from the top, through the surface of the diskette. **Azimuth misalignment** causes the head to meet the oncoming data on the rotating diskette at other than 90 degrees.

Backup A copy of a working diskette kept in a safe place to be used as a master in case of damage to the primary working diskette.

BASIC language Beginners All-purpose Symbolic Instruction Code. A powerful computer language that is intended to be easy to learn.

Baud rate A measure of serial communications speed equal to the reciprocal of the shortest signal element (usually one bit interval). For synchronous data transmission, the baud rate is equal to the clock period. The same is true for asynchronous transmission if there is only one stop bit.

Binary A numbering system based on the number 2. This numbering system, converted to on or off states of circuitry, allows a computer to carry out all its complex tasks.

BIOS Basic Input/Output System. Software used to enable communications between a monitor, keyboard, and disk drives. The BIOS lies between the programs and the actual hardware of the computer.

BIOS.COM The file which, when executed by the computer, provides the BIOS functions.

Bit Abbreviation for *binary digit*.

Block diagram A simplified overall diagram of system operation represented by interconnected blocks, each of which accomplishes a single task.

Blooming Presentation on a cathode ray tube that is dimmer than normal and larger in size than normal. Usually caused by lack of high voltage to the tube.

Boot record A short machine-language routine that starts the loading of the operating system from a diskette into memory for execution.

Booting up The process of loading the operating system into the computer memory and executing it.

Bootstrap A routine that, once begun, loads the rest of itself into memory.

Buffer A storage area in memory used to temporarily hold information on its way to another computer device. Often a specially designated portion of memory.

Bug An error in a program that causes undesired results.

Bus One or more connections, commonly eight, used for transmitting data between many sources and destinations.

Byte Eight bits of information as a unit. Can be used to represent 256 different values.

Card extender A plug-in card with parallel conductors used to raise a printed circuit up away from other cards for troubleshooting purposes.

Cassette interface A port provided for the saving and loading of computer programs and data from an audio cassette.

Centering The accuracy of rotating a diskette from its true center, thus making the data tracks available to the read/write heads without wobbling.

Centronics A wiring standard pioneered by the Centronics company for the purpose of interfacing a parallel feed printer to a computer.

Character A single printable letter, number, or symbol.

Checksum A number derived from a block of data to be transmitted that is used to verify the validity upon reception.

CHKDSK A command file that is used to test a diskette for gross errors.

Cleared (1) Set to logic 0. (2) A state where all data buffers are set to zero and operations begun from a new beginning.

CMOS Complimentary metal oxide semiconductor. A family of logic chips characterized by very low power requirements but high sensitivity to static damage.

Cold reboot Turning off the computer and turning it back so that all of the registers and the RAM memory is begun again from a totally fresh start. Often the only way to gain control of a computer that has crashed. Also called a *hardware reset*.

COM1, COM2 Designations for the first and second serial communications ports of a computer. When used in commands to the computer, must usually be followed with a colon, e.g. COM1: The COM refers to COMmunications.

Command files (.COM) Files stored on floppy diskettes or a hard disk that are intended to be loaded into the computer and executed as a program. Examples are a BASIC.COM file or a LOTUS.COM file. These files are in 8-bit binary format. Another type of command file is the .EXE file, which may also be loaded and executed directly.

COMMAND.COM A file used as part of the operating system of an MS-DOS or PC-DOS computer. This file contains interpreters for commands such as COPY, RENAME, DIR, and ERASE. Must be present to operate a computer with these operating systems.

Commands Typed words that mean that the computer is to carry out a specific task. Example: DIR. This command, when typed on the keyboard of a computer, is a command for the computer to display the directory of one of the diskette drives.

Communications port One of the serial input/output ports of a computer. Usually used to operate a modem or a serial printer.

Compatibility Standardized in order to work with or just like something else. Software may be called compatible if it works on all of a specific group of computers, such as the computers referred to as IBM-compatibles. Hardware may also be termed compatible if it is usable on all of a similar group of computers.

Component level Part of the term "troubleshooting to the component level." This is troubleshooting beyond the level of replacing equipment circuit cards and extends to the replacement of individual components such as integrated circuits, resistors, and capacitors.

CON: Designation of the control console consisting of the keyboard and the screen of a computer. Sometimes used in more advanced commands to manipulate data directly. Example: Typing CON: B:TEST.DOC at the operating system level will allow the keyboard input (seen on the screen, too) to be filed directly onto the b:diskette in a file called TEST.DOC. (To stop the keyboard input you must use a control-Z character.)

Concatenate Combine several files into a single file or combine strings of characters into one string. This is done by appending each one onto the end of the last.

Configuration A specific collection of hardware devices that work together. For instance, a monitor, keyboard disk drives and the system unit comprise a basic computer configuration. A different configuration might include a hard disk drive and only one floppy disk drive.

Console The console consists of the keyboard and monitor display used by the computer operator. It allows the control and feedback of computer status to the operator.

Control C The control character is used by a computer operator to abort a program and return to the operating system.

Control character A keystroke used to control rather than to pass data to a computer. It is invoked by holding down the CONTROL (Ctrl) key while hitting one of the character keys. The effect of doing this is to clear the D5 and D6 bits of the character key. For instance, the ASCII code for the letter H is 01001000. The code for h is 01101000. If either of these keys is hit while holding down the control key, the result is 00001000, the control code for backspace.

Controller A microcomputer chip dedicated to the control of a mechanical device. The Floppy Disk Controller is an example of this type chip, intended for the specific purpose of coordinating all of the control signals and directing data flow to and from a floppy disk drive.

Co-processor A microprocessor chip that specializes in a particular function, intended for use with another more general purpose processor. An example is the 8087 math co-processor used with the 8088 or 8086 general purpose microprocessors.

Copy protection Use of one or more of several different schemes to prevent the duplication of software. Used to prevent the unpaid proliferation of valuable software to those who don't pay for it. These schemes may consist of using deliberately misnumbered or duplicate numbers of floppy diskette sectors, deliberate manipulation of the cyclic redundancy check numbers on each sector of a diskette, or punching a tiny laser hole in the diskette. Despite these obstacles, many copy-protection methods can be bypassed using sophisticated duplicating software programs.

CP/M An operating system originally written for 8-bit computers. An acronym for Control Program and Monitor. Since it was intended for 8-bit computers having a maximum addressable memory of 64K, CP/M made the most efficient use of the limited memory available. Sixteen-bit operating systems such as MS-DOS, on the other hand, make operating a computer a bit easier at the expense of using more memory.

CPU Central processor unit. The "brain" of the computer. Eight-bit computers often use the Z-80 CPU and 16-bit computers the 8088 CPU.

Crash A condition of the computer where control has been lost and further operation of the computer is impossible. Symptoms include random characters and symbols on the screen and inability of the keyboard to respond to operator keystrokes. May be corrected by a warm boot in some cases. In others, only a cold boot will regain control.

CRC Cyclic Redundancy Check. A binary number placed at the end of a block of binary data that represents that block of data. Where a parity bit allows checking a byte of data, the CRC checks the validity of an entire block of information.

CRT Cathode ray tube. The monitor's picture screen, or TV tube.

CRTC Cathode ray tube controller. The sophisticated IC that takes the data from video memory and breaks it up into the pulses needed to control the electron beam of the CRT. Also generates the necessary pulses to initiate the horizontal and vertical scanning waveforms, called *sync pulses*.

Cursor The present active character position on the monitor screen. The placed marked by the blinking dashed line or block on the monitor screen.

Data Information. May consist of numbers, letters, or symbols. The information used by a *program* to accomplish a task. Example: A word processing program uses keyboard input to record *data* such as business letters. Both programs and data are stored together as *files* on a floppy diskette or hard disk.

Data-base management system A program used to keep track of similar data and to manipulate it. Consists of storing, manipulation, and retrieval of this data. An example would be all of the personal checking accounts at a particular bank. All of its branches would have access to the data base that has each persons information recorded within it. Each person would be a file and each item within the file such as the current balance would be a *record* within that file.

DDD Digital diagnostics diskette. Term coined by the Dysan company to describe its diskette used to analyze diskette operation by digital rather than analog means.

Decimal A system of counting based upon the number 10. An example is our use of dollars and cents (1/100th of a dollar). In contrast, we use the number 60 as a base with hours and minutes in keeping time (1/60th of an hour).

Default The value or location used if nothing to the contrary is provided. For instance, the default diskette drive of a computer may be shown at the system prompt as A>. Files may be accessed on either the A or the B drives, but the absence of a drive designator (such as B:) will result in the file being sought on the A drive only.

Device driver A program used to interface between a computer and the hardware of a peripheral device. A device driver receives computer commands and generates the proper signals for the hardware of the peripheral device.

Diagnostics Programs to assist in troubleshooting the computer and its peripherals. Consists of the ROM diagnostics that are executed at each power up and, for more detailed troubleshooting, the diskette diagnostics.

DIN The abbreviation for the association in West Germany that sets standards for electronic equipment there, the Deutsche Industrie Normenausschuss.

DIP Dual in-line plastic. Often used to refer to tiny switches that can be plugged into an IC socket: DIP switches. Also used to describe the packaging method for many ICs.

DIP switches See DIP.

Directory A table containing the names and other data related to the files on a diskette or hard disk.

Disk drives The mechanism that rotates a diskette, monitors the passage of the index hole, moves the read/write head to a specified position, and reads and writes data to the diskette.

Diskette A specially coated mylar material cut into a circle and placed within a protective envelope for the purpose of storing digital computer data.

Display Either the presentation observed on a monitor or the row of digits shown on a device such as a calculator.

DMA Direct memory access. A method of getting data out of memory without involving the CPU. Also allows faster access of data than using the CPU.

DOS Disk operating system. The software necessary to allow the writing and reading of data to and from a diskette drive. Since the retrieval and storage of data is a major function of a computer, the DOS portion of an operating system is a major portion of the software necessary to operate a computer.

DOS.COM The command program in a computer, often loaded from a diskette or a hard disk, that allows communications with the diskette drives.

Double-sided drive A drive outfitted with two heads rather than the one required for a single-sided drive. The two heads are on the bottom (side 0) and the top (side 1) of the diskette.

Down time Time that a piece of equipment is not available for use due to a failure within the system.

Drive exerciser A device used to generate appropriate commands to operate the mechanisms of a diskette drive for alignment or test purposes. Such commands include movement of the heads in and out along the diskette radius and the operation of the diskette rotating motor.

Dump Place data existing in RAM onto an external device such as storage or to a printer. Machine-level data from RAM to an output device for examination by a programmer.

Duty cycle A measurement of the time a device is actually working. A percentage obtained by dividing the on time by the time of an entire cycle. For example, if a soldering iron is operated for two minutes out of every ten, the duty cycle is 2/10 times 100 (to make it a percentage), a duty cycle of 20 percent.

Dynamic RAM Random access memory that operates by virtue of short-term storage of electrical charges. Dynamic memory must be automatically "refreshed" many times a second in order to retain memory data. Characterized by small chip size for number of memory cells available.

Erratic intermittent The worst kind of intermittent problem. Apparently will not respond to heating or mechanical stresses. Problem appears and disappears at random.

Error codes Binary or ASCII numerical codes generated by a computer as a shorthand means of informing of an error condition.

Executable files (.EXE) Files intended to be executed by a computer. Similar in structure (binary files) to a command file but occupies more disk storage space and runs slightly slower.

Expansion unit A means of providing additional expansion slots for a computer that has too many option cards to install in the system unit. The expansion unit consists basically of additional sockets in an appropriate chassis, with a cable that plugs into one of the system board expansion sockets. Additional cards are then installed in the sockets within the expansion unit.

Expansion sockets Sockets provided in a microcomputer for the purpose of installing optional printed circuit cards. These sockets, in a typical IBM-compatible computer, have 62 connections and include the address, data, and control lines from the CPU.

FAT File allocation table. One of two tables placed on a diskette for the purpose of keeping track of the chains of sectors belonging to a file and to mark bad sectors of the diskette to prevent their use. The FAT (two copies) are located on track 0 of a diskette.

FDC See *Floppy disk controller.*

FDD Floppy diskette drive. The mechanisms necessary to rotate the diskette, locate the read/write heads on the diskette, and monitor passage of the index hole. Often includes a printed circuit card for some of the control functions.

FET Field effect transistor. An amplifying semiconductor having very high input impedance and high gain. Remotely similar to the common bipolar transistor.

FIFO First in, first out. Referring to a type of memory organization that stores data in a stack. Reading that data results in the last item written being the first data read out of the stack. Often compared to the stack of plates in a cafeteria where the stack is loaded and unloaded from the top.

File A collection of information treated as a unit. May be a program or data file.

Filename An alphanumeric identification assigned by an operator to identify a file recognized by both the operator and the operating system of the computer.

Floppy disk controller The large-scale integrated circuit that takes commands from the CPU and converts them to the signals for the floppy diskette drive. Includes coding and decoding of track, sector, and side. Returns the data requested to the CPU.

Font A group of printable characters that are styled alike. For example, a standard roman text font is different from an italic font.

Format The arrangement of the individual elements that make up a field, record, file, or volume. A standardized form in which data is put together.

Graphics An information-passing mode in which pictures and other graphic information is processed, rather than ASCII characters. An example would be the production, storage, and printout on a graphics printer of a blueprint-style drawing.

Hall effect The resulting production of a voltage produced by application of a current and a magnetic field through a special semiconductor.

Handshake Signals used to control the flow of data. Data can be sent too fast for the receiving end. Handshaking is used to temporarily stop the transmission of data when necessary to prevent the overflow of the receiving equipment. Handshaking can be done using a separate signal line such as those used between a modem and a terminal, or they can be digital signals sent over the telephone lines between two modems. The first method is called hardwire handshaking and the second is software handshaking. See Chapter 13 for further explanations of protocols and software handshaking.

Hard copy A printed copy on paper, usually in readable form.

Hard disk A storage medium consisting of one or more specially coated plates rotating at high speed, read by read/write magnetic heads. In microcomputers, a hard disk may be installed with the system unit. Common rotational speed is 3600 rpm and storage capacity of 10 or 20 megabytes.

Hard-sectored Referring to diskettes that have multiple index holes. These holes fix the location of the sectors on the disk. Declining in popularity as soft-sectored diskettes gain.

Hardware Something you can handle: the physical portions of a computer such as the chassis, printed circuits, and IC chips.

Hidden files Diskette files not shown on a listing of the diskette directory, hidden to help prevent their erasure during normal file manipulation.

High impedance A relative term indicating a high internal resistance which limits the amount of current available from a given voltage source. A low impedance source, on the other hand, can supply relatively large currents. As an example, a series of penlight cells equaling 12 volts is a high impedance voltage source when compared to a 12 volt car battery.

Home position The beginning position to which a servo system such as the carriage of a printer moves when powered up. This position is then used as the starting point for all further incremental counting of the carriage movements back and forth on the carriage bars.

IC Integrated circuit. A collection of many transistors and circuits at a microscopic level, sealed within a plastic or ceramic package through which pins extend for connection to external circuitry. Commonly available with 14, 16, 20, 24, and 40 connections.

IEEE-488 A wiring standard for interconnecting one- or two-way digital equipment to a computer. An example is an automated electronic testing station.

Index hole A small hole through a diskette near the center spindle hole, used to monitor the rotation of the diskette and as a starting point for the sectors recorded on the diskette.

Index width The width of the pulse resulting from the reading of a light beam through an index hole in a diskette.

Initialize To "start from scratch." The loading of special registers within LSI IC chips to required values for using the chips in computer operations. Also the setting of other registers to zero for the same purpose.

Inputs Signals used to provide information to electronic circuitry. May be either analog or digital.

Interface A collection of electronic hardware and/or software necessary between two pieces of digital equipment to enable one- or two-way communication of commands and data signals.

Intermittents Problems in electronic equipment that come and go. They may be thermal, mechanical, or erratic.

Interrupt A single signal sent to a CPU which results in a jump to a specified location in memory required to service that interrupt.

Jumper A piece of wire or a small shorted connector to place on specific pins for the purpose of shorting them out. Used to select functions that are seldom changed.

Keyboard The set of switches used by a computer or terminal operator, most often called a QWERTY keyboard for the first keys on the upper left of the keyboard.

Language A means of providing humans a way to direct the operation of a computer with less effort than working directly with binary numbers. Common examples are assembly language, one step above binary programming. A more sophisticated, slower, but easier way to program is to use a higher-level language such as BASIC.

Light pen A light-sensitive attachment for a computer that enables it to tell where the human operator is touching it to the screen. It does this by noting when the light pen is activated versus the position of the CRT sweep at that instant. Coincidence of the light pen and the cursor is done by the CRTC.

Loading (1) Placing a resistance across a source of voltage. (2) Placing a program in RAM for CPU execution. (3) Converting a .HEX file into an executable form such as a .EXE file.

Logic levels The voltages within the acceptable high and low limits for a specific digital family. Voltage levels between these levels are not acceptable but are bad levels, not "nothing" levels.

Logic probe An electronic instrument that detects and indicates the voltages within the acceptable ranges of high and low logic levels, and those within the bad level range.

LPT1, LPT2, LPT3 The names assigned to the three parallel ports of a typical microcomputer to identify the three parallel ports used principally for printers. LPT refers to Line PrinTer.

LSI Large-scale integrated circuit. A microscopic, dense array of transistors, resistors, and other circuit elements necessary to perform a complex task. Examples: A Z-80 microprocessor and an 8255A I/O chip.

Memory chips ICs that are used for the storage of digital data. There are two types, RAM and ROM.

Microcomputer A small computer having many of the features of a minicomputer and even some of the mainframe computer capabilities. Commonly a desktop computer.

Microprocessor The central processor LSI chip of a microcomputer. Examples include the 8-bit Z-80 and 8085 and the 16-bit 8086 and 8088 microprocessors.

Modem An electronic unit necessary to send or receive digital information over standard telephone lines.

Monitor A visual means of providing digital information to an operator, most commonly a cathode ray tube.

Monochrome Having only one color. Refers to a black-and-white, green, or amber CRT screen as opposed to a color monitor.

Mouse An analog device used to input positional data to a computer faster than manipulating keyboard switches. By positioning the small object referred to as a mouse, the cursor on the monitor changes position. When the desired cursor position is reached the computer is notified to take the action requested at that position on the screen by pressing a button also located on the mouse.

MOV Metal oxide varistor. A discrete electronic component that clamps voltages at a defined level in either direction of current flow. Acts very much like a pair of zener diodes wired in series. Used to limit the amplitude of voltages.

MS-DOS Microsofts™ Disk Operating System. Similar to PC- DOS, the Personal Computer Disk Operating System. One of the popular disk-operating systems in use on 16-bit microcomputers.

Multiplexed Carrying bidirectional data flow, one way at one time, the opposite direction at another, or carrying different signals one way at different times.

Negative logic When a logic low is the required level to activate a logic circuit.

Network Two or more computers linked together to use a common source of data. Each computer in this configuration may be called a node.

Null modem A cable used in place of a modem when two digital equipments are located close enough together that telephone lines are not necessary. For instance, when two microcomputers in the same office need to communicate between themselves, a null modem would be used. Neither of the computers would "know" that a modem was missing.

Octal A numbering system based on the number 8. Numbers up to 7 would appear the same as a decimal number, but 8 would then be shown as a 10, or one 8 plus no digits; 9 would appear as 11, or one 8 plus 1 digit.

Off-line Not connected to the incoming data lines. A term often used to describe the status of a printer. When on-line, the printer is accepting commands and data from a computer. When off-line, some degree of local control may be possible, but all control from the computer is disabled.

Offset In addressing, the application of a positive or negative amount from a given base location in memory. For instance, an offset of three applied to a memory location of 0F231H would point to an address of 0F234H.

OK The prompt used in BASIC. The presence of an OK indicates that you are at the command level of BASIC. As a contrast, an A> is an example of the operating system prompt for most microcomputers.

On-Line Equipment which is under the control of the computer's CPU.

Operating system A program or collection of programs that organizes a CPU and all peripheral devices, including the operating console, into a working unit for the execution of application programs.

Operator problem An apparent failure of electronic equipment that is caused by inadvertent misoperation of the equipment by the system operator. A common problem in microcomputer operation.

Option cards Printed circuit cards purchased to perform one or more functions not provided for in a basic microcomputer unit. For example, an option card might be purchased to provide both additional memory for the computer and an additional parallel port for a printer.

Parameters Constaints used by a microcomputer system. For instance, the baud rate parameter for many microcomputers is set at 1200 baud.

Parity A method of checking the validity of 7 bits of data. This is done by using the most significant (eighth) bit to make the total number of set bits always come out to be even or odd, a parameter that is defined prior to a transfer of digital data.

Parity bit The most significant bit of an 8-bit byte. See *parity*.

Parity error An error condition detected by using the parity bit system of data checking.

Parser A software routine that "filters out" certain bytes or combinations of bytes. An example is the parser used in a printer that "catches" control-code bytes used to control the printer directly. All other bytes of data are sent to the print buffer for eventual printing on paper.

PC-DOS Personal computer disk operating system. An outgrowth of the MS-DOS (Microsoft disk operating system), bought by IBM for use in its personal computers.

Peripheral A device used with a computer which can either accept or provide input to the computer's central processor.

Physical device An input/output device or storage device connected to a CPU.

Pin feed A type of paper, often used with computer printers, that has holes along the paper edge. The holes provide precise alignment and indexing of the paper through the printer even after many sheets pass through it.

Pinout A listing of the connecting pins of a device, often either an integrated circuit or a connector.

Port collision Installing options cards in such a manner tha two or more ports have the same address. This usually results in the computer "locking up" when that port is accessed. Correct this situation by changing one or more of the conflicting addresses.

Positive logic When a high represents a true. In other words, the most logical way of thinking about logic circuits where, if a voltage is present (from 2.4 to 5 VDC for TTL, 70 to 100 percent of Vcc for CMOS circuits), the circuit is satisfied. As an example, an AND gate requires that both inputs be high at the same time for a high output. This is pure positive logic. A NAND gate, however, has a negative logic output that is true low.

Priority A number for a particular task that determines how important it is in relationship to the numbers assigned other tasks. The higher the priority number, the more preference is given.

PRN Standard designation for the printer connected to a computer. Also may be referred to as LPT1 or LPT2.

Processing Manipulation, consolidation, and the like of information to change it from one form to another or to make it more manageable.

Program A string of instructions that gives a CPU instructions to carry out a task.

Prompt A symbol used by a computer to indicate that it is awaiting input from the operator.

Protocol An agreed-upon set of parameters which, when used by both ends of a communications transfer, govern the exchange of data between two digital equipments.

Radial alignment The position of a diskette read/write head in relationship to the position in which it should be. If the head is exactly where it should be along a radial line to the center of a diskette it is in radial alignment.

RAM Random access memory. Now inaccurately taken as a term for static and dynamic memory in a modern computer, wherein data may be written and read at any location directly, without having to scan intervening data. Although also technically random access, ROM (read only memory) cannot be written into but is never referred to as RAM.

Random access A method of accessing computer memory data that does not depend upon the location of the previously accessed data.

Read/write heads The magnetic head assembly (or assemblies) of either a floppy diskette drive or a hard disk drive that puts magnetic data onto the recording surface of the media and later retrieves it for use by the computer.

Rectifier An electronic device that converts alternating current into pulsations of direct current.

Rf modulator In microcomputer applications, a very small oscillator that is modulated by a computer's composite digital information for the purpose of sending monitor signals through the normal tuner circuits of a television receiver. This enables the use of a television for a monitor, saving the cost of a separate monitor.

RGB Red, green, blue. An abbreviation commonly used to describe a color monitor that has direct drive, separate lines for each of these colors, as opposed to a composite color monitor, in which the colors are combined into a single signal.

Risetime The time required for a waveform to go from 10 percent of maximum amplitude to 90 percent of the same amplitude.

ROM Read only memory. Usually an integrated circuit chip, the ROM contains the necessary programs for a computer to begin loading the operating system. May also contain diagnostic routines.

Rotational speed The speed with which a diskette or hard drive turns. Common speeds are 300 rpm for a 5 1/4-inch diskette, 360 rpm for an 8-inch diskette, and 3600 rpm for a hard disk drive.

RS-232C A standard of interconnecting lines to pass serial digital data between a terminal or computer and a modem. Parts of this standard are commonly used for serial data transfer between other digital equipment such as printers and computers.

Scope Common abbreviation for *oscilloscope*.

Secondary storage Mass storage media such as floppy disk drives and hard disk drives. May also be tape or cassette storage.

Sequential access A method of data storage in which data must be accessed from one end toward the other when accessing specific addresses. An example is data storage on tape drives.

SET A binary value of high, as opposed to RESET or CLEAR, where the value is low.

Setup switches Switches set by a technician during system configuration that are later read by the computer at each power- up. These switches provide the means of letting the computer know what resources are available, such as the number of disk drives, amount of memory, type of monitor, and the like.

Shipping diskette A cardboard dummy diskette used to prevent a glass-to-glass contact of one read/write head against another during transportation. Prevents chipping of the heads. Must be removed before operation of the drive is attempted.

Skew The departure of the path of a read/write head from an exact radial line to the center of a diskette drive.

Soft-sectored Description of a diskette that has a single index hole and uses software to determine the number and location of sectors.

Software Computer programs stored on floppy diskettes or other secondary storage media. *Firmware* is software contained in a ROM.

Solid-state tester An instrument that provides an E/I curve of components and circuits during power-off circuit testing.

Static Without motion. Used to describe circuit operation wherein the voltage levels remain the same until manually tripped or incremented by the troubleshooting technician.

Static RAM The memory cells of a computer that retain data once written into them until that data is rewritten or the power is turned off. A series of many flip-flop circuits to accomplish this purpose.

Static stimulus tester A troubleshooting instrument that injects static DC logic levels into the CPU socket of a computer for the purpose of static testing of the control, address, and data busses.

Strobe A pulse of short duration used to indicate that data is stable and ready for use.

Subscript A letter or number below the normal level of printing, such as in the chemical formula for water, H_2O.

Superscript A letter or number above the normal level of printing, such as in a formula for squaring a number, $3^2 = 9$.

Suppressors Electronic components designed to clamp the incoming AC voltage below a specified value.

Surge A momentary increase in voltage, as a power-line surge.

Sync pulse A short pulse indicating the proper timing for an event to begin. For example, the horizontal sync pulse provided to a monitor indicates when the horizontal sweep should begin.

System board The main circuit board of a computer, sometimes called a mother board. The circuitry of a microcomputer exclusive of any optional boards.

Technoid A technically inclined person who consistently and eloquently overestimates his knowledge and/or ability.

Terminal Equipment that provides the input and output functions to enable an operator to communicate with a computer. Often monitor and keyboard, but may also be a printer with keyboard.

Terminating resistor A resistor connected to the end of a log line intended to minimize reflections by closely matching the characteristic impedance of that line.

Thermal intermittent An intermittent problem that is controlled by the amount of heat present in or on the circuitry. Either heating or cooling can affect the thermal intermittent.

Timer chips Integrated circuits used to provide digital waveforms or to provide timing functions through their counting ability.

Tractor feed The small pegs, used to drive the paper through a printer, that engage the holes in the edges of the printing paper. The mechanism that drives the pegs.

Transients Signals of short duration that are undesirable and may cause computer damage by puncturing semiconductor materials and circuit insulation.

TTL - Transistor-transistor logic Integrated circuits that depend mostly on interconnected transistors to perform circuit tasks. characterized by ruggedness, speed, and operation at exactly 5VDC.

UART - Universal asynchronous receiver-transmitter An integrated circuit that is used to convert parallel data bytes into serial strings, send that information over two or three lines, and at the other end reassemble the serial data into parallel again, using another of the same chips.

Utility A program for general use. An example is the utility program used to format new diskettes.

Varistor An electronic component that acts like two zener diodes wired in series. Used to clamp transients on power lines to safe level, it is often referred to as an MOV, or metal oxide varistor.

Video display card An option card that gets information from the system bus, places it into its video memory, then outputs it in a form suitable for use by a monitor.

Warm reboot Resetting of a computer from the keyboard to begin computer initialization from the beginning.

Word processing A program specializing in the manipulation of text data. Such a program makes text typing and editing much easier than typing with a typewriter.

Index